Pills, Profits, and Politics

UNIVERSITY OF CALIFORNIA PRESS

BERKELEY   LOS ANGELES   LONDON

No.

Milton Silverman
and
Philip R. Lee

PILLS, PROFITS,
AND POLITICS

Take one tablet every 3 hours

Dr. G.B.Heilbrunn

UNIVERSITY OF CALIFORNIA

No.178

University of California Press
Berkeley and Los Angeles, California
University of California Press, Ltd.
London, England
Copyright © 1974, by
The Regents of the University of California
ISBN: 0-520-02616-0
Library of Congress Catalog Card Number: 73-89166
Printed in the United States of America
Designed by Dave Comstock
Second Printing, 1975

CONTENTS

ILLUSTRATIONS

TABLES

NEARLY all of us alive today are witnesses to the miracles of modern prescription drugs—the infection-combating antibiotics, the steroid hormones to control arthritis and fertility, the psychoactive agents that influence the mind, and a host of others. Many of us *are* alive today because of those miracles.

Where these drugs are applied rationally, much credit must go to the scientists who discovered them, the drug industry that produced them, and the physicians who prescribe them.

But too often, the drugs are misrepresented, misprescribed and misused. The result has been a growing loss of confidence in the drug industry. Far more significant, there has been a loss of confidence in the ability of physicians to prescribe in the best interest of their patients. There is mounting indignation among physicians and patients alike who see the AMA and other medical organizations making themselves financially beholden to the drug companies.

Now something new has been added. Now there is evidence that irrational and misguided drug use involves more than the annual waste of hundreds of millions of dollars; it harms people, it puts many of them in hospitals—and some in coffins.

The price for all this waste of money and needless injury must be paid by the public as patients, and as consumers who pay premiums for health insurance.

The issues involved will not be decided easily, quickly, or comfortably. Some hallowed medical traditions must be questioned and some ancient practices curtailed. The needs of stockholders must be weighed against those of patients and consumers. At the same time, the present need of the public for safe, effective drugs at reasonable cost must be measured against the needs of future citizens for new drugs even better than those we possess today, and the research functions of the drug industry must not be crippled.

In the entire field of medicine, there are few subjects so vital to the health and even the lives of patients. Few so urgently call for action by an informed public.

And few authors are so well qualified to shed light on the subject as the authors of *Pills, Profits, and Politics*. For nearly twenty years, Milton Silverman and Philip Lee have been closely associated as patient and physician, as co-workers in the federal government and in university posts, as personal friends and now as co-authors.

Dr. Silverman is not only a distinguished science writer but also a trained scientist. Dr. Lee has had a notable career as family physician and medical leader. They bring together a most unusual combination of training, experience, and knowledge in the private practice of medicine, biomedical research, the planning and implementation of health policy at the highest levels of government, the background of the drug industry, and the politics of organized medicine. They share a driving interest in the quality of health care.

Pills, Profits, and Politics will quite possibly stir controversy. Drs. Silverman and Lee have emphatic views. Others may disagree, but the views expressed here deserve to be heard. The book is intended to outline a serious problem to the public and to indicate the options that are open.

John W. Gardner

Washington, D.C., February 1974

IN THEIR awesome power, modern drugs may be likened to nuclear weapons. Their discovery and application marks one of the most exciting chapters in the history of medicine. But, as one of our distinguished colleagues has noted, we are prescribing, dispensing, and using them as if we were dealing with bows and arrows.

To some, the misuse of these products is measurable simply in terms of dollars and cents. The problem may thus be dramatized by the plight of the poor and the elderly, and the burden on the taxpayers.

But this aspect is relatively unimportant. The goal of therapy is—or should be—not lower costs but better health. The prescribing of a drug should be based on the right drug for the right patient, at the right time and in the right amounts, with due consideration of costs. Too often, however, the wrong drug is ordered for the wrong patient, at the wrong times and in the wrong amounts, and with no consideration of costs. Too often, a drug—a safe drug, an effective drug, a magnificent drug—is prescribed when no drug at all is needed.

If such irrational prescribing resulted only in the waste of money—a patient's money, a health plan's money, or a taxpayer's money—this would obviously be regrettable. But the penalty is far higher. The price tag for irrational prescribing may now be calculated in terms of tens of thousands of needless drug-caused deaths each year, a million or more hospital admissions for adverse drug reactions, tens of millions of hospital days.

Much of the blame must be placed on the multibillion-dollar-a-year prescription drug industry and its incredibly effective promotional campaigns. But reprehensible as some of its huckstering has been, the industry cannot be made the only whipping boy. Others—physicians and patients in particular—must share in the responsibility.

The act of writing a drug prescription is one of the most ancient and visible symbols of the physician's knowledge and experience. It signifies the trust and confidence placed in him, not only by his patient but by society. How well each physician deserves this trust and confidence is now open to serious question. The majority of physicians appear to be largely unconcerned about the substantial involvement and continually growing influence of the industry in the training of medical students and the development of prescribing habits. Too many medical men are apparently unconcerned that their own professional organizations and medical journals may be linked to the industry with ties that, at the kindest, can be described only as undignified.

And finally, where irrational prescribing and drug use is concerned, it is the patient who may be not only victim but also culprit. Too often, he demands and even dictates the details of his own drug treatment or fails to follow directions and pays not only with needless expenses but sometimes with needless injury and possibly with death.

Since 1967, we and others have become increasingly aware of the nature, extent, and gravity of this complex and emotionally charged situation. In this book, we attempt to examine the roots of some of these issues, to describe and analyze the problems, and to diagnose a malady that affects physicians, patients, and the public alike. If our diagnosis is accurate, a new prescription for action is in order.

DURING THE three years this book was in active preparation and the four years before when we first began to look backstage at the remarkable world of drugs, we have received invaluable help from scores of our friends and colleagues. They opened their files and their memories to us, provided a wealth of information— much of it hitherto unpublished—and gave us their constant advice, counsel, criticism, and support. For all this, we are deeply appreciative —even for the occasional advice we did not accept.

Not everyone who assisted us can be mentioned here. Our particular thanks, however, go to the following:

CHARLES C. EDWARDS, M.D., MARK NOVITCH, M.D., JOHN JENNINGS, M.D., HENRY SIMMONS, M.D., WILLIAM GOODRICH, and PETER HUTT of the Food and Drug Administration.

DONALD RUCKER, PH.D., VINCENT GARDNER, and DOROTHY RICE of the Social Security Administration.

ALLEN BRANDS, chief pharmacist of the Public Health Service.

ROBERT MARSTON, M.D., and LEON JACOBS, PH.D., of the National Institutes of Health.

ALICE HAYWOOD of the National Center for Health Statistics.

ROBERT MARONDE, M.D., of the Los Angeles County–University of Southern California Medical Center.

PAUL STOLLEY, M.D., of Johns Hopkins University.

EUGENE FARBER, M.D., and FRED ROSEWATER, M.D., of Stanford University.

LEIGHTON CLUFF, M.D., of the University of Florida.

JOSEPH MC EVILLA, PH.D., of the University of Pittsburgh.

JERE GOYAN, PH.D., ROBERT DAY, PHARM.D., HENRY LENNARD, PH.D., LEON EPSTEIN, M.D., MICHAEL PARKER, ANNE SALTONSTALL and our other co-workers at the University of California, San Francisco.

WILLIAM APPLE, PH.D., GEORGE GRIFFENHAGEN, and EDWARD FELDMAN, PH.D., of the American Pharmaceutical Association, ROBERT JOHNSON of the California Pharmaceutical Association, and MARY LOU ANDERSEN of the Delaware Pharmaceutical Association.

BURT DAVIS, M.D., and LEO BROWN of the American Medical Association.

JAMES HAGUE and the late MARK BERKE of the American Hospital Association.

ARMISTEAD LEE and his associates of the Pharmaceutical Manufacturers Association.

JOSEPH PISANI, M.D., and JAMES COPE of the Proprietary Association.

JEAN WESTON, M.D., of the National Pharmaceutical Council.

JOHN BURNS, M.D., and the late V. D. MATTIA, M.D., of Hoffmann-La Roche; JOSEPH SADUSK, M.D., of Parke-Davis; FREDERICK ROLL and ABRAHAM SLESSER, PH.D., of Smith Kline & French; THEODORE KLUMPP, M.D., and MAURICE TAINTER, M.D., of Sterling-Winthrop; HAROLD UPJOHN, M.D.; and GEORGE SQUIBB.

MARC LAVENTURIER of Paid Prescriptions, Inc.

Attorneys PAUL RHEINGOLD of New York and JOHN WYNNE HERON of San Francisco.

PAUL DE HAEN of Paul de Haen, Inc.

FRED DANZIG of "Advertising Age."

The inclusion of their names does not necessarily indicate that any of these individuals approve or disapprove of our comments or our conclusions and recommendations.

In the same way, we express our deep gratitude to the Commonwealth Foundation and the Janss Foundation which provided financial support without seeking in any way to influence our statements.

Finally, thanks go to our respective families for their advice and assistance, and for putting up with us during these past years, and to Mia Lydecker, for whose unfailing help and cooperation we will long be grateful.

San Francisco,   MILTON SILVERMAN
January 1974   PHILIP R. LEE

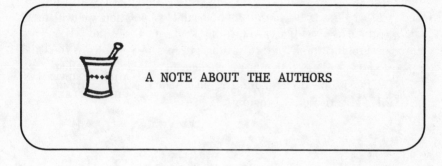

A NOTE ABOUT THE AUTHORS

MILTON SILVERMAN, PH.D., born in San Francisco in 1910, was trained in biochemistry and pharmacology at Stanford University and the University of California School of Medicine.

From 1934 to 1959, he won national recognition as science editor of the San Francisco *Chronicle*, and later as a science writer for the *Saturday Evening Post, Collier's, Reader's Digest*, and other magazines. He is the author of *Magic in a Bottle*, a history of drug discovery, a past-president of the National Association of Science Writers, and a winner of the Lasker Award for distinguished medical reporting.

His own research has included studies on synthetic sugars, anesthetics, the pharmacology of alcoholic beverages, and cultural drinking patterns in Italy, Brazil, France, Sweden, and the United States.

He served as a special assistant to Dr. Lee in Washington from 1966 to 1969, and again at the University of California, San Francisco, from 1969 to 1972. He is now research pharmacologist and lecturer in pharmacology at UCSF's Schools of Pharmacy and Medicine.

PHILIP R. LEE, M.D., a member of a noted California medical family, was born in San Francisco in 1924. He was trained at Stanford University, the New York University-Bellevue Medical Center, and the Mayo Clinic.

He joined the staff of the Palo Alto Medical Clinic in 1956, working primarily as a family physician. From 1963 to 1965, he was director of health services in the Agency for International Development, and from 1965 to 1969, Assistant Secretary for Health and Scientific Affairs in the U.S. Department of Health, Education, and Welfare.

He served as chancellor of the University of California, San Francisco, from 1969 to 1972, and has been professor of social medicine at UCSF since 1969.

During their years in Washington, Dr. Lee acted as chairman and Dr. Silverman as executive secretary and staff director of the HEW Task Force on Prescription Drugs. It was this group whose reports in 1968 and 1969 are now leading to significant changes in federal drug policies.

Dr. Lee is now director and Dr. Silverman a senior faculty member of UCSF's Health Policy Program.

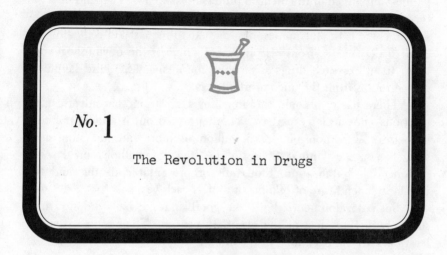

No. 1

The Revolution in Drugs

In 1935 a group of German scientists and physicians announced the discovery of a new drug for the treatment of staphylococcal, streptococcal, and other infections. Its generic or public name was sulfanido-chrysoidine. It was patented and put on the market under the brand name of Prontosil. This was the first of the so-called wonder drugs. Although Prontosil was an important agent, it was hardly the most important ever to be discovered. Its introduction, however, triggered a chain of events destined to open what medical historians may well call the great drug therapy era.

The nature of this remarkable period may be measured by many yardsticks: the exciting conquest of deadly infections, the relief of crippling, and the symptomatic relief of mental illness; or the skyrocketing increase in the number of prescriptions written by physicians, and in expenditures for drugs; or the mounting investment in drug research, the increasing sophistication and technical skill of drug investigators, and the soaring growth of the drug industry.

But there are other and more disquieting measurements: the avalanche of new prescription products introduced each year, the vast increase in drug promotion, the mounting confusion among prescribers, the impact of drug advertising on medical journal editorial policies, the strong ties between the drug industry and leaders of organized medicine, and the deep involvement of the industry—whether by accident or design—in medical education.

There is the expanding and carefully nurtured tendency of the public—and much of the medical profession as well—to depend on a pill for the solution of every problem of mankind, physical or mental or social. There is the inclination of a patient to request a specific drug, or even to demand it, from his physician. There is the obviously related trend to utilize such drugs as alcohol, marijuana, LSD, and heroin as escape routes from the uncomfortable realities of life.

There has also come the appalling realization that adverse drug reactions—due in large part to well-intentioned but irrational prescribing—are now responsible for a million or more hospital admissions annually in the United States alone, tens of millions of days of prolonged hospitalization, thousands of preventable deaths, and the resultant expenditure of *billions* of dollars each year.

Such developments, both the good and the bad, did not arise suddenly in the midst of the twentieth century. Their roots extend at least back to the beginning of recorded history.

TO DISCOVER A DRUG

As far back as any records go, it would appear that drug discoverers followed one basic rule: whatever the substance, be it animal, vegetable, or mineral, if it can be broken into bite-sized portions, or dissolved in a liquid concoction, or spread as a salve, try it on a patient. In some instances this version of research merely speeded the death of the victim. In others, the patient recovered or at least survived because of the treatment, or in spite of it.

By 1700 literally thousands of drug products had been tested and endorsed as useful at one time or another, but only about two or three dozen were actually effective.[1] The roots of male fern, pomegranate bark, santonin oil, and chenopodium oil were administered to exorcize intestinal worms. Mercury was applied as a purgative and diuretic, and later as a specific remedy for syphilis. Colchicum was given for rheumatic pains and particularly for gout. Cinchona bark from Peru was dispensed for malaria, and ipecacuanha root from Brazil for amebic dysentery. Chaulmoogra oil was used for leprosy. One household remedy, ergot, was widely applied to control the hemorrhage after childbirth, and another, digitalis, was highly recommended for a form of heart disease commonly called dropsy; also, but unaccountably, digitalis was even more highly recommended for the treatment of tuberculosis. Iron salts were found valuable for anemia, and iodine for goiter. The juice of the opium poppy and the leaves of hyoscyamus were acclaimed as sedatives and analgesics. Alcohol, taken first in the form of beer, wine, or mead, and later as distilled spirits, represented probably the first tranquilizer known to man.[2] In many of the ancient Egyptian, Greek, and Roman prescriptions, an alcoholic beverage was administered nominally as the solvent for other drugs, but often in such quantities that it alone would produce tranquility, sedation, and relief of symptoms.

Along with these agents were many more which, if not safe and effective, were certainly memorable. Among them were arsenic, strychnine, marijuana, alum, nettle juice, hemlock, fennel, wormwood, sassafras, lichens, and the moss growing from a gallows tree. There were various animal products which enjoyed at least brief popularity: earthworms rolled in honey for the treatment of gastritis; owl brain for headache; sheep brain for insomnia; deer heart for heart disease; fox lung for tuberculosis; goat liver for jaundice; powdered human skull or the fresh blood of a dying Christian gladiator for epilepsy; rabbit testicles for bladder disease and, of course, for impotence; and cow dung for eye infections.

While most of these early drugs were useless, the actually effective agents were often undependable. In most instances, they were crude products containing varying amounts of the active ingredient. With opium, for example, an eighteenth-century physician could never be sure that a standard dose would be totally effective, totally ineffective, or fatal.

A major change in this kind of drug discovery and drug use was signaled in 1805, when a twenty-three-year-old German pharmacist, Friedrich Sertuerner, reported the extraction of morphine from crude opium. This was the first isolation of a pure, powerful drug from a crude and generally unreliable product. It led during the next century to the isolation of a host of other valuable products: alkaloids like quinine, codeine, atropine, and cocaine, and a wide assortment of naturally occurring vitamins and hormones.

Starting in the mid-nineteenth century, the first important synthetic drugs made their appearance: nitrous oxide (1844), ether (1846), and chloroform (1847) as anesthetics; amyl nitrite (1867) and nitroglycerine (1879) for anginal pain; chloral (1869) for sedation; and antipyrene (1883), acetanilid (1886), and acetophenetidin (1887) for the control of pain and fever. Introduction of the last three marked the entry into the pharmaceutical field of the German chemical industry, which would dominate the world's drug production until 1914.

With the outbreak of World War I, the international drug situation suddenly changed. England, France, and the United States, cut off from their traditional supplies of German drugs and other synthetic chemicals, were obliged to create their own "fine chemical" industries, which first merely duplicated the products originally created by German scientists and then began developing new products on their own. (Until this time American contributions had been limited in number, but they included two of the first general anesthetics—nitrous oxide and ether—along with the discovery of Vitamin A and Vitamin D, and the isolation of epinephrine and thyroxin.)

Then came the Prontosil affair.[3] This brick-red chemical, of undoubted value in the treatment of infections, had been patented in 1932 by the I. G. Farbenindustrie, but was not introduced until 1935. The reasons for this delay in getting such a desperately needed lifesaving drug on the market have never been clearly established. A few months later a group of French scientists at the Pasteur Institute revealed that the complex Prontosil molecule consisted of two chief components: a reddish dye with no significant antibacterial value, and a powerfully active substance known as sulfanilamide. Ironically, it was quickly noted, sulfanilamide had been patented many years before as a dye-intermediate—by the I. G. Farbenindustrie—but this patent had long since expired.

These events had two immediate effects. First, the dramatic account of sulfanilamide was widely publicized in medical journals and in newspapers and magazines all over the world, and the demand for the new drug skyrocketed. Second, drug companies in England, France, Germany, and the United States, quick to see the potential sales in this new field, began to synthesize, test, and rush to the market a vast number of sulfanilamide derivatives which could be patented and promoted.

This approach, which began in the late 1930s with the sulfa-drugs, and which was intensified by the introduction of penicillin in the mid-1940s, heralded the start of the great drug therapy era. It was marked not only by the introduction of new drugs in great profusion and by the launching of large promotional campaigns, but also by the introduction of what are known as "duplicative" or "me-too" products—those which offer the physician and his patient no significant clinical advantages, but which are different enough to win a patent and then be marketed, usually at the identical price of the parent product, or even at a higher price.[4]

In addition, this era has been termed the period of "molecular modification." It must be emphasized that there is nothing necessarily evil or derogatory in molecular modification. In the case of all synthetic drugs, the new product can be created only by manipulation of a molecule. Occasionally, such a modification has yielded a major new type of drug, sometimes of breakthrough importance, as in the change from cortisone to prednisone, or in the apparently minor modification of the early antihistamines that led to chlorpromazine, the first phenothiazine tranquilizer. But such instances have been infrequent. Most molecular modifications have yielded only me-too products.[5]

The impact of the new-drug deluge on physicians—and therefore on their patients—has long been a matter of serious concern. It is difficult to comprehend how any physician can cope with some 200 sulfa-drugs, alone or in combination, or with 270 different antibiotic products, 130 antihistamines, or perhaps 100 major and minor tranquilizers.[6]

Part of the confusion is clearly the result of the increasingly rapid rate at which new drug products have been introduced. Of the two hundred prescription drug products dispensed most frequently by community pharmacies in 1969, only five had been introduced during the entire nineteenth century, five between 1900 and 1929, nine in the 1930s, eighteen in the 1940s, ninety-five in the 1950s, and sixty-six in the 1960s.[7] In addition, there were thousands of other prescription products available on the market and more or less widely advertised.

No physician could honestly claim he was able to be adequately informed on all of these drugs or able to select, on objective grounds, the best drug for his patient in every case. Even specialists testified, sometimes in anguish and sometimes in anger, that they were unable to learn enough about merely the new products in their own limited fields.[8]

Today it is clear that the great drug therapy era had brought the following changes:

(1) In place of the relatively few drugs, many of them of natural origin, available to physicians as recently as 1935, there were thousands of products, most of them created synthetically and most of these introduced since World War II. It was estimated, for example, that American physicians have available for prescription about 6,780 single drug entities and 3,330 combination products, giving a total of some 10,000 products in 14,250 different dosage forms and strengths, all

produced by only fifty-three manufacturers.[9] The number marketed by hundreds of other manufacturers, most of them relatively small, was unknown. An even larger number—more than 100,000 products—was available without prescription.[10]

(2) The locale of drug discovery had changed remarkably. During the nineteenth century and the early years of the twentieth, most new drugs had been discovered by individual investigators, who carried on their studies in their own pharmacies or clinics and worked in such European countries as Germany, France, and England. Since 1938 most new drugs had been discovered by teams of scientists, who worked in drug industry laboratories and mainly in the United States. Whether this American domination will continue is, however, now a matter of some doubt.

(3) Unlike many of the older agents, which were by and large relatively ineffective but also relatively safe, the new drugs were often far more powerful—and far more toxic. The era of "pink pills for pale people," which rarely helped but even more rarely harmed, had evidently gone forever. Physicians were accordingly faced not only with an astounding array and complexity of drugs, but with drugs possessing an equally astounding potential for curing—or for killing.

(4) The impact of these new drugs on the public health had been extraordinary, although they were often given somewhat more credit than they deserved.

THE IMPACT ON HEALTH

The germ-killing sulfa-drugs and the antibiotics helped to slash the death rates from the once-dreaded streptococcal diseases, such as acute rheumatic fever (figure 1), and puerperal sepsis or childbed fever, and from pneumonia (figure 2). Similar victories were achieved against scarlet fever, erisypelas, streptococcal septicemia, meningococcal meningitis, staphylococcal infections, and typhoid fever. It may be noted, however, that although sulfanilamide became generally available in 1938 and penicillin in 1945, the mortality rates for most of these infections had been steadily dropping in the United States since about 1910. Nonetheless, these new agents manifested a striking effect in making recovery not only more certain but far smoother and quicker. Patients suffered less pain, tissue damage, and disability, and required less hospitalization—or none at all. As costly as some of these new drugs may have been, the total cost of medical care in the treatment of an illness was substantially

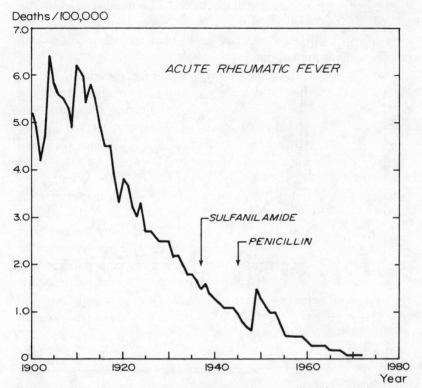

FIGURE 1. Acute Rheumatic Fever: Deaths per 100,000 Population—Impact of
Sulfanilamide and Penicillin
SOURCE: U.S. Department of Health, Education, and Welfare, National Center
for Health Statistics, "Births, Deaths, Marriages, and Divorces—Annual Sum-
mary for the United States," *Monthly Vital Statistics Report*, various years;
National Center for Health Statistics, *Vital Statistics of the United States*, 1968
(Washington, D.C.: U.S. Government Printing Office, 1971), Vol. II, Sect. 5.

lower, and patients were able to return to normal activity in a fraction of
the expected time.

In the "good old days"—the mid-1930s, for example—the complete expenses for a case of severe streptococcal infection might be $500
or more. Such an amount would cover days or weeks of hospitalization,
the doctor's bill, nursing care, medication, and perhaps a good share of
the funeral costs. Now the drugs alone may cost as much as $50, but the
necessary physician care is reduced, hospitalization and nursing care are
seldom required, and the patient is usually back at work in a few days.
His total bill will probably be under $100, and the services of an

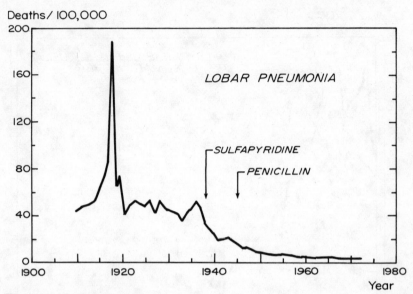

FIGURE 2. Lobar Pneumonia: Deaths per 100,000 Population—Impact of Sulfapyridine and Penicillin
SOURCE: See figure 1.

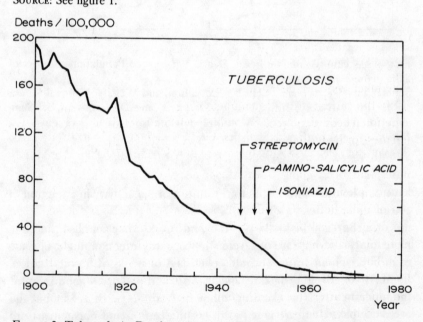

FIGURE 3. Tuberculosis: Deaths per 100,000 Population—Impact of Streptomycin, p-Amino-Salicylic Acid, and Isoniazid
SOURCE: See figure 1.

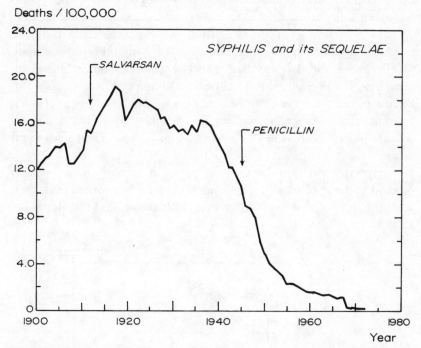

FIGURE 4. Syphilis and Its Sequelae: Deaths per 100,000 Population—Impact of
Salvarsan and Penicillin
SOURCE: See figure 1.

undertaker will not be needed. (Such a case has often been used to
justify the current price of many lifesaving drugs—an argument that has
sometimes been denounced as biological blackmail. These and similar
defenses for high drug prices will be considered later.)

In the case of tuberculosis (figure 3), death rates in the United
States had been going down steadily since at least the turn of the
century, presumably as the result of improved sanitation, the pasteuriza-
tion of milk, better nutrition and housing, and the use of lung-collapse
and other surgical procedures. With the introduction of streptomycin,
para-amino-salicylic acid, and isoniazid, the rates were forced even lower.

The syphilis death rate, which had continued to rise even after the
discovery of Paul Ehrlich's "magic bullet," arsphenamine, dropped
dramatically after the introduction of penicillin (figure 4). The drop,
however, had actually begun in this country as early as 1935, in part as
the result of a nationwide drive by Dr. Thomas Parran, then the surgeon
general of the Public Health Service, together with Paul de Kruif and

other science writers, to bring the facts of syphilis prevention and syphilis treatment into the open.

In the tropics, death rates from malaria were slashed by the combined application of new quinine derivatives and other antimalarials, DDT sprays, and swamp drainage. The combination of these approaches—better drugs, insect control, and improved hygiene, and also the use of vaccines—served to control such age-old infections as cholera, bubonic plague, dysentery, typhus fever, yellow fever, and a host of parasitic infections that had long flared in both tropical and subtropical areas.

Hypertensive heart disease, once one of the most deadly killers, was brought under control, allowing patients to live more normal lives, soon after the discovery of hexamethonium, hydralazine, and the Rauwolfia alkaloids (figure 5).

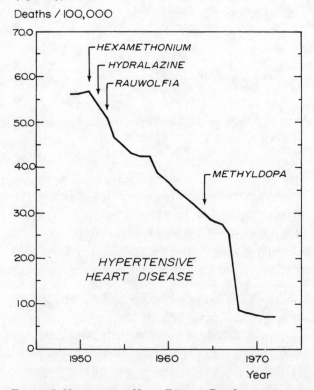

FIGURE 5. Hypertensive Heart Disease: Deaths per 100,000 Population—Impact of Hexamethonium, Hydralazine, Rauwolfia, and Methyldopa
SOURCE: See figure 1.

Deaths / 100,000

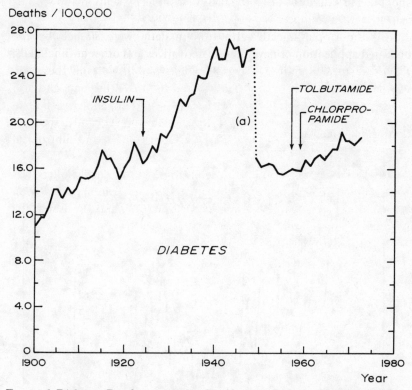

FIGURE 6. Diabetes: Deaths per 100,000 Population—Impact of Insulin, Tolbuta-mide, and Chlorpropamide
SOURCE: See figure 1. Note : (a) indicates change in reporting methods.

The discovery of insulin, and later that of tolbutamide, have had no appreciable effects on the diabetes death rate per hundred thousand (figure 6), which has continued to climb (perhaps as a reflection of the growing percentage of the elderly in the population) but these drugs have made it increasingly possible for diabetics to live longer and more comfortably. Figures from the Joslin Clinic show that the duration of life after the onset of diabetes was only 4.9 years during the preinsulin period 1897–1914. Since 1956 it has been 16.7 years. Even more startling are the effects in diabetics below the age of twenty; in the period 1897–1914, the average survival for them was only about 2 years after the disease was first detected, but by 1960 the average survival period had gone up to 24 years.[11]

Similar triumphs in increased longevity or in prolonged control of symptoms have been achieved with new drugs in the treatment of epilepsy, parkinsonism, asthma, thyroid disease, and even certain types of cancer. The new steroid hormones have provided useful weapons against arthritis and, in the form of oral contraceptives, against unwanted pregnancies. New vaccines have come close to wiping out poliomyelitis (figure 7) and offer the promise of eradicating mumps, measles, and rubella.

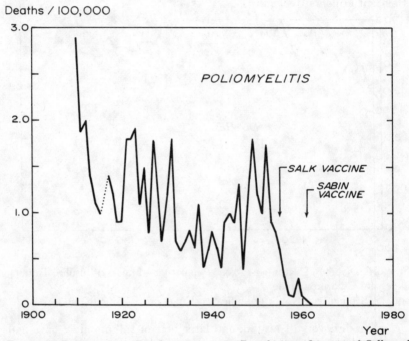

Deaths / 100,000

FIGURE 7. Poliomyelitis: Deaths per 100,000 Population—Impact of Salk and Sabin Vaccines
SOURCE: See figure 1.

With the advent of the new tranquilizers and other psycho-pharmacologicals, it has become possible for the first time to reverse the ominously growing number of patients in mental hospitals (figure 8), and consequently to slash the high costs to society for prolonged institutional care. In recent years the reduction in the number of patients in mental hospitals may also reflect the tendency to treat such individuals on an outpatient basis in their home communities. There is at least some evidence that new attitudes and approaches in these hospitals may have played an equally important role.[12] But although the tranquilizers and related drugs have significantly controlled mental symptoms, they have thus far failed to cure mental illness, and there is growing apprehension that their frequent use to cushion or camouflage what are simply the normal problems of living may be seriously harming many millions of patients.[13]

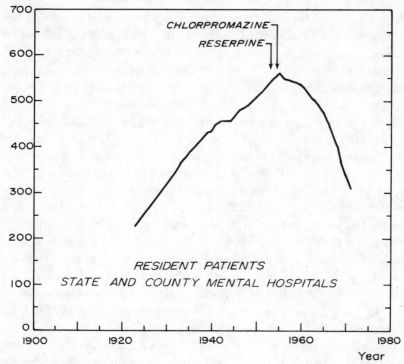

Resident Patients (thousands)

FIGURE 8. Resident Patients, State and County Mental Hospitals—Impact of Reserpine and Chlorpromazine
SOURCE: U.S. Department of Health, Education, and Welfare, National Institute of Mental Health, Biometry Branch.

Still other drugs, by making possible smoother anesthesia and safer operations, have in turn made possible the development of a wide variety of advances, including open-heart surgery, tissue and organ transplants, more effective cancer surgery, and the surgical treatment of epilepsy.

At the same time, the use of new drugs, particularly antibiotics and other antibacterial agents, has resulted in a reduction in the frequency of what were once common surgical procedures. In a number of hospitals, for example, operations for such diseases as osteomyelitis have been significantly reduced, and the once fearsome operations for mastoid infection, brain abcess, and lung abcess have nearly disappeared. As two surgeons at the University of California in San Francisco put it, "When we were taking our residencies here thirty years ago, we used to do one or two mastoidectomies a day. Now we do one or two a year. And now we do so few operations for brain abcess and lung abcess that it's tough to teach our young surgeons how to handle these problems."

The use of these and similar new drugs has had an impact on the economic costs of illness that amounts to savings of many billions of dollars a year. Thus, one cost analysis showed, the reduction in hospitalization made possible by new antituberculosis drugs yielded gross savings of roughly $4 billion during the period 1954–1969. Estimated savings resulting from the use of polio vaccine are now of the order of $2 billion per year. The new measles vaccine has given annual savings of about $180 million, in addition to averting millions of cases of acute measles and thousands of cases of mental retardation each year.[14]

It is difficult for many modern workers to realize that most of these accomplishments have been recorded during only the past forty years, a period in which more practical advances were made in medicine than during the preceding forty centuries. Largely as a result of such therapy, along with the widespread use of vaccines to provide immunity against such infections as diphtheria, whooping cough, tetanus, and smallpox, the average life expectancy at birth in the United States has risen from fifty-four years for a child born in 1920, and sixty for one born in 1930, to seventy for a child born in 1970.[15] The change can be shown similarly by maternal mortality rates, one of the most widely used health indicators. In 1930 there were about 680 maternal deaths per hundred thousand live births in the United States; in 1940 there were 376; in 1950 there were 83; in 1960 there were 37; and in 1969 there were 25.[16]

As Dr. Walsh McDermott, Professor of Public Health at Cornell, has emphasized, the change has also been reflected by the population growth in this country. In 1968 he testified:

> The doubling of the United States population in the past fifty years is largely attributable to the biomedical advances made during this period and in the one immediately preceding. . . . It should be noted that during the past fifty years, and especially during the past twenty, there has been little change in the [total] U.S. death rate. To a public accustomed to think of both medical advances and population growth in terms of a

lowering of death rates, it might seem that our massive biomedical effort has not had very much influence. On the contrary, its influence has been great. For this doubling of the U.S. population in fifty years has occurred not only with little change in death rate, but with a birth rate that would be classified as low.

Immigration was not a significant factor; thus the only way this doubling of the population could be attained was by minimizing the wastage of early death and by insuring that each person born into our society had the maximal chance to survive through the childbearing period and on into late middle, or old age.

Perhaps no illustration is more vivid than the fact that a newborn child today has an average life expectancy of seventy years, whereas in 1900 in New York City a seventy-year-old man had a better chance of surviving the next year than did a newborn infant.[17]

Much of the credit for these accomplishments belongs to the drugs themselves, and to the skill of the scientists who created them and the physicians who used them, even under increasingly confusing conditions. But credit also goes to the growing public awareness of medical advances, and to the social and economic changes that have enabled millions of men and women, for the first time, to obtain access to good medical care.

Gratifying as these triumphs have been, the record is not all good. On the other side of the ledger are such entries as the following:

—The avoidable deaths from reactions to penicillin and other drugs in patients known to be allergic to these agents

—The gastrointestinal hemorrhage deaths caused by aspirin

—The fatal blood damage caused by prolonged use of butazolidin for the control of arthritis

—The gastrointestinal disturbances and massive bleeding, the increased susceptibility to infection, the psychoses, and the bone-softening osteoporosis caused by steroid hormones

—The needless deaths resulting from the use of chloramphenicol for infections in which it is without value

—Deaths (hundreds and perhaps thousands a year) attributable to the combination of tranquilizers and alcohol

—The waste of perhaps 25 percent of prescription drug expenditures on products that are now classified as ineffective, or on products that are effective but not justified by the patient's clinical condition.

The blame for these and similar clinical and economic tragedies must also be shared. Part goes to the drug industry, part to pharmacists, part to physicians, and certainly part to the victims themselves.

THE RISE IN DRUG USE

The mounting interest of Americans in their health may be demonstrated most vividly in the amount of money they have invested annually in hospital care, medical and dental services, drugs, and other personal health services and supplies. That investment doubled from 1950 to 1960, rising from about $11 billion to $24 billion, and then more than doubled again to reach $62 billion in 1970.[18] The estimate for 1972 is in excess of $75 billion. (Expenditures for medical research and construction of medical facilities are not included.)

Only a small portion of the rise may be explained by population growth. The average per capita cost was about $76 in 1950, $137 in 1960, and $316 in 1970. A larger portion may be attributed to inflation and the reduced purchasing power of the dollar. If the annual costs are calculated in terms of constant 1950 dollars, however, the boom in the health care industry is still apparent—$11 billion in 1950, $19 billion in 1960, and $37 billion in 1970. Similarly, in terms of constant 1950 dollars, average per capita cost increased from $76 in 1950 to $107 in 1960 and $191 in 1970.

During those two decades much of the rise in costs was the result of greater use of hospitals and physician services, along with increased prices charged by both hospitals and doctors. At the same time, the number of prescriptions dispensed and the total cost of those products to purchasers have both soared at an unprecedented rate. This growth was understandably gratifying to drug manufacturers, but somewhat upsetting to those concerned with the ramifications of a drug-oriented society.

In general, it has been accepted that prescription drug expenditures amount to roughly 8 percent of the nation's health care costs. Such a figure is often presented as *only* 8 percent. It is based, however, only on sales in community pharmacies. The full accounting is far different.

According to a Social Security Administration analysis,[19] in the year 1972 an estimated 1,161 million prescriptions were dispensed by community pharmacies (independents and chain stores), 174 million by pharmacies in department stores, supermarkets, and discount stores, and 108 million by dispensing physicians. The total for these retail outlets— 1,443 million prescriptions at an average price of about $4 apiece— would indicate an expenditure of approximately $5.7 billion.

An additional 938 million prescriptions—752 million for inpatients and 186 million for outpatients—were filled by hospital pharmacies. At an average price of $4 each, which is probably far below the actual case, these would represent an expenditure of about $3.8 billion. In addition, the amount paid by taxpayers for drugs purchased and dispensed by governmental institutions was approximately $0.5 billion.

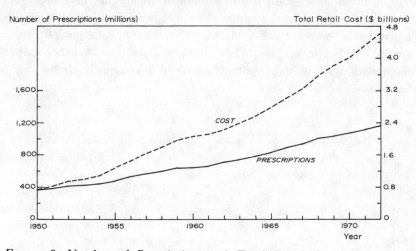

FIGURE 9. Number of Prescriptions and Total Retail Cost, Community Pharmacies
SOURCE: *American Druggist*, various issues.

The total prescription drug bill for 1972 would thus be approximately $10.0 billion. To this may be added roughly $4.0 billion paid by the public for nonprescription or over-the-counter health products (see chapter 9), giving a bill for all drugs of $14.0 billion. And finally, the cost of adverse drug reactions, estimated in 1971 to be at least $3.0 billion and now perhaps as much as $4.5 billion for hospital charges alone (see chapter 11), should also be included in any aggregate appraisal of total drug costs. *On this basis, the real annual drug bill to the public was at least $17.0 billion, or approximately 20 percent of all health care expenditures.*

For community pharmacies only, slightly different figures are given for the period 1950–1970 by *American Druggist*. As is shown in figure 9, the number of prescriptions dispensed by such pharmacies has risen from about 363 million a year in 1950 to 634 million in 1960 and 1,200 million in 1970. (During that year, there were an estimated 1,500 million patient-physician visits.) At the retail level, these purchases carried a price to the consumer of $0.7 billion in 1950, $2.0 billion in 1960, and $4.8 billion in 1970.[20]

Of the 1970 total, approximately 89 percent of the prescriptions called for a brand-name product, and 10 percent for a generic-name product, while about 1 percent required special compounding by the pharmacist.[21] The small proportion of generic-name prescriptions, even though it has been rising steadily for more than a decade, does not necessarily indicate that American physicians are overwhelmingly unwilling to prescribe generically. This situation also reflects the fact that about 75 percent of the most frequently prescribed prescription drugs on the market were still under patent and could be obtained only from the brand-name manufacturer.

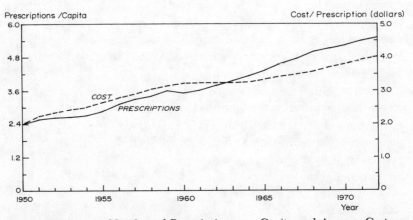

FIGURE 10. Average Number of Prescriptions per Capita and Average Cost per Prescription, Community Pharmacies
SOURCE: *American Druggist*, various issues.

The average cost per prescription, as shown in figure 10, rose from $2.00 in 1950, to $3.22 in 1960, $3.78 in 1970, and $4.00 in 1972.[22] Perhaps more significant is the rapid rise in the average number of new prescriptions or refills obtained per capita each year: 2.4 in 1950, 3.6 in 1960, 5.4 in 1970, and 5.5 in 1972.

These changes in prescriptions dispensed by community pharmacies—more and more prescriptions, at higher and higher prices—were paralleled in hospital pharmacies. In American hospitals the period 1950–1970 was marked by the following enormous increases: The total number of beds, in both governmental and nongovernmental hospitals, increased only from 1.5 million in 1950 to 1.6 million in 1970. But total annual admissions rose from 18.5 million to 31.8 million. And total hospital expenditures soared from $3.9 billion to $28.0 billion a year.[23]

No detailed nationwide survey has yet been conducted on the total number of prescriptions dispensed by hospital pharmacies, and their total cost to patients. Usually, drug costs are listed in the patient's bill but are considered relatively unimportant when viewed against such traumatic items as $100 or more a day for room charges. Only when a patient finds he has been billed $1.00 for two aspirin tablets, or $3.75 for three sleeping pills, and must pay the bill himself, is he likely to protest.

From a preliminary study conducted on a number of nongovernmental, nonprofit hospital pharmacies in California,[24] we estimate that a typical hospital pharmacy in 1970 dispensed an average of about 350 inpatient prescriptions per occupied hospital bed per year, at an average charge of roughly $5.30 to the patient or to his insurance carrier, union health plan, Medicare, or other third-party agency. Such a pharmacy also dispensed half as many prescriptions during the year to outpatients, at an average charge of $4.95 per prescription. This estimate represents only average figures; some hospitals were found to be dispensing an average of 500 or more inpatient prescriptions per occupied bed per year, and some were charging an average of $9.00 or more per prescription. One charged a *minimum* of $7.50. Here it must be emphasized that the average price per prescription charged by a hospital cannot be properly compared with that charged by a community pharmacy, since the nature of the drugs prescribed and the quantities involved may be far different.

A CHANGING PUBLIC

Buried in the seemingly drab statistics on drug use are significant reflections of the changes that have occurred since World War II—changes in disease prevalence, the entry of new drugs, changes in public attitudes, and differences in the composition of the population.

The elderly, for example, have increased from about ten million, or 7.5 percent of the population, in 1945 to more than twenty million, or nearly 10 percent, in 1970. In spite of their relatively small number, they account for approximately 25 percent of all out-of-hospital prescriptions. Where the typical American under the age of 65 now acquires an average of 5 prescriptions per year from community pharmacies, at an annual cost of about $20, the average elderly individual receives 13.4 prescriptions at an annual cost of $60.[25] With the growing proportion of the elderly, there has also come an increase in the incidence of the chronic diseases with which the elderly are particularly afflicted, and thus an increase in the number of prescriptions written for the control of arthritis, heart disease, high blood pressure, and diabetes.

In the same way, the proportion of women in the population has been steadily increasing. This, too, has had an impact on the use of prescription drugs, since the average per capita cost of these products for women is about 50 percent greater than that for men.[26] The greater use of drugs by the elderly and by women has also been noted in other countries. It has likewise been reported that, at least in some countries, married and divorced men and women use drugs more often than do single individuals of the same age.[27]

Although the proportion of the poor in America has decreased substantially during the past two decades, their per capita use of prescription drugs has risen markedly. According to a 1964–1965 survey, the average number of prescriptions per capita was 6.4 per year for those with an income under $2,000, in comparison with about 4.5 for those over that income level.[28]

Whether such dramatic changes have been uniformly beneficial to patients, or to society in general, is not altogether clear. The widespread use of oral contraceptives, for example, has been bitterly attacked not merely on religious grounds, but also on the basis that these drugs— effective as they are—can be at least slightly more dangerous than other contraceptive methods. Stronger misgivings have been expressed in the case of psychopharmacological agents.

"I have become deeply concerned about the use, overuse, and abuse of the psychic drugs—particularly the ones most commonly called tranquilizers," a distinguished general practitioner declared in 1966. "I believe these drugs are not only used wrongly, to excess, and without adequate indication but that in many instances their indiscriminate use has led to dependency, habituation, and addiction with all of the consequent results."[29] In 1971 a group of scientists put it this way: "The introduction and spread of psychoactive drugs in the human population may represent another kind of pollution, one which may also have the potential for precipitating an ecological catastrophe." [30]

Even more significant than drug developments or changes in the composition of the population have been changes in public attitudes. During the past third of a century, Americans by the millions have become aware of medical progress. Some perceived this progress during their wartime moves from the rural slums of the south to defense industries in the north, and through their discovery of industrial medicine. Some learned about it during military service. Others learned about it in school, or through press, radio, and television. They found that many of the ills that had plagued them and their families for generations could be controlled and even cured by modern medical care, and they wanted that care for themselves and their children. The concept that good medical care is not a privilege but a right—an idea that was viewed as fantastic, and probably subversive, in the 1930s—had become broadly accepted as logical and obvious in the 1960s.

At the same time, through a variety of approaches, it became increasingly feasible for Americans to obtain access to such care. Economic barriers were reduced by the growth of health insurance programs, union health plans, prepaid systems, and such government programs as Medicare and Medicaid. Some of these programs covered drug costs; some did not. All of them, however, had one feature in common: they made it economically possible for more patients to visit more physicians, and these visits in turn led inevitably to more drug prescriptions. Other barriers needed to be removed—hurdles involving racial discrimination, geographical distances, ignorance, and superstition. These, too, are being overcome, and with the same results—more patients visiting more physicians, and obtaining more prescriptions.

Finally, there has been the reporting of new drug discoveries, primarily by newspapers and magazines. Here the impact of headlines— "New Wonder Drug for Pneumonia," "Scientists Discover Super-penicillin," "Breakthrough Reported Against Cancer," "Doctors Announce New Asthma Cure"—has been of enormous importance. Some of the newspaper and magazine accounts have faithfully and accurately reported important research. Some have reported—unfortunately, with equal prominence—unimportant or faulty research. Some have trumpeted the results of animal tests, and have built up the false hopes that a new drug would work equally well in human subjects. Some have emphasized only the favorable aspects of a new product and ignored its toxic characteristics.

Where this reporting was done well, it usually represented the efforts of a competent writer who based his account on a well-written report of well-performed research. Where it was done poorly, the blame could be assigned to bad reporting, bad research, or both. Whether the report presented to the public was accurate and dispassionate, or disgracefully incompetent, however, the overall result was the same. It led to an unprecedented demand by patients for the latest wonder drug.

That demand has been heightened in part by the torrent of over-the-counter-drug advertising aimed directly at consumers and carried not only in newspapers and popular magazines but particularly on radio and television. Increasingly, it has become evident that these products—headache remedies, sedatives, antitension products, vitamin preparations, antacids, cold and cough remedies, antiallergy products, tonics for the elderly, laxatives, medicinal gargles, iron preparations, and even hemorrhoid "cures"—are promoted too often with claims that are false, misleading, unsupported by scientific data, and esthetically repulsive. Too often they have puffed up a minor change in an aspirin product into a major breakthrough ranking at least with the discovery of penicillin, a veritable pharmaceutical moon-landing. Perhaps far more significant, the promotion of such over-the-counter drugs has contributed to the convincing of large sections of the public that there is a pill for every ill, and that there is—in fact, there *must* be—a chemical answer to every physical, emotional, and sociological discomfort of mankind. In addition, widespread medication by modern "pill-popping" parents may have played a role in inducing young people to avoid unpleasant aspects of life by turning to marijuana, the amphetamines, the barbiturates, mescaline, and LSD.

Not too many years ago the *New England Journal of Medicine* commented that a patient's first desire in consulting a doctor was to get a surgical operation. If this were not recommended, he would accept a prescription for a drug. If no prescription were forthcoming, he would settle for a diet.[31] It now appears that the order of priorities may have changed and that the patient's first goal is a prescription.

These mounting pressures have had a disconcerting effect on prescribing physicians. For example, a physician will complain, "My patients read the latest issue of *Reader's Digest* and then tell me what to prescribe." Or, "My patient really doesn't need a tranquilizer. He needs to grow up and cope with his family problems like a man, but it's easier for him—and for me—to give him a prescription for a hundred Librium capsules." Or, "My patients come in with a cold, or influenza, and demand penicillin. I know penicillin is no damn good in such conditions, but they say if I don't give them a prescription for it, they'll go to another doctor."

In the years when physician incomes were lower and such threats could be viewed as potent economic blackmail, it might have been possible to sympathize with doctors who yielded and wrote the worthless prescription, perhaps comforting themselves with the thought that "it won't hurt the patient." But in these days, with physician incomes at an all-time high, with the clear-cut evidence that virtually any drug can hurt a patient, and with the realization that an adverse reaction to an irrational prescription may be an invitation to a malpractice suit, such a policy would appear to be economically unjustifiable and clinically unacceptable.

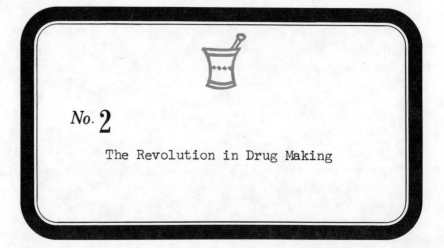

No. **2**

The Revolution in Drug Making

ON A number of counts the drug industry is truly remarkable. Few if any other industries have contributed so magnificently to the health and welfare of the public, to the control of pain and sickness, and to the prolongation of life. In comparison with other manufacturers, its record in refraining from polluting lakes, rivers, and the air has been exemplary. Its relations with labor have been only rarely marked by serious disputes or strikes. It has aided universities and medical schools, often without any selfish ends. It has developed products needed by relatively few patients afflicted with certain rare diseases, and has continued to make these available, sometimes at no profit and perhaps at a financial loss. It has supported basic research, certainly with no immediate prospect of financial gain, at the current rate of about $90 million a year.

At the same time, it has been able to capture financial rewards beyond the most optimistic dreams of its founders. If it exists secondarily for profits but primarily to benefit mankind, as some spokesmen have claimed, then the drug industry is much like the early missionaries who reportedly went to Hawaii to do good—and did exceedingly well.

In addition, the drug industry has been subjected to intense criticism. This is scarcely an unusual phenomenon on the American scene. During the past decade criticism and abuse have also been heaped on steel companies, automobile manufacturers, the oil industry, the railroads, public utilities, and practically all other big businesses—and on physicians, pharmacists, lawyers, undertakers, columnists, and college professors. Most such target groups have learned to accept these public denunciations with resignation if not good grace, to make those reforms that seemed inescapable, and in general to live with the situation. Yet the drug makers have manifested a distinct feeling that what is good for the drug industry must be good for the public, and they have sometimes reacted to criticism—justified or not—with a hypersensitivity that, to some observers, verges on the paranoid.[1]

THE COMPANIES

It must be recognized that, in reality, there is no such monolithic entity as "the drug industry." There are many segments of the industry composed of different companies doing different things at different times, possibly for different reasons, and achieving different results. Accordingly, the fact that one drug firm was found guilty of deliberately committing fraud in reporting its research results,[2] or has allegedly connived with other firms in illegal price-fixing,[3] should not necessarily indicate that all or even many companies have engaged in such reprehensible activities in the past, or are so engaged at present. Similarly, the fact that some companies have continued year after year to conduct honest, imaginative, and productive research should not provide a protective umbrella over those drug companies whose research is less useful.

The fact that some American industry spokesmen have claimed credit for discovering drugs actually discovered in other countries—notably reserpine, chlorpromazine, and tolbutamide—may raise questions concerning the veracity of its promotional claims, but this does not mean that the American industry and American investigators contributed nothing to the use of these drugs. Thus the widespread application of reserpine (isolated and first demonstrated to be effective in hypertension and mental illness by CIBA in Switzerland) was made possible in large part by supportive research financed by CIBA in the United States. The use of the tranquilizer chlorpromazine (synthesized and first demonstrated to be effective by Rhône-Poulenc scientists and clinicians in Paris) was unquestionably stimulated by the American studies financed by Smith Kline & French. The use of the oral antidiabetic tolbutamide (synthesized by the Hoechst firm in Germany and first demonstrated to be effective by European workers) was significantly aided by the testing program supported in this country by Upjohn.

In general, the prescription drug companies in the United States—there are believed to be about 800 of them, although no one knows for certain—may be divided into the 135 members of the Pharmaceutical Manufacturers Association and the 650 or more non-PMA companies. Both groups produce or sell prescription drugs, which are not generally advertised to the public. For this arbitrary reason they are sometimes known as ethical drug companies.

The PMA members may be relatively few in number, but they wield substantial power. Together they are responsible for approximately 95 percent of all prescription drug sales in this country, and thirty of them have about 70 percent of the market. Among them are the American-based firms representing Swiss, British, and other foreign companies, which together have between 10 and 15 percent of the American market. Not only do the PMA companies account for most of the sales, but they also carry on most of the industry's research, control most of the existing drug patents, market most of the brand-name products, conduct most of the industry's advertising and other promotion, and make most of the profits.[4]

In contrast, the non-PMA companies, which account for only 5 percent of the sales, do little research and conduct only minimal promotion. While a few of them control some drug patents and market brand-name products, most of their business involves drugs distributed under their generic or public names. The PMA and non-PMA companies cannot be separated simply on the basis of whether or not they handle generic-name products. For example, Eli Lilly, a major producer of brand-name drugs, is also one of the nation's largest suppliers of generics.

Among the large drug companies there has been no standard route for entering the field.[5] Some, such as Upjohn, Abbott, and Lilly, are the modern outgrowths of small operations set up originally by physicians to provide drugs for their own patients. Others, including Merck, CIBA-Geigy, and Pfizer, are the outgrowth of chemical firms that started with dyestuffs, fertilizers, explosives, and similar products, and then added pharmaceuticals to their production lines. Some, like Bristol, began as patent-medicine makers. Several antibiotic makers, such as Schenley Laboratories (now part of Riker Laboratories), grew from an early interest in fermentation processes. Some, as in the case of McKesson and Smith Kline & French, developed from wholesale drug distribution, and others, like Barnes-Hind, grew out of pharmacies. A few, like Armour, grew out of the packing industry as a source of hormones and other animal products. One, Syntex, resulted from the discovery that the root of a Mexican yam could serve admirably as a source of valuable steroids.

Regardless of the differences in their backgrounds, virtually all of these companies have done moderately well and some have been spectacularly successful. Few, if any, have failed financially or gone out of business, although there have been some corporate changes. Some drug companies have merged with others, while others have been merged into huge industrial conglomerates.[6] Some have expanded into nondrug fields, such as medical electronics instrumentation, cosmetics, plastics, agriculture, and publishing; for this they have given the reason that the prescription drug industry has become entirely too risky. On the other hand, some major chemical companies, including DuPont, Dow, and Monsanto, have felt that the risk is not so alarming and have moved into drug development.

In most of the major American drug firms, top management has become significantly different.[7] Relatively few of the present directors and top officials have come from the traditional disciplines of drug development or medicine. Instead, many seem to represent banking, investment firms, and professional management.

SALES AND PROFITS

Under such direction, the performance of the companies has brought general satisfaction to their stockholders. Year in and year out, in times of depression or prosperity, inflation or deflation, the industry has steadily built up its overall sales and profits. Annual sales at the manufacturer's level, as is shown in figure 11 and in table 1 in the Appendix, have risen from about $1 billion in 1950 to about $4.3 billion in 1970 and $5.0 billion in 1972 for the United States alone. Sales to foreign markets have increased even more dramatically, reaching about $2.6 billion in 1970 and $3.0 billion in 1972. Total sales were thus roughly $6.9 billion in 1970 and $8.1 billion in 1972.[8]

In the United States the sales involve approximately ten thousand different products on the market. As will be noted later, this abundance of products has created certain difficulties. An even greater abundance, however, faces physicians practicing in such countries as France.[9]

Detailed information on the breakdown of the manufacturer's dollar is difficult to obtain. Some companies, such as the subsidiaries of Swiss firms, publish no financial statements. Others are merely units of

Dollars (billions)

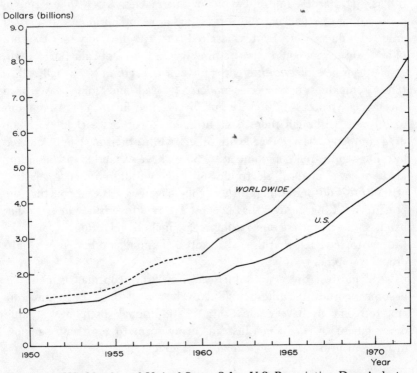

FIGURE 11. Worldwide and United States Sales, U.S. Prescription Drug Industry
SOURCE: *Annual Survey Report* (Washington, D.C.: Pharmaceutical Manufacturers Association, 1973).

large industrial complexes, and separate statements of their pharmaceutical operations are not readily available. Estimates from various industry and government sources suggest a 1972 distribution based on sales as shown in figure 12. Here it would appear that slightly more than 40 percent goes for the cost of goods sold and for administrative expenses. The industry's vital and also highly publicized quality control program, intended to assure unvarying purity, safety, and effectiveness, takes about 2.5 percent. The large sums donated by the industry to universities and medical schools—about $45 or $50 million a year—represent about 0.7 percent. Research, involving both human and veterinary products, takes approximately 9 percent. (It is not known what portion of these research expenditures are used for the development of new drugs and what for the development of more pleasing flavors and colors and for general market research.) Approximately 20 percent, and possibly much more, goes for

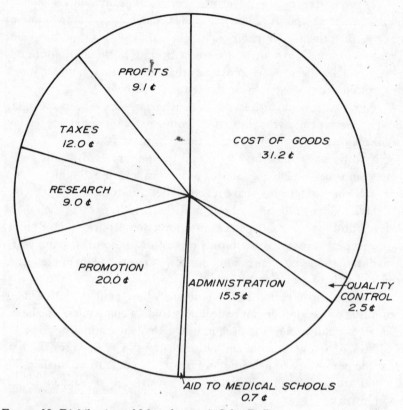

FIGURE 12. Distribution of Manufacturer's Sales Dollar
SOURCE: Derived from extrapolation of data in U.S. Department of
Health, Education, and Welfare, Task Force on Prescription Drugs,
The Drug Makers and the Drug Distributors (Washington, D.C.:
U.S. Government Printing Office, 1968), p. 13.

promotion. Finally, 12 percent goes for taxes, and about 9 percent is left
as net profit. Within the drug industry the profit rate is probably higher
for PMA companies than for non-PMA companies.[10]

In contrast to the average 9 percent profit after taxes for the drug
industry, the average for all other manufacturing industries in the United
States has usually been less than 6 percent.[11] Investment analysts have
been struck by the fact that, unlike the situation in other major
manufacturing industries, few if any of the leading prescription drug
companies have reported an annual net loss in many years.

The reported 9 percent average company profit rate on sales, it should be noted, applies to overall company operations. Since most of the large brand-name companies market not only prescription drugs but also other products on which price competition is hotter and profit rates are presumably less, it is probable that the actual net profit on prescription drugs alone is even higher than 9 percent.

Based on investment, drug profits after taxes have been averaging about 18 percent per year since 1960, compared with about 11 percent for all major manufacturing corporations. In most years since 1955 the drug industry has ranked first or second in profitability. In some years, some companies—including Sterling, American Home Products, Norwich, Schering, and Searle—have recorded net profits of 30 to 39 percent per year. Carter-Wallace, Rohrer, and Smith Kline & French have achieved profits of 40 to 47 percent. Marion Laboratories, A. H. Robins, and Syntex have reported net profits of 51 to 54 percent in some years. Even during the severe depression years of 1930 to 1935 Upjohn reported profits of at least 30 percent.[12]

Some companies and some economists have argued that ordinary accounting procedures do not really apply to drug companies. The heavy research expenditures of the drug industry, they say, should be regarded as additions to capital investment rather than ordinary expenses. On that basis, the percentage of net drug profits would appear to be smaller, but it would still be substantially higher than the average for all manufacturing industries.

Table 2 in the Appendix indicates the average net profits as based on investment for the drug industry, compared with those for all American manufacturing industries. Tables 3, 4, and 5 show the profits for some of the leading individual American prescription drug companies for 1972 and for the period 1956–1971.

Not included in these tables are subsidiary divisions, such as the Lederle Laboratories division of American Cyanamid, for which separate statements are not available. Also omitted here are such Swiss-based firms as Hoffmann-La Roche, Sandoz, and CIBA-Geigy, which do not generally divulge details of their financial operations. Recently, Fortune magazine presented a profile of one of the Swiss firms, Roche, formally known as F. Hoffmann-La Roche & Co., A.G., and described as "the world's largest ethical drug manufacturer, undisputed world market leader in vitamins and psychopharmaceuticals, and a company that is currently one of the most profitable enterprises on earth." [13]

The Fortune portrayal of Roche operations was at least startling.

The company's capital investment was given as nearly $2.5 billion, with each share of stock priced at roughly $55,000. Roche's cash position was such that it had no need to seek financing from Swiss and American banks; instead, banks and various industries borrowed from Roche. Sales in 1970 were given as almost $1.2 billion, with about 60 percent representing sales of prescription drugs and vitamin specialties, and nearly 25 percent from sales of bulk vitamins. A major portion of the company's drug sales came from Librium and Valium, which together accounted for about one-half of the sales of all tranquilizers. Approximately 40 percent of Roche's worldwide sales came from the operations of its American subsidiary, based in Nutley, New Jersey.

Recently, some American drug companies have established portions of their operations in Puerto Rico, thus giving them a tax-exempt status on such activities, and enabling them to achieve net profits of as much as 40 percent after taxes. As one security analyst commented, "The most important recent discovery of the research-minded drug industry was Puerto Rico." [14]

The industry has never denied that its profits are high, but it has vehemently denied that they are too high. Such a view is not unexpected, since few industries are ever inclined to admit that their profits are too high. In the same way, it would be unreasonable to expect consumers to agree that a company's prices and profits are too low. Whether drug profits are reasonable and justifiable is, however, another matter, and this is, and probably will remain, a subject of considerable controversy.

THE QUESTION OF RISK

Drug earnings have been defended largely on the premise that high profits are essential in any high-risk industry, and the drug industry is a very high risk business indeed. For example, it is asserted that an apparently successful, profitable product may rapidly become obsolete if a superior product is developed by a competitor. Similarly, such a product may be removed from the market if an unanticipated side effect or social misuse appears, or if an unanticipated lack of efficacy is discovered.

Such events are far from hypothetical. For example, Lederle's enormous investment in the development of antipneumonia serums had to be scrapped when the sulfa-drugs were introduced. Lederle was hit again when its diuretic product acetazolamide (Diamox) was largely replaced by Merck's thiazide diuretics. Merck was similarly affected when cortisone was made almost obsolete by Schering's prednisone.

Cutter suffered heavy financial losses when its polio vaccine was found to be unsafe. Several companies, including Syntex, Searle, and Parke-Davis, sustained losses when it was revealed that the early oral contraceptives could increase the chance of serious or deadly blood clots.

The risk of such disasters is obvious. The record shows, however, that they occur only infrequently.[15] A product may be rendered obsolete by a new discovery, but often the new product is developed by the same firm that created the original drug. The risk of unexpected lack of safety or efficacy is still present, but the danger has been minimized by new and tighter drug-testing regulations established by the federal government. Moreover, when a company loses heavily on one item, it usually more than compensates with the profits from its successful products.[16] As one of the industry's most important supporters, economist Simon Whitney of New York University, told a conference in 1969, "Whatever the risks have been or are, I have to assume that the profits have more than offset them." [17] The major exception in recent years has been Parke-Davis, which ended more than a decade of dismal earnings by merging with Warner-Lambert. Insiders in the industry placed the blame mainly on two factors: the company's insistence on tying most of its efforts to one product, chloramphenicol, later shown to have serious or even fatal side effects, and the refusal of its top management to support an aggressive research program.[18]

In the same way, the industry has emphasized that its high profits are also justified by its heavy investment in research. Clearly, this worldwide investment is large, reaching $619 million in 1970 and an all-time high of $728 million in 1972. In that last year the net profits for the industry, after all research costs, taxes, and other expenses were paid, also reached an all-time high of more than $800 million.

In recent years industry spokesmen have occasionally used its research program not merely as an explanation but also as the basis of a threat. As one observer put it, "If you ask any drug company official what would happen if the government should . . . , he'd interrupt you by saying, 'We'd have to cut down on our research.' " [19]

The industry has also declared that it must have high profits in order to attract investment capital. But, as the chief economist of the Federal Trade Commission has testified, drug companies rarely if ever need to go into the money market to obtain financing. He said:

> There is no reason to conclude, on the basis of advice being given investors by investment analysts, that the drug industry is a uniquely risky

industry. On the contrary, the generally glowing reports of investment analysts suggest that large drug companies should have little difficulty obtaining adequate capital should they choose to go into the market for it. Actually, however, their profits are so large that drug companies seldom need to go to the capital market for equity capital. And there is no reason to expect that drug companies would have difficulty getting adequate capital even if they enjoyed profit rates comparable to most other American industries.[20]

Finally, the industry has defended its prices and profits by stressing the fact that there are many failures for each successful drug, and the successful product must compensate for all the failures. To this one former drug company research director commented, "This is true since it is the very essence of research. The problem arises out of the fact that they market so many of their failures." [21]

Thus, although the industry's spokesmen have continued to insist that theirs is a high-risk business, tied to the unpredictable results of research, these dire warnings have not been notably convincing to various professional observers, security analysts, and investment counselors. As *Chemical and Engineering News* commented editorially, the situation is "singularly unfrightening." [22]

RESEARCH TRENDS

As the drug revolution has progressed the very nature of drug research and development has undergone significant alterations. In industry, drug investigations have been transformed from what were largely product control studies to competitive drug development. The growing complexities and sophistication of this research have brought growing emphasis on an understanding of the mechanisms of drug action, at the cellular and even the molecular level. The individual research worker has been replaced in considerable part by the large and expensive research team. At Upjohn, for example, the staff of scientists was increased from twelve in 1938 to about four hundred in 1970. Simple laboratory procedures have mushroomed into complex and more effective but far more costly research techniques. Expensive equipment has become essential. New requirements for proof of safety and efficacy have demanded prolonged and costly clinical trials. Together these factors have priced the development of a new drug product far beyond the financial capabilities of most universities and nongovernmental research institutions.

In governmental research, centered mainly in the National Institutes of Health, drug-related investigations now are budgeted at more than $100 million a year, either for studies conducted in government laboratories and clinics or for research grants and contracts to universities and other nongovernmental institutions (see also chapter 10). This relatively modest sum—modest at least in terms of NIH's $1.5 billion budget—is, however, only one part of the story. In addition, many hundreds of millions of dollars are invested annually in NIH's basic research programs, which have made possible the later development of new drug products. Such basic research contributed significantly to the development of the first practical vaccine against German measles, important new antileukemia agents, the antihypertensive methyldopa, *l*-DOPA for the treatment of parkinsonism, and such anticancer drugs as arabinosyl cytosine, methramycin, and BCNU. Government funds and facilities have been utilized to conduct clinical trials of still other new products developed for the treatment of arthritis, cancer, and heart disease, and to maintain the quality, purity, safety, and efficacy of all vaccines.

But since government drug research for the most part is deliberately not product-oriented, and since product development has become far too costly for most universities, the drug industry has been virtually alone in undertaking the development of nearly all new products. This is indicated by the constant rise in the industry's annual research investment. A portion of that increase, as was noted above, is the direct result of the higher cost for facilities and manpower. Another portion may be attributed to the 1962 Kefauver-Harris Amendments that require the manufacturer to present acceptable evidence of both safety and efficacy. Under that legislation a manufacturer can no longer launch a new product based mainly on unsubstantiated testimonials purchased for a few thousand dollars each,[23] but rather is obliged to conduct the necessary—and usually costly—research and to submit the actual evidence.

As a result of these and other factors, the price tag for discovering and getting to market one new drug product is now a minimum of many hundreds of thousands of dollars, and may run to $7 million or more.[24] In 1971, for instance, Lederle reported that the development of its new antibiotic minocycline had taken ten years, $7 million for research, and $3 million for new facilities. Presumably no company can afford to risk such an investment without being awarded a period of protective monopoly in which to recoup. This protection has been provided by means of the patent system. Whether drug patents are inherently beneficial and essential—to the public as well as to the industry—or needless and evil, has been endlessly debated. Unquestionably, the intricacies of the patent system have significantly colored the methods and results of drug research.

PATENTS AND DRUG NAMES

In the United States the system is covered in Article I, Section 8, of the Constitution, which gave the first Congress the power "to promote the progress of science and useful arts by securing for limited times to authors and inventors the exclusive right to their respective writings and discoveries." The Congress quickly acted on this power by allowing an inventor to have seventeen years of exclusive rights over his discovery. Some have considered this seventeen-year period to be as sacrosanct as Holy Writ. Others have commented that what the Congress has given, the Congress can take away.

In the case of drug products, protection under the American system is remarkably complete. Only two other countries, Belgium and Panama, are believed to offer comparable coverage.[25] In these nations it is possible to obtain a patent on a drug product, or a patent on a manufacturing process, or both. There are a few loopholes and inconsistencies in the system. For example, no patent was allowed on penicillin, on the grounds that it is a naturally occurring product. On the other hand, patents were granted on such other naturally occurring antibiotics as streptomycin and tetracycline.

As airtight as this protection may be in theory, it practically never lasts for seventeen years in practice. In many instances a company may be forced to devote four or five years, or sometimes more, in testing for safety and efficacy, thus leaving only about twelve years or so of actual protection. Further, within a few years after a new drug is put on the market, it may be rendered obsolete by the discovery of a superior chemical, and again the period of meaningful patent protection may be reduced. On the other hand, a patent on a new drug can be combined with one or more patents on processes to manufacture the drug, and thereby provide a substantially longer period of protection. The impact of such possibilities is difficult to assess, since most companies will recoup their total investment on a drug within about three years after it reaches the market.[26]

Intimately related to drug patents is the matter of drug names. Each drug may carry three names. First is its *chemical* name, which shows its molecular structure and usually is understandable to and pronounceable by chemists only. One such chemical name is 10-(3-di-methylaminopropyl)-2-chlorphenothiazine hydrochloride. Second is its so-called established, public, or *generic*, name. This is the name most commonly used in the scientific literature, supposedly indicating its general chemical nature, and the one under which physicians and pharmacists generally learn about a drug in medical or pharmacy school. The generic name of the substance indicated above—a widely prescribed tranquilizer—is chlorpromazine hydrochloride. Finally, the drug may be known by its trademark or *brand* name, which is usually simple, easy to remember and spell, and short enough to fit on a prescription blank. In the example here the brand name is Thorazine. At the end of seventeen years, when the patent expires, the product may be produced and marketed under its generic name by any qualified company. The original brand name, however, may be monopolized by the original company forever.

It is a matter of accepted business strategy that a company introducing a new, patented drug product will use the period of patent protection to mount a full-scale promotion campaign. This is aimed not only at selling the drug under its brand name while the patent lasts, but also at permanently imprinting that brand name on the memories of prescribing physicians. The goal is obvious: to associate the brand name with the product so that the physician will continue to prescribe it by that name long after the patent has expired.

In most instances the results are equally obvious. Brand-named Miltown and Equanil are far more widely prescribed than meprobamate. Brand-named Lanoxin is more widely prescribed than unpatented digoxin. Serpasil is more widely prescribed than reserpine. Seconal and Nembutal are more widely prescribed than secobarbital and pentobarbital, respectively.

As an important part of this strategy, there seems to have been an effective effort to select public or generic names that are far more complex than their respective brand names, and far more difficult to remember, spell, or pronounce. Thus, most physicians find it easier to call for Kynex rather than sulfamethoxypyridazine, Daricon rather than oxyphencyclimine-hydrochloride, and TAO rather than triacetyl-olean-domycin. As we have commented elsewhere, once the patent on TAO expires, anybody can market it under the name of triacetyl-oleandomy-cin—but who would want to?

Regrettably, the business of naming drugs has had an impact beyond the marketplace, and many physicians have been dangerously confused. For a patient known to be allergic to penicillin, they have prescribed a "different" antibiotic such as Abbocillin or Duracillin, apparently without recognizing the fact that these products are merely penicillin under different brand names. They have prescribed Panalba for patients allergic to novobiocin, seemingly unaware that Panalba is a combination of novobiocin and tetracycline. Even after the thalidomide disaster had become widely publicized, physicians in Europe and South America, though not in the United States, continued to prescribe the drug to pregnant women, probably because it was marketed under brand names that failed to reveal the thalidomide content.[27]

About ten years ago it had become apparent to just about everyone involved that this name-game had reached ridiculous levels. Until then both the generic name and the brand name had been assigned by the manufacturer. Since 1964 this baptismal function has been assigned to the United States Adopted Names Council, which includes representatives from the American Medical Association, the U.S. Pharmacopeia, the American Pharmaceutical Association (as publisher of the National Formulary), and the Food and Drug Administration. The council is authorized to negotiate with the manufacturing firms to select both brand names and generic names. These names will presumably be adopted by the World Health Organization and the major pharmacopeias of the world.

In such negotiations the secretary of HEW, represented by the commissioner of FDA, has veto power. He can turn down any proposed name if he feels it is unsuitable. If the council cannot reach unanimous agreement, the commissioner of FDA is authorized to select the names by himself. To date, however, these powers have rarely been utilized, and some tongue-twisting generic names continue to appear.

In this deadly serious business, finding the right name for a new drug is only one element. Far more important is the discovery of the new product in the first place. Here, depending on the point of view, the record has been either magnificient or terrifying. In the past twenty years the American drug industry has developed and put on the market some six thousand new prescription drug products. These may be considered in two major categories. Most frequent among these new arrivals have been the so-called fixed-ratio combination products. These generally consist of two or more agents—for example, a sulfa-drug plus an antibiotic, or an antihistamine plus an antibiotic, or two antibiotics—on which the respective patents have run out. Generally, they are formulated and marketed under a new brand name, and their supposed virtues are extolled by large promotion campaigns. The value of such fixed-ratio combination products has now become a matter of serious concern (see chapter 5). Second are the new *single-drug entities*. These are new, individual, and almost always patented substances, available only from the patent-holder or his licensees, and almost invariably under a brand name.

Number of New Drugs

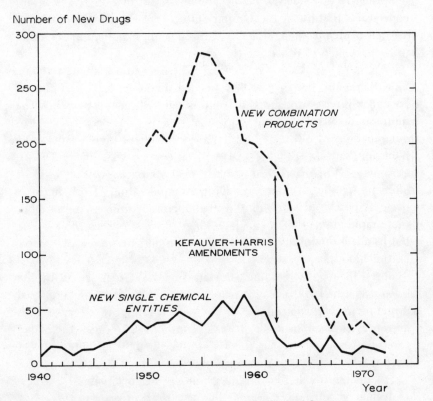

FIGURE 13. New Drugs Marketed Annually in the United States
SOURCE: Paul de Haen, Paul de Haen, Inc.

Since 1955 the number of new combination products introduced each year has dropped precipitously. The number of new single entities has also dropped since 1959. Some industry spokesmen have placed the blame on the throttling requirements of the Kefauver-Harris Amendments, which now require a drug manufacturer to present convincing evidence that each new product is both safe and effective. But, as is indicated in Figure 13, the precipitous drop began three years or more before the new legislation was enacted by the Congress, and about five years before proof of efficacy was required in actual practice by regulation. In fact, the drop in new single-drug entities submitted to FDA for approval was obvious as early as 1956.[28] For another explanation, it is possible that some manufacturers intending to introduce new combination drug products may have realized that the mounting costs of proving their safety and efficacy have made the economic rewards less tempting. In addition, as at least some commentators have noted, it is conceivable that the creators of new drug products may have temporarily run out of steam.

THE MATTER OF "ME-TOO" PRODUCTS

It has also been recognized that all the new single entities, which presumably represent the real triumphs of drug research, may not be quite so remarkable. Most of them represent only *minor* molecular modifications of older and accepted products—a sodium rather than a potassium salt of an antiallergy drug, for example, or a butyl rather than a propyl ester of a tranquilizer. In most cases such a minor modification offers no significant clinical advantages over the parent form. It may be twice as potent per gram, but also twice as dangerous. It may offer a more rapid absorption, which is of possible interest only to statisticians but totally unimportant to clinicians—for instance, reaching a peak level in the blood in an average of thirty minutes rather than thirty-one minutes. It rarely holds any promise of financial savings for the patient, since it is usually priced at the same level as the parent compound and sometimes even higher. These minor modifications have become widely known as duplicative, congener, or "me-too" products. Some manufacturers have reacted with displeasure to such appelations. Some physicians have reacted with displeasure to the products.

Finally, among the new single chemical entities, are the *major* molecular modifications, some of them amounting to virtual breakthroughs. They are not created in great numbers. Some authorities have indicated that they appear at the rate of perhaps four or five a year.[29] An independent assessment by FDA covering the period 1950 through 1971 put the number at about seven a year.[30] While they are uncommon, they represent the stuff that medical miracles are made of.

The nature and the number of duplicative or me-too products, and the enormous efforts seemingly necessary to promote them, continue to be a thorny problem for manufacturers and physicians alike. Although it seems generally agreed, even within the industry, that too many of these products are on the market, there is no agreement on their precise identification. One manufacturer may scornfully but privately point to the large number of me-too drugs produced by his competitors, but he will strongly insist that no such products are marketed by his own firm. Each drug company apparently views its own new product in the way a parent regards its own new offspring—as undoubtedly the greatest thing of its kind ever created—and responds to any criticism with unbridled ferocity.

Since at least 1960 such criticism has been mounting steadily, both outside and inside of industry. One Pfizer researcher, for example, assailed management for wasting the time of drug scientists. "Their talents," he said, "should not be expended on patent-bypassing chemical manipulations, or on ridiculous mixtures of drugs, or inconsequential additives to established drugs. Since the number of well-trained capable scientists is severely limited, their potential should not be wasted." [31]

Dr. Dale Console testified that "with many of these products, it is clear while they are on the drawing board that they promise no utility. They promise sales. It is not a question of pursuing them because something may come of it . . . it is pursued simply because there is profit in it." [32] Dr. Console, for many years director of research at Squibb, told a Senate committee that the new drugs which make old drugs obsolete are in most instances merely new. They are not better.

> Since so much depends on novelty, drugs change like women's hemlines, and rapid obsolescence is simply a sign of motion, not progress. With a little luck, proper timing, and a good promotion program, any bag of asafoetida with a unique chemical side-chain can be made to look like a wonder drug. The illusion may not last, but it frequently lasts long enough. By the time the doctor learns what the company knew at the beginning, it has two new products to take the place of the old one. . . . The pharmaceutical industry is unique in that it can make exploitation appear a noble purpose. [33]

During his tenure at Squibb, Dr. Console estimated, approximately 25 percent of its research funds were devoted to "worthwhile" projects, and 75 percent to the development of me-too drugs and unimportant combination products. And the record in his firm, he added, was no worse than that in other drug companies.

Some industry leaders have declared that the development and introduction of such products is an inescapable phase of drug research, since it is difficult if not impossible to determine whether a new product will be a breakthrough discovery or merely a me-too modification until after it has been prescribed for many years. An FDA official testified recently that "a firm often does not know when it starts research on a particular drug that it will end up with just a 'me-too' product. You know, it is very difficult to know before you do the study what you are going to end up with." [34] But a one time research director of Merck, Sharp and Dohme had this to say:

> We cannot ignore the criticism that we have created an abundance of new drugs related structurally and therapeutically, which in the opinion of many serious-minded clinicians contribute little but confusion. . . . In viewing the congener-drug developments of recent years, I have often wondered why medicinal chemists in so many laboratories had chosen to direct their efforts into molecular modification of new drugs discovered by others. Although this massive surge has created new knowledge for the medicinal chemists at an almost explosive rate, its productiveness in the field of medicine can be questioned. [35]

Pierre Garai, an advertising expert, who has been described as "one of the drug industry's most eloquent spokesmen," presented this view:

> No manufacturer of drugs can afford to restrict his production to genuinely significant pharmaceutical innovations. . . . It should therefore surprise no one that we find slight modifications of existing products marketed by the bushel, a veritable blizzard of parity products slugging it out as each company strives to extend its share of the market, endless polypharmaceutical combinations of dubious merit, and a steady outpouring of new chemical entities whose advantages, to say the least, remain to be established. [36]

In 1969, after many months of study conducted with the aid of consultants from the drug industry, medicine, and pharmacy, the Department of Health, Education, and Welfare's Task Force on Prescription Drugs presented these conclusions:

> The Task Force is convinced that the directions and quality of some industry research programs deserve careful consideration.
>
> We have noted the serious and increasing concern expressed by practicing physicians, medical educators, pharmacologists, and economists —and even some industry leaders—at the number of molecular modifications of older drugs introduced each year. Some of these modifications undoubtedly represent significant advances, but most appear to be so-called "me-too" drugs—substances which are not significantly different from other drugs, nor significantly better, and represent little or no improvement in therapy, but which are sufficiently manipulated in chemical structure to win a patent.

We have noted the comparable concern expressed at the number of new fixed combinations of old drugs introduced each year. Although these combinations may offer some convenience to elderly patients in particular, clinicians and pharmacologists have cautioned that they also involve obvious hazards and combine drugs in a "locked-in" proportion which may or may not fill the needs of individual patients.

The numbers of duplicative and combination drug products introduced in recent years have been decreasing, but they still represent the great majority of all so-called new drugs.

It is evident that these duplicative products, along with combination products, are used widely by some physicians, perhaps on the basis of the industry's exceedingly effective marketing and promotion activities. . . . But it is also evident that the need for this overabundance of drug products has not been convincing to some medical experts. Thus, in many of the Nation's leading hospitals, when expert physicians have served on pharmacy and therapeutics committees to select the drugs needed for both inpatient and outpatient therapy, they have generally found many if not most of these duplicative drugs and combinations to be unnecessary. These products have been found generally unnecessary by physicians providing medical care to the armed forces. They have been found generally unnecessary by leading clinical pharmacologists.

If these items were offered at prices substantially lower than the products they duplicate, they would provide at least an economic advantage, but in most instances they are introduced at the same or even higher price.

The development of such duplicative drugs or combination products cannot be considered an inexpensive, fringe benefit. Each requires laboratory research, clinical trials, and the accumulation of sufficient data to demonstrate to the Food and Drug Administration that the new product—although it may not represent any therapeutic advance—is at least safe and efficacious.

Since important new chemical entities represent only a fraction—perhaps 10 to 25 percent—of all new products introduced each year, and the remainder consists merely of minor modifications or combination products, then the Task Force finds that much of the drug industry's research and development activities would appear to provide only minor contributions to medical progress.

We likewise find that to the extent the industry directs a share of its research program to duplicative, noncontributory products, there is a waste of skilled research manpower and research facilities, a waste of clinical facilities needed to test the products, a further confusing proliferation of drug products which are promoted to physicians, and a further burden on the patient or taxpayer who, in the long run, must pay the costs.[37]

The dominant position of the American pharmaceutical industry has often been attributed to the protection of the American patent system. But other countries also provide strong patent protection for drugs and yet have not achieved any brilliant record in drug discoveries. "No doubt this country has been a leader in discovering drugs in recent years," says Dr. Harry Dowling,

> but surely we are dealing here with more than one variable. America has also had the greatest resources to finance the drug industry. It has had the largest supply of trained personnel, and if we are to believe the complaints of the "brain-drain" from Great Britain, America's higher salaries, higher standard of living, and superior facilities for research continue to attract foreign scientists to this country. Finally, America has the largest number of top-flight universities whose scientists are working in fundamental areas relating to drugs. Many of them have been teachers of drug company scientists, and many of them function as consultants to industry.[38]

Many critics have claimed that the problem of the production and promotion of me-too drugs in avalanche-like proportions, and the related matters of drug prices and drug industry profits, may be alleviated by conducting radical surgery on the American patent laws. Among the proposals have been the following:

—Abolish all patents on drugs
—Reduce drug patent protection from the present seventeen years to ten years, five years, or less, on the grounds that a drug company will normally recoup its investments in a new product in the first three years after it reaches the market
—Permit the manufacturer to have exclusive use of his brand name only until the expiration of his patent, at which time any qualified manufacturer may produce the drug and market it under its original, highly publicized name
—Abolish brand names on all drugs and allow them to be promoted only under their generic names
—Permit patents only on new drugs that offer clear-cut clinical or price advantages to the patient
—Require a manufacturer to license other companies to produce and distribute his patented products under an appropriate royalty agreement.

These and similar proposed maneuvers have already engendered some heat. At present it appears that the total abolition of drug patents would harm the public—not to mention the drug industry—far more than it would help. Until now almost every important new product has been discovered in countries with one type of drug patent system or another. American physicians apparently are unaware of any important new drugs coming from the Communist bloc nations, which offer no drug patents of any kind; and only a very small number have come from Italy, the only major Western European country without drug patent protection. Retail drug prices in Italy, incidentally, are among the highest in Europe.[39]

The other proposals, however, seem to call for careful consideration on the part of industry, the health and legal professions, and the government. Attention should be directed particularly to the success or failure of moves now under way in other countries. In England, for example, efforts are being exerted to keep drug prices at a reasonable level through a voluntary price agreement hammered out jointly by the British drug industry and the National Health Service. Compulsory licensing is already authorized in such countries as Canada, Great Britain, and Sweden; there the original manufacturer has a limited number of years for the exclusive sale of his new product, and thereafter may be required to license other firms to market it under a royalty agreement.[40] This approach appears to be overly cumbersome and certainly has been applied only on rare occasions. Its major significance may lie in its power to induce companies to keep their prices within reason. The industry has demonstrated no great enthusiasm for such a system, but American companies have managed to sell their products profitably in foreign countries that have compulsory licensing laws, and some industry leaders have indicated that they could survive if such laws were enacted in the United States.[41]

Perhaps the most promising approach lies in the direction of requiring all new drug products to be introduced only under their generic names. This in itself could induce manufacturers to moderate their huge campaigns to promote a name that would become public at the end of the patent. It might even dissuade some manufacturers from flooding the market with clinically unimportant me-too products.

Such a compromise modification would unquestionably be bitterly opposed by most segments of the drug industry, many medical journals, and advertising agencies, and certainly by those members of the American Bar Association who have steadfastly opposed any major change in patent or trademark laws. Similarly, it would not satisfy those consumer groups which have demanded nothing less than the abolition of all drug patents. Further, this concept—marketing under generic name only—would not provide protection to the public in case a manufacturer should patent a lifesaving breakthrough drug—for example, a specific chemical cure for all solid cancers—and sell it only at a truly extortionate price.

The public, however, has another protection against such medical blackmail. Involved here is the little-known but vitally important Section 1498 of Title 28 in the U.S. Code. This is the law which, when the lives or welfare of its citizens are at stake, empowers the federal government to authorize any manufacturer, domestic or foreign, to produce a product in violation of patent. The intriguing possibilities of applying this authority in the matter of drugs is discussed elsewhere (see chapter 7).

To a considerable extent, the matter of drug patents, along with brand names, prices, and profits, has provided the juiciest targets for the drug industry investigations that have been conducted by the Congress in this country and by governmental groups in Canada, England, and other countries. In the United States the investigations were spearheaded mainly by Senator Estes Kefauver between 1959 and 1962, and by Senator Gaylord Nelson beginning in 1967, and involved particularly the Pharmaceutical Manufacturers Association and its member companies. To these firms the Senate hearings represented nothing less than an unjustified inquisition—and one which was all too widely reported to the public.

Obviously, those hearings were not stacked heavily in favor of the drug industry, and the real or purported misdeeds of the industry were exposed repeatedly. Some newspaper reporters and nationally syndicated columnists added to the woes of the industry by conducting their own investigations and publishing their own findings. Such powerful figures as senators Russell Long of Louisiana, chairman of the Senate Finance Committee, and Joseph Montoya of New Mexico unleashed their own attacks on the industry. The drug makers were saddened to find they were berated not only by labor unions and other consumer groups but also by such professional groups as the American Pharmaceutical Association and the American Public Health Association. As one PMA official put it, "We're the ideal target. We can't hit back.".

But the situation has not been entirely one-sided. In the Senate the industry has had the staunch support of such powerful men as Hugh Scott of Pennsylvania, Roman Hruska of Nebraska, Vance Hartke of Indiana, and the late Everett Dirksen of Illinois. It has had columnists and editorial writers or their publishers who were sympathetic to the industry's views. It has had the backing of the American Medical

Association and of most medical journals, especially those that carried drug advertising. It has had the advice and counsel of some of the most competent and influential attorneys and lobbyists in Washington, and of the most experienced advertising and public relations firms on Madison Avenue.

The warm editorial support so frequently given to the industry by some medical journals may be related to the fact that among the associate members of the PMA have been the publishers of such journals as *Medical Tribune, Medical Economics,* and *Modern Medicine.* Other associate PMA members are the AMA itself and the American Academy of General Practice—a curious situation that apparently is not widely known among American doctors.

Repeatedly in the Senate hearings the issue has been the presence or absence of competition and of risk in the prescription drug industry. In the sessions chaired by Senator Nelson, for example, the industry stubbornly insisted that competition is both present and intense, and supported its stand by presenting testimony from such prominent economists as Gordon Conrad and Irving Plotkin of Arthur D. Little, Inc., Paul Cootner of the Massachusetts Institute of Technology, Jesse Markham of Princeton, and Simon Whitney of New York University. In opposition, equally distinguished economists—Leonard Schifrin of William and Mary College, Henry Steele of the University of Houston, Irving Fisher and George Hall of the Rand Corporation, and William Comanor of Harvard—testified that competition is minimal.[42] Using one set of yardsticks, the pro-industry experts concluded that the risk in the drug business is large. Using a different set, the anti-industry experts concluded that it is small.

The debate, which was prolonged, complex, and sometimes bitter, did little to budge either side from its original position. A similar impasse was reached in similar hearings conducted in Canada and England, with the same issues at stake, the same arguments presented, and a difference only in the cast of participating characters. On one issue, however, the battle lines were clearly drawn:

If competition is defined as depending on competitive prices (as it does with automobiles, sandwich spreads, some nonprescription drugs, and whiskey), then there is little competition in the prescription drug industry. But if competition depends on product rivalry with little or no price difference involved (as it does with brand-name cigarettes and airline transportation), then the competition in the drug industry is fierce.

Thus, while the experts failed to agree, while industry leaders claimed that they had little or no protection against the merciless attacks of Kefauver and Nelson, and while these two senators claimed in turn that they were unprotected against the attacks of the powerful drug lobby, it appears that the continuing drug industry controversy may be a reasonably well balanced confrontation in the finest American traditions of adversary proceedings. This is, however, no tempest in a test tube. The lives of too many Americans are at stake.

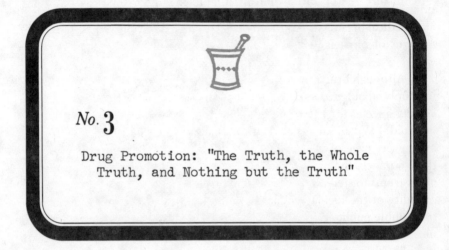

No. 3

Drug Promotion: "The Truth, the Whole Truth, and Nothing but the Truth"

FOR more than forty years a noisy dispute has raged in the United States over the issue of government interference in medicine. This controversy still goes on, but some aspects have been settled. It has been accepted, for example, that the government rather than medical organizations shall have the authority to license and unlicense physicians; that the government may properly help finance the construction and operation of medical schools and hospitals; that the government shall provide or help finance health care for its own employees, the elderly, the indigent, military veterans and those in the armed services, and other special groups; that the government may properly finance student loan funds; that the government shall help finance research in hospitals and medical schools, and in its own facilities; and that it shall exert some control over the quality and marketing of drugs.

At the same time it has been generally accepted that there are some things that the government should not do. For instance, it should not dictate—except in unusual circumstances, such as during wartime—where a physician should get his training, where he should set up his practice, what if any specialty he should follow, and how he should diagnose or treat an individual patient.

Now it is evident that an equally bitter and perhaps more serious controversy has arisen, this time involving industry intervention or interference in medicine, and notably interference by the prescription drug industry.[1] At the core of the issue is the promotion of prescription drugs: its nature, its extent, its reliability, its impact on medical journals and medical organizations, its influence on the education and prescribing patterns of physicians, and its effect on the quality and cost of health care.

Although drug promotion apparently began to raise serious misgivings only about a decade ago, it has drawn the fire of some medical leaders since at least the turn of the century. In 1902 Sir William Osler declared, "We all know too well the bastard literature which floods the mail, every page of which illustrates the truth of the axiom, the greater the ignorance, the greater the dogmatism. Much of it is advertisements of nostrums foisted on the profession by men who trade on the innocent credulity of the regular physician, quite as much as any quack preys on the gullible public. Even the most respectable house is not free from the sin." [2]

In this country, what seemed to be the first corrective move came in 1914, when Congress authorized the Federal Trade Commission to stamp out false and misleading advertising. Most products were covered, but not all. Perhaps in the belief that medical men—because of their education, experience, and superior intelligence—are experts who cannot be fooled, the Congress specifically exempted any advertising distributed to physicians. Although some physicians disagreed with this flattering evaluation of their astuteness and later attempted to do something about the problem, it evidently remained the sense of the Congress until well after World War II.

By that time, when the introduction of new drug products, and the accompanying drug promotion, had begun to rise to torrential proportions, the battle over promotion broke out in earnest. In that dispute certain charges and countercharges have been made repeatedly. Critics claim, for example, that advertising and other promotion may be appropriate for cereals, detergents, and deodorants, but not for drug products that may be of life-and-death importance. Industry defenders have retorted that this objection is simply a throwback to the days when advertising was the mark of a quack remedy.[3]

Some critics assert that drug promotion in moderation might be acceptable, but the present volume has reached the point of over-kill. "One has to be blind, deaf and dumb, to lock his office if he wishes to avoid being deluged with direct mail advertising, visits by detail men and more recently heavy promotion in 'throwaway' unsolicited journals which, for the most part, serve as advertising vehicles," said Dr. Calvin Kunin, then of the University of Virginia. "I have no objection to ethical promotion of products, but the matter is out of hand." [4]

But Pierre Garai said, "As an advertising man, I can assure you that advertising which does not work does not continue to run. If experience did not show beyond doubt that the great majority of doctors are splendidly responsive to current ethical advertising, new techniques would be devised in short order." [5]

And a group of drug company presidents said in a joint statement, "Often one hears 'there is too much advertising.' Perhaps this is true, but what is too much? The advertiser knows when the return does not justify the expenditure. . . . Dignity, common sense, professional acceptance and business judgment have a way of exerting a leveling influence in time." [6]

More disconcerting is the influence of this promotional flood on the prescribing habits of physicians. There can be no doubt that its impact is considerable. Numerous surveys have shown repeatedly that many if not most medical men are first induced to prescribe a new product not by a scientific report in a medical journal but by a drug advertisement or, most often, by the presentation of a detail man.[7] Among community pharmacists, there has long been the belief that "just by looking at the new prescriptions that come in each day, you can tell which detail man has been through town."

In theory, a physician could check the reliability of promotional claims by going to the library and looking up the published reports in the scientific literature. In practice, this is generally impossible. "It might be said that the physician has available to him the scientific literature and can make his judgment about the relative value of drugs from the literature," it was noted by Dr. Harry L. Williams, professor of pharmacology at Emory University. "This is just not so—the physician does not have the time. I am a pharmacologist, and my professional role is to keep up with drugs, and I am unable to do so. I subclassify myself as a neuropharmacologist. . . . I wonder if I even accomplish keeping up with this narrowed field." [8]

The critics insist that massive promotion adds to the cost of the product, but ⸗industry defenders claim that it makes possible mass production, which in turn leads to lower production costs. It is, of course, probable that the cost per unit is lower with a production of a hundred million rather than ten million tablets or capsules. In the case of those few drugs introduced without patent protection, such as penicillin and nicotinic acid, production savings have clearly benefited the public. But with patented products, accounting for the overwhelming proportion of all drugs, there is no convincing evidence that any substantial proportion of production savings is passed on to patients. In most instances the price of a new patented product, regardless of any increase in sales, remains essentially the same until the patent expires or a superior product appears on the market. Even after patent expiration or the entry of a competitive product, the price of the original drug may be kept pegged at the original level.

With chlorpromazine, introduced in 1954 under the brand name of Thorazine, for example, the original price to pharmacists listed by Smith Kline & French was $6.06 per 100 25-mg tablets. By 1965, at least partly because of the demonstrated clinical value of this tranquilizer and partly because of the exceedingly effective promotional campaign staged by the manufacturer, sales of chlorpromazine had skyrocketed. If these increased sales, and the increase in production, yielded any savings in production costs, the savings were not apparent to patients, for the 1965 price was still $6.06. Only in 1969, when other effective tranquilizers had long since had an impact on the market, was the price reduced.[9]

Another charge has emphasized that too many promotional campaigns are based on false, misleading, puffed-up claims, and a covering-up of hazards. Against such an allegation the industry has presented a variety of defenses:

—The charge has always been untrue.
—The charge may have been true in the past, but essentially all such unhappy promotion has now been halted.
—All promotional claims traditionally include a modicum of puffery to whet reader interest ("An apple a day keeps the doctor away," "The beer that made Milwaukee famous," "You can't buy a better vodka for love nor rubles," "Not a cough in a carload," etc.) and the inclusion of such unimportant little exaggerations is not inappropriate in drug advertising.
—If drug advertising claims were misleading, the advertising would not be accepted by medical journals.
—Physicians are experts who cannot be fooled.

The drug companies have emphasized that advertising and similar promotional activities make it possible to inform physicians quickly on new drug products. This is obvious, but it is also obvious that enormous promotion was not needed to inform doctors about penicillin, polio vaccine, and similar unpatented products, nor about the development of new surgical procedures, diagnostic techniques, and cancer-detecting methods.

The industry has stressed the fact that, without drug advertising, some medical publications would need to raise their subscription price, and others—the so-called throwaway journals—might have to go out of business. For example, the total loss of advertising would cost the *Journal of the American Medical Association* more than $7 million a year; to continue its operations at the customary level, *JAMA* would therefore need to raise its subscription rate to each subscriber by about $1 per week. The impact of such a price rise on the average practicing physician, now earning a net income of more than $40,000 a year, would probably not be cataclysmic. In the case of throwaway magazines, the loss of drug advertising would require the publications to charge each physician for the magazine he now obtains free, or to suspend operations. To some outspoken critics the latter would not represent total clinical catastrophe.[10]

Various industry representatives—joined by some physicians, advertising agencies, magazine editors, congressmen, and others—have said that attempts to control the extent or quality of drug promotion represent censorship and government interference and dictatorship, and may well lead not only to government control of the prescribing practices of physicians, but to socialized medicine.

"Whenever the suggestion is made that the consumer deserves more protection from unrestrained promotion, cries of 'censorship' are heard from the captains of industry and the masters of the mass media," said Dr. Charles D. May, of Columbia University. "This word 'censorship' is made more repulsive by opposing it to 'freedom' and the sanctity of 'self-regulation.' . . . Self-regulation is a myth not likely to be realized outside of Utopia." [11]

The arguments invoking the specters of government dictatorship and socialized medicine are scarcely new. In one guise or another, they have been put forth for years in efforts to block voluntary health insurance, compulsory health insurance, the use of quack cancer remedies, the strengthening of the Pure Food and Drug laws, the application of federal funds to the expansion of medical schools, and the development of governmental programs to provide health care for the poor and the elderly. Such attempts to discredit moves aimed at improving health care may be regrettable, but they are understandable. One newsman observed, "Obviously, a fox would take a dim view of using federal funds to build a stronger fence around the chicken yard."

Whether control of drug promotion might result in a further spread of government-financed health programs now seems of only moot importance. The adoption of a national health insurance or health service program in the United States—now one of the few major industrialized countries in the world without one—appears to be a matter not of whether but rather of what kind and when.

More worthy of consideration is whether control of drug promotion might influence prescribing patterns. This, however, is only one aspect of a broader problem: are those patterns in need of change? An acrimonious debate has continued to rage over the assertion that the drug industry, through its promotional activities, has accidentally or deliberately managed to assume an important or even dominant role in the postgraduate education of physicians on drug prescribing. Here the charge has often been made that the nation's medical schools and medical societies, by failing to keep practicing physicians up-to-date with objective information on drugs, left a vacuum, which was promptly filled by the industry's campaign of advertising and other promotion.[12]

This upsetting problem has caused concern not only in the United States but also in other countries. One British medical writer said, "The medical profession has to a great extent lost control. That commerce should attempt to take over the task of academic instruction, using its immense resources in the palatable presentation of scientific facts, is a matter of deep significance. For if doctors are in fact reduced to receiving instruction from trade, what becomes of their claim to be considered a learned profession?" [13]

In this connection, a curious falling-out has resulted from a failure to agree on the basic nature of drug advertising. In the late 1960s the drug industry—perhaps stung by criticisms of its creeping take-over of medical education—declared that its advertisements were clearly to be regarded not as "educational" but rather as "informative reminders." [14] An advertising agency official put it bluntly in this fashion: "Advertising is a selling force, not a postgraduate course in medical education." [15] But at the same time, the AMA—anxious to maintain its status as a tax-exempt educational institution—testified before the House Ways and Means Committee that the revenue from its advertising should not be taxed, since this advertising was unquestionably "educational." [16] The AMA view was rejected.

Finally, and of most significance, there is the growing fear that the major evil of excessive drug promotion may be not the hundreds of millions of dollars involved each year, but its effect in leading to excessive, irrational prescribing. "There is nothing automatically bad about drug advertising," Dr. Louis Lasagna told a 1969 drug research conference.

> In the vacuum that's been created by the failure of the academic world to take seriously its responsibility for educating doctors about old and new drugs, somebody has to get the information across to the doctor that new drugs are available. And if an exciting, unique drug comes along, and it is not applied promptly and properly to all those people who require its use, then that drug is being underused and the public is suffering. If, on the other hand, drug advertising pushes excessively a drug that is no better than those on the market and perhaps is inferior, or if the drug is so successfully plugged that patients who don't need it at all get it, then I think the drug is overused and the public is ill served.[17]

EXTENT

Perhaps no other aspect of drug company operations is the subject of such widely disparate estimates as is the extent of drug promotion. On one hand, the head of a market survey group declared that total drug promotion changed from $433.9 million in 1968 to $436.9 million in 1969 and $430.1 million in 1970. Of the last figure, he claimed, about $102.0 million was earmarked for journal advertising, $48.0 million for direct mail, and $281.0 million for detailing.[18]

In striking contrast, the commissioner of FDA estimated that the total for drug promotion was roughly $600 million in 1966—about $3,000 per practicing physician per year—and $900 million in 1968.[19] His figures are reasonably in line with those of one leading pharmaceutical advertising expert, who stated in 1963, "In absolute terms, approximately three-quarters of a billion dollars is spent every year by some sixty drug companies in order to reach, persuade, cajole, pamper, outwit, and sell one of America's smallest markets—the 180,000 physicians." [20] According-ing to a Social Security Administration analysis, in 1971 the prescription drug industry spent more than a billion dollars on all forms of promotion in the United States alone: $700 million for all costs associated with detailing, including sampling; $167 million for professional journal and direct mail advertising; $150 million for other direct and indirect forms of promotion, such as films, pamphlets, seminars, plant tours, convention displays, and entertainment; and $3 million for institutional promotion. More than 85 percent of this billion-dollar expenditure, it was charged, "must be classified as an economic waste." [21] Yet the president of PMA declared that the direct outlay for medical journal advertising, direct mail advertising, and detailing in 1971 was only $425 million.[22]

Such promotional expenditures to reach primarily the prescribing doctors in the country may be compared with the industry's highly publicized annual research expenses, slightly less than $700 million in 1971. They may likewise be compared with the $977 million spent by the nation's medical schools during the academic year 1970–71—the latest period for which figures are available—to support all their educational activities.[23] (This last sum does not include about $480 million for medical school research supported by governmental and private funds.)

The 1971 figure for industry is based on the estimate that the industry puts into United States promotional activities at least 20 percent of its United States sales, and possibly far more.[24] In comparison, the industry invests about 9 percent of its sales in research.

By far the largest share of these promotional funds is used for the operations of the drug detail men who periodically visit physicians and also call on pharmacists and hospital purchasing agents. On the basis of PMA estimates that some 25,000 individuals are so employed, and estimates that each detail man now costs a company at least $25,000 a year, it appears that these activities would total more than $600 million a year. Technically, they are not salesmen, and a PMA spokesman has suggested that their function is "more comparable to that of sales engineers or customer service representatives." [25] Unquestionably, some detail men have provided invaluable help to physicians and therefore to their patients. They have supplied prompt information on new products. They have served as effective intermediaries between the medical staffs of their companies and physicians who request particular information. They have helped to instruct physicians, pharmacists, and nurses in the use of new products and devices. But most are paid at least in part on a commission basis. As Fortune magazine commented, "You wouldn't expect them to knock their own product." [26] A former Squibb official declared that at least some detail men make their presentation on this basis: "If you can't convince 'em, confuse 'em." [27] From its own experience as well as from various marketing surveys, the industry has long recognized that detailing—expensive as it may be—represents the single most effective method of drug promotion.

The amount devoted to advertising in the medical journals may seem low, at least when compared with detailing costs, but it is scarcely insignificant. In 1970, of the five trade journals carrying the largest amounts of paid advertising, four—*Medical Economics, Modern Medicine, Medical World News,* and the *Journal of the American Medical Association*—were medical journals. Only *Machine Design* ranked among them. Gross advertising revenues were estimated to be about $11 million for *Medical Economics,* $9 million for *Modern Medicine,* $8 million for *Medical World News,* and $7 million for *JAMA. Medical Economics* alone carried some four thousand pages of advertising during the year.[28]

"This is a peculiarly intriguing situation," a longtime observer of the prescription drug scene has said. "The drug companies are well aware that the best way to push prescription drugs is through detailing, not through magazine ads. In that case, why spend $100 million or more a year in advertising? Perhaps there is a fringe benefit. Perhaps if those millions of dollars of ads don't convince many physicians, they convince the magazine publishers and the fellows who write their editorials."

Since 1968 or 1969 there are indications that several of the larger drug companies have decided to modify their promotional activities. Some major firms have practically eliminated direct mailings to physicians, reduced their advertising in medical journals, and changed the nature of their detail-man presentations. As measured by the total numbers of pages involved, advertising volume in *Medical Economics, Modern Medicine,* and *JAMA* dropped by about 2 to 5 percent between 1969 and 1970. But it dropped by 12 percent in *Medical World News,* 16 percent in *Medical Times,* 21 percent in *Hospital Physician,* and 51 percent in *Medical Tribune.* Few important medical journals reported any substantial increase in advertising.[29]

According to one industry insider, overall industry expenditures for promotion in some companies had been cut by a third. "Some people in the industry," he said,

attributed this change to the crunch of the economic recession. That was probably of only minimal importance. Much more effective have been the Nelson hearings, the reports of the HEW Task Force on Prescription Drugs, the press outcry, growing recognition that the newer physician is getting to be far more sophisticated and cynical than his predecessors, and the industry's discovery that promotion to the extent of over-kill is simply not economically justified.

Other promotion expenses include those for exhibits, hospitality suites and cocktail parties at medical conventions, all-expense tours, the staging of conferences or symposia that may or may not be related to a product, gifts, and public relations campaigns.

There are still other activities that warrant consideration, although it is not clear in each case whether they should be classified as representing promotion, education, research, or some combination of these areas. Seldom are they tied rigidly to a specific drug product. Among them are the distinguished CIBA Symposium series, the educational programs of the Wellcome Museum, the foreign fellowships and the closed medical TV programs sponsored by Smith Kline & French, the fundamental research of the Roche Institute of Molecular Biology, the diabetes detection campaign supported by Upjohn, and many others.

Some critics have attempted to minimize the importance of these and similar efforts, and have claimed they represent "guilt payments" by the companies, but there is no evidence to support any such charges. No company is obliged to undertake these activities, all of them have represented valuable contributions to health, and all of them have won the respect of most medical workers.

RELIABILITY: THE MESSAGE

The extent of prescription drug promotion is only one aspect of the problem. More important is the reliability of that promotion, and its influence on health care. Industry and medical leaders have grudgingly admitted that there may have been some unfortunate lapses during the pre-1962 days—the period before the Kefauver-Harris Amendments—but they insist that this situation has long since been remedied.[30] Industry leaders, along with spokesmen for the American Medical Association, have likewise insisted that physicians are experts who cannot be hoodwinked, and thus efforts to promote a drug by means of misleading claims would be doomed to failure.[31]

The degree of unreliability in drug promotion before 1960 cannot be determined with precision. In 1961, however, Dr. Solomon Garb—then at Albany Medical College—and his colleagues compared the claims made by twenty-six major drug companies and compared these with the scientific evidence available to support them. They concluded that only eleven of the firms could be considered reliable.[32] Seven years later he suggested that the situation had been greatly improved and estimated that about eighteen could be rated as reliable.[33]

At such institutions as the School of Medicine at the University of

Virginia[34] and the University of California at San Francisco the problem
of drug advertising reliability was judged sufficiently important to justify
the development of special courses to build a heightened sense of
skepticism among medical and pharmacy students. The subjects highlighted in these and other courses have involved a variety of important
drug types.

For example, increasing criticism has been directed against the
enormous advertising for tranquilizers and other psychoactive drugs,
even though numerous studies have indicated few if any significant
differences among competing products.[35] Great concern has been
expressed at the recommended use of these products to "treat" the
sadness of a death in the family, the nervousness of a child's first day at
school, the apprehension of a visit to the dentist, and other ordinary
problems of living, and to make "medical" out of "nonmedical"
problems.

Typical of this variety of promotion is the advertisement for the
Sandoz tranquilizer Serentil that appeared in medical journals in 1971:

> For anxiety which comes from not fitting in—the newcomer in town who
> can't make friends and the organization man who can't adjust to altered
> status within his company, the woman who can't get along with her new
> daughter-in-law, the executive who can't accept retirement, these common
> adjustment problems of our society are frequently intolerable for the
> disordered personality who often responds with excessive anxiety. Serentil
> is suggested for this type of patient.[36]

Such drugs, declared FDA commissioner Charles Edwards, are actually
intended for patients suffering from severe anxiety and tension. "These
are psychiatric conditions which require careful diagnosis and management," he said. "They do not include the ordinary frustrations of daily
living." [37]

A similar charge has been leveled against the promotion of
sedatives for the treatment of what Roche Laboratories described as a
"sleep cripple."

"The imperative to sleep, and within the prescribed time, has in
America, become a puritanical obsession which drug companies are
happily encouraging and profiting from," said Dr. Robert Seidenberg of
New York's Upstate Medical Center.

> They continue to frighten people, knowing full well that sleeplessness,
> except in rare and extraordinary instances, is not harmful to mind or body.
> . . . The physician is told that if his patient does not have "her proper

sleep," she may have a "nervous breakdown," clearly an exploitation of the "old wives' tale" that deserves being put to an everlasting sleep itself. This is the type of fear technique that promotes addiction. What do we gain when our "sleep cripple," through medical intervention, becomes a "drug cripple"? [38]

He and other authorities have expressed their deep concern over the use of psychoactive drugs to manage or "pacify" elderly men and women, mental hospital patients, and uncooperative school children, not to benefit the patients but to make life quieter and more comfortable for doctors, ward attendants, and teachers.

There is no doubt but that tranquilizers, sedatives, and other psychoactive drugs have a role—and sometimes a vital role—in medical practice. But turning to them as a drug solution for every ache, discomfort, or social annoyance does "damage to the human spirit." In effect, Dr. Seidenberg claimed, the public is now told to "reach for a pill instead of a thought."

In the same way, the promotion of "extra vitamins" has come under mounting attack. In the United States there has long been convincing evidence that most people have no need for extra amounts of these substances and fill their daily vitamin requirements by their ordinary daily diet. The major exceptions are those who are unable to afford to buy enough food—and presumably are also unable to afford to buy vitamin products. Further, as one expert pointed out, since excess vitamins for the most part are not stored in the body but are excreted promptly, "we have the most nutritious sewage in the world." [39] Another exception, now the subject of considerable controversy, may be the value of Vitamin C in very large dosages in preventing the common cold.

Perhaps the most carefully documented study in this connection concerns the promotion of chloramphenicol, the potent antibiotic put on the market in 1949 by Parke-Davis under the brand name of Chloromycetin. (A further account of the Chloromycetin promotion campaign, and of how physicians responded to it, is given in chapter 12.) By 1952 it had become evident that the drug could cause fatal aplastic anemia and other blood disorders. Some physicians felt that it should therefore be taken off the market, but FDA—after careful consideration by the National Research Council and a nationwide panel of experts— decided that it should remain available, but only for cautious use in certain serious or potentially fatal conditions in which no other antibiotic was effective. Such life-threatening applications were very uncommon, and included those primarily for typhoid fever, hemophilus influenza, and a few other infections which at the time could not be satisfactorily controlled by any other agent.

The risk of fatal aplastic anemia from Chloromycetin is not alarmingly high, ranging from about 1 in 25,000 to 1 in 40,000 users, depending on the dose.[40] Children appear to be especially susceptible. If the antibiotic had been promoted only for those conditions, such as typhoid fever, in which it then was the drug of choice, probably little alarm would have been expressed. What did arouse concern were the efforts exerted by the company in encouraging physicians to use Chloromycetin in conditions for which safer antibiotics were available, and in minimizing its hazards.[41] Thus, when the early reports of Chloromycetin toxicity were reported, Parke-Davis hinted at a devious plot marked by "the unethical tactics being employed by representatives of certain competitors," [42] and assailed newspapers and magazines for "careless or illogical deductions, lack of scientific understanding, use of material out of context, and lack of proper perspective." [43]

For a brief period the FDA decision—well publicized to the medical profession—had some effect. Leading medical journals urged practitioners to use utmost discretion and prescribe Chloromycetin only when absolutely necessary. Sales of the product dropped significantly.

Parke-Davis meanwhile issued an extraordinary statement which indicated that the FDA-NRC warning actually represented an endorsement and was, in fact, "undoubtedly the highest compliment ever handed the medical staff of our company." [44] It embarked on an even more intensive promotion campaign. Its advertising continued to extol Chloromycetin and to minimize the hazards. Its detail men were instructed not to mention toxicity "unless the physician brings up the subject." [45]

Although it is difficult to monitor the presentation of a detail man, FDA obtained at least some insight into the Chloromycetin detailing campaign when two Parke-Davis representatives called upon a practicing physician in San Francisco and told him there were no more dangers of blood damage with this drug than with any other antibiotic—a claim that was totally without foundation.[46] Only later did the detail men discover that the physician was also a part-time FDA employee.

By 1964 Chloromycetin sales were soaring once again. Various surveys indicated that the overwhelming majority—perhaps 90 percent or more—of the patients treated with Chloromycetin should never have received it. About 12 percent of the Chloromycetin prescriptions were for the common cold and 2 percent for acne,[47] a record that raises serious questions about the judgment of the physicians involved.

Since 1966, as will be noted below, new regulations have improved the situation, and any company is now legally required to limit its claims to those which it can prove, and to give adequate prominence to the dangers of the drug. Interestingly, this holds mainly for advertisements published in the United States. In medical journals published in nearly all other countries no such warnings are included in Chloromycetin promotion. Japanese doctors, for example, were urged to use a combination of seven vitamins and Chloromycetin—described as "a remarkably ideal antibiotic"—for the treatment of gonorrhea and measles, the prevention of pre- and postoperative infectious diseases, and an array of other conditions.[48] This double standard has been denounced as immoral,[49] but Parke-Davis spokesmen have defended it on the grounds that the inclusion of warnings is not required by the law of other countries.[50] Such a double-standard approach has not been monopolized by Parke-Davis. Other companies have also engaged in exaggerating benefits and minimizing dangers, especially in Latin America, perhaps in the belief that their products are safer and more effective south of the Rio Grande.[51]

Unfortunately, unreliable or misleading drug promotion was not limited to Chloromycetin. In 1963, for example, Merck staged a full-scale campaign to herald the introduction of indomethacin, marketed under the brand name of Indocin. Although the company had submitted adequate evidence to demonstrate Indocin's efficacy in only four types of arthritic disease, it was promoted for use in many others.[52] It was described repeatedly as "safer" and "more effective," but the advertising failed to indicate safer or more effective than what. The company stated that "since the experience with Indocin in children is limited, it is recommended that this drug should not be administered to pediatric age groups until the indications for use and dosage have been established." The experience had not been that limited; the company was already aware that the drug had been tried in children and had evidently caused several deaths. It was claimed that Indocin does not increase susceptibility to infection, but Merck neglected to mention that the claim was based on experiments with a few rats challenged not with infections but with bacterial endotoxins. When human trials were undertaken, it was found that Indocin increases susceptibility to infection. The company's advertising converted the FDA's approved statement that "Indocin itself may cause peptic ulceration" into "Ulceration of the stomach . . . has been reported."

The quality of Indocin promotion was illuminated further when Senate investigators obtained a set of printed instructions distributed to detail men by the head of Merck's Los Angeles office.[53] In addition to emphasizing claims for safety and efficacy that far exceeded FDA-approved material, the instructions added, "It is obvious that Indocin will work in that whole host of rheumatic crocks and cruds which every general practitioner, internist, and orthopedic surgeon sees every day in his practice." The instructions to the Merck detail men, according to testimony before a Senate hearing, continued as follows:

> "Tell 'em again, and again, and again."
>
> "Tell 'em until they are sold and stay sold!"
>
> "For these entities [presumably the rheumatic crocks and cruds] he is presently prescribing steroids, aminopyrine-like butazones, aspirin, or limited analgesics like Darvon and the almost worthless muscle relaxants. . . ."
>
> "You've told this story now, probably 130 times. The physician, however, has heard it only once. So, go back, and tell it again and again and again and again, until it is indelibly impressed in his mind and he starts—and continues—to prescribe Indocin. Let's go. . . ."
>
> "Let's stand on our little old two feet this month and sell the benefits of Indocin."
>
> "Take off the kid gloves. If he wants to use aspirin as base line therapy, let him use it. Chances are the patient is already taking aspirin. He has come to the physician because aspirin alone is not affording satisfactory, optimal effects. . . ."
>
> "Now every extra bottle of 1,000 Indocin that you sell is worth an extra $2.80 in incentive payments. Go get it. Pile it in!!!"

When Merck was invited to clarify such an untidy situation, the company's president made this statement: "Language is not a perfect method of communication, and it may well be that words and phrases that we used in the belief that they mean one thing may have been interpreted by some physicians to mean something else. Such are the complexities of semantics." [54]

Eventually it became evident that the whole Indocin affair represented a case of much pharmaceutical ado about very little. Although the drug had made its debut with such headlines as "Indomethacin: Welcome Breakthrough in Arthritis," later studies led a group of experts to conclude that "what we had in indomethacin was another aspirin-like compound." [55]

At about the same time Searle introduced the first of the oral contraceptives by claiming, "The effects of birth control pills have been studied possibly more thoroughly and for a longer continuous time in the same persons and in more women than any other drug. Evidence of their safety and effectiveness has been continuously observed." [56] The study was actually based on only 66 women who had taken The Pill for twelve to twenty-one consecutive menstrual cycles, and 66 others who had taken it for twenty-four to a maximum of thirty-eight consecutive cycles, or a total of 132 subjects.[57] Later calculations showed that The Pill was responsible for producing a serious or fatal blood clot in some 2,000 women during the first three years after it was introduced.

The problems faced by FDA and other governmental agencies in controlling or at least minimizing this kind of unreliable or blatantly false promotion have been due in considerable part to legal complications. In 1914, as was noted above, the Federal Trade Commission was authorized to halt all false and misleading advertising except what was distributed to physicians, presumably in the belief that physicians are too astute to be taken in by such promotion. In 1938 the situation became more confusing when Congress assigned primary jurisdiction over drug *advertising* to FTC, but jurisdiction over drug *labeling* to FDA.

In 1948 FDA proposed a new regulation that would define labeling to include all written, printed, and graphic material used in the promotion of drugs and medical devices. Furthermore, the regulation stated, this promotional material would be considered labeling *whether or not the product and its labeling were contained in the same interstate shipment.* In short, at least in the case of drugs, the word *label* did not apply only to printed matter wrapped around the bottle. It could also apply to a drug advertisement carried separately in a medical magazine. The new regulation was strenuously opposed by the drug industry, which declared that it would carry the fight all the way to the Supreme Court. The Supreme Court finally got the case. It ruled in favor of FDA.

At first, FDA took advantage of its new authority primarily to halt the interstate shipment of drug products which were "mislabeled" because they contained subpotent, contaminated, or otherwise unacceptable material. Only rarely did the agency challenge a company on the basis of its advertising, and then almost always on the ground that the advertising included scientifically unsupported claims of safety.

In 1966 a new approach was signaled by Dr. James Goddard, who had just been appointed commissioner of FDA. He told the annual convention of the Pharmaceutical Manufacturers Association that his agency had been investigating complaints involving nearly one-third of the PMA members. "Some advertising cases have been quite abusive of regulations," he said. "They have trumpeted results of favorable research and have not mentioned unfavorable research; they have puffed up what was insignificant clinical evidence; they have substituted emotional appeals for scientific ones." [58]

Under its new leadership, and with strong support from the secretary of HEW, FDA decided it would no longer attempt to attack misleading promotion only by seizing misbranded products—a procedure that often required a complex, time-consuming, and expensive court fight. Instead, it expanded the use of what have become known as the "Dear Doctor letters." In essence, a company found to be making false, misleading, or unsupportable claims would be obliged either to face a costly seizure and court case, or to amend its advertising claims and send a letter to that effect to every practicing physician in the United States.

The number of these "Dear Doctor letters" issued each year ranged between two and nine during the years 1961–1965. There were twenty-eight of them in 1966 and twenty-seven in 1967. In 1968, when Dr. Goddard resigned as commissioner, they dropped to twelve, and then continued to decrease in 1969 and 1970. During those years most of the major prescription drug manufacturers were required to issue at least one "Dear Doctor letter." To one AMA spokesman, many if not most of these incidents represented merely "nit picking." [59] To many physicians and other health workers, the significance may be somewhat greater.

For example, Wallace Pharmaceuticals was required to state that the advertised claims for its tranquilizer Deprol, ostensibly supported by twenty-one clinical studies, were actually based on only ten studies, of which nine were admittedly uncontrolled. In many of the patients said to have been helped by Deprol, the diagnosis had not been clearly established, or the recommended maximum daily number of tablets had been exceeded, or the patient was simultaneously receiving other tranquilizers or electroshock therapy.[60]

Pfizer was required to notify physicians that the advertisements for its meclizine and hydroxyzine products failed to note that the substances were teratogenic in experimental animals and accordingly should be used only with great caution in pregnant women.[61] Among the products were the tranquilizers Atarax and Vistaril, and such antinauseants as Bonamine and Bonadoxine, both widely recommended at the time to control the nausea of pregnancy.

Bristol was required to modify its advertising for Tegopen, an antibiotic approved for use primarily against penicillin-resistant staphylococci but promoted as a "new everyday penicillin for common bacterial respiratory infection." [62]

CIBA was obliged to retract its claims for Ismelin, which asserted, without adequate supporting evidence, that the drug would prevent strokes.[63]

Ross Laboratories had to change its promotion for Pediamycin, which was featured as being especially safe for infants, but with no supporting evidence submitted.[64]

Parke-Davis was brought into the limelight again for its advertising of Ponstel, which was promoted as being equal in efficacy to codeine. The evidence submitted by the manufacturer demonstrated that it had no superiority over aspirin.[65]

Lilly was called to task for its advertised claims that its tranquilizer Aventyl was effective in the treatment of "behavioral drift," a diagnosis apparently invented on Madison Avenue and not clearly understandable elsewhere.[66]

Abbott was chastised for claiming without adequate proof that its product Enduron was better than rival products, and was required to send a corrective letter to every physician in the United States. A year later, however, Abbott was reported to be making the same unsupported claims to every physician in Canada.[67]

In yet another incident, Parke-Davis was involved with its Norlutin, which had been recommended for use in pregnant women to prevent threatened abortion. After the drug had been on the market, a disturbing report revealed that "during the past year or two, Norlutin has caused a fetal masculinization with sufficient frequency to preclude its use or advertisement as a safe drug to be taken during pregnancy." It was the *Journal of the American Medical Association* which carried this report and which also continued to carry Norlutin advertisements for three months after the report had been published.[68]

One promotional campaign that attracted attention involved a million-dollar series of advertisements published in the *Reader's Digest* during the late 1960s by the Pharmaceutical Manufacturers Association, and later distributed in the form of more than a million reprints to physicians, pharmacists, legislators, and others. Intended to demonstrate the unquestionably great contributions of the drug industry, the campaign was later criticized on a number of grounds.

The PMA gave credit to American drug companies for discovering two drugs—reserpine and chlorpromazine—that had actually been discovered in Europe.[69]

It properly credited American drug company research for reducing the death rates from many diseases, but it asserted that there had not been one death from diphtheria in the United States during the past five years. One call to the Public Health Service would have revealed that there had been forty-one diphtheria deaths reported in this country in 1962, forty-five in 1963, forty-two in 1964, thirteen in 1965, and an estimated forty in 1966.[70]

It sought to show the superiority of brand-name products over low-cost generic-name drugs by revealing the dismal results achieved with a generic-name antidiabetic agent used in Canada. Unfortunately, the advertisement omitted mention of the fact that the generic product involved had failed to meet the Canadian pharmacopeia requirements and thus was on the market illegally.[71]

Finally, the reprints failed to carry the word *advertisement*, thus possibly leading some readers to believe that the material represented the unbiased account of a *Reader's Digest* reporter rather than paid advertising.

The commissioner of FDA testified that he was distressed by the situation but was powerless to act under existing laws, since PMA is not a drug company shipping products across state lines but rather a trade association.[72]

Not all members of the PMA endorsed the campaign in the *Reader's Digest*. Dr. V. D. Mattia, the late president of Hoffmann-La Roche, the fourth largest manufacturer of prescription drugs in the United States, revealed afterwards that he had "violently objected" to the PMA advertising program and had refused to help pay for it.[73]

Against this record, it may be worthwhile to consider the widely publicized concept that physicians are experts who cannot be fooled by false claims. As one industry spokesman put it, "The doctors, of course, have . . . the power to reject the advertiser that misleads—and woe to the manufacturer in whom the doctor loses confidence!" [74]

But the record is clear that, during the past decade, many of the major prescription drug companies have been required to admit that their promotion was not the truth, the whole truth, and nothing but the truth, and to so notify every physician in the United States. The record is also clear that, during the past decade, the sales and profits of practically every major drug company have continued to increase. And the record is clear that many of the drug products shown by FDA to have been promoted on the basis of false or misleading claims have been ranked, and continue to be ranked, among the drugs most frequently prescribed by American physicians.

RELIABILITY: THE MEDIUM

For at least a half-century physicians have evidently acted in the comforting belief that if a drug product is advertised in a medical magazine, the advertising has been checked for reliability by somebody —the editors, an advertising review board, the Food and Drug Administration, or some independent panel of experts—and thus may be accepted as pharmacological gospel. The situation has actually been far different. For example, under existing regulations, FDA usually undertook a review of drug advertising only *after*, and sometimes long after, it had appeared in print. The policy followed by the hundreds of medical journals published in the United States varies greatly from one publication to another.

In general, medical journals can be divided into three major groups: the scientific society journals, the journals published by official state and national medical organizations, and the "controlled circulation" or throwaway journals. These may differ widely in the nature of the articles they publish, the size and nature of their audiences, the relative amount of advertising they contain, and their editorial attitudes.

The scientific journals, such as the *Journal of Laboratory and Clinical Medicine, Endocrinology, Circulation Research*, and the *American Journal of Physiology*, are usually nonprofit publications owned by a nonprofit scientific society. Most carry little advertising—perhaps a dozen pages or less per issue—and the advertising matter is generally segregated from the text pages. None of these is distributed without cost. The subscribers must pay for them, and their circulation is usually small. Among these specialized publications are several devoted primarily to consideration of relative drug safety and efficacy. Included in this category are *The Medical Letter* in the United States and *The Prescriber's Journal* in England. Neither carries any advertising.

The second group encompasses the major publications of the various national and state medical societies, including the *Journal of the American Medical Association*. Some of the state journals publish few if any significant scientific articles, while others—headed by the *New England Journal of Medicine*, official publication of the Massachusetts State Medical Society, and the California Medical Association's *California Medicine*—rank among the most highly regarded medical journals in the world. These are normally distributed to all members of the organization, with the subscription cost included as part of membership dues. They carry substantial amounts of advertising, which in many cases is so distributed that the reader can scarcely look at a technical article without being accosted by advertising claims in an adjoining column. The sums received for advertising may far surpass the cost of publishing the journal, and the excess is used to support the various clinical, educational, organizational, and even political activities of the association.

The situation involving the *JAMA* is especially illuminating. In 1967, for example, the AMA's income from advertising—largely though not exclusively for drugs—reached a new high of nearly $14 million, representing about 43 percent of the total AMA income. An additional 2 or 3 percent came from commercial exhibits at AMA conventions, and about 5 percent from the use of AMA mailing lists. In short, the AMA was dependent on its advertisers for about one-half of its income.[75] By the early 1970s, however, AMA advertising revenues had dropped substantially, and the association was facing serious financial problems. Nevertheless, the AMA was still looking to the drug industry for a substantial portion of its support. This was not pleasing to all its members. As Dr. James Faulkner warned, "No organization which purports to represent the medical profession should allow itself to get in a position of being largely dependent on income from drug advertising." [76] Dr. Seidenberg put it even more strongly:

> There is bitter irony in this acceptance by the AMA of virtual partnership with the drug industry. For many years, the AMA, in its costly and militant campaign against "socialized medicine," promoted the image of the sanctity of the doctor-patient relationship. We recall the painting of the compassionate physician at the bedside of his patient. The public was advised to keep the third party (government) out of this picture. We were not told that another third party was waiting in the wings; the drug industry was deemed a more acceptable (or more generous) bedfellow.[77]

In the third group are the throwaway journals. Most, if not all, are privately owned and highly profitable. In most, the advertising content is exceedingly large. They are circulated free to tens of thousands of physicians, and in some cases to a hundred thousand or more. Several are sent to only a particular target group known as the HPPs, the "high-prescribing physicians," who are reported by their local pharmacists or drug detail men to write well over one hundred prescriptions per week.

Among the leading throwaway publications are *Medical World News, Current Therapeutic Research, Medical Economics, Modern Medicine, Massachusetts Physician, Medical Times,* and *Private Practice.*[78] *Current Therapeutic Research* carries no advertising; it is distributed without cost to medical schools, hospitals, and medical societies and is subsidized largely by the sale of reprints to drug manufacturers for distribution to physicians. *Massachusetts Physician* is subsidized entirely by advertising and is distributed free to some eleven thousand doctors in Massachusetts, Vermont, and New Hampshire. On occasion, it has included a guest editorial signed by a drug company president, has carried a portrait of the industry leader on its front cover, and has frequently denounced generic prescribing. Its editor has staunchly insisted that this total dependence on drug advertising has had absolutely no effect on editorial policy.

Another noteworthy member of this group is the *Medical Tribune* family of publications, which have been described as "all but inseparable" from a leading medical advertising agency, William Douglas McAdams, Inc.[79] Dr. Arthur Sackler, the former board chairman of the McAdams agency, was a founder of *Medical Tribune* and in 1973 was listed as its international publisher. For many years Dr. Joseph Gennis served as both executive vice-president of McAdams and executive editor of *Medical Tribune.* Although the American Association of Advertising Agencies forbids ownership of news media by advertising agencies, in order to prevent an obvious conflict of interest, the McAdams organization has avoided trouble by the simple expedient of not being a member of the AAAA.

Recently, *American Family Physician/GP*—the publication of the American Academy of General Practice—has become a member of the throwaway group by having copies distributed without cost to physicians. Earlier this publication attracted attention when it was testified that the journal had sought to increase its drug advertising by circulating to drug companies a compilation of its editorials on drugs, all of which seemed to be favorable to the industry.[80]

Most of the throwaway magazines are marked by the following characteristics:

—Skillful and sometimes superlative reporting and editing, and colorful, imaginative illustrations

—An inordinate portion of space devoted to drug advertising

—The provision of space to nationally known physicians and even an occasional congressman, and the commissioning of articles by writers, all of whose admiration of the brand-name drug industry has long been evident

—A discreet silence on such matters as the "Dear Doctor letters" and the conviction of companies on the grounds of false and misleading advertising, violations of antitrust laws, and similar offenses. In the case of the *Medical Tribune*, however, observers have noted that this solicitous treatment has not always been extended to companies that do not advertise in the publication[81]

—A uniformly unfriendly attitude toward proposals for the use of generic drugs, changes in drug patent laws, and FDA controls on misleading drug promotion.

For example, Dr. Morris Fishbein—the former editor of the *JAMA* and later the editor of *Medical World News*—declared on the basis of some fifty-four years of experience that the proposed FDA advertising controls in 1967 represented "an invasion of medical practice and medical education that is wholly unwarranted." [82] In the same vein the late Dr. DeForrest Ely, president of the McAdams agency, declared that the FDA advertising regulations would "jeoparadize freedom of the press." [83]

The relationship between editorial attitudes and the reliability of drug advertising carried in medical journals would seem to invite an analysis of the advertising review methods employed by these publications. Here again the case of the *JAMA* is of particular significance.

After the Congress authorized the Federal Trade Commission in 1914 to halt all false and misleading advertising except what was directed to physicians, the leadership of the AMA decided to take action on its own and set up a rigid advertisement-screening program under its distinguished Council on Pharmacy and Chemistry (later renamed the Council on Drugs). In 1929 this screening method became what was known as the Seal of Acceptance program.[84]

Under this program no drug product could be awarded the AMA Seal until all its claims for safety and efficacy had been carefully reviewed by the council and its associated experts. The council was empowered to seek all technical data in a company's files, and even to inspect manufacturing plants. It exerted some control over generic names and usually insisted that these be simple and short. Finally, no drug could be advertised in the *JAMA* unless it carried the Seal of Acceptance. Such an approach was not foolproof, but it marked a significant advance. Most physicians could feel reasonably confident in prescribing drug products advertised in AMA publications.

Then, in the early 1950s it became apparent that the *JAMA* was lagging behind other medical journals in advertising. In a four-year period advertising revenues for the *JAMA* had risen only about 3 percent, in comparison with roughly 40 percent in other and perhaps more tolerant journals. Accordingly, in 1952 the AMA retained Ben Gaffin and Associates of Chicago to find the explanation. The Gaffin survey soon indicated that most physicians and small drug firms thought well of the AMA's advertising policy, but the large companies—the potential large advertisers—were critical, particularly on two counts. First, they were unhappy with the Seal of Acceptance program. Second, they were displeased with the long-standing attitude of the Council on Drugs that the use of most fixed-ratio combination products was irrational, unnecessary, and unsafe, and therefore these products should not be approved for advertising in the *JAMA*. The Gaffin organization recommended that the Seal program be dropped, and that advertising control be liberalized.[85]

In 1955 the AMA took all advertising control out of the hands of the Council on Drugs and stopped the council—or any other AMA group—from demanding full disclosure from manufacturers. The Seal of Acceptance program was abolished.

Within a year or two the impact of these changes was evident. Advertising in the *JAMA*,which now included combination drug products, began a dramatic rise, increasing from about $5 million in 1955 to $10 million in 1963 and about $15 million in 1969. At the same time, however, the reliability of drug advertising became increasingly questionable. In an effort to remedy this situation, some of the smaller drug firms, which had valued the old Seal of Acceptance program, set up a small group of medical experts known as the Physicians' Council, which would review advertising and award a special insignia to be carried in approved advertisements. But, as the Physicians' Council began to win support from practicing doctors, it was viewed with growing suspicion and hostility by the American Drug Manufacturers Association (now part of PMA). Enough pressure was applied so that the new council lost its financial support, and the insignia program was aborted.[86]

Thereafter, the *JAMA* embarked on a program of having proposed

advertisements screened only by an internal review group. The nature of
this process was indicated later in testimony before a Senate committee
by Dr. Edward Pinckney, who served as an associate editor.

> While on the editorial staff I noted many discrepancies in the ads
> published within *JAMA*'s pages. I brought these to the attention of the
> editor and each time I was referred to the "advertising review committee,"
> which was not part of the editorial department of *JAMA*. In reality, the
> "advertising review committee" (and this was after the abolishment of
> council review for all AMA-advertised products) was nothing more than
> one woman, medically untrained, who glanced at the ads, and seemingly
> did nothing more than admire them for overall appearance. I can say,
> therefore, that although the AMA claimed to have "advertising princi-
> ples," such principles never really existed in fact.[87]

At least equally serious is the possible relationship between the
JAMA's advertising and the editorial policies of the magazine. Editorially, the *JAMA* had taken forceful stands until about 1955 in favor of
generic prescribing. Thereafter, in a noteworthy reversal of editorial
policy, it has taken vigorous stands against generic prescribing, and
against FDA's attempts to control misleading advertising and inadequate
warnings against potential side effects and other hazards. While it did
carry strong warnings against the dangers of Chloromycetin in 1952, it
gave little prominence during the 1960s to warnings against other
products that were shown to be ineffective or unduly dangerous.
Although the AMA's Council on Drugs continued to emphasize the
irrationality of most fixed-ratio combination products, the *JAMA*
continued to carry advertisements for them.

As one reflection of such policies, the *JAMA* published in 1968 an
editorial attacking the prescribing of generic-named products.[88] The
editorial appeared in the same issue that carried a lengthy, detailed
article which reported that a generic version of the antidiabetic drug
tolbutamide compounded with less than the standard amount of a
dispersing agent was far less effective than the tolbutamide marketed by
Upjohn under the brand name of Orinase. The paper, entitled "The
Generic Inequivalence of Drugs," had been written by a member of the
Upjohn staff.[89] It failed to disclose that the inferior product had never
been marketed or even proposed for clinical use, but was merely an
artificial laboratory freak.

The *JAMA* also was involved with a report on the hazard of
products containing antibiotics and other substances in fixed-ratio

combinations. The paper, submitted by a panel of thirty distinguished scientists and clinicians representing the National Academy of Sciences and the National Research Council, was rejected by the editors of *JAMA*, on the grounds that it was not in publishable form.[90] It was promptly accepted and published in the prestigious *New England Journal of Medicine.*[91]

AMA leaders have steadfastly denied that their huge advertising revenues have had any influence on the association's policies. Dr. Edward Annis, a former AMA president, made this statement in the *AMA News*: "The American Medical Association's programs and policies have never been, are not now, and will never be shaped by any dependence on the drug industry. And to insure that there is no conflict of interests, the AMA has consistently separated the editorial management, advertising acceptance, and business management of each of its scientific publications." [92]

Other journals have been more willing to express their inability to perform adequate screening of drug advertisements. For example, the editor of the *New England Journal of Medicine* said, "A respectable journal . . . can and does create its own advertising committee or some comparable group to evaluate both the product and the . . . advertising claims. Such a committee, however, functions better in theory than in practice. Most journals cannot command the expertise necessary to cover the broad range of pharmacology." [93]

He and other editors have agreed, however, that their continued publication depends on continued advertising support, as uncomfortable as this may sometimes be. One editor indicated the dilemma by replying to an angry physician: "I agree that the advertisement in question was offensive and possibly misleading, but we had to accept it. We need the money."

In 1971 the editor of a journal directed primarily at interns and residents wrote: "Concern about the pernicious effects of advertising on *The New Physician* audience has prompted demands that *TNP* create its own advertising standards and review board, or that *TNP* eliminate pharmaceutical ads altogether. The latter suggestion, while it has a certain romantic appeal in some quarters, would leave the journal morally rich and financially defunct. Fifty-four percent of the journal's advertising revenues come from pharmaceutical companies." [94]

Other physicians have testified that some medical journals had "refused to publish articles criticizing particular drugs and methods of therapy, lest advertising suffer," and some journals have been exposed to pressures so great as to cost the jobs of editors who have incurred the wrath of the drug industry.[95]

Since the enactment of the Kefauver-Harris Amendments in 1962, and FDA's implementation of more rigid drug advertising regulations commencing in 1966, the situation has been somewhat different. The new regulations require that a drug advertisement must normally include the following: [96]

    (1) A fair summary of the effectiveness of the drug in the conditions for which it is offered, and a similar summary of all the side effects, contraindications, precautions, and other warnings that are applicable

    (2) A fair balance in presenting the information on effectiveness and the information on hazards

    (3) A reasonably close physical association of the information on effectiveness and the information on hazards, together with a discussion of the adverse data in the same degree of prominence that is used for the claims of effectiveness

    (4) The use of only those promotional claims which have been cleared in advance upon approval of the drug by FDA.

Normally, the various claims and warnings must be printed in the so-called package insert that accompanies all drug shipments. The package-insert material, approved by FDA before the drug may be put on the market, is then supposedly established as a guide for all advertising related to the product.

These regulations, which have been implemented for more than seven years, were originally opposed strenuously by most of the major drug companies, the agencies that handled their advertising, and the medical journals that published it. It seems evident now that, somehow or other, most of the interested parties have learned to live with the new laws. The value of some of the regulations has been questioned—notably on the grounds that the required warnings are so lengthy and detailed that many physicians may not bother to read them, and that physicians may not even see the package insert—but they have given medical magazine publishers at least some assurance. If a proposed advertisement carefully follows all of the material approved for the package insert, it will probably not be found to be false or misleading. Unfortunately, however, no one can be sure until *after* the advertisement has been published. At present FDA does not have the money or the manpower to require and conduct preclearance of all advertisements.

Although there are many loopholes that need to be closed, the problem of unreliable drug advertising has apparently been somewhat alleviated. As the commissioner of FDA testified in the summer of 1967, "I may be an optimist but I begin to feel that I am seeing some improvement in journal advertising. I look at these journals and I have greater difficulty in finding violative ads just on quick inspection."[97]

What remains essentially unabated is the problem created by the sheer bulk of drug advertising and other promotion, and its relation to over-prescribing, needless prescribing, and other irrational practices on the part of physicians.

PDR: BIBLE FOR PRESCRIBERS

Although the fact is not widely recognized, the throwaway group also includes *PDR*, or *Physicians' Desk Reference*, which is used by many physicians as the virtual bible of prescription drugs. Published by *Medical Economics*, *PDR* is in fact simply a compilation of *paid advertising purchased by the major brand-name companies.*[98] Over a period of more than twenty years, *PDR* has won a reputation that verges on sanctity. A survey conducted a few years ago by the Opinion Research Corporation for PMA revealed that it was the source of prescribing information most often used by 82 percent of physicians in a selected sample.[99] In a more recent survey conducted by the AMA on its own members, with 96,950 doctors replying, their prescribing was reported to be "markedly" influenced by direct mail promotion in 1 percent, by medical journal advertising in 2 percent, by detail men in 11 percent, by package inserts in 17 percent, by FDA notices and publications in 18 percent, by the AMA's own *AMA Drug Evaluations* in 20 percent, by the opinions or recommendations of other physicians in 30 percent, and by *PDR* in 37 percent.[100]

Many physicians appear convinced that the products included in *PDR* have been specially selected or screened by an expert review board. Actually, the products included in each annual issue are merely those that an indivudual manufacturer wishes to advertise. The advertising material is essentially that which has been approved by FDA for use in the package insert, and is thus technically regarded as labeling that must conform to the FDA's full-disclosure requirements.

In general, even though they also meet FDA requirements, generic-name products are rarely promoted in *PDR*. A manufacturer of such a generic product as phenobarbital, for example, would find it illogical to advertise a drug that is marketed by many of his competitors under the same name. But many physicians seem to believe that the absence of a generic-name product from *PDR* is a sign that the product is of low quality or otherwise inferior.

The advertising revenues obtained by *PDR* make it possible for the publication to be distributed free each year to practically all practicing physicians and hospitals.

THE GIFT GAMBIT

Another promotional device—and one that is unequivocally tied to the company name—is the free-gift method. Many companies have generously offered free medical bags to medical students, free drugs for students and their wives, free baby foods for their children, free textbooks, free class steak parties and beer busts, free weekends in Manhattan, and even part-time jobs as detail men. To practicing physicians they have offered cocktail parties, golf tournaments, free golf balls, free prescription pads (sometimes with the name of the company's product already printed on the sheets), hospitality suites at medical conventions, and unlimited supplies of free drug samples. They have offered such rewards as microwave ovens, color television sets, and wristwatches to physicians who purchase minimum dollar amounts of drugs for their office use—a practice that the AMA's Judicial Council had denounced as "rebating." [101]

Some medical students and some physicians have openly sought such presents. Others have rejected them with more or less passion. The significance of these gifts in influencing the long-term prescribing patterns of a doctor remains open to question, but the advisability of the practice, which has been attacked as an unsubtle form of bribery, seems to be limited. "When we returned the gifts to Eli Lilly, which was perhaps ungentlemanly and rude and in a sense inconsistent," one student said, "Lilly responded by saying they thought we were very ungrateful, which brings up the whole problem: why should we be grateful to a company whose products we have to prescribe for our patients?" [102]

A distinguished physician commented in these words: "Granted that the line between attracting attention and seducing is a fine one, these extremes are not worthy of an industry and a profession whose actions are so closely bound up with the health, the safety, and the lives of the public." [103]

ADVERTISEMENTS WITHOUT ADVERTISERS:
THE PROBLEM OF "UNDER-THE-COUNTER" PROMOTION

When a physician begins reading an advertisement carrying the name of a drug company, or listening to a company detail man, he is—at least in theory—on notice that the accompanying presentation may be a more or less biased sales presentation. This is identifiable advertising.

Totally different is the situation when the source is not readily identified—when the advertising is offered in the guise of a news report carried by the Associated Press or United Press International, published in the *New York Times*, the *San Francisco Chronicle*, or other newspaper, included in an ostensibly objective article in the *Reader's Digest*, or incorporated in the lecture of a seemingly independent scientist or practicing physician. This approach, with the source of the advertising not readily ascertainable, may well be termed under-the-counter promotion. The propriety of such a technique may be in doubt; its efficacy is not.

One customarily practiced device is the drug-industry-sponsored conference or symposium devoted either to a particular new drug product or to a clinical problem in which the product may seem to have value. The nominal host may be a medical group, a medical school, or a medical or scientific academy. The speakers may include various Americans, although European participants supposedly provide desirable glamor. It is generally considered useful to include a hundred or more physicians in the audience, but it is far more desirable to have the largest possible attendance of newspaper, magazine, and trade journal writers. The indoctrination of the doctors in the audience is viewed as helpful, but more importance is placed on the accounts filed by the press representatives present and on the formal published proceedings of the conference, which may be used for months or years thereafter as "scientific" background.

In the case of psychiatry, for example, Dr. Natalie Shainess of the William Alanson White Institute told a Senate hearing, "The extent of drug advertising, and the rewards which drug companies have used, have so taken over psychiatrists, that it is really frightening. There is virtually no meeting, no publication, no event that is not funded in part or in whole by the drug companies." [104] When the company financing such a program is openly identified, the physicians in the audience—and the press representatives—are appropriately alerted. When the sponsorship is less evident, physicians and the public may be led astray.

A related technique involves the participation of seemingly un-biased scientists or clinicians in a conference, symposium, or postgradu-ate education program, especially when this participation involves extolling the use of a drug for purposes that cannot be supported by evidence submitted to FDA. When such a recommendation stems from a competent and truly independent speaker, the value to the scientific community may be apparent. But that community is entitled to know if the speaker has accepted financial support from the drug company.

At least in the past, numerous physicians, scientists, medical school faculty members, and even governmental officials have participated in this manner. In some instances they have apparently spoken from sincerity, and incidentally—but quietly—have accepted travel expenses, entertainment, a consultant fee, an honorarium, a research grant, or other remuneration from the drug company. In other instances they have allowed the company to review or actually censor their text beforehand, or have even had a company representative write the speech.[105]

These kept scientists and doctors, known in the trade as "the stable," [106] have also been employed in the preparation of articles for medical journals. An editor of a reputable journal would presumably reject such articles, but some have apparently slipped through the editorial screening process. In throwaway publications owned or con-trolled by a drug company or its advertising agency, however, these articles may be printed and then quoted thereafter as scientific evidence.

An equally effective method may involve the direct publicizing of a product to the public. Although a company may not legally advertise a prescription drug to the public, it may provide information to a newspaper or magazine writer. When this has been done properly, the results have usually been informative to both the public and the medical profession and beneficial to the company. Here the ingredients generally include a company spokesman who will provide all the facts, good and bad, without making any attempt to puff up claims or gloss over hazards, and a competent medical or science writer.

But this procedure has not always been followed. Some products have been publicized while they were still undergoing controlled laboratory or clinical tests, and long before they were available to the public. Some—notably a number of cancer and arthritis "cures"—have been extolled far beyond the scientific facts. Some have been praised with little or no mention of their dangers. Science writers have long been accustomed to receiving press releases on some new drug that, on guinea pigs and other experimental animals, has had a remarkable effect in controlling cancer—"thus promising an early breakthrough"—but that never is found to be effective in human beings.

In recent years particular criticism has been directed toward the publicizing of drug products in the so-called news columns of throwaway medical journals. Many of these accounts have been marked by exaggerated claims, but since the purported source of the news is generally an independent physician—or one whose connection to the company cannot be proved—the article is technically not an advertisement and is therefore beyond the reach of FDA.

Sometimes the source of such exploitation has been a drug company. Occasionally it has been an overly enthusiastic individual or group of practitioners. Among the products involved in these various types of non-advertiser advertisements have been Indocin for "tennis elbow," DMSO for the alleviation of arthritis and a host of other conditions, Chloromycetin for trivial infections, MER/29 for atherosclerosis, diphosphopyridine nucleotide (DPN) for alcoholism, amphetamines for long-term control of obesity, and Vitamin B_{12} for anything except pernicious anemia. In some instances the publicizing of such products has led only to the waste of a few dollars—or sometimes a great many—by the patient. In others, however, the result has been the tragic creation of false hopes, or complete catastrophe.

OPTIONS FOR ACTION

Many proposals have been offered to control the quantity of prescription drug advertising and improve its quality. For example, both in the United States and in other countries, it has been suggested that limitations be placed on the amount of drug advertising expenditures that can be accepted as business expenses for tax purposes. It has been frequently urged, both here and abroad, that detail men should be licensed by governmental agencies and required by law to give factual, unbiased presentations. Some industry critics have offered the idea that "truth squads," composed of qualified clinical pharmacologists or other professionals, should call regularly on physicians to rectify any misleading claims made by detail men. Repeatedly, there have been demands that all prescription drug advertising, or at least the basic theme of each campaign, should be precleared by FDA. More and more, there are recommendations that each physician should be furnished a publication —prepared by either a governmental agency or a medical group—containing objective, up-to-date information on the relative value of drug products and the reliability of the claims made for them. One such publication is the new *AMA Drug Evaluations*, which is discussed in chapter 12.

These and other approaches are considered in chapter 13. None of them, however, can be as effective as a hard core of critical judgment and skepticism, built into each medical man while he is in medical school and maintained throughout his professional career.

No. 4

The Impossible Dream: Search for the Absolutely Safe Drug

SINCE at least the time of Hippocrates it has been the cardinal rule that a physician should never administer or prescribe a drug more dangerous than the disease afflicting his patient. Except perhaps during the period of homeopathy, when drugs were given in such extreme dilution that they had essentially no danger—and essentially no physiological effect—this rule has been constantly violated.

There are many reasons underlying this centuries-old record. Under ordinary conditions, whether they be those of the fifth century B.C. or those of the twentieth century A.D., the maker of a drug product would rarely be inclined to place much emphasis on its hazards. Under ordinary conditions a patient seeking medical care would apparently prefer to get a prescription for a potentially risky drug than no prescription at all. And under ordinary conditions most physicians would be loath to admit that they—or any of their colleagues—had ever prescribed a drug with undue dangers.

These attitudes may be illustrated by the almost incredible story of morphine,[1] which was carelessly marketed, prescribed, and used during the last half of the nineteenth century, and even into the twentieth, in spite of seemingly overwhelming proof of its dangers. Many physicians staunchly refused to believe that it could be addicting. Or, they said, it might contribute to the "morphine habit" when given by mouth, but was perfectly safe when injected. Patent-medicine makers made fortunes advertising and selling pain-killers, cough mixtures, consumption cures, and remedies for "pelvic conditions of women," cancer, rheumatism, neuralgia, diarrhea, cholera, and even soothing syrups for babies, without informing the public that the major ingredient of their products was opium or morphine.

At the same time, cocaine—or an extract of coca leaves—was widely advertised as an almost universal cure.[2] A major figure in the cocaine business was Dr. Angelo Mariani of Paris, who prepared the material in the form of wines, elixirs, pastilles, lozenges, and even tea. One of his colleagues said, "Thanks to Mariani wine, I have been able to restore the voice of many lyric artists who would have been unable without this potent agent to give their performance." Another testimonial read, "This young woman complained of weakness and general atony, headache, dizziness, vertigo, tendency to lipotynie caused by sorrows, sitting up late at night, and general depressing influences. . . . There was insomnia and a tendency to night sweat. I prescribed Mariani wine. At the end of a month's treatment, her state was most satisfactory." In medical circles Mariani's advertising was generally considered to be accurate, since he gave the strict warning: "Beware of substitutes." Until nearly the end of the nineteenth century many physicians denied that cocaine could be dangerous. In fact, some—among them was Sigmund Freud—recommended the use of cocaine for the treatment of morphine addicts.

Perhaps the most remarkable event in this portion of history came in 1898, when Heinrich Dreser of Bayer announced a new morphine derivative that, according to his claims, was nonaddicting, effective in controlling pain, and so safe that it could be used to treat morphine addiction. The new product, known technically as acetyl-morphine, performed so heroically that it had been named heroin.

THE 1906 LEGISLATION

Attempts to guarantee the safety and purity of drug products—and even their efficacy—have long concerned physicians, pharmacists, drug manufacturers, and governmental agencies. During the 1700s fumbling efforts were made to set and enforce standards, and during the 1800s, especially in France and England, the first modestly effective laws were

passed. What was probably the first practical legislation to control the
purity of both foods and drugs was enacted in England in 1872.[3]

In the United States the spirit of reformers was present at an early
date, but the willingness of Congress was not. From 1871 to 1905 nearly
two hundred bills to require the purity of foods and drugs were
introduced, yet not one important measure was passed. In the waning
years of the nineteenth century, however, the stage was set for action.
(For a detailed account of these events the reader is referred to the
colorful and carefully documented histories by James Harvey Young,
The Toadstool Millionaires and *The Medical Messiahs*.[4])

At the outset this battle was waged largely by a few reputable food
producers, a few congressmen from food-producing states in the Mid-
west, and small groups of consumers who were outraged by the
marketing of flour contaminated with weevils and rodent droppings,
adulterated cooking oils, putrefying meat, meat laced with inordinate
amounts of chemical preservatives, and other contaminated, mislabeled,
unsafe food products. At the same time the American Medical Association was angrily denouncing many nostrums and quack remedies—some
totally ineffective, others containing mainly narcotics or alcohol—that
were widely exploited as cures for cancer, diabetes, tuberculosis, "female
complaints," and essentially all the ills of man and beast.

The drive for corrective legislation was spearheaded by one man,
Dr. Harvey Wiley, chief of the Bureau of Chemistry in the Department
of Agriculture—chemist, indefatigable crusader, and curmudgeon. Although he had some interest in controlling impure drugs, his major
target was impure food. Periodically he issued reports from his laboratory to indicate the real nature of so-called food products that were
being widely advertised to the American public and pushed into the
American gastrointestinal tract. He attacked the manufacturers of
adulterated foods, and the lawyers, lobbyists, and congressmen who
defended them. He battled the publishers of newspapers and magazines
who were profiting handsomely from the advertising of impure foods. He
called for new and potent laws at the federal level, and for strong
enforcement.

Year after year Dr. Wiley and his supporters failed to make any
significant progress. Then backing came from an unexpected source, the
so-called muckraking press. Reporters like Samuel Hopkins Adams,
writing in *Collier's*, Mark Sullivan in the *Ladies' Home Journal*, and
William Allen White in the influential *Emporia Gazette* began reporting the revolting facts to the public. Of particular strategic significance

was Upton Sinclair's *The Jungle*, which revealed the appalling unhygienic conditions in the Chicago stockyards. Together these muckrakers created a public demand which could no longer be denied. The result was the Pure Food and Drugs Act, passed by the Congress and signed by Theodore Roosevelt in 1906.

The new legislation, often known as the Wiley Law, received its baptism under legal fire in a case involving a potent headache remedy called Cuforhedake Brane-Fude. Advertised as giving "a most wonderful, certain and harmless relief," and containing "no . . . poisonous ingredients of any kind," it was composed of acetanilid, antipyrine, caffeine, sodium and potassium bromide, and 24 percent alcohol. Profits had reputedly reached the $2,000,000 mark. In a memorable and perhaps prophetic decision, the manufacturer of the Brane-Fude was found guilty of misbranding and fined $700. One commentator calculated that this left the manufacturer $1,999,300 ahead.[5]

The Wiley Law closed a few loopholes in the marketing and promotion of impure, unsafe products, but it was marked by three serious flaws. First, as Dr. Wiley himself quickly admitted, although it provided some measure of control against impure foods, it had little impact on impure or unsafe drugs. Second, many people felt reassured that passage of a law meant that the problem was essentially solved. And third, enforcement of the law was assigned primarily to Dr. Wiley, who was a magnificent crusader but a less than adequate administrator. He was soon embroiled in bitter disputes with Roosevelt and his secretary of agriculture, and later in similar feuds with President Taft, and was obliged to resign.

An additional problem involving drug promotion stemmed from a Supreme Court decision that the Congress had really meant to control false and fraudulent representations but not to regulate "mistaken praise" for drugs. As a result, the more ignorant the drug promoter, the more likely he was to escape legal restraint.[6]

Dr. Wiley was succeeded first by Dr. Carl Alsberg, a distinguished and tactful chemist, and then by Walter Campbell, a competent attorney, an expert on enforcement, and a magnificent administrator. It was Campbell who directed operations while they were the business of the Bureau of Chemistry, later to become the Food, Drug and Insecticide Administration, in the Department of Agriculture. Still later, the agency—retitled the Food and Drug Administration—would become part of the new Federal Security Administration, and then part of the Department of Health, Education, and Welfare.

After its enactment the Pure Food and Drugs Act was bulwarked here and there by occasional minor changes, but these were inadequate, and major new legislation seemed essential. The campaign began one morning in 1933, when Campbell met a young Columbia University economics professor, Rexford Tugwell, who had been brought to Washington as assistant secretary of agriculture and one of Franklin Roosevelt's new "brain trust." Campbell told Tugwell of the need to strengthen the law, particularly to improve the control over unsafe drugs. On the afternoon of the same day, Tugwell told Campbell that he had already discussed the problem with President Roosevelt and that FDR had given his blessings to the drafting of a new law.

The proposed legislation was drafted and eventually introduced by Senator Royal Copeland of New York, a conservative Tammany Democrat, homeopathic physician, one-time health commissioner of New York City, and author of a health column for the Hearst newspapers. Even with his distinguished backing, the bill could make no progress through the Congress. One reason was that it was popularly known not as the Copeland bill, but as the Tugwell bill, and Professor Tugwell—who had once spent two months in Russia and who openly expressed his belief in a planned economy—was viewed as an archenemy of big business.

The need for tightened control seemed only too obvious. Unsafe drugs were still on the market—manufacturers had found numerous ways to get around the 1906 law—and products were being exploited with unsupportable claims. Drug advertising in newspapers and magazines, and now on the radio, was blatant and booming, and most publishers were not visibly in favor of giving up this lucrative revenue. Although a few responsible drug companies saw the need for improvement, most drug makers bitterly fought against the Tugwell bill and sought even to weaken the 1906 law. In support of Tugwell and Dr. Copeland were the ardent women's organizations and consumer groups. The AMA backed portions of the bill, though with no great enthusiasm. There was also an important muckraking book, 100,000,000 Guinea Pigs, written by F. J. Schlink and Arthur Kallet of Consumers' Research.

Meanwhile, Tugwell became disenchanted with Roosevelt and left Washington. Dr. Copeland had fallen out with the president over FDR's attempt to pack the Supreme Court. The bill itself, which had undergone constant modifications in one congressional session after another, was denounced by consumer groups as too soft and by the drug industry as too harsh. Then came a catastrophe that was destined to make history.[7]

THE ELIXIR SULFANILAMIDE AFFAIR
AND THE 1938 LEGISLATION

In 1937 the fame of sulfanilamide had spread around the world, and millions of tablets of the new drug were being used each year. One firm in Tennessee, Massengill & Co., tried a different marketing approach. On the theory that most people in the South prefer to take their medicaments in liquid form, the company sought some way to get sulfanilamide into solution. Unfortunately, the substance does not dissolve readily in water, alcohol, or any of the usual biological solvents. It would, however, dissolve in di-ethylene glycol. To such a solution a little coloring matter and raspberry flavor were added, and the product was put on the market under the name of Elixir Sulfanilamide. So far as can be determined, no one at Massengill tested the Elixir for safety on human subjects or experimental animals, or even looked up the toxicity of di-ethylene glycol in the textbooks.

Soon after marketing began, Dr. Morris Fishbein at the AMA received a telegram from Tulsa, Oklahoma, reporting that six people had died, all with the same unmistakable signs of kidney damage. All had taken Elixir Sulfanilamide. Did Dr. Fishbein know the ingredients of that Elixir? He did not know, but he proceeded to find out. He called the factory, but the Massengill people declined to give away a trade secret that might benefit their competitors. Finally, under insistent prodding, they admitted that the product contained di-ethylene glycol. To Dr. Fishbein the shocking answer was clear: di-ethylene glycol, which in the body turns into kidney-destroying oxalic acid, was the cause of death—a slow and exceedingly agonizing death.

The Food and Drug Administration in Washington was notified immediately, and FDA field men were ordered to confiscate every bottle of the deadly Elixir that had already been distributed to pharmacies and physicians. Newspapers, radio stations, and posters covered the South with warnings, but in too many cases these came too late. Salesmen lied about their customers, druggists altered their records, and panicked physicians crept into pharmacies at night to destroy their prescriptions.

At the end, when nearly every bottle had been tracked down, the total of known deaths stood at 107. Many of the victims were children. All that could be done to the manufacturer under the law as it then stood—the old 1906 law—was to penalize him for misbranding his product. According to the law, an elixir is a solution in ethyl alcohol. Di-ethylene glycol is not ethyl alcohol. The manufacturer later told reporters: "My chemists and I deeply regret the fatal results, but . . . I do not feel there was any responsibility on our part." His chief chemist felt differently. He committed suicide.

The public reaction to the Elixir Sulfanilamide tragedy quickly brought action by the Congress. The new Food, Drug, and Cosmetic Act was passed by both houses of Congress in June 1938 and signed into law by President Roosevelt. Ironically, Dr. Copeland collapsed on the Senate floor and died on the last night of the session, never knowing whether Roosevelt would sign the bill.[8]

Although the 1938 law did not incorporate all the new authority that FDA had wanted, it did provide the agency with important new powers. The regulations against false and misleading advertising were stiffened, appropriate warnings had to be included in the labeling, excessively dangerous drugs were banned, enforcement procedures were strengthened, and penalties for violations were made more severe. Of particular importance, no new product could be put on the market until the manufacturer presented convincing evidence to FDA that it was relatively safe. Significantly, the new law did *not* require the drug maker to produce convincing evidence of efficacy.

Although industry spokesmen had charged repeatedly during the congressional hearings that the new rulings would cripple their research, slow the introduction of new drugs, and thus injure patients, it quickly became evident that the industry could live—and continue to prosper— under the 1938 law. Although some physicians had asserted that taking any drugs off the market would represent destructive government interference in the practice of medicine, medicine continued to be practiced successfully and profitably. And although some publishers had denounced advertising restrictions as a violation of freedom of the press, drug advertising revenues continued to rise each year, and freedom of the press did not disappear.

Perhaps the most unhappy influence of the 1938 law was its effect in reassuring many laymen and physicians that drug safety was now guaranteed by federal law and that therefore all drugs legally on the market were absolutely safe. Repeatedly, physicians and scientists have emphasized that absolute drug safety is practically impossible to achieve. With few if any exceptions, there is no biologically effective drug that, under certain conditions, cannot injure or destroy tissues, or kill. *The goal, therefore, must be relative safety—a drug which is less dangerous than the disease against which it is used.*

It is clearly imperative that its safety must be painstakingly assayed before any new drug is released for use. As Dr. Chauncey D. Leake of the University of California put it, "There is no shortcut from chemical laboratory to clinic, except one that passes too close to the morgue." [9] In this respect, it is essential to recognize that three loopholes are always present with any drug product: (1) Relative drug safety cannot be achieved if the dangerous side effects of the drug are not known. (2) It cannot be achieved if these side effects are known to the manufacturer but not honestly reported to physicians. (3) It cannot be achieved if the side effects are reported to physicians, but ignored by them.

THE CHLORAMPHENICOL AFFAIR

Here the case of chloramphenicol—marketed by Parke-Davis under the brand name of Chloromycetin—deserves attention. Introduced in 1949, this antibiotic was quickly found to be effective in the treatment of such infections as typhoid fever, hemophilus influenza, and a number of diseases caused by staphylococci and other organisms. Similarly, by the early 1950s there was little doubt but that the use of chloramphenicol was occasionally associated with the development of serious or fatal blood destruction. The problem was not merely that another useful drug turned out to have unpleasant side effects, but rather what the manufacturer and prescribing physicians did about it.

As is indicated in chapters 3 and 12, the record of the manufacturer is open to serious question. For about fifteen years Parke-Davis promoted its product in such a way that its evident dangers were minimized or totally ignored. It was recommended directly or by implication for use not merely in typhoid and other diseases for which no other agent was then suitable, but also in conditions for which other antibiotics—practically as effective and far safer—were available. As a result, in the United States, where experts estimated that chloramphenicol should have been properly prescribed for less than 200,000 patients a year, it was actually administered to more than 3.5 million.[10] Many of these were suffering from mild infections in which safer drugs, or no drugs at all, could have been used, while others were afflicted with such diseases as the common cold and virus pneumonia in which chloramphenicol had never been shown to have any value.[11]

The number of known deaths caused by the drug (several hundred in the United States) was relatively small. Each, of course, was a tragedy. Perhaps more tragic is the fact that most of those fatalities were needless, since most of the use of the drug was irrational. To the extent that such irrational prescribing was the result of misleading advertisements or overly enthusiastic promotion by detail men, the manufacturer deserves condemnation. But the dangers of chloramphenicol had been widely publicized by FDA and by leading medical journals. Accordingly, the prescription of this drug to millions of patients a year who could have been treated effectively and more safely with other agents warrants the indictment of the physicians involved.

THE MER/29 AFFAIR

Somewhat different was the affair of triparanol, a new drug developed by the William S. Merrell Co. of Cincinnati, a subsidiary of Richardson-Merrell, and introduced as an agent to reduce blood cholesterol levels. The hope was that it would prevent atherosclerosis and coronary disease. Marketed under the code name of MER/29, it seemed to represent another but not unusual case of a presumably safe drug which later was found to possess totally unforeseen and unpredictable hazards.

According to the official records, the new drug application for MER/29 was submitted to FDA in July 1959 and approved in May 1960. By late that year physicians were reporting that use of the drug in their patients was causing baldness and an alarming number of instances of skin damage, changes in the reproductive organs and the blood, and serious eye damage, including the production of cataracts. On December 1, "in cooperation with the Food and Drug Administration," Merrell was obliged to send a warning notification to all physicians. On April 12, 1962, Merrell withdrew the drug from the market. But, as later investigations revealed, that was not the whole story.

During the late 1950s, when Merrell was conducting intensive laboratory trials—mostly on rats, dogs, and monkeys—a young laboratory technician, Mrs. Beulah Jordan, the wife of a Cincinnati telephone company engineer, was hired to undertake the tests on a group of monkeys. One day she observed that one of the monkeys being administered MER/29 was losing weight, and that it was no longer able to jump from its cage to the laboratory scales for the once-a-week weighing procedure. It leaped, but it landed in the wrong place. The animal seemed to perform as if it were partially blind. "Its eyes did not look right," she said.[12]

Mrs. Jordan reported this to her supervisor, a "Dr." William King (it later appeared that he had not yet been awarded his doctor's degree) who in turn informed Dr. Evert van Maanen, a Dutch-trained physician who was serving as Merrell's director of biological sciences.[13] "Dr. van Maanen, with the concurrence of Dr. King," it was later testified,

> then decided to throw out the sick male drug monkey mentioned above from the experiment and substitute another control monkey in his place which had never been on MER/29.
>
> After this decision, Dr. van Maanen called Mrs. Jordan into his office and instructed her to make this substitution in working up the weight charts. . . . Mrs. Jordan resented being asked to . . . render a false report, and refused to sign her charts. Dr. King ordered her to never mention the substitution. She was told that this was the way the Company wanted it and to forget it. She was told that this order had come from higher up and there was nothing she could do about it but obey the order and do as the "higher-ups" wanted.[14]

Mrs. Jordan did not forget about it, and soon quit her job. Early in 1962, after Merrell had warned physicians that "recent discoveries" disclosed the dangers of the drug, she mentioned to her husband the curious events of two years before. Her husband then happened to mention it to the members of his car pool. Among his fellow riders was Thomas Rice, who happened to be a supervisory inspector from the Cincinnati office of FDA. Rice found the situation not merely curious. He immediately called FDA headquarters in Washington, D.C., and a three-man inspection team was instructed to visit the Merrell laboratories.[15]

The results of that inspection brought to light a shocking record of fraud and deceit. The laboratory notebooks, once the FDA men managed to obtain them, showed that the death rates among groups of experimental animals were far higher than those reported to FDA. Even before the new drug application was approved, the company was aware that relatively low doses would produce tissue damage and interfere with fertility in experimental animals. Before the application was approved, at least some Merrell scientists knew that the drug could wreck the eyes of rats and monkeys.[16] None of these findings was reported to FDA. At that time, some FDA experts had expressed concern that, even on the basis of the incomplete data submitted by Merrell, the drug showed "little margin of safety." [17]

Late in 1960 Merrell had invited other firms to study the drug. In

November scientists at Merck told Merrell that MER/29 could damage the eyes of rats and dogs.[18] In July 1961, while Merrell jubilantly announced that 300,000 human patients had been treated with the drug, scientists at Upjohn made a similar report to Merrell on eye damage.[19] Neither of these findings was transmitted to FDA.

The FDA search of Merrell's files also unearthed correspondence indicating the company's relationship with supposedly independent investigators. One grant was recommended for a Los Angeles physician, primarily to keep him busy for a while longer "rather than take a chance on his reporting negatively." [20] An early approach to military hospitals was explained on this basis: "We were not thinking here so much of honest clinical work as we were of a pre-marketing softening prior to the introduction of the product." [21]

An interdepartmental memorandum noted that a paper signed by a New Jersey physician—"prepared for the most part by us"—had been rejected by the *American Journal of Cardiology* but accepted by the *Journal of the Medical Society of New Jersey*. "We have received permission to purchase reprints," the memorandum stated.[22] Another internal memorandum recommended continued payment of a personal consultation fee to a physician, largely on the basis that the company could not afford to chance alienation of the physician at that time. "Perhaps," it was noted by a Merrell worker, "I shouldn't regard this as blackmail." [23]

One FDA investigator found that a group of physicians at the Cleveland Clinic had prepared a scientific paper describing "extremely toxic effects" produced by the drug in test animals. Merrell representatives, however, had intervened and allegedly "prevailed upon" the Cleveland group to withhold publication for more than two years.[24]

In still another memorandum, it was evident that one distinguished investigator, Dr. Irving Wright of New York, was less cooperative, and had refused to submit a copy of his manuscript to the company. A Merrell representative said, "I realize that this circumstance is unavoidable at times but in view of our relationship with Dr. Wright, the monies which we have expended to support the man and his work, and the importance of our knowing in advance what such a man will say, all indicate that we should still make some effort to get hold of this manuscript." [25]

Merrell's withdrawal of MER/29 did not mark the end of this unsavory and no doubt unusual episode. In December 1963 the company and three of its officials were indicted on criminal charges in federal court. In June 1964 the company pleaded nolo contendere, was found guilty, and was fined $10,000 on each of eight counts for a total of $80,000. The three individuals were given suspended sentences of six months each.[26]

In other legal actions the company did not escape so lightly. In case after case it was sued for damages by victims who asserted they had been blinded or otherwise injured by MER/29. Many of these patients were represented by lawyers who formed an unprecedented association, which became known as the MER/29 Group. Under the direction of Paul Rheingold, a New York attorney who had been a Harvard classmate and later a close personal friend of Ralph Nader's, the members of the group pooled their efforts and information in their suits against Merrell.[27]

Although most of the suits were settled out of court, about a dozen went to trial and reached jury decisions. Time after time, witnesses brought out the same details, testifying that some of the highest officials of the company had known of the drug's toxicity, and even revealing how company detail men had been instructed to cover up facts about the side effects.[28] And time after time, juries brought in verdicts for damages. In one New York case the jury called for a judgment of $1,200,000, although this was later reduced by the judge to $235,000.[29] In a California case the judgment was for $675,000—$175,000 for compensatory damages and $500,000 for punitive damages—but this was reduced by the judge, with the agreement of attorneys for both sides, to $425,000.[30] By the time the statute of limitations had run out, it was estimated that Merrell had been subjected to about 1,500 suits, involving 490 cases of cataracts alone, with court judgments and out-of-court settlements running to about $45 or $55 million.[31]

It was believed in some quarters that the suits, with all their attendant publicity, would at least temporarily wreck Merrell's good name among physicians, that these physicians might be less likely to prescribe Merrell products, and that accordingly the company's sales and profits would sink. Attorneys for the company even warned that the heavy damage verdicts might destroy the company. At first the company's stock plummeted on the New York Stock Exchange and remained depressed for several years. But, as figure 14 shows, the company's sales, net worth, and net profits all continued to *rise*.

During the brief period of only two years that MER/29 was on the market, its promotion was noteworthy. So was the effect of that promotion on physicians. The campaign was kicked off by distribution of

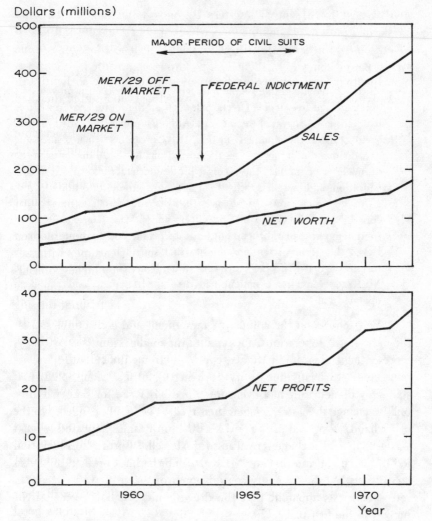

FIGURE 14. The Impact of MER/29 Litigation: Richardson-Merrell Sales, Net
Worth, and Net Profits, 1956–1972
SOURCE: Derived from data reported by Federal Trade Commission, Security and
Exchange Commission, First National City Bank of New York, Value Line
Investment Survey, and other sources.

a MER/29 manual, sent via Western Union to some hundred thousand physicians, plus direct mailing pieces and publication of multipaged advertisements in leading medical journals. "In true Madison Avenue form," Paul Rheingold of the MER/29 Group commented,

> all this material had one simple message: MER/29 had been proved safe, non-toxic and free of side effects. Salesmen on the routes and even a free handout movie repeated the message. Although proving intent to mislead the doctor was therefore easy in the MER/29 cases, it remains surprising that doctors did in fact rely on the advertising. MER/29 thus proved the oft-made criticism that the medical profession had come to rely for its education on drug sellers rather than on its own studies or common sense. . . . The proof shows, to be sure, that doctors faced a company that concealed its knowledge of side effects and provided false answers to routine inquiries about them, but nevertheless the doctors appear to have lacked the normal scientific curiosity that should have led to an early realization that MER/29 was a toxic drug. Some continued to prescribe MER/29 even after a patient had developed cataracts and had been operated on!

Few reports on the company's indictment and conviction, and on the nature of its operations, appeared in the medical journals. Attorneys representing the injured patients reported extreme difficulty in inducing practicing physicians to testify for the plaintiffs. Many physicians staunchly denied they had even prescribed MER/29 for their patients, only to change their stories when their records were subpoenaed. On the other hand, an official of the AMA's Bureau of Drugs appeared as what was described as a character witness for Merrell.[32] Further consideration led to the conclusion that the MER/29 affair had not brought any great credit to FDA, and a deputy commissioner of the agency admitted, "In retrospect, it is apparent that the drug should not have gone on the market in the first place." [33]

THE THALIDOMIDE AFFAIR AND THE 1962 LEGISLATION

A far more tragic affair, and one destined to have remarkable repercussions, was the case of thalidomide. Introduced in 1958 by a German firm, Chemie-Grünenthal, it quickly won acceptance as one of the safest sedatives ever discovered. It produced a normal, refreshing sleep with no morning-after grogginess. It was widely administered to fretful infants. It was apparently free from any significant side effects and seemed to be virtually suicide-proof. Nowhere is there any evidence that Grünenthal had failed to test it for safety by the then required testing procedures, although later the company was charged with failure to conduct adequate tests. It was approved for use in practically every major country, often for purchase without a prescription. But there were a few exceptions. For what were later described as "technical reasons," France refused to accept thalidomide. Israel delayed its approval until only three weeks before the dramatic revelation of its dangers.

In the United States the thalidomide license was obtained by the Merrell Company, which requested FDA approval to distribute the drug in this country under the name of Kevadon. On September 12, 1960, the application was assigned for routine processing to a newly arrived medical officer, Dr. Frances O. Kelsey.[34]

Under the law as it then stood, Dr. Kelsey was obliged to reject the application within sixty days, primarily on the grounds that the drug was unsafe, or it would be approved automatically. For some reason, she was suspicious. The European data seemed unimpressive. Accordingly, for sixty-day period after sixty-day period, she managed to delay a decision on the only other legal grounds available to her: the application, she said, was not complete.

The basis of her suspicions was exceeding nebulous. About the only important side effect that had been reported was a kind of peripheral neuritis, a "tingling of the nerves," that had appeared in a very small percentage of patients. When it did occur, the patient merely needed to stop using the drug and the tingling disappeared. About fifteen years earlier, however, Dr. Kelsey had done some research on a number of other drugs that can produce peripheral neuritis in experimental animals and had found that some of these substances can occasionally cause the birth of a paralyzed, stunted, deformed fetus. But there was no evidence that thalidomide had caused this effect in any of the rats, mice, and other experimental animals tested by Grünenthal. Nevertheless, Dr. Kelsey continued her delaying tactics, and Merrell, which had won approval to market Kevadon in Canada, applied increasing pressure on FDA.

Then, starting in Germany, there came the first reports of children born with phocomelia, a strange deformity marked by seal-like flippers in place of arms and legs. This was an exceedingly rare phenomenon, but suddenly 12 cases appeared in 1959, 83 in 1960, and 302 in 1961. Similar rises were soon noted in Australia, Japan, and other countries.[35]

In Germany a Hamburg pediatrician, Dr. Widekund Lenz, finally came upon the explanation. At least 50 percent of the mothers of the deformed babies, he found, had taken thalidomide during their pregnancies.[36] On November 15, 1961, he warned Grünenthal and urged the company to take immediate action. On November 26 Grünenthal withdrew the drug from the market and notified all its licensees. Two days later the West German government issued a public warning. At about the same time another physician, Dr. W. G. McBride in Australia, had independently made the same discovery and had published his findings in *Lancet*, the distinguished British journal.[37] Although the Canadian government issued a cautious warning in December, Merrell continued to market thalidomide in that country until March 2, 1962.[38]

At the end, it was estimated that the thalidomide tragedy had afflicted some ten thousand babies in at least twenty different countries.[39] Efforts to halt the use of the drug were handicapped by the fact that it was sold under dozens of different trade names and often with labels that did not disclose the thalidomide content.

Strangely, these developments remained largely unknown in the United States until the first scientific report was made to the American College of Physicians in April 1962, and reporter Morton Mintz published a dramatic account of Dr. Kelsey's role in the *Washington Post* on July 15.[40] Although the product had not been approved for sale in the United States, American families were also involved. In some cases the mothers had obtained thalidomide while they were living or traveling in Europe. In addition, samples had been widely distributed by Merrell detail men, and a large proportion of the victims were born to the wives of American physicians.

The thalidomide tragedy had three other effects. First, it made a national heroine out of Dr. Frances Kelsey. Second, it induced the Congress to take another look at the proposed Kefauver-Harris Amendments—which seemed doomed to certain defeat—and to put the proposed legislation into law. And third, it brought a change in testing for drug safety. (Later it became evident that thalidomide does not produce noticeable fetal deformities under ordinary test conditions in pregnant mice, rats, and other common laboratory animals, but causes phocomelia mainly in a few species of rabbits.) Since then, at least in the United States, no new drug can be approved until its safety in pregnancy can be adequately demonstrated.

Although the tragedies involving Elixir Sulfanilamide, Chloromycetin, MER/29, and thalidomide were important, they were not the only instances in which unsafe drugs have been promoted and prescribed. Another case was disclosed during the Kefauver hearings, when Senate investigators received a tip that they might well look into a new antidiabetic drug marketed by Pfizer. The product, chlorpropamide, or Diabinese, was competing briskly with Upjohn's antidiabetic Orinase. It was advertised as "the oral antidiabetic most likely to succeed," with an "almost complete absence of side-effects." John E. McKeen, president of Pfizer, testified before the committee that it had been investigated with great care.

On the morning before McKeen spoke, however, two documents prepared by Dr. Domenic G. Iezzoni, the company's associate director of research, were slipped under the door of the investigators. One of the reports disclosed that side effects had been noted in 27 percent of treated patients. In the second, a personal memorandum to McKeen, Dr. Iezzoni had written: "In evaluation of Diabinese we have encountered an incidence of toxicity which, at the least, is not less than that seen with Orinase. . . . Of the side-effects noted with Diabinese medication, the jaundice and exfoliative dermatitis are particularly outstanding when one realizes that, to date, there has been no reported instance of either of these complications in patients treated with Orinase." Senator Kefauver put the documents in the record. He was promptly denounced by senators Everett Dirksen and Roman Hruska for attempting to evaluate the worth of a particular drug.[41]

In still another case, Wallace & Tiernan developed a new tranquilizer known as Dornwal, and put it on the market over the strenuous objections of the company's own medical director, who felt that the drug was therapeutically ineffective. Other company experts warned that it could cause serious and possibly fatal blood damage. In October 1961, more than two years after Dornwal had been introduced, the same Dr. Kelsey who figured in the thalidomide affair was attending a medical meeting when she heard the first disquieting rumor. The company, it seemed, had failed to notify FDA that blood damage had actually occurred in at least one Dornwal-treated patient. "Before this concealment was finally discovered by the Food and Drug Administration," it was later reported, "eleven cases of blood dyscrasia attributable to Dornwal had occurred." [42] The company was found guilty on criminal charges in federal court and was fined $40,000.[43]

Another firm, McNeil Laboratories, was denounced by FDA for concealing the vital information that its drug Flexin had apparently caused serious liver damage in six patients (five of whom died) and meanwhile claiming that "Flexin has produced no irreversible toxic reactions when administered to patients daily for periods of six months." [44] The company escaped prosecution when the Justice Department ruled that the statute of limitation had already expired.[45]

THE AFFAIR OF "THE PILL"

In the recent history of drug safety, probably no products have created more furore and controversy—at least as measured by the emotional heat generated—than the oral contraceptives, known popularly and collectively as The Pill. Based on a series of new synthetic sex hormones created by Carl Djerassi and his co-workers at the Syntex Laboratories in Mexico, the first commercial version of The Pill was G. D. Searle & Co.'s Enovid. It was field tested in Puerto Rico during the late 1950s and was approved by FDA for general use in 1960.

According to FDA estimates, Enovid and competitive products that soon entered the field were being used by some 400,000 women in 1961, 1.2 million in 1962, 2.2 million in 1963, 4.0 million in 1964, and 5.0 million in 1965.[46] By 1970 the estimated number had risen to 8.5 million. From the outset the efficacy of The Pill was obvious. When used properly, it prevented pregnancy in virtually all users. From the evidence submitted to FDA, it also seemed obvious that The Pill was sufficiently safe for its widespread, prolonged use as a contraceptive.

Almost from the outset it was recognized that The Pill posed a highly unusual problem. While most drugs (the vitamins and most hormones are notable exceptions) are used for relatively brief periods, a contraceptive pill would be used by millions of women during most or all of their childbearing years. While most drugs are used to control a disease, a symptom, or other pathological condition, a contraceptive would be used to prevent an unwanted pregnancy. (Whether such a pregnancy should be defined as an illness has been endlessly debated.) While most drugs are used on patients who are ill—or who think they are ill—contraceptives would be used by women who presumably are in good health. Under these conditions, with the possibility that women might be taking The Pill regularly, month after month, for twenty or thirty years, the problem of long-term safety was destined to build up a storm of controversy.

The first signs of trouble appeared in 1961. A British physician, Dr. W. M. Jordan, reported in *Lancet* that a forty-year-old nurse taking The Pill had suffered a severe though not fatal pulmonary embolism.[47] At about the same time, Dr. Edward Tyler in Los Angeles observed that two young women taking The Pill had been stricken with similar blood clots, and both had died.[48] In Cranford, New Jersey, Dr. Edmond Kassouf found a serious case of clotting and vein inflammation in one of his patients who had been on a high dosage of The Pill. He telephoned the company and later testified, "They assured me there was no evidence to implicate The Pill." [49]

By the summer of 1962 rumors were beginning to spread in medical circles and were even mentioned in the British press. In September Searle quickly organized a conference, which concluded that there was no available evidence to show that The Pill increases the risk of blood clotting. One outspoken critic, however, later described the situation in these terms: "Within several hours of convening this meeting, before participants had an adequate opportunity to study and discuss the data presented at the meeting, the Chairman called for a vote that would, in effect, be a whitewash of The Pill. He commented, '. . . so far there has not been a single shred of evidence that has been presented in any of these figures to suggest that it contributes to a greater incidence of this disease. . . . Will everyone agree with that?' The Chairman ultimately got the vote he requested." [50] Of the participants, twenty-seven voted in favor. Only one physician voted in opposition.

The conference decision, widely publicized, did not quiet the growing uneasiness, and a special committee under the chairmanship of Dr. Irving Wright of Cornell was appointed by FDA to investigate. In August 1963 it turned in its report, concluding that no significant increase in the risk of thromboembolic disease could be demonstrated.[51] There had been 272 cases of serious blood clots reported among users of The Pill, including 30 deaths, but such clots also occurred in women not using oral contraceptives. There was, it seemed, not enough evidence to prove that The Pill involved any added risk.

For the next five years the controversy continued to grow. A Senate committee headed by Hubert Humphrey, monitoring the operations of FDA, unearthed the disquieting fact that the Puerto Rican study on which the original FDA approval was based had included only 132 women studied for at least twelve menstrual cycles—a number so small that it was later described as "scientific scandal." [52] At the same time, Dr. Kassouf—the New Jersey physician who had earlier faced a serious case of blood clotting in one of his own patients—found that among the first Puerto Rican group there had been at least two or three deaths which had never been adequately explained. Two of the women, it was claimed, had died suddenly with signs of severe chest pain. Neither of these victims had been autopsied. "To my surprise," he said afterwards, "FDA had no records of these deaths." [53]

But there were other statements that seemed to offer reassurance. Dr. Irwin Winter of Searle told the Humphrey committee, "It is difficult to reach any other conclusion but that Enovid is not only one of the most intensively investigated drugs available, but is also one of the safest." [54] Dr. John Rock of Harvard, one of the pioneers in testing The Pill, claimed that it was perfectly safe when it was taken under the supervision of a competent physician and directions were followed.[55] He assailed those who emphasized the dangers of The Pill as "irresponsible and uninformed." [56] Another Harvard authority, Dr. Robert Kistner, declared that "scrutiny of the available data by experts . . . has completely exonerated the drug as the causative factor." Another pioneer in the field, Dr. Gregory Pincus of the Worcester Institute of Experimental Biology, reviewed such possible side effects as a tendency to blood clotting and concluded, "When subjected to careful scrutiny, all of these conditions have been found to be unrelated to the use of the contraceptives." [57]

A Searle booklet stated, "The effects of birth control pills have been studied, possibly, more thoroughly and for a longer continuous time in the same persons and in more women than any other drug. Evidence of their safety and effectiveness has been continuously confirmed." [58] Another Searle promotional campaign claimed that the incidence of clots in users of The Pill was even *lower* than normal.[59] Dr. Alan Guttmacher, president of the Planned Parenthood Federation, was quoted as saying that fears of thromboembolic involvement in women taking oral contraceptives have no basis in proven medical fact.[60] In 1966 a special task force of the World Health Organization voted "unanimously" that The Pill was safe, although it was later revealed that the task force vote had been 7 to 6, and was reported as unanimous only because this was a WHO requirement.[61]

Regardless of these pacifying reassurances, there were some experts who were not pacified. Dr. James Shannon, head of the National Institutes of Health, offered his opinion that women using The Pill were "really taking a chance," [62] and Dr. Louis Lasagna of Johns Hopkins declared, "While I cannot prove it, I am convinced that women [using The Pill] have died because of clots forming in the vessels of the heart, brain, the lungs, and the intestines." [63]

In one memorable court case, Searle was sued following the death of a young South Bend, Indiana, woman who had died from a pulmonary embolism after taking Enovid. The jury found Searle not guilty of negligence or breach of implied warranty, but ended its verdict by recommending that the company should immediately warn physicians of the "dangers of the possibility of phlebitis, thrombotic and embolic phenomena." [64] In essence, as one newsman commented afterwards, the jury told Searle, "You're not guilty—but don't do it again."

Then, commencing in 1967, a series of reports from Great Britain produced the first sound basis for alarm. As to the possibility that The Pill could induce serious or fatal blood clots, a British Medical Research Council task force concluded, "The sum of evidence . . . is so strong that there can be no reasonable doubt that some types of thromboembolic disorder are associated with the use of oral contraceptives." [65] Dr. M. P. Vessey and his colleagues reported that "the risk of hospital admission for deep vein thrombosis or pulmonary embolism is about nine to ten times greater in previously healthy women who use oral contraceptives than in those who do not." [66]

While Dr. Celso Ramon Garcia—another pioneer in the Puerto Rican tests—declared that "there is no evidence whatsoever" to connect the use of oral contraceptives with clots,[67] and Searle spokesmen insisted that the British data did not necessarily apply to American women,[68] a new FDA committee report essentially confirmed the British findings. This group, headed by Dr. Louis Hellman of New York's Downstate Medical Center, concluded that the excess risk was less than that reported in England—about four and a half times, as compared with nine or ten times—but it was unquestionably present.[69] It now seems clear that clots occurred in one out of two thousand Pill users, and that death struck about thirty of each one million users. In nonusers, fatal clots occur in five women per million.[70]

In his report Dr. Hellman concluded that the oral contraceptives could be designated as "safe within the intent of the legislation," and need not be taken off the market.[71] It was a conclusion that upset some members of his committee, and that was cited, on the one hand, by Pill manufacturers to support their claims of safety and, on the other, by Pill opponents to support their warnings of danger.

At the heart of the dispute was the meaning of "safe within the intent of the legislation." To some it signified that The Pill was safe enough to be acceptable, but there was no agreement on who should decide acceptability. Should it be each practicing physician, or organized medicine, or a federal agency, or the patient herself? To others it meant that The Pill was comparatively safe, but there was no agreement on whether the risk of The Pill should be compared with the risk of other available contraceptive methods, or with the risk of diseases or death that may occur during pregnancy.

Early in 1970 the controversy flared during hearings held by Senator Nelson. Some witnesses testified that the risks of The Pill were minimal when compared with its convenience, its obviously high effectiveness, and its acceptability by women—although it was apparent that 20 percent or more of women using The Pill had given it up after a brief trial. Others testified that The Pill was less dangerous than pregnancy or even than driving on a freeway, although the relevancy of the latter fact seemed dubious.

Some physicians angrily denounced Senator Nelson's hearings as causing needless anguish among women and "interfering with the doctor-patient relationship." Leaders of the Planned Parenthood Federation warned that the attendant publicity was imperiling worldwide attempts to control the population explosion.[72] In this connection, it is noteworthy that Nelson had long been an advocate of population control and family planning.

In one heated exchange, Phyllis Piotrow, a former official of the Population Crisis Committee, suggested that the hearings would so interfere with the use of The Pill that there would be a crop of "Nelson babies." She was supported by a Republican member of the committee, Senator Robert Dole of Kansas. Morton Mintz, of the *Washington Post*, later said that the tragic effects of The Pill might therefore be personalized as "Piotrow strokes" or "Dole thromboembolisms." [73]

Midway in the hearings, *Newsweek* published the results of a Gallup Poll which disclosed that two-thirds of the women taking The Pill had never been told by their physicians of any possible hazards.[74] At least partly in response to this startling revelation, FDA announced that it was taking an almost unprecedented step: it would require a warning to be attached to each bottle, directed not to the physician or the pharmacist, but to the patient herself. The text of the proposed warning went through at least four drafts, each vehemently opposed by the AMA and the PMA. On occasion the two organizations differed strongly on the text they would approve. The final version, watered down but still opposed, was required for use in June 1970.[75]

Even as the warning requirement was put into effect, the AMA's House of Delegates passed a resolution that stated: "The proposal to supply information on side effects . . . intrudes on the patient-physician relationship and compromises individual medical evaluation. . . . The proposed statement would confuse and alarm many patients. The package insert is an inappropriate means of providing a patient with information regarding any prescription drug; the most effective way to inform the patient is through the physician." [76]

Later studies have indicated that use of The Pill may also lead to the greater risks of suffering a stroke[77] or developing gallstones.[78] Most recent evidence suggests that such risks may be minimized by utilizing newer dosage forms containing relatively small amounts of the active hormones.

THE AFFAIR OF THE ORAL ANTIDIABETICS

A comparable controversy—again involving how much the patient should be told—arose more recently when the safety of oral antidiabetic drugs came into question. According to a report by the University Group Diabetes Program (UGDP), a cooperative, long-term controlled trial conducted by twelve university clinics, the risk of dying from cardiovascular disease is more than twice as high in diabetic patients taking tolbutamide than in those taking insulin or controlling their diabetes only by special diets.[79] Essentially the same findings were reported later for phenformin. The UGDP reports were vigorously denounced on two grounds. First, it was claimed by other clinicians, the research was poorly planned and the results were not scientifically sound. Second, it was declared, the results should not have been made public in any case, since they needlessly alarmed patients.

Once again, this dispute put FDA on the spot. On the one hand, it was pressured by some members of Congress and consumer groups to take the "dangerous" oral antidiabetic drugs off the market. On the other, it was advised to take no action at all, or at least await the completion of confirmatory studies. Under the circumstances, FDA took what seemed to be a reasonable position: it called the UGDP reports to the attention of all physicians and recommended that diabetic patients should be given the oral drugs only if they could not be helped by diet alone or by diet plus insulin. It was a view that did not please everybody. "We had no other choice," an FDA official said. "We could not ignore the UGDP results. But without further research, those results certainly didn't justify banning the drugs. We decided to keep physicians informed, and let them make the decision for each of their diabetic patients." [80]

One dissenting physician, Dr. Irving Graef of New York University, told a reporter that most diabetes experts did not disagree with the intent of FDA's warning. What they resented was the fact that FDA was the one doing the telling. "We don't mind FDA putting a warning on a label that says this drug is not indicated for this or that purpose," he said. "But in this case, FDA is taking our hand and guiding it, saying do this, do that, and if that doesn't work, it may be all right to try the oral drugs. I think that is what the physicians are objecting to." [81]

By late 1973 the vital research to prove or disprove the UGDP findings was incomplete, and the manner in which the possible hazards should be called to the attention of physicians was still being disputed in the courts. Of interest to some observers of the litigation was the fact that the major suit aimed at blocking FDA was brought not by Upjohn or any other major manufacturer of oral antidiabetics, but instead by a committee of physicians. Yet, Dr. Max Miller of the University Hospitals of Cleveland noted, the attorney who filed the suit was also an attorney for *Medical Tribune*, which was closely tied to William Douglas McAdams, Inc., which in turn was an advertising agency for Upjohn.[82]

Left hanging was the question of what voice diabetic patients should have in the decision. Was it reasonable to let an individual decide that the ease and convenience of taking an oral drug would justify an apparently added risk? Or should the physician alone decide?

ON THE MINIMIZING OF MISADVENTURES

Whether this "father knows best" attitude will largely prevail is yet to be determined, as is the question of how—or whether—the success of medical care depends on the knowledge or on the blissful ignorance of the patient. It is our conviction that, in most instances, the patient's welfare will be best served if he can be given all the significant information he is intellectually, emotionally, and culturally able to absorb. The "father knows best" tradition may have worked well with patients in the past. It presumably added to the ego-satisfactions of physicians. But it does not seem to be so palatable to patients today. Certainly when it is a matter of taking a calculated risk involving drug safety, it would appear that the patient—the one taking the risk—might well have a voice in the decision.

Remaining for future solution is the problem stemming from widespread demands that a new drug must be not merely relatively safe but absolutely safe—demands that cannot be met. Here the issue is not simply the fact that no drug can be absolutely harmless. Rather, it is essential to understand that the relative safety of a drug may depend on the reasons for its use. Thus, a drug that causes death in five out of one hundred patients may nonetheless be acceptable in the treatment of inoperable malignancies for which no other therapy is known, while a drug that causes death in only one out of ten thousand patients would probably be unacceptable for treatment of the common cold. Further, it is essential for both patients and physicians to understand that a toxic side effect that occurs only rarely—for example, once in ten thousand patients—may not be recognized until at least fifty thousand patients have used the product. And a drug that causes long-delayed side effects—say, only after ten or twenty years of use—may escape implication until it has been used for ten or twenty years, or even longer.

What cannot be postponed or ignored is the problem of known or suspected hazards that are not quickly and accurately reported to the medical profession. From even the few instances discussed in this chapter it seems obvious that the mere passage and enforcement of laws and regulations has not yet succeeded in keeping all relatively unsafe drugs from use. It appears unlikely, but it is nonetheless possible, that other unsafe products may reach the market in the future, as the result of insufficient testing, fraud or deceit, the deliberate or unconscious minimizing or concealing of side effects, the venal drive of an unscrupulous manufacturer, or sheer stupidity.

It is a painful fact of pharmaceutical life that acceptable testing for safety even in the experimental animal stage is time-consuming and costly. "It is not at all unusual," a British expert stated in 1969, "for a complete program on testing toxicity of one drug to involve well over 1,000 animals, over 1,200 hemograms, about 5,000 different laboratory tests, over 700 autopsies, and histologic examinations of over 6,000 organs." [83] But these studies, and the subsequent studies in human subjects, must be done, and they must be done honestly.

In 1966, shortly after he became commissioner of FDA, Dr. Goddard told the Pharmaceutical Manufacturers Association convention:

> Now, I will admit that government employees do not have a corner on all wisdom. I will admit that there are gray areas in the IND [Investigational New Drug] situation. But the conscious withholding of unfavorable animal or clinical data is not a grey-area matter.
>
> The deliberate choice of clinical investigators known to be more concerned about industry friendships than in developing good data is not a grey-area matter.
>
> The planting in journals of articles that begin to commercialize what's still an investigational new drug is not a grey-area matter.

These actions run counter to the law and the ethics governing the drug industry.[84]

Such misadventures may not be completely preventable, but they can be minimized. This can be accomplished only by the ceaseless vigilance of physicians, patients, drug manufacturers, and governmental agencies alike. Any relaxation in that vigilance may bring another Elixir Sulfanilamide disaster or another thalidomide tragedy.

Further, there is growing recognition that the future evaluation of drugs and other chemicals ingested by human beings may require measurement not merely in relation to efficacy but also in terms of their contribution to the chemical and psychological pollution of man's internal environment. This view, which may call for a "second level" of testing, has been stressed in a 1971 manifesto signed by some of the most illustrious scientists of our times: Peter Beaconsfield, Rebccca Rainsbury, Julian Huxley, and Rudolph Peters of England, Jacques Tréfouël, Jacques Monod, and Raymond Paul of France, and Hugo Theorell of Sweden. They said:

> If the present trend continues, within the next decade almost every person in the technologically developed countries will—according to the pharmaceutical industry—be on some type of daily drug regimen for the improvement or maintenance of his positive health.
>
> This habit is becoming modern Man's response to his over-anxiety, over-weight, over-indulgence, and over-population. In addition, it is inevitable that he will be consuming an ever increasing number of food additives and substitutes the use of which is the result, in large measure, of modern economic dictates concerning demand and supply, storage and distribution.
>
> The problem of this continuous ingestion of synthetic products, their possible effects on Man, on his disease patterns, and on his physiological adaptibility to the ever increasing demands of environmental change are beginning to be recognized.[85]

The effects of environmental pollution, of physician-caused diseases, of the so-called diseases of civilization, are among "the monumental issues of our day," they said. They are all technically soluble. But while halting and correcting pollution of the external environment may be technically feasible, the cost will be astronomical. In contrast, the prevention of further internal pollution is not only relatively inexpensive but also practical, providing the problem is recognized and attacked now. "These," the scientists said, "are causes for concern not only to the specialist but also to the general biologist and all those having any responsibility for the physical and psychological well being of mankind."

No. 5

Drug Efficacy: The Case of the Emperor's Old Drugs

"But," a little child said, "the emperor isn't wearing any clothes at all!"
HANS CHRISTIAN ANDERSEN, *The Emperor's New Clothes*

IT IS in the nature of things that the overwhelming majority of people who become ill are afflicted with such minor complaints as headache, indigestion, or the common cold. Most will recover regardless of the remedies they take or do not take. Similarly, most patients with certain chronic ailments—for example, arthritis, asthma, peptic ulcer, and even some forms of emotional disease—will undergo some periods of intense discomfort and others in which the symptoms tend to disappear for a time. Even in such serious diseases as cancer and tuberculosis, medical men have long observed that some patients will inexplicably show temporary signs of improvement without treatment.

If, in any of these conditions, a patient should be given a drug—*any* drug—just at the time his symptoms were about to diminish or vanish spontaneously, it may be tempting for him or his doctor to conclude that it was the drug that deserved the credit. In all the thousands of years of drug use, few other situations have represented a more dangerous trap for the unwary. Few have provided a richer opportunity for the unscrupulous drug maker or the clinical crook.

The willingness of physician and patient alike to attribute any improvement to the therapy most recently administered was presumably responsible for the long acceptance of mistletoe, turpentine, and similar remedies as cures for epilepsy, the use of bloodletting as the established treatment for pneumonia, and the use of gelatine in the treatment of malaria. It was responsible for the nearly unbelievable period, more than a century, during which generations of physicians dosed and overdosed patients with digitalis, not for heart disease—for which it is effective—but for tuberculosis.

These and scores of other ancient remedies had seemingly withstood the test of time. They had been applauded and prescribed by many if not most medical men. Yet all of them, in the way they had been used, were utterly worthless. In some circles there is the comforting belief that all such inefficacious remedies have long since been discarded, and that every product prescribed by modern physicians must have proven value. Regrettably, this is not altogether true.

There are still some older physicians, along with their young disciples, who recommend strychnine as a tonic, port wine as a treatment for anemia, and bonded bourbon for snakebite. There are supposedly more scientific practitioners who prescribed various anticholinergic drugs—at one time, there were about 120 of these products on the market under various brand names—for the treatment of duodenal ulcer, although a leading gastroenterologist has charged that, in controlled studies, not one had demonstrated any significant value.[1] One drug has been widely prescribed for the control of nausea, although it has been reported to be no more useful than saline.[2] Amphetamines and other appetite suppressants have been prescribed for obese patients for months at a time, or even indefinitely, although there appears to be ample evidence that their effect on appetite wears off after about eight weeks.[3]

During the past few years it has been reported that cancer of the vagina—ordinarily an exceedingly rare type of malignancy—was detected in almost a hundred young girls whose mothers had been given stilbestrol to prevent an apparently imminent spontaneous abortion. The first use of the drug for this purpose dates back to 1946. In 1953 two controlled trials demonstrated its complete lack of efficacy. Yet, the director of the Clinical Center of the National Institutes of Health testified, in the late 1940s, 1950s, and 1960s, without proof of benefit, thousands of pregnant women underwent stilbestrol therapy.[4]

At one time, antihistamines were widely accepted by physicians—and still are by many patients—as effective in the control of the common cold, although their value as a cold cure was debunked many years ago.[5]

Such irrational prescribing may appear of trivial importance in some instances, at least on clinical grounds. In the case of the common cold, for instance, the death rate—with or without treatment—is reasonably close to zero. What may not be dismissed as trivial is the fact that the purchase of these products represents an expenditure of funds amounting to many hundreds of millions of dollars a year,[6] plus the fact that none of these products may be considered absolutely safe.

In this connection, special interest has been focused on so-called fixed-ratio combination products. There is, of course, nothing new about drugs in combination, for they have been prescribed and compounded for centuries, with the proportion of each ingredient tailored by the prescriber to fit the apparent needs of each individual patient. Quite different are the *fixed-ratio* combination products, with the proportion of ingredients established, not on an individual basis by the physician, but across the board by the drug manufacturers.

These fixed-ratio products have been marketed for decades, but for many years over the strenuous objections of the American Medical Association. Beginning in 1909, the AMA's prestigious Council on Pharmacy and Chemistry (later renamed the Council on Drugs) held that most of these products offered few if any advantages, most posed needless risks, and their use was irrational. The council later refused to award its impressive Seal of Approval to most fixed-ratio combinations, and such products therefore could not be advertised in the *JAMA*.

In 1955, when the Seal of Approval program was jettisoned by the AMA—largely as a result of industry pressure—the production, the promotion, and the prescription of fixed-ratio products all went into high gear. Combinations of penicillin with streptomycin and of penicillin with sulfa-drugs had already been on the market and now were backed with huge advertising campaigns. A combination of penicillin, aspirin, phenacetin, codeine, and various antihistamines was heavily pushed for treatment of the common cold, although neither the combination itself nor any of its ingredients had any demonstrable effect on the infection. Then, with the Seal of Approval program out of the way, new combinations made their appearance on the market, and in drug advertisements and in the sample cases of detail men: tetracycline with vitamins; tetracycline with aspirin, phenacetin, codeine, and antihistamines for the common cold; tetracycline with oleandomycin; tetracycline with novobiocin; and tetracycline with amphotericin.[7]

By the mid-1960s, it was estimated, fixed-ratio combinations accounted for about 40 percent of the most frequently prescribed drug products on the market.[8] The shotgun antibiotic combinations—sometimes known as "piggy-back antibiotics"—by themselves represented sales of about $200 million a year.[9] In the absence of any substantial evidence of their value, how did it come to pass that any of these products achieved and continued to maintain such popularity? "Simple," an experienced detail man explained. "Doctor A used it because we told him Doctor B used it. Doctor B used it because Doctor C used it. And Doctor C used it because Doctor A used it. For further evidence, we could mention that the product was advertised in all the best medical journals. And we could emphasize that it was selling like hotcakes. What doctor is going to question a success record like that?"

When a product did not live up to expectations, the "success record" was rarely questioned. Instead, the physician was likely to feel that the dosage had been inadequate, or the patient uncooperative. Rarely, too, was he likely to confess to his colleagues that the treatment had been ineffective. If all his brother physicians were obviously using the product successfully, any admission of failure might cast doubt on his own professional competence.

A few doctors did actually question the record. The AMA's Council on Drugs continued to battle against what it felt were irrational products, but the council's power had gone. Scores of experts, mostly in top hospitals and medical schools, spoke out in the same fashion, but they were dismissed as theoreticians and ivory-tower types who had not the least comprehension of the realities of day-by-day medical practice. It is probable that never before in history had so many physicians—all of them supposedly trained as scientifically knowledgeable professionals—been so effectively and profitably brainwashed. Ironically, the solution stemmed not from the activities of scientists or medical men, but mainly from the efforts of a mumbling, drawling, implacable attorney, Estes Kefauver, the senior senator from Tennessee.

THE KEFAUVER HEARINGS

A graduate of Yale Law School, Kefauver had first been elected to the House of Representatives in 1939 and to the Senate in 1949. As a senator, he had been a leader in the investigation of organized crime, one of the first to demand censure of Senator Joseph McCarthy, and one of the first members of the Senate to call for civil rights for black Americans, a fact that did not exactly endear him to his southern colleagues. Beginning in 1957 as the chairman of the Senate Subcommittee on Antitrust and Monopoly, he had already conducted probes on the pricing structure of the steel and automobile industries.

Late in 1957 Kefauver asked his top staff assistants to suggest the next area for investigation. Irene Till, a onetime Federal Trade Commission economist, urged him to undertake a study in depth of prescription drugs. Dr. Till had been anxious to look at prescription drug prices since 1951, when she had found that the price of an antibiotic prescribed for her husband seemed to be exorbitant, and further that the prices of all competitive products were precisely the same. To her this smacked of price-fixing, but she had been unable to induce any federal agency to look into the situation. Not even Kefauver seemed interested. Then, beginning in the summer of 1958, came two events that were destined to bring on a full-scale investigation.

First, the Federal Trade Commission for the first time reported the profit statements of major drug companies separate from the statements of the chemistry industry in general. Here it was evident that the profits of the drug companies after taxes were about 11 percent as based on sales and 19 percent as based on net worth—far above the average percentages for nearly all other manufacturing companies. Second, early in 1959 John Lear—the science editor of the *Saturday Review*—published the first of his reports on the false, misleading, and avalanche-like promotion of some drug products.[10]

Shocked by these disclosures, Kefauver and his staff members—notably Dr. Till, Dr. John Blair, and Paul Rand Dixon—decided that some dredging in depth was clearly indicated. Since adequate information, even on drug company sales to the federal government, was not then available, the senator issued subpoenas to the top drug manufacturers in the United States.[11]

From the moment that the subpoenas were mailed, Kefauver realized that he would be under substantial pressure either to quash the investigation entirely or to treat the drug industry with the greatest delicacy. Across the country, and especially in his home state of Tennessee, he quickly learned that his investigation was not viewed with any great enthusiasm by drug companies, some medical leaders, local chambers of commerce, and especially local retail druggists. He was assailed as a coonskin-hatted hillbilly publicity seeker and an enemy of free enterprise.

The opening set of hearings, which were held off and on between December 1959 and October 1960, at first were ridiculed by some industry executives. "They thought they'd come in there with all that high-priced legal and public-relations talent and mop up the floor with him," Richard Harris quotes one industry lobbyist as saying. "They simply refused to believe that he was tough and smart as hell." [12]

Kefauver was also a master strategist in conducting committee hearings. At the first session, with Francis Brown, the president of Schering, on the witness stand, he brought out at the last moment—just before the newspapermen were preparing to leave and write their first-edition stories—the curious fact that Schering's prednisolone cost about 1.6¢ per tablet to produce, but was sold to the pharmacist for 17.9¢ per tablet and to the patient for 28.8¢. He and his staff members calculated that this represented a markup of 1,118 percent, a figure that was quoted in newspaper headlines the next day from coast to coast.

Another hormone, estradiol progynon, was purchased from a French firm, Roussel, and marketed in the United States by Schering at a markup that Kefauver estimated to be 7,079 percent. That figure, too, attracted attention from the press. The Schering president claimed such markups were necessary to support the company's program of research and development and informing the medical profession. "You did no research on this drug," the senator told him. "You bought a finished product from Roussel. All you did was put it in a tablet, put it out under your name, and sell it at a mark-up of 7,079 percent." [13]

This opening exchange signaled the nature of the rest of the hearings. In session after session Kefauver and his aides disclosed the markups on one product after another, the lack of price competition in the industry, the inordinate net profits, the amount of money—an average of about 24 percent of sales—devoted by the big brand-name companies to promotion, and the apparently inexplicable fact that many American companies were selling drugs in foreign countries at a fraction of the price charged consumers in the United States.

As the investigation continued to make headlines Kefauver turned his attention from hormones to tranquilizers and then to oral antidiabetic drugs and antibiotics. Medical experts appeared as witnesses to denounce the promotion of Parke-Davis's Chloromycetin, the advertising and widespread use of combination products, and the apparent unwillingness of physicians to prescribe low-cost generic-named drugs.

Not all of the witnesses were friendly, and the hearings were vigorously attacked by spokesmen for industry and for organized medicine. Kefauver himself faced potent opposition from several of his fellow senators, notably from Roman Hruska of Nebraska and the late

Everett Dirksen of Illinois, who once described Kefauver as having the charm of a Victorian lady and the single-mindedness of an Apache Indian. Further, Kefauver felt that he was not receiving adequate support from either President Kennedy or the Food and Drug Administration.

A possible explanation for some foot-dragging by FDA officials came when John Lear published another report in the *Saturday Review*, this time disclosing the sorry story of Dr. Henry Welch.[14] Head of the antibiotic division in FDA, Dr. Welch was also editor in chief of *Antibiotics and Chemotherapy* and *Antibiotic Medicine and Clinical Therapy*, two journals owned by MD Publications of New York. He was also co-owner of the *Medical Encyclopedia*. The other co-owner was Dr. Felix Marti-Ibañez, a highly regarded medical historian, who also was the owner of MD Publications. Lear was unable to get any estimate of Dr. Welch's earnings from these extracurricular activities.

Tipped off by Lear's article, Kefauver and other investigators probed more deeply into Dr. Welch's operations and found that he was working with such firms as Parke-Davis and Pfizer with what seemed to some observers to be undue closeness. Although he admitted he was receiving "a small honorarium" for his editorial duties, government investigators later discovered that his honorariums between 1953 and 1960 totaled $287,142.40.[15] He offered to retire from FDA. The offer was accepted. Both Dr. Welch and Dr. Marti-Ibañez demanded the right to appear before the Kefauver committee and clarify the record. Kefauver notified them on May 5, 1960, that they would have such an opportunity at the hearings scheduled for May 17. Neither appeared then or at any subsequent session, both pleading illness.[16]

At the end of the investigative phase Kefauver was convinced that new corrective legislation was essential. There should be, he felt, a requirement that a drug should not be allowed on the market unless adequate evidence were submitted to FDA to show that it was not only relatively safe but also effective. The advertising and labeling of each drug should include not only its brand name but also its generic name. Advertising and labeling should include adequate warnings of contraindications and potential side effects and other hazards. Drug manufacturing plants should be regularly inspected by FDA. FDA should have ample time—not the sixty days then stipulated by law—to evaluate the evidence before clearing a new drug for marketing. Finally, provisions should be made to require a drug patent holder to license other manufacturers.

This last proposal—the one which seemed to offer the best way to reduce drug prices—was based on the feeling of some of his staff members that countries without drug product patents had discovered just about as many new drugs as had countries with drug product patents. (Later it would be emphasized that most major countries without drug *product* patents did, in fact, provide quite adequate protection through drug *process* patents. For many years thereafter this lapse was used both in the United States and abroad in efforts to discredit *all* of Kefauver's findings and recommendations.)

The proposed amendments to the law were eventually incorporated into a package known as Senate Bill 1552, introduced by Kefauver in April 1961. Senate committee hearings on the bill commenced in July and continued for seven months. To a considerable extent, these sessions were a replay of the earlier investigative hearings, but there were some notable exceptions.

To Kefauver's delight, the liberal segment of PMA—particularly Eugene Beesley, president of Lilly and chairman of the PMA board, and John Connor, president of Merck, along with PMA's special counsel, Lloyd Cutler—found much in S. 1552 that they approved. They were, however, strongly opposed to the compulsory licensing provision or any other changes in the drug patent laws.[17] On the other hand, it seemed there was little in the bill that was acceptable to the AMA. Spokesmen for the medical group opposed even the proof-of-efficacy proposal. Only the individual practicing physician, they insisted, could determine the efficacy of a drug—a claim that was later derided as "making every physician his own Pasteur."

As the hearings continued, a strong coalition developed between the AMA and the less liberal wing of the PMA. To many insiders it seemed evident that the PMA wanted AMA help in defeating the Kefauver bill, while the AMA wanted PMA assistance—and the money from drug advertisements—in defeating the Medicare bill that was also being considered by the Congress.[18]

Within the AMA there was a division of opinion that did not become public knowledge at the time. The AMA's Board of Trustees was strongly opposed to the Kefauver bill and attempted to get its own drug experts to join in the opposition. "One of the AMA attorneys came to the Council on Drugs . . . with the request that we go on record against the Kefauver-Harris Amendments," said Dr. Harry C. Shirkey. "I brought up the question, 'Does this mean we should go on record as being against safety and efficacy?' Well, this did not go over with the Council, and we turned the idea back." [19]

The reaction within PMA was described as follows:

> There was a hard-line group that wanted to sweep into Washington and try to buy up the necessary votes, and there was a more liberal group [led by Connor of Merck and Beesley of Lilly] opposed to such statehouse tactics. . . . The Kefauver hearings had all but indelibly besmirched the pharmaceutical business, they felt, and they held that the best counter-measure would be to encourage a certain amount of remedial legislation. Perhaps their most compelling argument was that history had shown drug legislation to have a way of getting stronger the longer it lay around Capitol Hill, so the chances were that if the companies succeeded in blocking Kefauver's bill, they would sooner or later get something worse.[20]

In the Senate hearings Kefauver fought virtually alone against such potent adversaries as Senator Dirksen and Senator Hruska, who had consistently supported the more reactionary stand of the PMA, and James Eastland of Mississippi, whose intense personal dislike of Kefauver was commonly known. At one point these opponents—with the apparent connivance of some administration workers—reported out a version of S. 1552 that had been so weakened that it was assailed as the "double-cross bill." It was then, however, that the story of the thalidomide tragedy swept across the country, and Congress was deluged with demands for protection. Even President Kennedy, in a letter to Senator Eastland, called for a strong bill.

In August 1962 the strengthened Kefauver bill was passed by the Senate, and in September a companion bill introduced by Oren Harris of Arkansas was approved by the House. The bill, now known as the Kefauver-Harris Amendments, was signed a few weeks later by the president. The compulsory licensing proposal had been stricken from the law, but most of the other important proposals were intact.

The outcome was due in part to the thalidomide affair, but it seems evident that most of the credit must go to Kefauver and his aides, and to the small group of senators and representatives who fought at his side. Senator Paul Douglas of Illinois put it this way when he addressed the president of the Senate:

> The Senator from Tennessee has waged a long and lonely fight for an adequate drug bill. He has been attacked by the powerful drug industry, and . . . he has not received a great deal of help from some of his colleagues. . . . But now, Mr. President, because of the many terrible

tragedies which have occurred in European countries from the use of the drug thalidomide and the cases which have occurred in this country, it has been proved that the Senator was right all the time. . . . Men who had openly and secretly fought him now flock to get on the bandwagon and pretend that they were always his supporters. As a humble American citizen, I wish to commend the Senator from Tennessee and all those who helped him, for fighting all these months and years for this great reform. Certainly, the American people will eternally be grateful to him.[21]

Kefauver did not live long enough to savor much of this gratitude. He died the following year, in August 1963.

The new law was long overdue. Many useless or irrational products had already been introduced, either by outright charlatans or by overly enthusiastic individuals or companies sincerely convinced that their product was a boon to suffering mankind. For many years FDA—like comparable agencies in many other countries—had struggled arduously but often unsuccessfully to keep worthless remedies off the market and to remove those already in use. "Ordinarily," an FDA official recalled, "it was difficult if not impossible to stop these ineffective drugs unless you could prove the company was guilty of false advertising—and that usually meant months or years of delay and costly court trials."

The problem had been especially thorny in the case of worthless cancer treatments. Thus, it took more than twenty years to stop the infamous "Hoxsey treatment" [22] and more than forty years to stop the "Koch treatment." [23] In 1970 the so-called Laetrile treatment[24] was rejected once again by FDA, after nearly twenty years of promotion by its proponents.

One of the memorable cases is that of Krebiozen, a horse-serum product introduced in 1951 with the blessings of the highly regarded physiologist and physician, Dr. A. C. Ivy, vice-president of the University of Illinois. This alleged cure had reportedly been developed by a Yugoslavian refugee, Dr. Stevan Durovic, who had worked on it for twenty years at the University of Belgrade, perfected it while working in an Argentine laboratory, and then brought it to the United States. He refused to disclose the secret of his formula to anyone—even to Dr. Ivy—because the communists might steal it. When samples of Krebiozen were tested in this country by cancer experts, the material was described as worthless—a report that ushered in more than a decade of bitter controversy. Early in the dispute one inquisitive reporter, intrigued by the Argentine background of the story, telephoned a friend in Buenos Aires—a distinguished surgeon and scientist—who assured the newspaperman that he had indeed known Dr. Durovic, that Dr. Durovic had indeed worked in the same hospital with him, and that Dr. Durovic had indeed been studying a serum; but the serum had been tested only against high blood pressure—in which, tragically, it did not work.[25] In 1973, in spite of the lack of any scientific evidence to demonstrate its value, Krebiozen was still being demanded by patients.

Another case involved arginase, a natural body enzyme, which was promoted for the treatment of cancer in the early 1950s by a California group that included a dentist who had taught at the University of California College of Dentistry until he was "not recommended for reappointment"; an Indian research worker who had been studying at Stanford University and who, in 1948, only three months before he could win his Ph.D. degree, was "disqualified for good cause"; the operator of a San Francisco college for morticians and a school for naturopaths; a San Francisco physician; an attorney; and a surgeon and onetime chief of staff at a major Los Angeles hospital. In November 1950 human trials began in Los Angeles, and eventually about 127 patients were treated. A few others were treated at a hospital in Oakland.

"The results they obtained were beyond our expectations," a spokesman for the arginase group claimed. "In every case positive results were attained, demonstrated by laboratory tests before and after treatment, by the reaction of the patients themselves, and by hospital clinical records. . . . Many near-miraculous results have been achieved."

In April 1952, after months of painstaking study by independent cancer experts, the California Cancer Commission, and a team of newspaper investigators, the rest of the story was revealed. The "hospital clinical records" were a catastrophic shambles. X-ray films and pathology reports were often incomplete, undecipherable, inconclusive, or missing. In some cases there was no evidence that the patient actually ever did have cancer. In some, the arginase had been given to patients who were simultaneously receiving X-ray treatment and other therapy. In some, it was difficult or even impossible to locate the patients or to determine whether they were dead or alive.

At the end, fifteen patients were selected for detailed study. All unequivocally had cancer. They had been given no other treatment except arginase. Of the fifteen, six had died—of cancer. Nine were still alive, but their conditions were described by experts in such terms as "tumor growing," "unfavorable progress," "tumor larger than two months ago, patient going downhill," or "patient alive but anemic, emaciated, weaker, tumor extending." [26]

In most instances, attempts by the government, the AMA, or any other group to drive these worthless remedies off the market were bitterly opposed by some people. "Generally," a reporter commented, "any producer of a useless drug—particularly a useless cancer remedy— can count on recruiting dozens or even hundreds of 'cured' patients who will gladly sign testimonials, picket government offices, and write angry letters to the editor."

Frequently the defenders of the products under attack blamed the venal machinations of the AMA or other "medical monopoly," which presumably would stoop to any means in order to keep an effective anticancer treatment from the afflicted victims who needed it. Such an argument, of course, overlooks the fact that medical men—and their wives and children—are also among the victims of cancer, and might appreciate the development of a more effective cancer treatment, no matter who discovers it.

EASY ROUND: THE PRE-1938 DRUGS

Under the terms of the Kefauver-Harris Amendments, FDA was finally given the authority to take suitable action against quack cancer remedies and all other ineffective products. The drugs involved, it was decided, should be considered in three different categories: (1) those on the market before 1938 (the year in which proof of drug safety was first required); (2) those first marketed between 1938 and 1962; and (3) those first marketed after 1962.

The first group—the pre-1938 products—were all tentatively accepted as effective under a kind of grandfather-clause agreement. This meant that such long-used and well-tested drugs as morphine, codeine, digitalis, insulin, thyroid, quinine, and the early sulfa-drugs could remain in use without further ado. Also blanketed in were a few old drugs that may not have been well established as effective, but it was believed that these were so few in number and so infrequently prescribed that they would pose no serious clinical problem. For the more recently introduced products—those first marketed after 1938—the situation was somewhat different. It was, in fact, dynamite-laden.

DIFFICULT ROUND: THE POST-1962 DRUGS

To handle new drugs coming on the market for the first time, FDA set up a complex procedure that was soon assailed by the drug companies as far too complex, too time consuming, and too expensive. "What they really were objecting to," FDA commissioner Goddard said afterwards, "was that it made them do their homework a little more carefully."

Under the new procedure no company could introduce a new drug until it had gone through two key steps, the Investigational New Drug (IND) plan and the New Drug Application (NDA) process. In submitting an acceptable investigational plan, the company was first required to provide such information as the physical and chemical properties of the drug, the process by which it was to be manufactured, the results of all preliminary test-tube and animal studies, a proposed plan for clinical trials in human subjects, and information on the training and experience of the proposed investigators.

Once the IND notification had been cleared, clinical trials could be started—first on a limited number of individuals, and usually in a research center, and then on a larger number of subjects by more physicians. All results bearing on safety and efficacy had to be collected for submission to FDA. In all but exceptional circumstances, informed consent had to be obtained in advance from all subjects participating in the trials.

With the completion of the IND study, the company could then submit the formal New Drug Application. Still more information was required: scientific evidence that the drug was relatively safe and effective, proof that the manufacturer could produce batch after batch with unfailing quality, and the proposed labeling, with ample evidence to show that any claims to be made were supported by factual evidence. "The various phases of IND and NDA may require several years," it was reported. "Five years to complete all the requirements is not considered unusual." [27]

The impact of these requirements on a drug maker was considerable. For example, a Parke-Davis official reported that when the company first marketed a particular epinephrine preparation in 1938, all it had to submit was a 27-page report concerned primarily with safety. In 1948, when it introduced a new expectorant, only a 73-page report was required. Another new drug marketed in 1958 needed a 430-page submission. But in 1962, when Parke-Davis requested FDA approval of its contraceptive Norlestrin, it had to present a report amounting to 12,370 pages. And in 1968, when approval was requested for its new anesthetic Ketamine, the required documents totaled slightly more than 72,000 pages in 167 volumes. [28]

Approximately the same amount of data was required by the Food and Drug Directorate in Canada, and nearly as much by health authorities in Japan. In Great Britain, France, and other European countries, far less supporting data was demanded, and often the decisions were rendered quickly after a relatively relaxed and informal consideration. In some instances the review system employed in these European countries meant that a new product could be cleared for use in Europe many months or even years before it was approved for use in the United States. But with the memory of the thalidomide tragedy still fresh in their minds, many physicians and scientists—both in Europe and in the United States—were not sure that such a quick and easy method of drug approval is necessarily in the best interest of the public.

There is no evidence to indicate that the health of Americans has been adversely affected to any significant degree by the so-called delaying tactics of FDA. In practically every case in which FDA has postponed its decision on a new drug for prolonged periods, equally effective products were already available for prescription. "These delays," said Dr. Goddard, "may have proved painful to a drug company anxious to market a new drug and start cashing in on its research investment, but they have not done injury to patients or interfered with the delivery of high-quality medical care."

It is significant that the new FDA requirements called not merely for more material but for a higher quality of data far different from the incredibly unscientific testimonials that once had passed as objective evidence. Dr. Goddard told a PMA meeting, "I have been shocked at the quality of many submissions to our staff. The hand of the amateur is evident too often for my comfort. So-called research studies are submitted by the carton-full, and our medical officers are supposed to take all this very seriously. I cannot." [29]

A number of companies found that much of the money and time they had expended for testimonial-type research was wasted, since FDA would not accept it, and they protested with anguish against the additional costs placed on them, and the delay in getting a potentially profitable new product on the market. Dr. Goddard told them, "If the sponsoring company is imprudent enough to waste stockholders' money on low-quality work, then that company must bear the consequences of such waste." [30]

The FDA investigations turned up various sorry aspects of what was touted as research: the submission of detailed reports and claims involving a series of two patients; claims of therapeutic miracles on patients who had not even been adequately diagnosed; the use of private physicians as drug company experts who were delighted—at a price—to sign any endorsement, provided that somebody would tell them what to report. As one reporter noted, "Some drug companies went so far as to design the 'clinical' experiment, write the testing physician's reports, and then pay him for use of his name." [31]

At the outset FDA was subjected to constant abuse—from the drug companies for moving too slowly, and from consumer groups for approving drugs too readily. By now, however, it appears that the IND and NDA procedures—although they are probably unduly complex and cumbersome in most instances—are tolerable. They have delayed the arrival of some new products on the market, although FDA has demonstrated that it can move very quickly with such high-priority items as drugs needed for the treatment of certain types of cancer and parkinsonism. The new regulations have irritated many drug company officials—although company scientists have demonstrated more under-standing—and they have required companies to invest more money in their research operations. But the companies, even though they once proclaimed that the proof-of-efficacy requirements would put them out of business, have found that they can get their good drugs approved—and their earnings have not been catastrophically depressed. One company research director said, "We really shouldn't complain too much. After all, the new regulations merely make us do what we said we were doing all along."

Further, the drug makers learned that inordinately lengthy applications running to ten thousand pages or more were not invariably required. "When the research has been properly planned and executed, and all the material submitted is cogent," a former FDA official has noted, "a report of only two or three hundred pages will be completely adequate." [32]

EXPLOSIVE ROUND: THE 1938–1962 DRUGS

The new law required FDA to wait until 1964 before demanding proof of the efficacy of drugs introduced between 1938 and 1962. The two-year period was intended to give both the government agency and the industry a breathing spell before this highly sensitive area would be touched. "This was a totally different ball game," an industry official recalls.

The drugs in question here were all on the market. They were being sold, sometimes in amounts of tens of millions of dollars a year. They represented a source of profits which industry felt were practically guaranteed. And they were being prescribed by physicians, sometimes in terms of millions of prescriptions a year. The doctors were accustomed to using them, and any question of the efficacy of these products would be a god-awful blow to their professional judgment. The whole thing was packed with dynamite.

An industry research director said, "By and large, our industry represent-atives said they welcomed any investigation, and were confident all our products would be found effective. That was whistling past the graveyard. A lot of us were nervous."

At FDA there was also some trepidation, and for nearly a year and a half the agency was in no great hurry to flex its newly acquired muscles. Then in 1966 Dr. Goddard became commissioner and decided that the time had come for action. Convinced that FDA did not have the necessary manpower to do the job itself, he arranged—with the blessings of industry—to have the study conducted independently by the most prestigious scientific groups in the United States, the National Academy of Sciences and its research arm, the National Research Council. Any decision reached by such highly regarded institutions would presumably have the best chance of acceptance by the medical profession and the industry. In July 1966 a contract was signed between FDA and NAS/NRC. In that same month the industry was invited to submit all the necessary supporting data for all therapeutic claims on the 1938–1962 drugs.

Eventually, some two hundred experts—both research authorities and practicing physicians—were assembled in thirty panels to consider roughly sixteen thousand therapeutic claims involving more than four thousand products marketed by nearly three hundred different compa-nies. About 15 percent of these were such over-the-counter products as mouthwashes, dentifrices, and cold remedies. Available to the panels for consideration were all the articles on each product published in the medical literature, all the information in the FDA files, all the additional data that the manufacturer might wish to submit, and any personal experience they may have had in their own clinical practice. It was eventually agreed that each product would be put in one of six different categories:

> *Effective*—those with "substantial evidence" of effectiveness
> *Probably effective*—those for which some additional evidence was required to rate the drug as effective

Possibly effective—those which might eventually be shown to be effective, but for which little evidence of efficacy could be found

"Effective but . . ."—those rated as effective for some recommended uses, but not for all, and which therefore would call for labeling changes

Ineffective as a fixed combination—those fixed-ratio combination products for which it was felt that one or more components might be effective if used alone, but which were not acceptable in combination for reasons of safety or because of the lack of evidence of the contribution of each component to the claimed effect

Ineffective—those with "no substantial evidence" of effectiveness.

The NAS/NRC panels were clearly faced with an enormous task. It was obvious from the outset that their decisions would not win universal approval. It soon became evident that this prediction would be amply fulfilled. In the summer of 1968 the first report was issued. This concerned a group of substances known as citrus bioflavinoids, promoted and widely prescribed for the control of capillary fragility. The NAS/NRC experts reviewed the evidence and concluded that the bioflavinoids might work admirably in guinea pigs but had no value in man. The decision: *ineffective.*

Dr. Goddard had no choice in taking the next step. Under the law as enacted by Congress, he announced that FDA was requiring the bioflavinoids to be removed from the market. He was promptly denounced as a dictator, and there were demands that he should be fired. In an apparently spontaneous campaign—at least there was no immediate proof that any manufacturer had started it—patients wrote angry letters to their congressmen and local newspaper editors and voiced their complaints on radio "talk shows."

This, however, was only the opening foray. As the months passed, the NAS/NRC panels completed more of their assignments and reported their decisions. By the end of 1970 about 360 prescription drugs—roughly 7 percent of all those considered—were listed as lacking substantial evidence of efficacy, and about 200 were rated as only possibly effective. Many more *products* were so described, since many of the drugs were marketed in different strengths and dosage forms and often by different companies.[33]

A number of companies were especially hard hit. Of the products categorized as "ineffective," twenty-nine came from Squibb, twenty-seven from Upjohn, twenty-one from Pfizer, twenty from Lederle, nineteen from Lilly, fifteen from Wyeth, and fourteen from Merck.

Nearly every major producer was involved, as were many of the smaller firms. Of the sixteen thousand therapeutic claims made for these products, about 66 percent were described as unsupported by substantial evidence as required by law.

The PMA was quick to report that about two-thirds of the "ineffective" drugs had been withdrawn from the market before the NAS/NRC list was published, and that some had been taken off several years before.[34] But, FDA officials noted, all of these products had been approved previously and could be reintroduced at any time unless government action was taken. It was the consensus of the NAS/NRC panels that

> many of the presentations submitted by manufacturers in support of the claims made for their drugs were far from convincing. The lack of evidence based on controlled studies by seasoned investigators was conspicuous. In its place, we were asked to evaluate bulky files of uncontrolled observations and testimonial-type endorsements. Moreover, independent searches of the medical literature indicated that there exists little or no scientifically convincing evidence to support many of the claims made for many drugs that have acquired a significant place in medical practice.[35]

The panels found that too many product labels, which were intended to serve as guides to the physician, were "poorly organized, repetitive, out-of-date, evasive and promotionally oriented." The whole situation, they said, was "deplorable." [36] The NAS/NRC panels generally found little value in most antibiotic combinations, antibiotic-containing cold remedies, combinations of antibiotics and sulfa-drugs, and thyroid-amphetamine combinations for use in obesity.

In the case of propoxyphene (Darvon), the experts ruled that there was enough evidence to establish its efficacy in easing certain types of pain, but they urged that the labeling of this product—one of the most heavily promoted and widely prescribed drugs in the country—needed alterations. Even in large doses, they said, Darvon had not always been found to show any superiority over aspirin or a placebo, and in smaller doses it was often indistinguishable from a placebo. Further, they noted, the labeling had failed to disclose either its close chemical relationship with such narcotics as methadone or the potential addicting properties of Darvon.

In a more recent analysis a team of University of Chicago workers declared, "We think it is reasonable to conclude, on the basis of our review, that propoxyphene is no more effective than aspirin or codeine and may even be inferior to these analgesics. . . . It appears that factors other than intrinsic therapeutic value are responsible for the commercial success of propoxyphene." [37] Similar findings were also reported from a study at the Mayo Clinic.[38]

From the time the first NAS/NRC findings were reported, and the announcement that FDA would move to take ineffective products off the market, strong protests emanated from industry. These were not tempered by the FDA policy that manufacturers of "probably effective" products would be given an additional twelve months to provide additional supporting data, and manufacturers of "possibly effective" products would get six months. Manufacturers of "ineffective" products would get thirty days to provide supporting data from their files; they could, of course, undertake new clinical trials at their leisure. With increasing vigor, industry leaders asserted that FDA had not given them enough time to prepare their cases (although they had known since 1962 that the governmental ax was eventually going to fall) or that the agency had no legal authority to act, or that its judgments had been capricious, discriminatory, inconsistent, dictatorial, and very possibly un-American. As one FDA official put it, "We find that the support we once had from industry has, in some instances, been diluted." [39]

Nowhere was the problem more intense than in the case of fixed-ratio combinations of antibiotics. Three such combinations figured with particular prominence in this controversy. One was Achrocidin, one of the most widely prescribed antibiotic products for colds and similar infections. Another was Squibb's Mysteclin-F, containing tetracycline and amphotericin, which was selling at more than $14 million a year at the retail level. The third was Upjohn's Panalba, a combination of tetracycline and novobiocin. Its sales were about $9 million a year.

Marketed by the Lederle Laboratories division of American Cyanamid and other firms, Achrocidin was a combination of tetracycline, caffeine, chlorothen, phenacetin, and salicylamide. FDA officials estimated that it was being sold in quantities more than enough for a complete course of treatment for more than 2 million patients a year. The manufacturers defended its use by presenting a survey of 274 "specialists" who overwhelmingly considered the product to be safe and effective. Dr. Henry Simmons of FDA noted later:

> Of those surveyed, 6.9 percent were pediatricians; none of their comments mentioned the inappropriateness of using tetracycline in children with developing teeth which it stains. . . . 11.6 percent of those surveyed were

obstetricians, none of whom mentioned the hazard to the fetus of using
tetracycline in the latter part of pregnancy. . . . Some of the comments of
the specialists referred to the effectiveness of the particular product for
influenza and colds, despite the fact that both are caused by viruses for
which tetracycline is ineffective.[40]

FDA ruled that Achrocidin must be withdrawn from the market. The
manufacturers appealed to the federal court of appeals, and finally
petitioned two Supreme Court justices to stay the order. Both justices
refused.

When FDA announced its decision on Mysteclin-F, it received less
than a dozen letters of commendation from physicians and more than
two thousand letters of denunciation. It struck FDA workers as a rather
curious coincidence that many of the denunciations, although typed on
the individual office stationery of physicians in many parts of the United
States, incorporated almost identical phrases, terminology, and even
punctuation. The general tenor was somewhat as follows:

Mysteclin-F has had a definite useful place among the antibiotics
prescribed in my practice, particularly for those types of patients prone to
candidal infections. I have been using Mysteclin-F for (5) years and the
FDA order to withdraw Mysteclin-F from availability for prescription use
would create an unnecessary and inconvenient restriction on my prescribing freedom to the detriment of my patients.

A possible explanation for some of the similarities in this torrent of
protests came when one physician revealed that a friendly detail man
had kindly offered to type the letter on the physician's own stationery, all
ready for signing and mailing to FDA.[41]

Dr. Herbert Ley, who had by then succeeded Dr. Goddard as
commissioner, sent a telegram to Squibb, notifying the company that he
had received many communications of protest from physicians, but was
still awaiting receipt of results of well-controlled studies as called for by
the statute.

The controversy that flared over Panalba was even more intense.
When the decision was announced that this product had flunked its
NAS/NRC test—but while the ruling was still being challenged—a
vice-president of Upjohn sent the following letter to several thousand
selected physicians:

Because of misleading and possibly misunderstood statements which
have appeared in the lay press, we would like to take this opportunity to
clarify our position and to assure you that Panalba remains available.

In the Federal Register of December 24, 1968, the Food and Drug Administration published a notice about Panalba and certain other combination antibiotics. The question is whether certain combinations of drugs should be allowed to remain on the market.

Approximately 40% of the drugs prescribed today are combinations of one form or another. In principle, if the physician's right to prescribe is denied for one category of useful drugs, it is conceivable this same right may be denied for others. We believe the decision as to whether these drugs are used should rest in the hands of the practicing physician.[42]

The letter, which closed with an invitation to the physician to write his sentiments to FDA, was itself denounced as outrageous. Among other matters, it ignored the fact that a physician who, for whatever reason, wanted his patient to get both ingredients of Panalba, tetracycline and novobiocin, could get his wish by writing prescriptions for each component separately.

A few months later the situation became even more unhappy when Commissioner Ley introduced into evidence a letter concerning some reports an FDA inspector had happened to find in Upjohn's files. "For approximately ten years," it was testified,

> it has been observed from blood serum level studies that the "Panalba" (novobiocin and tetracycline) combination results in markedly lowered and occasionally zero blood serum levels of novobiocin and the tetracycline serum level is slightly lowered. This would serve to defeat any purposeful effectiveness the two drugs may have had in combination and certainly leaves a great doubt whether this combination has ever been more or even as effective as tetracycline alone.[43]

Upjohn's officials, Dr. Ley stated, had never reported these findings to FDA as required by law. "The failure to make a report," said an FDA lawyer, "is both a ground for suspending the product from the market and for regulatory action of a criminal nature." [44]

Upjohn's letter to doctors was not its only maneuver. Company representatives carried their appeal to members of the Congress, and even to the secretary of HEW, and filed suit in federal court to block FDA from removing Panalba from the market. In July 1969 a federal judge issued a temporary injunction in favor of Upjohn, holding that the drug could not be banned until the company had a full opportunity to appeal to FDA. Early in 1970, however, a federal court of appeals handed down a decision against Upjohn. A three-judge panel reviewed the matter, including the company's argument that thousands of physicians had prescribed Panalba in hundreds of millions of doses, and decided that Congress had meant what it said when it passed the Kefauver-Harris Amendments. The court stated: "We hold that the record of commercial success of the drugs in question, and their widespread acceptance by the medical profession, do not, standing alone, meet the standards of substantial evidence prescribed by the law." [45] Later the case was carried to the Supreme Court, which declined to overrule the judgment of the lower court.

It would be nonsensical to damn all fixed-ratio combination products. In many instances they provide convenience for the patient, a reasonable guarantee that he will not take one drug and forget the other, and sometimes a significant saving in cost. In many instances the efficacy of the combination has not been seriously questioned, as with the combination of an anesthetic with epinephrine for local anesthesia, the combination of hormones in oral contraceptives, the combination of certain antituberculosis agents for use in underdeveloped countries, and the combination of different sulfa-drugs.

What has aroused the most passionate controversy here has been the combination of two or more antibiotics in a single product, or the combination of an antibiotic with a sulfa-drug. Such products, it has been argued, can provide a greater range of activity; that is, one component may be effective against one invading microbe while the other may combat a different organism. But almost from the time these products were introduced with noteworthy fanfare—the antibiotic combinations were heralded as ushering in the "third era of antibiotic therapy"—they came under heavy attack. The major arguments that have been repeatedly presented against them include the following:[46]

—The fixed ratio of the components makes it impossible for the physician to tailor the proportion to meet the needs of an individual patient.
—The ratio is established by the manufacturer rather than, as has been traditional, by the physician.
—Rarely are two drugs needed to produce the desired clinical effect. When they are, they can be prescribed separately.
—The combination is generally marketed under a brand name that does not readily disclose the ingredients.
—Most important, the simultaneous use of two or more drugs increases the risk of a serious or fatal adverse drug reaction.

(It is obvious, as Dr. Lasagna has noted, that some of these fixed-ratio combinations are no more irrational than individual prescriptions written by some doctors.)[47]

In reaching the decision that these combination products were ineffective under the meaning of the law, the NAS/NRC panels did not rule that the components were ineffective individually. Rather, on the basis of all the evidence they could find, it was judged that the combinations carried a greater risk than could be justified by any increase in efficacy.[48]

On its side, the drug industry—staunchly supported by spokesmen for the AMA and many medical journals that happened to be carrying drug advertising—insisted that due consideration should be given to the clinical impressions of physicians accumulated over a period of years, involving millions of doses administered to hundreds of thousands or even millions of patients. But FDA maintained the position that these constituted only unsubstantiated opinion and did not satisfy the requirements of the law.

Similarly, FDA was not visibly swayed by a survey conducted for the PMA that showed that most physicians—100 percent of them in the sample polled—were accustomed to prescribe at least one of a list of eight combination products brought to their attention.[49] Observers were quick to note, however, that the list included only one product, Mysteclin-F, that had been rated by NAS/NRC as ineffective. The others—Tetrex F, Darvon Compound, Empirin Compound with Codeine, Ser-Ap-Es, Diupres, Hydropres, and Salutensin—were in little or no danger.

The popularity of most combination products that were under attack was undisputed. "No one can argue that these drugs are not widely employed," said Dr. Heinz Eichenwald, head of the department of pediatrics at the University of Texas Southwestern Medical School.

> In the case of some of them, such as Signemycin and Panalba, this amounts, in my mind, to a strong indictment of the ability of many physicians to judge what is effective and what is not. All of us are aware that the great majority of conditions for which these drugs are employed are, in fact, self-limiting; many represent viral infections of the respiratory tract which run their course totally unaffected by any type of therapy.
>
> I cannot overemphasize the fact that the demand for these agents was created by advertising which made claims which are still, a decade or so later, unsubstantiated on the basis of controlled observations.[50]

In yet another move to challenge the NAS/NRC findings—the so-called Town versus Gown gambit—members of the panel were described as ivory-tower academicians, teachers, and research workers who were unaware of the realities of everyday medical practice, although many of the "academicians" were also engaged in the treatment of patients. One critic declared that neither FDA nor the NAS/NRC held a monopoly on all knowledge and demanded that these crucial decisions should be made by some medical group like the AMA. It was not clear, however, which in this instance was the real AMA: was it the AMA's advertising department, which accepted promotion for combination products? or was it the AMA's Council on Drugs, which steadfastly opposed most of them?

While this dispute continued to rage, the industry was hit by what seemed to be an unnecessarily low blow. Dr. Jesse Steinfeld, surgeon general of the Public Health Service, announced on December 11, 1970, that he was ordering the PHS to cease purchasing not merely those products listed as ineffective but also those listed as only possibly effective. Similar regulations, he indicated, would eventually apply to drugs provided under the Medicare and Medicaid program.

The president of PMA strongly opposed this policy and declared that it was "extremely unfair" to the drug industry.[51] Dr. Steinfeld promptly replied: "I do not agree that the Departmental policy is unfair to the drug manufacturing industry as you allege. Even if it were, I would then have to weigh that against the unfairness of giving sick people drugs that have not been shown to be effective. I would have to decide in favor of the sick people." [52]

At about the same time other federal agencies moved to block the purchase and use of ineffective products. For example, the surgeon general of the Air Force told all Air Force medical officers that drugs found to be ineffective "will be removed from the stocklist and local purchase of such items will not be authorized." In addition, he called attention to the prescribing of high-cost drugs when equally effective but much less expensive products are available. "Many experts are convinced that Librium and Valium are vastly over-prescribed today," he said. "Similarly, Darvon probably has no greater analgesic effectiveness than aspirin and there are totally effective low-cost alternates for Ornade. Therapeutic committees must regularly review their own drug consumption data to insure that formularies not only satisfy the needs of the staff but also accurately reflect the judgments of current medical literature and the harsh reality of austere finances." [53]

One serious charge leveled at the whole NAS/NRC review and its implementation by FDA came from Dr. Lasagna, who himself was a panel member. "To begin with," he said, "the study was of necessity imperfect. Its panels were chosen from scientists nominated by the chairmen, allowing for parochial biases. The magnitude of the task . . . precluded exhaustive attention to detail or the presentation of extensive supporting information from the manufacturers. The rating classifications established for the guidance of the panels . . . were not clearly defined or easy to apply. Panels were inconsistent in their use of the terms." [54]

FDA itself had been inconsistent in the past in setting up guidelines to demonstrate efficacy, and was inconsistent in acting on the NAS/NRC recommendations, he claimed. In some cases the judgments were made not on the basis of efficacy but on that of *relative* efficacy, which had not been authorized by the Kefauver-Harris Amendments.

Also attacked was the FDA policy to order products off the market by summary judgment, without giving the companies an ample opportunity for public hearings. In defense, an FDA spokesman claimed that such open hearings could be dragged on for decades. The only logical procedure would be to get these presumably ineffective products off the market quickly and then afford each company an opportunity to seek any redress through the courts.

By mid-1973 the final outcome was yet to be determined, and the removal of some less-than-effective products was still being blocked by legal maneuvering or the submission and analysis of additional data. It seemed likely that final decisions would not be rendered until well into 1974. Yet certain points were already clear:

Approximately 2,000 of the 4,000-odd 1938–1962 products had been cleared as "effective," and 760 had been categorized as "ineffective" or "ineffective as a fixed-ratio combination." The remainder were still classified as "probably effective" or "possibly effective," awaiting final adjudication. Approximately 600 had been banned from the market, and hundreds of others had been approved but only with significant changes in their labeling.[55] Over the years, the products now taken off the market had cost American patients and taxpayers many billions of dollars. But if these products had not been prescribed, the public would not necessarily have saved any substantial amount, since presumably other drugs would have been prescribed in their place.

More important than the money involved was the effect of their use on medical care. It seemed only too apparent that these "ineffective" products had been given to hundreds of thousands of patients annually who could have been treated better with more effective or safer drugs—or with no drugs at all.

Removal of these "ineffective" products from the American market meant that a few drug companies were hard hit, but the industry as a whole suffered no disastrous financial trauma. When an "ineffective" product was barred, physicians generally prescribed in its place another product made by a different company, or perhaps by the same company. And even though the companies were stopped from selling these "ineffective" products in the United States, they could still promote and market them generally in Europe, Africa, Asia, and Latin America.

The good name of a few firms had been sullied, but probably without lasting harm. As shown only too well by the continuing prosperity of companies even after the FDA's "Dear Doctor letters," after the demonstration of misleading drug advertising, and even after the disclosure of fraud in research, the memory of most physicians appears to be short-lived.

In reporting the drug efficacy studies, the editorial attitude of most medical journals seemed geared primarily to consideration for the sensitivity of drug advertisers. Nearly all such journals at first either ignored the situation, or gave only a cursory summary of the NAS/NRC findings, with no identification of the products rated as "ineffective." Many viewed with scorn or alarm the panel findings and the FDA actions, and some aided in fomenting the Town and Gown squabble. In striking contrast, some metropolitan newspapers felt that the matter was so vital that they carried the detailed drug ratings in their columns.

Perhaps most disconcerting were the disclosures that much of the drug industry's vaunted research had been shoddy; that much of its publicized scientific evidence consisted only of testimonials; that well over half of its therapeutic claims were unsupportable; that many industry spokesmen and physicians were content to determine drug efficacy by a popularity vote; that many medical journals seemed less anxious to inform physicians than to protect advertisers, and had been publishing supposedly scientific reports that could not withstand the scrutiny of experts; and that thousands of physicians had often been prescribing drugs without adequate proof of their value.

"How, then, has this deplorable situation developed?" asked Dr. Keith Cannan, of NAS/NRC. "I suggest that it is because an aggressive industry, a harried profession and a bureaucratic agency of government are trying to work together to satisfy an exuberant public demand on an inadequate factual and conceptual base. They are making a rather poor job of it." [56]

To a considerable extent, the whole affair brings to mind Hans

Christian Andersen's *The Emperor's New Clothes*. If everyone else seems convinced that the Emperor's new garb is present and beautiful— or that the efficacy of a drug has been scientifically established—it is sometimes difficult to object.

THE SUPREME COURT DECISIONS

While the drug efficacy battle was being fought drug by drug, or product by product, from 1969 onward—with heated arguments at FDA hearings, pressures applied on congressmen and by congressmen, incendiary statements by representatives of medical organizations, strong editorials in medical journals, emotional appeals in the press, mail campaigns, demands by consumer groups to move faster, dire warnings from the drug industry against moving too quickly, and the formalized, gavotte-like appeals in the lower courts—another and perhaps more significant series of fundamental questions was being posed:

When the Congress enacted the Kefauver-Harris Amendments, did it really mean what it said? Did FDA actually have the authority to crack down on products classified as less than effective? Could FDA ban a product before the courts had ruled on the merits of each individual case? If scientific evidence indicated that a parent drug was ineffective, could FDA rule, in the absence of other evidence, that me-too versions of the parent compound were similarly ineffective? Which should carry more weight, scientific evidence or popularity polls?

Early in 1973 the Supreme Court agreed to consider these questions. Among the attorneys for FDA and the drug industry there could no longer be any doubt: this would be the moment of truth. In June, considering four related cases in a package, the Supreme Court handed down its decisions, voting 7 to 0.[57]

—The Congress, the court ruled, clearly meant what it said when it passed the Kefauver-Harris Amendments.

—FDA clearly has broad power to order drugs off the market on the grounds of ineffectiveness.

—When a drug is ordered withdrawn, the same action applies to all me-too versions.

—The "grandfather clause" approach on which industry had long depended to protect many older prescription and over-the-counter drugs from FDA action was greatly weakened or essentially scrapped.

—In one instance the Court ruled against FDA and decided that industry was entitled to more hearings than FDA had been willing to grant.

—Most important, the Supreme Court rejected anything less than adequate and well-controlled clinical evidence to demonstrate safety and efficacy. Reliance upon clinical impressions or anecdotal evidence —or, as some cynics put it, "sales figures"—in place of hard-nosed scientific data was described by Justice William Douglas as "treacherous."

Some industry representatives described the Supreme Court rulings as "unmitigated disaster," and predicted that the decisions would inevitably wreck the American pharmaceutical industry, cripple research, slow the introduction of new drugs, wipe out America's preeminence in drug development, and work to the detriment of the health of Americans. But one drug company attorney said:

> The trouble with that line of chatter is that the industry has been using it too long, and we've lost our credibility. For nearly seventy years, the industry has bucked almost every proposed new drug law by warning that it would wreck the industry, make us cut down on research, destroy American medicine, ruin the public health, and probably bring on communism. The problem now is that there are too many people—especially in the Congress—who won't swallow it. They know only too well that, with all the new laws, drug industry profits are higher than ever. Drug research has been expanded. American medicine has never been more productive. And the health of the public has never been better. For too many years, the drug industry has been crying "wolf." Now, we're convincing each other—but nobody else. The new Supreme Court decisions? Our people can live with them.

THE FORGOTTEN ONES: DRUGS FOR CHILDREN

For reasons that are not altogether clear, most new drugs introduced during the past decade carry labels or package inserts with such statements as "not indicated for use in pediatric patients," "should not be used in patients under the age of 12," or "should not be used in children since adequate data to establish safe conditions of use are lacking."

Dr. Harry Shirkey, professor and head of the department of pediatrics at Tulane, has indicated the untenable position in which these and similar instructions place a practicing physician.

> He has a patient with an illness for which a certain drug has been most efficacious in adults, and let us say the patient is a child eleven years of age. . . . If he withholds a valuable drug, he is a criminal. If he does not follow the package insert, which says there have not been adequate studies, and then there is an adverse reaction . . . then he has used a drug which has

been clearly contraindicated for the use of children. So he is in a bad situation. He is damned if he does and damned if he does not.[58]

There is no standard manner in which physicians have reacted to this problem. Some physicians, possibly fearing the legal consequences of using such drugs on their young patients, have withheld drug therapy. Others have refrained from using such drugs on the clinical grounds that the safe and effective dose level for children is unknown, and even the dose-per-pound ratio established for adults may not apply to children. Some have declined to use these drugs in the fear that some chemical agents react far differently in children than they do in adults. On the other hand, some physicians—perhaps most of them—have gone ahead and treated their young patients with drugs even though they know that they might thereby be inviting charges of malpractice.

There is no simple explanation for how this situation has arisen. Certainly no blame can be directed toward the drug industry, the Congress, or FDA. Somehow, in both the 1938 and the 1962 legislation, the Congress decided not to grapple with the sensitive question of drug-testing in children. It is long since time for society to face up to the problem. This, however, requires more than the enactment and implementation of the necessary laws and regulations. It involves consideration of such ethical questions as these: Should all new drugs be tested on children, or only those most likely to be important in pediatric practice? Should these drugs be tested only on children who are ill, and thus may have need for drug therapy, or should they be measured on healthy "volunteers" in order to determine proper dosages, routes of administration, and the possible occurrence of side effects and adverse reactions?

If these tests on children are to be conducted under the standard "informed consent" regulations, have parents not only the legal but also the ethical right to give this consent for their children? In a suit filed before the California state superior court in 1973, attorney James Nielsen, a faculty member of the University of California's medical center in San Francisco and a member of UCSF's committee on human experimentation, asked the judges to rule on whether parents may legally give "informed consent" for research to be conducted on a *well* child, one who is not suffering from a disease and who therefore cannot expect to benefit directly from the tests.[59]

Until these difficult questions are answered, Dr. Shirkey has claimed, children will not be able to obtain the full value of drug treatment. They will continue to be "therapeutic orphans." [60]

FUTURE TRENDS

It is clear that from the time the new proof-of-efficacy requirements were put into effect by FDA they irritated and perplexed many drug companies and physicians—and even some staff members of FDA itself. The IND and NDA processes were cumbersome and time-consuming, forced the companies to undertake additional and costly research, and deprived at least some companies of the chance to market a newly discovered product quickly. But there is no evidence that they deprived American patients of urgently needed new drugs to any significant degree. Similarly, there is no evidence that patients in foreign countries, where American-discovered drugs could often be marketed more quickly than in the United States, were getting superior care.

Nevertheless, it has long since become apparent that many of the original review processes were inordinately complicated and laborious, and some of these have already been modified. For certain classes of drugs, for example, FDA developed the Abbreviated New Drug Application process, which appears to be helpful in clearing new generic-name products. An incentive to heightened efficiency has been the agency's policy to give priority not merely to urgently needed drugs, such as those for the treatment of cancer, but also to drug applications that are submitted in proper form the first time.

Other possible improvements warrant consideration. A greater reliance could be placed by FDA on selected drug research studies conducted in foreign countries. Similarly, it has been proposed that all required drug testing to prove safety and efficacy should be done by the federal government itself, either in FDA or the National Institutes of Health. Such a procedure, it has been held, would remove much of the bias which has marked at least some industry-supported research in the past. Presumably the cost would be borne by the taxpayers, and the drug company—spared the need to conduct the expensive testing itself—would, or at least could, market the product at a lower price. It has likewise been proposed that the necessary testing should be done in specially designated nongovernmental institutions such as university medical centers. The costs would be paid by industry, but the selection of the center to carry on the research would be determined by FDA. This, too, it has been suggested, would minimize bias and essentially guarantee that all the results, both favorable and unfavorable, would be openly and honestly reported.

In any consideration of these and similar proposals, it should be noted that serious manpower problems will almost certainly be involved. Testing a new drug for safety and efficacy—especially a drug that somebody else has discovered—is not generally regarded as a particularly exciting occupation. Few competent research workers have been inclined to devote much time to it. Further, it has been claimed, unless such an investigator is alert and highly motivated, he may well overlook an unexpected side effect that could lead to an unsuspected new use for the product, or the development of a better drug.

Finally, it has been proposed for at least a decade that a new drug should not be approved unless it is demonstrably better than any competitive product already available—safer, or more effective, or less expensive. Such a policy would unquestionably do much to reduce the output of me-too products, make it easier for physicians to keep up with new drugs, and cut drug costs.

This approach has never been greeted with visible enthusiasm by most drug manufacturers. It could, they say, reduce competition, lead to restraint of trade, and thus increase prices. They say it would obviously force the companies to cut down on their research. They note that no other industry in the United States has yet been saddled with such a requirement. Such a policy, however, has been applied—and applied to prescription drugs—in Norway for many years, with apparent success.[61]

It may be concluded that although the new ground rules for proving the safety and efficacy of a drug have been undoubtedly burdensome for the industry, the industry has not been crushed by the burden. At least some ineffective or worthless products have been removed from the market. There have been delays in getting new drugs approved, but the health of the public has not been significantly harmed. In spite of the added costs of more careful drug testing, the prices of individual drugs on the market have not yet skyrocketed. And as a result of all the furore during the past ten years or so, at least some physicians have been induced to question all promotional claims and even to question their own prescribing practices. This last development alone may have justified all the furore.

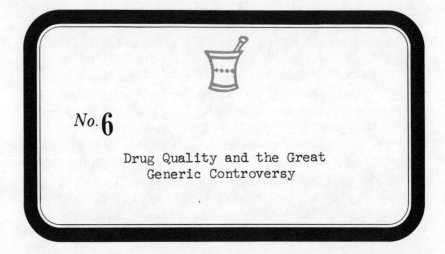

No. 6

Drug Quality and the Great Generic Controversy

WHEN A physician orders a drug for a patient, rarely does he prescribe—or does a pharmacist dispense—a *drug*. What the patient receives is a *drug product*. On how well it is formulated may depend whether the product will be effective, worthless, damaging, or fatal. Such products contain not merely the desired drugs, the so-called active ingredients which presumably have already been shown to be both relatively safe and effective. They may also include such additional ingredients as fillers, binders, dispersing agents, buffers, flavors, and coloring matter. The active ingredients may be present in different crystal forms or particle sizes. The product may be put up in liquid form, packed into a capsule or other coating that will disintegrate more or less rapidly, or formed under one pressure or another into a tablet.

These and similar factors may have a remarkable effect in determining how much of the active drug is actually absorbed, and how rapidly it reaches the appropriate tissues and organs in the body. In some instances, these differences in absorption may be readily discernible and may be enthusiastically exploited in advertising, but have only trivial clinical significance. Thus, few physicians—and probably few patients—

would be greatly concerned if a headache remedy reached the bloodstream in two and a half rather than two minutes. In other instances, a seemingly minor difference in absorption—as with a drug to control blood clotting—may threaten the patient's life.

The problems involved here, the problems of drug product quality, are far from theoretical. Even in the mid-twentieth century, tablets of iron compounds prescribed for the treatment of anemia have been compressed under such great pressure or have used such excessive binding agents that they failed to disintegrate in the intestinal tract and were excreted unchanged from the body. Antibiotics have been combined with supposedly inert ingredients that actually reacted with the active agent and blocked its absorption. Some manufacturers have marketed products with dangerously more or less of the active agent than was indicated on the label. Some have used ingredients so distasteful that patients refused to take the prescribed medicine. Some have used formulations that quickly decomposed on the pharmacist's shelf. Some have had label mix-ups, with a drug distributed under the label of a totally different product. And some have allowed their products to become tainted with dangerous or even lethal contaminants.

These and similar quality failures are scarcely new. In 1789 a group of Philadelphia physicians pointed out to their colleagues "the absolute necessity of some standard amongst ourselves to prevent that uncertainty and irregularity which in our present situation must infallibly attend on the compositions of the apothecary and the prescription of the physician." [1]

During the past century and a half, some of the needed standards and control methods have gradually been developed. The major official compendia of standards in this country, the *United States Pharmacopeia* (USP), published since 1820, and the *National Formulary* (NF), published since 1888, now cover between them some two thousand drug forms, giving the best available information on applicable laboratory tests, procedures for assay, and the like.[2] These standards have provided invaluable guidelines for drug manufacturers and research-minded physicians and pharmacists. (By law in some states, every pharmacist is required to have copies of the publications. He is not, however, required to read them.) As new knowledge has become available, and as new needs have become apparent, they have been updated, improved, and made more sophisticated. USP and NF are admittedly not perfect. They do not cover all drug products on the market. The fact that some three thousand drug products are marketed without either USP or NF standards has been denounced by critics as a national disgrace. It is charged now that they have paid inadequate attention to the burning issue of generic equivalency—although, as will be noted below, this issue reached the fiery stage only about ten years ago.

On its part, the federal government has become increasingly active and forceful in intercepting low-quality products and clamping down on slovenly production methods, but this governmental control has not been foolproof. For example, approval of each vaccine product has long been required on a batch-by-batch basis, but this approach did not manage to prevent the distribution of polio vaccine contaminated with virulent polio virus.[3]

Under existing laws, FDA has no authority to require inspection and approval of every drug manufacturing plant *before* it goes into operation, and a company may operate for as long as two years before it must undergo FDA inspection. The authority of FDA applies only to products in interstate commerce and ordinarily does not touch companies whose products do not cross state lines. Even with these limitations, and with the restrictions stemming from inadequate manpower and finances, FDA has managed to get thousands of low-quality products off the market. Here, the most practical device has been what is euphemistically termed "voluntary recalls." "What this actually means," says an FDA official, "is that we offer the drug company two alternatives—either take your bad product off the market voluntarily or you go to court to face civil or criminal charges."

During a six-year period, as table 6 in the Appendix shows, there were about 752 recalls involving subpotency or superpotency, 377 because of label mix-ups, and 806 because of contamination or adulteration. In some instances the products were recalled before they had reached the pharmacies of the nation, but in others they were actually being dispensed to patients. Both large and small companies, brand-name and generic-name makers, were concerned. Although most of the recalls involved only tens or hundreds of thousands or a few million tablets or capsules, in 1971 a single drug company had to recall a total of 957 *million* digoxin tablets. In some of these cases it was possible to get back nearly all of the recalled product, but in others only a small portion could be recovered.

During the past few years, FDA found bottles of Vitamin B_1 mislabeled as B_{12}, erythromycin mislabeled as a pain-killer, $\frac{1}{4}$-grain phenobarbital tablets mislabeled as $\frac{1}{2}$-grain, and 5-mg warfarin tablets (for the control of blood clotting) mislabeled as $2\frac{1}{2}$-mg tablets. One liver preparation approved only for veterinarian use was mislabeled and marketed for injection into human beings. FDA tests picked up nitroglycerin tablets (for the control of anginal pain) with as little as 16 percent of the labeled amount, prednisone (for arthritis, asthma, and other conditions) with 30 percent, reserpine (for hypertension) with 25 percent, and morphine with 68 percent. The FDA tests similarly disclosed ophthalmic ointments contaminated with metal particles, injectable Vitamin B_{12} containing fragments of metal and glass, sulfa-drugs with mold, and hormone solutions with unidentified fever-producing contaminants. One lot of an antihistamine solution was shipped in bottles that reportedly exploded because of the gas produced by contaminating bacteria. In a report on one lot of more than a million digitalis tablets, an FDA report said, "Potency cannot be determined; unknown interfering substance caused premature deaths among test animals."[4]

In the case of most recalls, few patients were known to have been injured or killed, but the record is admittedly incomplete. No one knows how many cases of injury or death charged to an adverse drug reaction, a toxic side effect, or "drug failure" were actually caused by the use of a mislabeled, subpotent, superpotent, or contaminated product. The blow to the pride of the companies involved—many of which had long boasted of their unblemished reputation for reliability and high quality —could have been traumatic. Fortunately for most such firms, American physicians and their patients are not generally made aware of which companies had recalled what products. In other instances the problem was more widely reported. For example, in 1963, products manufactured by Squibb were found to be so contaminated with penicillin—to which many people are dangerously allergic—that it was found necessary to close down one of the company's manufacturing plants.[5]

Even more shocking was the discovery that sterile intravenous solutions bottled by Abbott—the world's largest producer of such solutions, mainly for hospitals—could be contaminated by bacteria when they were opened and then resealed. By April 1971, according to FDA, the blame had been placed on the use of a new lining for the screw caps on the bottles.[6] According to the Public Health Service, administration of the contaminated solutions to hospitalized patients had resulted in many cases of septicemia and even some deaths.

After insistent prodding by the *Washington Post*, FDA released a "regulatory history," which disclosed that, in fact, there had been troubles with Abbott's solutions for intravenous administration since

1964.[7] At first it had been an apparent label mix-up, with bottles of sodium chloride solution incorrectly labeled as "Dextrose 5% in Water." Later it was reported that bottles of "Dextrose 10% Saline" had been incorrectly labeled as "Dextrose 2½% in Lactated Ringer's Solution." Abbott was obliged to telegraph warnings to hospitals and physicians, at a cost estimated to be between $750,000 and $1,000,000. In addition, some bottles were found to be contaminated with mold; FDA asked for a recall, but Abbott refused and claimed that the bottles had been damaged after they had been delivered to the hospitals. In April 1969 FDA learned that Abbott had been receiving an increasing number of complaints of contamination over the previous seven months. "Inspection of the firm . . . disclosed that the firm did not have sufficient control to assure that defective large glass bottles would be at an absolute minimum and that any defective bottles actually received would be detected." But it was the feeling of FDA that "Abbott had fully corrected the causes of the difficulties and that no criminal action would be recommended to the Department of Justice."

From this whole unhappy affair, and others like it, one conclusion seems inescapable: where drug products are concerned, neither the size nor experience nor good repute of the manufacturer can serve as a complete guarantee of product quality.

Another and quite different flaw in drug quality control appeared in the 1950s, when it seemed that a number of important drugs—most still under patent—were facing competition from black-market products made illicitly by manufacturers in this country and abroad.[8] These illegal products, often shaped, colored, and labeled exactly like the legitimate drugs, were generally priced far less to pharmacists, but at the usual price to patients. It seems obvious that their appearance on the market— whether this was a flood or a trickle has never been satisfactorily demonstrated—required not only an illicit manufacturer to produce them but also a larceny-minded wholesaler or pharmacist to buy them and then sell them at an exorbitant profit to his customers. It likewise seems obvious that, if the manufacturer of the legal drug had set a price reflecting the cost of production plus only a reasonable markup, the incentive to produce illegal versions would have been far less tempting.

This loophole was apparently plugged during the 1950s and early 1960s by a nationwide campaign spearheaded by the National Pharmaceutical Council, a specially formed organization composed of some of the nation's leading brand-name drug manufacturers. As a result of this campaign, most of the state legislatures passed what were known as "antisubstitution laws," which made it a crime for a pharmacist to dispense a product other than the one specifically prescribed by a physician. For example, if a physician ordered Luminal—the brand name for phenobarbital controlled by Winthrop—the pharmacist was obliged to dispense the Winthrop product, even though the patent on phenobarbital had long since expired and many low-priced generics were available. This same rule held if the prescription order called for "phenobarbital Winthrop." Only if the physician called simply for "phenobarbital" could the pharmacist choose among the generic phenobarbitals legally on the market.

Later it became evident that there were two aspects of these antisubstitution laws that would warrant further attention. First, although they were accepted by most state legislatures as measures to protect the public health, there is at least some reason to believe that they were utilized later by the big brand-name companies to protect themselves against price competition. And second, Alaska, Missouri, and the District of Columbia refused, at least until recently, to enact such laws, without any visible damage to the health of their citizens, though to the evident discomfiture of the National Pharmaceutical Council and the major companies it represents.

Up to this point, attention has been directed mainly toward drug products manufactured by a single producer—in most cases, therefore, products that are still under patent. While there have been serious lapses in their quality control, these have been relatively infrequent. Most companies developing a new product have demonstrated that, with good personnel, good manufacturing practices, and good testing and quality control methods, they can learn how to prepare a product so that, batch after batch, it will perform reliably. Physicians will come to depend on it. But eventually the patent will expire and other companies can then legally manufacture the product. This may signal the start of a totally different drug game.

THE GENERIC CONTROVERSY

Once generic-name versions come on the market, not only quality but also relative price become vitally significant. Usually, although not invariably, the generic-name product is priced substantially less than the brand-name version. Under such conditions, if the generic-name product is clinically as safe and effective as the more costly brand-name product, there would seem to be no reason for a physician with any consideration for his patient's pocketbook to order the more expensive form. During the 1930s and 1940s this was largely a matter of academic interest. Professors of pharmacology and other educators urged their colleagues to prescribe generically wherever possible, but their recommendations excited neither warm support nor hot opposition, and in fact were generally ignored.

In the late 1950s and early 1960s, especially during the Kefauver Committee hearings, the generic controversy began to generate somewhat more heat. There were disclosures that a few manufacturers of generic products were what became known as *schlock* houses; one reporter described them as "dreadfully unhygienic operations—something like two men and a bathtub—turning out dreadful products." But it was also noted with increasing concern that some makers of brand-name drugs were also guilty of turning out dreadful products. At the same time, Senator Kefauver observed that certain brand-name drugs were priced eight, ten, fifteen, and even twenty times higher than apparently equivalent generic products. Physicians were nevertheless prescribing the higher-priced brands, perhaps partly because "most detail men hinted darkly at the substandard quality of drugs put out by small companies." [9]

The Kefauver hearings were enlivened at one point by disclosures that, in 1944, Dr. Austin Smith, then the highly esteemed editor of the *Journal of the American Medical Association*, had come out strongly in favor of generic prescribing, mentioning the "enormous profits" to be made from brand-name drugs, and condemning the "absurd practice" of prescribing them when less expensive generic equivalents were available. Fifteen years later he came out against generic prescribing, but then he was no longer editor of the *JAMA*; he had become president of the Pharmaceutical Manufacturers Association.[10]

So far as the generic controversy was concerned, the Kefauver hearings produced a considerable amount of fireworks but few significant changes. At the time there seemed to be no way that the Congress could alter the traditional preference of most practicing physicians to prescribe by brand name, regardless of cost. For the next few years the controversy continued to seethe. One noted pharmacologist described the situation in these terms:

> The small house that capitalized on other people's discoveries is, in a sense, parasitic. A society with nothing but such firms would be in a sad fix. . . . On the other hand, much of the attack by the ethical houses on generic drugs has been below the belt. Many such drugs are perfectly

satisfactory products, and not the sort of hopelessly inferior junk pictured in campaigns against them. An occasional preparation, to be sure, is sufficiently off the mark to interfere with medical care, but the same can be said of the products of large firms.[11]

THE NELSON HEARINGS: THE MATTER OF PRICE

In 1967, a new chapter began, marked by another series of hearings in the Senate, and the simultaneous investigations by a task force in the Department of Health, Education, and Welfare. The Senate sessions were not simply replays of the Kefauver hearings, since a new and important element had been added. In the summer of 1966, two multibillion-dollar programs had been implemented as amendments to the Social Security Act: Medicare, which provided federal funds to pay for hospital and medical care for the elderly, and Medicaid, financed in substantial part by federal funds, which paid for health care provided to the poor who were receiving public assistance. With its investment in these two programs, along with health expenditures by the Department of Defense, the Veterans Administration, the Public Health Service, and similar operations, the federal government was paying for prescription drugs at the rate of more than $500 million a year.[12]

With federal tax funds at stake in such quantities, this had suddenly become a different situation. The government had an obligation to see that these funds were spent wisely. Accordingly, proposed laws to induce or require the prescription of inexpensive generic-name products in federally supported programs wherever possible were introduced by three Democratic senators—Russell Long of Louisiana, Joseph Montoya of New Mexico, and Gaylord Nelson of Wisconsin. Enactment of such legislation, Long declared, would save the taxpayers a minimum of $100 million a year.[13]

Probably the most important hearings were those conducted by Senator Nelson. An attorney, twice governor of Wisconsin, elected senator in 1962, and chairman of the Subcommittee on Monopoly of the Select Committee on Small Business, Nelson was a hardened veteran of investigations into big business and a leader of campaigns for tire safety, auto safety, and conservation. His hearings on prescription drugs and the drug industry, which would eventually fill more than twenty-five volumes of testimony, were marked by controversy which spilled out into the halls of Congress, newspaper columns, medical journal editorials, and medical meetings. During the hearings, Nelson ran for reelection and let it be known in Wisconsin that elements of the drug industry were eager to have him defeated. He won by the largest vote in his career.

On one point, the hearings showed, the situation was inescapable: prices of apparently equivalent products varied by 3,000 percent or more. In the case of prednisone, for example, Schering priced its product under the brand name of Meticorten at $17.90 for a hundred tablets, while generic prednisones marketed by competitors were listed as low as $0.59 per hundred. Since then, as is shown in table 7 in the Appendix, relative prices have changed somewhat, but the differences between brand-name and generic-name products are still startling.

A parade of industry witnesses failed to produce adequate justification for these enormous price differences. Certainly they could not be readily explained by the fact that brand-name companies were investing only about 9 percent of their sales in research and only about 2.5 percent of sales in their vaunted quality control procedures.[14] Significantly, it was noted, such major brand-name companies as Lilly, Squibb, Upjohn, Merck, and Smith Kline & French—which also maintained effective research and quality control programs—were among the makers of low-cost generic products.

There was ample evidence to demonstrate that many governmental institutions, notably the Department of Defense, were buying generic products at substantial savings. Many hospitals had adopted formularies based on the use of generics. One such program was instituted, over strenuous objections, at Grady Memorial Hospital in Atlanta, municipally owned and operated, with its medical services under the direction of the medical school of Emory University. "It was not easy in the beginning," testified Dr. Harry Williams.

> As you might imagine, the medical profession is conservative. This was a radical departure of performance at Grady Hospital. There were complaints that the committee was trying to dictate the type of medicine practiced at the hospital, that Grady Hospital patients would be poisoned by cheap, inferior drugs, that the change from one color of pill to another would upset the Grady Hospital patients in an irremedial manner, that we should buy trade-named expensive items to support the research done by the large drug companies, and that the committee was attacking the American free enterprise system.[15]

But introduction of the formulary did not unduly disturb the hospital physicians, upset or poison the patients, or fracture the free enterprise system—although it caused some consternation among drug detail men—and it yielded savings of $150,000 on a drug budget of $480,000 during the first year.

During the subcommittee hearings on drug prices, the American Medical Association conducted its own survey in Chicago and reported that a generic prescription was no guarantee of low prices to the patients.[16] The AMA's announcement, however, was so unhappily worded that it laid the blame for the nation's high prescription drug bill on the shoulders of the pharmacist, an allegation that brought instant and scathing denunciations from both the American Pharmaceutical Association and the National Association of Retail Druggists. But, in part, the AMA statement was true. A generic prescription order is in itself no guarantee of a low price. Receiving such an order, a pharmacist could legally fill it with a high-cost brand-name product and charge accordingly. Or he could actually dispense a low-cost generic but charge a patient the price of a brand-name drug.

Thus, on the matter of prices, the hearings had established two basic facts that were beyond dispute: Most generic products were undoubtedly less expensive than their brand-name counterparts. But there were some generic products that offered little or no financial savings, while a few were actually more costly. Moreover, prescribing generically would not in itself necessarily guarantee savings. Also required was the willingness of the pharmacist to stock and dispense low-cost generics and charge accordingly.

In general, the issue seemed clear enough, so that, in his 1968 Health Message to the Congress, President Johnson said, "We must make certain that the American taxpayer does not pay needlessly high and exorbitant prices for prescription drugs used in federally supported programs. . . . The taxpayer should not be forced to pay $11 if a $1.35 drug is equally effective. To do this would permit robbery of private citizens with public approval."

THE NELSON HEARINGS: THE MATTER OF EQUIVALENCY

Far more confusing, and far more bitterly contested, was the issue of clinical equivalence. The generic products merely had to pass the chemical and physical tests specified by USP and NF. Except for injectable products, no tests in animals or human subjects were required. Were they, then, as effective as the more expensive products in treating disease? What would be the effect on the quality of medical care of requiring physicians to prescribe generic products?

Month after month, these questions were disputed with vast quantities of rhetoric but remarkably little scientific evidence. Clouding the issues were such matters as the heartrending problems of the poor and the elderly, the traditional rights and privileges of prescribing physicians, the humanitarian goals (or extortionate practices) of the drug industry, and the necessity (or dreadful dangers) of government interference.

Even failures to agree on definitions became pertinent. Thus, early in the hearings, Durward Hall, congressman from Missouri, himself a physician and widely considered to be a spokesman for the AMA on Capitol Hill, appeared before Nelson and presented a moving attack against generic prescribing. But, to the acute dismay of his fellow physicians and the brand-name drug industry, he replied to a question by defining generic prescribing as "using the Latin chemical or molecular formula name." [17]

The denigrating activities of some brand-name companies and of PMA came under constant attack. "It is obvious there has been a campaign to throw questions upon the efficacy of generic drugs," declared Dr. Martin Cherkasky of New York's Montefiore Hospital. "I think that doctors and the public have been intimidated." [18] George Squibb said, "Not only has the pharmaceutical industry been successful in maintaining the conviction with many physicians and buyers that not all drugs are alike, but it has even succeeded in persuading them that all products are different, which is a much more effective argument from a sales point of view." [19]

Nelson himself made constant use of a report published in *The Medical Letter* which stated that twenty-two brands of prednisone, priced from $17.90 to as low as $0.59, had all been found to meet USP standards and, according to the impression of experts across the country, had performed adequately in patients.[20] Time after time the senator utilized these figures to belabor industry representatives, and challenge them to present any evidence that any one of these twenty-two products was better than another. (At the time, no industry official could reply to this challenge. Only recently was it reported that there were actual differences in absorption among the twenty-two prednisones.)[21]

Charges had been made earlier, and were repeated before the Nelson subcommittee, that some generic products were being produced by *schlock* houses and other incompetent companies, and obviously could not be expected to perform dependably. This subject flared when FDA released the results of a survey disclosing that about 7 percent of a sample of generic products actually on the market failed even to meet USP or NF requirements for potency. But, to the consternation of brand-name manufacturers, the survey also revealed that essentially the same percentage of brand-name products had similarly failed to meet potency requirements.[22]

These findings were strongly attacked by the PMA, and FDA was obliged to state that the percentages were based on only some 4,500 samples and did not necessarily apply to all brand-name products and all generics. Nevertheless, the conclusion seemed obvious: brand-name or generic, the name of the manufacturer could not necessarily serve as a guarantee of quality.

Much emphasis was placed on the vital necessity of a physician to prescribe a product with which he had become familiar over many years, and the sanctity of brand names was repeatedly stressed. Nelson eventually accepted the concept that a physician could continue to prescribe such a product, providing he felt this essential for a particular patient and providing further that he would prescribe it by generic name plus the name of the manufacturer—that is, not "Meticorten" but "prednisone Schering."

More recently the sanctity of brand names came into question when it was noted that Pfizer had requested permission to apply its brand name of Antivert—long used for the combination of meclizine and niacin—to a different product containing only meclizine as the active ingredient. In the same way, Abbott's brand name of Sucaryl originally applied to cyclamate, later to a mixture of cyclamate and saccharine, and then to a product that contains only saccharine as the active ingredient.[23]

As the hearings continued it finally seemed to be generally understood that a great many things could go wrong to affect the quality of a drug product. But there was no agreement on how often such failures occurred, nor on the significance to the overall use of drugs. According to Dr. Edward Feldman of the *National Formulary*, as of late 1967 there were probably less than five scientifically proved cases in which two or more prescription products meeting accepted chemical and physical standards had failed to perform equivalently in patients.[24] Dr. Lloyd Miller of the *U.S. Pharmacopeia* put the number at less than twelve and possibly not more than six.[25]

As of that date, the documented cases of clinical nonequivalency were few, and some of those went back to the 1930s. In each instance, FDA officials assured, the unacceptable products had been promptly removed from the market, and no serious injuries had occurred. Industry spokesmen described such low estimates as representing only the tip of the iceberg and at least intimated that there were many more such instances, all of which were menacing the public health. To such allegations Nelson said, "Prove it."

The industry representatives were apparently unable to supply the requested proof. During the hearings, for example, the senator put the question flatly to Henry DeBoest, vice-president of Lilly. "What I am asking you, sir," he said, "is whether any drug company in America has any evidence to prove the continually repeated assertion that even if two drugs meet USP standards, therapeutic equivalency may not exist. I have heard that time after time. I have asked each witness whether he has any clinical evidence at all from anyplace in the world. I have not received any yet." DeBoest replied that he had no such evidence.[26]

It was at this point that an additional example of nonequivalency appeared. The drug was chloramphenicol, marketed only by Parke-Davis under the brand name of Chloromycetin until 1966, when the patent expired and a number of other companies began marketing the same drug under its generic name. The possibility that all of these products might not be equally effective was not reported by practicing physicians. Instead, a Parke-Davis official came to the office of the secretary of HEW in Washington one day in 1967 and related the curious case of a West Coast tropical-fish fancier. "This gentleman," the official said, "had been using our Chloromycetin in his aquarium to protect his fish against infections. When these low-cost generics came out, he switched to one of them. But he found that the product—instead of dissolving in the aquarium water—just stayed on top like some kind of a scum." [27]

Tipped off by this report, Parke-Davis scientists had checked the products on human subjects and found that some of the new generics were absorbed into the bloodstream of human volunteers as poorly as they dissolved into a tankful of tropical fish. FDA workers quickly confirmed the company's findings, and the low-quality products were immediately ordered off the market until they could be properly reformulated. Throughout this entire affair, it seems interesting that no complaints of clinical failure for these low-quality products were ever received from practicing physicians.[28]

One imposing advocate of the use of generics, who repeatedly claimed that instances of nonequivalency were infrequent, was Dr. John Adriani, professor of surgery and pharmacology at Louisiana State University, chairman of the AMA Council on Drugs, and one of the most esteemed drug experts in the world. "The paucity of convincing and well-documented data of clinical significance," he said, "causes one to suspect that the situation has been grossly exaggerated." [29] Later Dr.

Adriani was under consideration for appointment as director of the Bureau of Medicine in FDA, but the appointment was reportedly blocked. Insiders suggested that his support of generic prescribing, and his opposition to fixed-ratio combination drugs, had won him the enmity of the pharmaceutical industry (see chapter 10).

Although agreement had not been achieved on the seriousness of the generic nonequivalency problem, it seemed obvious that some failures had unquestionably occurred in the past. Similarly, it seemed obvious that—regardless of the quality control programs of industry and government—such failures might possibly occur in the future. What appeared far more important than ascertaining the number of past failures was preventing or minimizing breakdowns in drug quality in the future. Gradually there appeared recognition of the need for even more rigorous and sophisticated testing before any new product—certainly any new life-and-death product—would be allowed on the market. But if more sophisticated testing were to be required, who should pay the costs? Should the brand-name manufacturer be forced to prove—at considerable expense—that his product was better than generic competitors? Or should the generic manufacturer be forced to prove—also at great expense—that his product was as good as the brand-name version? As the president of the PMA put it, this became a matter of deciding where the burden of proof should be placed.[30] In the Department of Health, Education, and Welfare, this and other equally ticklish problems were already under study.

The first hearings of the Nelson subcommittee were held in May 1967. In that same month, on the basis of a directive from President Johnson, John Gardner—then secretary of HEW—established what was to become known as the HEW Task Force on Prescription Drugs. We were chairman and staff director, respectively, of the Task Force. Our mission was broad: to undertake a comprehensive study of the problems of including the costs of prescription drugs, both in-hospital and out-of-hospital, under the Medicare program. Inextricably involved was the controversy over generics. The primary goal was obviously the provision of the highest possible health care to the elderly. Only secondary, but nonetheless important, was the development of approaches that would utilize federal funds with all reasonable economies.

As the Task Force undertook its studies, and as the simultaneous hearings were being conducted by Senator Nelson, it became increasingly evident that the controversy over generic equivalency would not be solved quickly, readily, or to the satisfaction of all parties involved. On the one hand, most of the brand-name drug manufacturers, many representatives of organized medicine, and their adherents in Congress hailed the appointment of the Task Force and openly predicted that the group would inevitably support their stand, and find that "generic nonequivalency" was so frequent and so dangerous that it represented a serious menace to health. On the other hand, proponents of generic prescribing were confident that the Task Force would support *their* stand and find that "generic nonequivalency" was so unimportant that it could safely be ignored.

At stake, of course, was whether the government might eventually rule that Medicare—and other federally supported programs—should cover the costs of only inexpensive generic products where they were available, or instead cover the cost of whatever product the physician might prescribe.

At the outset, the Task Force took one significant step to bring some semblance of order into the dispute. This involved terminology.[31] "The term *generic equivalents* is not used in the body of this report," it was stated. "Although it has been widely utilized, it has been given so many different interpretations that it has become confusing." Instead, three different and quite specific definitions were proposed:

Chemical equivalents would be considered to be those multiple-source drug products which contain essentially identical amounts of the identical active ingredients, in identical dosage forms—that is, tablets, capsules, elixirs, and the like—and which meet existing physico-chemical standards in the official compendia. If they failed to meet USP or NF standards, they would be illegally on the market.

Biological equivalents would be those chemical equivalents which, when administered in the same amounts, will provide essentially the same biological or physiological availability, as measured by blood levels, excretion rates, and the like.

Clinical equivalents would be those chemical equivalents which, when administered in the same amounts, will provide essentially the same therapeutic effect as measured by the control of a symptom or disease.

To the pleasure of the Task Force, these three definitions were accepted by essentially all participants in the controversy. It was one of the few times that such unanimity was achieved. The basis of the controversy then could be presented as follows:

Given two products containing essentially the same amount of the same active ingredient in the same dosage form—that is, two chemical equivalents—will they produce essentially the same clinical effects?

On the answer—or answers—depend medical and economic decisions of considerable importance.

If the physician can be given reasonable assurance that two such competitive products will, in fact, give predictably equivalent clinical effects, then his choice between the two may well be based on relative costs. Under such conditions, there would be little justification for prescribing a relatively expensive brand of a drug when an equally effective counterpart is available at substantially lower cost.

But if the physician cannot be given this assurance, his clinical judgment would dictate that he use only the product which can be expected to yield the desired clinical effects—regardless of cost or any other nonmedical factor.

In attempts to find answers and develop policies which will lead to desirable economic savings, without lowering the quality of medical care, it has been held that the only crucial factor is whether or not the product in question can meet all official standards. If two tablets, for example, both meet the specifications for identity, strength, quality, and purity published in the official standards, it has been proposed, then—regardless of any other factors—they will assuredly yield identical clinical results.

Experts on drug standards and controls have stated repeatedly that, on the basis of available evidence, for the vast majority of drugs, this assumption is indeed correct. But the fallibility of existing standards has been shown by the finding—in rare cases—that different physiological effects can be produced by two different products, each formulated by a different manufacturer but both conforming to the same official specifications.

The answer to the question posed above thus must be: *Given two drug products containing essentially the same amount of the same active ingredient, the two products may not in all cases produce the same clinical effects.*[32]

This was admittedly only a partial answer. It was still essential to determine how often this lack of clinical equivalency is likely to occur, which drug products are involved, what factors are responsible, how serious was the problem, and what steps should be taken to correct the situation. Later it was emphasized that the essential assurance given to the physician should be not in the form of advertising, promotion, or the established image of the manufacturer involved, but wherever possible in the form of objective, scientific data.[33]

The Task Force devoted twenty months to this investigation. It sought out every bit of pertinent evidence, published and unpublished. It sought and received the advice and counsel of more than a hundred experts, both American and foreign, in the fields of clinical medicine, pharmacology, pharmacy, and drug manufacturing. It assigned specially selected staff members to make firsthand studies of drug insurance and drug quality control programs throughout the United States and in Canada, Great Britain, France, Sweden, and Belgium. Other studies were conducted on programs in Denmark, Norway, and Italy. Later these on-the-spot investigations were expanded to include Holland, Australia, and New Zealand.

At the end, the Task Force presented its conclusion: "*On the basis of available evidence, lack of clinical equivalency among chemical equivalents meeting all official standards has been grossly exaggerated as a major hazard to the public health.*" [34] Behind this finding were these factors:

Low-cost generics had been used in many leading nongovernmental hospitals. In such institutions, instances of clinical nonequivalency had seldom been reported, and few of these have had significant therapeutic importance.[35] They had been used with similar results in Veterans Administration[36] and Public Health Service hospitals.[37] They had been used with similar results in American military operations. (Here, it should be noted, the success of this program may be related to the intensive inspection system used by the Department of Defense.)[38] They had been used with similar results in state welfare programs.[39] They had been used with similar results in foreign drug programs.[40]

In addition, the Task Force could not help but note what was probably one of the most poorly kept secrets in medical circles—the efforts of drug company detail men, operating on their own or on orders from their firms, to secure from practicing physicians and pharmacists any possible clues to the clinical failure of generic products. These efforts did lead to the discovery of some generic products—and some brand-name products as well—that did not meet USP or NF standards and thus were being marketed in violation of the law. But, so far as all available evidence would demonstrate, they did not result in any significant number of disclosures of clinical failures with products legally on the market.

Another noteworthy development came in August 1968, when the PMA published a bibliography of 501 articles in the medical literature[41] —supposedly a bombshell that would demolish the Task Force conclusions. "This unique publication," said PMA's president, C. Joseph

Stetler, "refutes the astonishing myth that there are not significant differences among dosage forms of the same drug." That statement in itself was somewhat astonishing. We were not aware of any responsible scientist or clinician who did not agree that there might be significant differences. The question was how often do they occur and what threat do they pose to patients. In response to a request from Senator Nelson, the Task Force and its technical consultants reviewed the "bombshell" of 501 references cited by PMA and came out with the following analysis:[42]

Of the 501 studies, only 221 were actually conducted in human subjects. Of the 221, only 76 were—by PMA's own evaluation—"adequately designed or controlled experiments." Of the 76, only 12 represented comparisons between what might seem to be different brands of the same chemical equivalent. And of these final 12, most compared different dosage forms (such as tablets versus effervescent solutions), or different salts (such as sodium derivatives versus potassium derivatives), or different coatings (such as delayed release products versus rapid release products). Some of these final products failed to meet existing USP or NF standards and thus would be illegally on the market.

"At the most, Task Force staff and our consultants agree, there were only two or three which demonstrated statistically-significant lack of biological equivalency, and in one case, the differences were described as being without any practical clinical importance." One drug company public relations official later quipped, "The PMA should be charged with treason in time of war. Their damn bibliography merely gave aid and comfort—and a lot more ammunition —to the enemy."

There were, nevertheless, those documented cases in which generic products had met USP or NF standards and yet failed to perform properly in controlled human trials. Few of these were on the record when the Task Force began its operations in 1967, and in that same year chloramphenicol was added to the list. "Even though such cases are few, and others may well be reported in the future," the Task Force said, "these cannot be ignored, and the problem deserves careful consideration because of the medical and economic policies which are involved." [43] This consideration, it was felt, should not involve further polemics. There was an urgent need for less rhetoric and more scientific data.

THE TASK FORCE EQUIVALENCY TRIALS

Ideally, any definitive comparison of equivalency would involve a study of supposedly comparable drug products in human patients afflicted with a specific disease—that is, a measurement of *clinical equivalency*. In most cases, such a comparison would be impractical and possibly unethical. It would be time-consuming and costly. It would be complicated not only by human differences but by differences in the symptoms of diseases under consideration. Furthermore, it would involve human experimentation under conditions in which an unexpected lack of clinical equivalency might well have disastrous results. Equivalency studies could be conducted in experimental animals, but the nature of specific diseases and the nature of drug absorption and action in animals and human beings may not be comparable.

Instead, as a practical alternative, it appeared that attention should be directed to objective measurements of *biological equivalency*—or relative physiological availability—measured in normal subjects as a proxy for the direct measurements and comparisons of clinical effects. This was based on the general agreement among pharmacologists that in the case of most drugs—certainly most of those taken orally for their effects in the blood, the liver, the brain, or other internal organs—their therapeutic effectiveness will be substantially related to their absorption into the blood stream. Thus, if two preparations yield the same blood concentration of active ingredients, presumably they will yield the same therapeutic effect.[44]

On the basis of these factors, the Task Force embarked in the fall of 1967 on a determination of the biological equivalency of a number of chemical equivalents. This program was warmly endorsed by some drug companies. Other firms, however, were less enthusiastic and supportive; some of these stressed the point that nothing would be accomplished by testing only a number of products, and that *all* generics must be assayed before *any* decisions could be reached. Such a task might well take decades. It is at least conceivable that this latter attitude stemmed from the fact that the longer any governmental decision could be delayed, the longer the profit structure of brand-name drugs could be protected.

But the prospects were not that forbidding. Although there were many drugs on the market, most of them—about three-quarters—were still under patent, and no generic versions were being produced. Of those that were available as generics, some provided the active agent already in solution, and it was believed that these would offer few problems of absorption. Still others were drugs prescribed mainly for the relief of mild, temporary symptoms, and it appeared that even substantial differences in clinical effect would have minimal importance for the public health.

Accordingly, in the Task Force trials, which were begun by FDA and the Public Health Service, top priority was given to products that met the following criteria:[45]

—The product is generally considered to be a "critical" or "life-and-death" drug—that is, one required for the control of a disease rather than for the alleviation of temporary or trivial symptoms.
—It is generally dispensed in solid form, as a tablet or capsule, rather than in solution.
—The active ingredient itself is relatively insoluble.
—Particular attention should be given to those drugs which had previously been the subject of a reported or suspected nonequivalency or therapeutic failure.

After consultations with clinicians and scientists, and off-the-record meetings with representatives of most major drug companies, it was determined that the tests should begin with about two dozen compounds: aminophylline, bishydroxycoumarin, chloramphenicol, chlortetracycline, diethylstilbestrol, diphenhydramine, diphenylhydantoin, erythromycin, ferrous sulfate, griseofulvin, hydrocortisone, isoniazid, meperidine, meprobamate, oxytetracycline, para-amino-salicylate, penicillin G, penicillin V, prednisone, quinidine, reserpine, secobarbital, sulfisoxazole, tetracycline, thyroid, tripelennamine, and warfarin. (Digoxin, which was later to figure prominently in this matter, was not included, largely because at the time there seemed to be no practical assay method to measure its absorption in the body.)

The Task Force itself was guilty of an error based on excessive overoptimism, and predicted that the tests on many if not most of these drugs would be completed within eighteen to twenty-four months. The technical problems involved were, however, so complex in some cases that the investigation had not been completed in four years.

In 1971 the situation was analyzed in a searching review by Dr. John Wagner of the University of Michigan. His survey went back to 1954. It included only controlled studies using the same drug in the same dosage form in human subjects. The results showed that large differences had been demonstrated in six "critical" products: para-amino-salicylic acid, chloramphenicol, diphenylhydantoin, tetracycline, oxytetracyline, and warfarin. Similar differences had been demonstrated in two other products of less critical importance, aspirin and riboflavin.[46]

Some industry spokesmen nevertheless continued to insist that the reported cases of lack of equivalence understated the problem. Dr.

Wagner himself said that "to assume there is no problem with any of the other drugs or to even guess at the extent of the problem there really is—is unscientific in the extreme." But Dr. Edward Feldman of the *National Formulary* said in 1971:

> During the past five years or more, therapeutic equivalence and nonequivalence have been the subject of more discussion, attention, and study than probably any other issue in the history of modern pharmacy and therapeutics. Industry, government, academia, and the professions have all directed intensive efforts of an unparalleled degree in an attempt to compile evidence and to arrive at a valid assessment of the extent of therapeutic nonequivalency. Examination of the resulting record reveals only very meager evidence which documents therapeutic nonequivalence.[47]

In Canada, where parallel equivalency studies had been undertaken, Dr. Eldon Boyd, a consultant to the Food and Drug Directorate, stated that "92 to 97 percent of different brands of drugs sold in Canada are sufficiently absorbed to be clinically equivalent. The initial indications," he added, "are that in Canada, as in the U.S. of America, lack of physiological equivalency in brands of drugs meeting all other statutory requirements is not extensive and is not a major hazard to public health." [48]

Probably the most upsetting instance of proved nonequivalency came to light late in 1971, when a team of Columbia University investigators using a newly developed technique reported enormous discrepancies in the absorption of digoxin from several generic-name versions of the drug [49] This was clearly a case involving a critical drug, which in one form or another was being used regularly by some five million heart disease patients. Used properly, it can be lifesaving, but as all physicians knew, or should have known, it can be extremely dangerous, and it has been held responsible for many cases of serious drug reactions and many deaths. One of the trickiest aspects of its use is the determination of the precise dosage for each individual patient. For these reasons, the Columbia group's report was especially serious, since it showed that the different products—all of which had met existing USP standards—gave blood levels varying by as much as 700 percent. Large differences were found even in different batches produced by the same manufacturer. "With a potent drug like digoxin," an FDA official said, "you're playing Russian roulette unless you have some assurance of tablet uniformity."

But it soon became apparent that FDA had been having digoxin troubles long before the Columbia group published its findings. Tests showed that whereas the brand-name manufacturer, Burroughs-Wellcome, had been producing its Lanoxin with excellent standardization, many other firms were marketing generic digoxin products with as little as 12 percent or as much as 276 percent of the amount specified on the label. Since 1970, when tablet-by-tablet analysis became practical, FDA scientists had found that a bottle of digoxin tablets might have an *average* value meeting USP requirements, but the variations from one tablet to another could be extremely large. Even earlier, going back at least to 1966, FDA had been aware that some bad batches of digoxin were reaching the market, and had ordered recalls of the defective products. But the agency had failed to notify the public, or even to alert all physicians, of these earlier findings. A major reason was the fear of arousing needless public concern, Theodore Byers of FDA said afterward, and added, "Looking back at the experience, I'd have to say that we goofed." [50]

Whether these developments dispelled either the "myth of generic equivalency" or the "myth of generic nonequivalency" may be endlessly debated, but this does not appear to be important. In this slightly less than perfect world, there can never be absolute guarantees that *all* generic products will inevitably be biologically or clinically equivalent. There can never be such guarantees of such equivalence for *all* batches of the same product made by the same manufacturer. This is scarcely an unprecedented situation. There is no absolute guarantee that all physicians, merely because they passed licensing examinations five or ten or twenty years ago, are equivalently competent—or even adequately competent—to practice medicine.

THE TASK FORCE RECOMMENDATIONS

In a utopian world no drug of any kind would be permitted on the market unless samples of each batch were tested on human subjects. Such a monumental task would be needless in many and perhaps most instances, would raise drug prices to an intolerable level, and would pose a risk to the test subjects that could not be justified. As a practical compromise, other steps were recommended:

The biological equivalency trials should be continued by the government with high priority. According to a recent report by the Surgeon General, these trials are being continued.[51]

The USP and the NF should continue to improve their standards, adding sophisticated new methods and requiring proof of biological equivalency—where necessary—on animals or human subjects. Both official publications are reviewing their standards, adding such additional methods as measurement of dissolution rates, and—at least for such "critical" drugs as antibiotics—considering *in vivo* measurements as a routine requirement.

No company should be allowed to produce and market drugs until it had first been inspected, approved, and licensed by FDA. Legislation requiring these vital steps has already been introduced in the Congress.[52]

Acceptable quality control systems should be required in all drug manufacturing plants. Some companies are already utilizing such systems, and would merely be required to continue them. Some manufacturers might not elect to institute these systems, and their products would be banned from interstate commerce; certainly they should be declared ineligible for purchase or reimbursement in any government-financed program. (Whether these products were banned from intrastate commerce would be determined by the individual states.) Other manufacturers might decide to institute and maintain acceptable quality control procedures; this would result in slightly higher production costs, which the manufacturers would presumably cover by setting slightly higher prices on their products—an increase that would be unquestionably justified by the improvement in quality.

FDA has already made significant advances in this direction, tightening its rules for so-called "good manufacturing practices" and operating its new Intensified Drug Inspection Program. The latter, aimed at improving overall industry performance by concentrating on specific manufacturing firms, has made it possible to bring marginal operations into line and to identify and eliminate what seem to be hopeless cases. From 1968 to 1971, FDA has reported, some 287 drug manufacturers and associated testing laboratories were inspected. In most cases acceptable performance was achieved. "In some 44 remaining cases," FDA commissioner Charles Edwards said, "are 23 firms which are now the subject of legal action, and 21 firms which are giving up the drug business because of their inability to come into compliance." [53]

In 1970, soon after Dr. Edwards had taken office, he won the plaudits of the brand-name companies and many medical journal editors when he told a pharmacy meeting, "We have found that comparable bio-availability frequently does not exist for products that are otherwise, so far as currently available methods are concerned, identical." [54] But less than a year later, after he had investigated the situation further, he told the PMA, "We think it is a disservice to the public to use a few episodes where drug equivalency was drawn into question to imply that the whole drug supply is in doubt. We disagree with your conclusion that because a few instances have occurred, this is probably a very frequent phenomenon." [55] At about the same time, he denounced companies for claiming they were financially unable to correct deficiencies in their processes, for failing to perform even physico-chemical tests on every batch of product, and for skimping on technical and scientific personnel.[56]

Finally, when in the future the patent expires on a drug, and it becomes possible to produce generics, none of these generic-name products would be permitted on the market unless (a) it met all the USP or NF requirements and (b) when required by the Secretary of HEW—as would be the case for "critical" or "life-and-death" products —adequate test data were supplied to demonstrate essentially equivalent biological availability. Here it was the Task Force's belief that continuation of the ongoing clinical trials on current generic-name products would eventually offer a practical solution to the present problem, and that the new requirement would minimize the problem in the future.

A similar recommendation was approved late in 1969 by the American Pharmaceutical Association:

> Prior to the initial distribution of a drug product or modifications of an existing product, every manufacturer should be obligated to perform tests which are appropriate and sufficient to demonstrate the clinical safety and efficacy claimed for that manufacturer's product, and to make a summary of this information readily available to the medical and pharmaceutical professions. In particular, in the absence of such tests, it cannot be assumed that the product will exhibit clinical acceptability.[57]

The National Academy of Sciences/National Research Council in 1970 presented its views in a position paper which closely paralleled the earlier recommendations of the Task Force:

> All producers of drugs should be required, as they are now, not only to provide evidence of composition, purity, and quality, but also evidence of physical availability as judged by tests of disintegration, dispersion, and dissolution rates in appropriate solvents. In the majority of cases, this should suffice, but in every case in which there may be doubt of biological equivalence, biological tests should be required.[58]

Late in 1970 FDA proposed to implement these recommendations by requiring biological equivalence tests on selected products—probably those of life-and-death importance, and in cases where lack of equivalency might be suspected.[59] These FDA plans won little enthusiasm from small generic-product firms, but they were greeted with praise by most brand-name companies, the PMA, the *JAMA*, and other medical journals. Then, to the astonishment of many observers, most of the major pharmaceutical companies and the PMA—which had long insisted on the crucial importance of testing for biological equivalency—suddenly switched sides and protested to FDA that "such testing is not current good manufacturing practice and that adequate methods do not exist to make such testing practical and meaningful." [60]

In the summer of 1973 Dr. Simmons of FDA reviewed thousands of tests conducted by the agency—especially by its National Center for Drug Analysis in St. Louis—and said, "We cannot conclude there is a significant difference in quality between the generic and brand-name products tested." He declared that he was constantly discouraged by the quality of the dialogue on the subject. "The pronouncements made by members of the various camps," he emphasized, "are often biased and, occasionally, frankly and intentionally misleading or exaggerated." [61]

Thus, in the great generic controversy, the debate and the rhetoric may be expected to continue. If it is to be terminated, this will probably result not from the accumulation of all of the evidence that the various parties would like to have but more probably from the entry of more and more brand-name drug makers into the generic business. "If your company is making and selling generics itself—and making a damn good profit selling them," one brand-name company official said, "you're going to think twice before spending your money supporting a campaign to knock all generics."

THE ANTI-ANTISUBSTITUTION LAWS

Beginning about twenty years ago, most state legislatures passed the so-called antisubstitution laws concerning drug products. In 1971, after more than two years of study, the American Pharmaceutical Association approved a resolution that declared that these laws were no longer necessary—if they ever had been—and therefore should be repealed.[62]

It could safely be predicted that the APhA recommendation would stir up about the same intensity of controversy that was generated by the proposal to repeal the laws against liquor. Within pharmacy, the proposed repeal was opposed by the powerful National Association of Retail Druggists, several state pharmacy associations, and even a sizeable minority of the APhA itself. It was similarly opposed by the AMA—this time including the AMA's Council on Drugs—and by many state medical groups. The *JAMA* declared that revocation of the antisubstitution laws would "turn order into chaos." [63] The PMA claimed that physicians alone are in a position to know both the patient's health problems and the drug products of possible value (and possible harm) to him.[64]

Seemingly at the heart of the matter were the issues that had already marked the generic controversy in general—the rarity or frequency of nonequivalence among generic products, and the ability of FDA to keep low-quality generics off the market. In addition, and as might have been expected, some opponents of repeal warned that, without the antisubstitution laws, drug research would be slashed and the quality of health care would suffer. Others warned that a pharmacist substituting one brand for another would be liable to costly malpractice suits. Carl Roberts, director of the legal division of the APhA, countered by stating, "Our research reveals that there is not a single reported case, either before or after enactment of state antisubstitution laws, involving a claim that a pharmacist was negligent where he had dispensed a different brand drug product than that prescribed. . . . Pharmacists who dispense only quality drug products from reputable sources should have little to fear about potential harm to patients and consequent liability." [65]

Some defenders of the antisubstitution laws claimed that repeal would allow pharmacists to substitute a different *drug* in place of the one prescribed—in place of phenobarbital, for example, substituting pentobarbital, chloral hydrate, or even aspirin. No such proposals had been presented; rather, repeal would allow the pharmacist only to substitute one *brand* of the same drug for another. Some even proposed the absurd notion that the physician would prescribe "antibiotic," and it would be up to the pharmacist to decide whether to dispense penicillin, tetracycline, chloramphenicol, or streptomycin.

Some claimed that a physician would be unable to specify a particular brand even when he felt that this was essential for the appropriate care of a patient, as in the control of blood clotting or the use of a product that could safely be taken by an allergic patient. But provisions were made for the physician to order a specific brand for a specific patient whenever this was clinically necessary.

In addition to these real or imagined arguments—and the expected denunciation of repeal as "socialistic"—there was another issue of far more importance. Who was better able—the physician or the pharmacist—to select the best brand of a drug? The classical argument of many physicians, "We can observe the effects of the products on patients, and so we are the only ones to decide," no longer had the impact it once possessed. Many so-called judgments made at the bedside were no better than clinical impressions that could not stand up under scientific scrutiny. Confidence in the ability of many physicians to select effective products had been shaken by the embarrassing disclosures that many drugs rated as "ineffective" by the National Academy of Sciences/ National Research Council study had been widely prescribed for years. And many physicians were freely admitting that the whole subject of drug selection had become far too complex and required more time than they could afford.

"It would appear that in this day and age, the physician does not have the time or background to be familiar with each pharmaceutical company or the quality of its various products," said an editorial in the *Delaware Medical Journal*. "Logically, this responsibility should be delegated to the pharmacist, the member of the medical team with the necessary training and experience in pharmacology." [66]

It thus became a question of whether pharmacists—especially the new breed of intensively trained clinical pharmacists—were willing and able to undertake the responsibility for selecting the best brand of a prescribed drug. Some pharmacists did not want such a responsibility, but others did—and in fact argued that they had long since won the right to utilize their abilities for the patient's benefit.

The AMA protested strongly and threatened retaliation, but Dr. William Apple, executive director of the APhA, retorted, "It is inconceivable to me that AMA would believe that organized medicine can dictate subservience for pharmacy and other health professions while demanding absolute freedom for medicine. The AMA may be the captain of the health team, but . . . AMA doesn't own the team." [67]

Regardless of the furore, it appears that the issue will be settled sooner or later, with the antisubstitution laws repealed in spirit or in fact. The signs are now evident:[68]

> —In many major hospitals, especially those with effective formularies, agreements have already been reached for the physicians to prescribe generically (except when a particular brand is needed by a particular patient), and the pharmacist is authorized to select the brand.
> —Similar arrangements have already been implemented in federal and state health plans, group practice clinics, and health insurance programs.
> —In many cities, community pharmacists have already been authorized

formally or informally by individual physicians to select the best brand
and to dispense accordingly to their patients.

—A growing number of private physicians are accustomed to prescribing
generically.

—During the past decade, it has been estimated that more than a billion
prescriptions have been dispensed on the basis of the pharmacist's
choice of brand.[69]

As another indication, Squibb recently adopted an intriguing
approach when it guaranteed that if a pharmacist should face any
liability action for filling a prescription "properly" with one of *its* generic
products, Squibb would "provide legal advice and/or defense as necessary." Although the company's statement did not recommend violating
any antisubstitution law, it revealed what a trade journal termed the
growing awareness among major pharmaceutical firms of the need to
compete for so-called generic business, and of the pharmacist's increasing
importance in product selection.[70]

Yet another sign, and one that probably produced no joy in either
AMA or PMA headquarters, appeared in the *San Francisco Examiner* in
August 1973. "What I do," Dr. Russell Roth of Erie, Pennsylvania, told
a reporter, "is write down the generic name of the drug and hope that
the druggist will give the patient the best price for it. Generally,
physicians are supposed to encourage the druggist to pick the company." [71] Dr. Roth was the newly-installed president of the AMA.

When a national health insurance system or health service plan is
adopted in the United States, with substantial financing through federal
taxes, it seems a certainty that the Congress will set up guidelines in an
effort to give the highest quality of health care at the lowest reasonable
cost. Those guidelines will almost certainly call for the use of generic-
name products except where there are medical reasons for specifying a
brand-name product.

One indication of what the future holds came in Kentucky, where
in 1972 the legislature repealed its antisubstitution law—the first state to
take such action. Two years earlier such a move had been proposed, but
it was defeated by a coalition of the state medical and pharmacy
associations, supported by the drug industry. In 1972 the pharmacy
association changed its stand and urged passage of the bill. It was
supported by many physicians—although not by the medical society—
and by organized labor and other consumer groups, and the potent
Louisville Courier-Journal.

"The PMA went all out to beat us," a Kentucky pharmacist said.

"They had so many lobbyists and industry leaders running up and down the corridors of the state capitol that if somebody had dropped a bomb, it would have wiped out half of the pharmaceutical vice-presidents in the country. But times had changed. The people wanted it, and the legislators knew it, and we won—and won big."

Under the new Kentucky law, when a pharmacist receives a prescription for a brand-name drug that is also available under generic name from other sources, he is authorized to substitute a generic product, providing it is listed in a formulary prepared by a state drug formulary council. It is up to the council to select only those generic products that are believed to be of high quality and are relatively inexpensive.

A somewhat similar bill was enacted in Maryland in 1972, after five years of effort by the state pharmaceutical association and by some medical leaders. During the final year of the campaign, tremendous industry pressure against the bill was exerted on the medical society, the state pharmacy board, the legislature, and the governor, but without success.[72] The new law permits a pharmacist to substitute one brand for another, unless the physician explicitly prohibits any substitution, and provides that the pharmacist must notify the physician of the brand actually dispensed, the product must be on a state formulary list, and the pharmacist must pass on to the patient the full savings in cost.

Perhaps in recognition of these trends, such important brand-name companies as Smith Kline & French, Robins, and Parke-Davis have already introduced lines of so-called "brand-name generics," carrying a brand name but priced more reasonably to meet the competition of low-cost generics.

GENERICS AND DOLLAR SAVINGS

Another issue in the generic controversy, and particularly in the battle over antisubstitution laws, concerns prices and profits. As was shown above, the prices of some brand-name products, although certainly not all of them, are higher than those charged for their generic-name competitors. The maintenance of these brand-name prices is obviously vital to the present profit structure of the pharmaceutical industry.

Similarly, the antisubstitution laws—although they were enacted ostensibly to protect the public health—have become important in maintaining the use, prices, and profits of brand-name drugs. Any tampering with these laws could mean that the brand-name industry's huge promotion campaign, costing hundreds of millions of dollars a year and directed primarily to advertising and detailing brand-name products, would have been largely wasted and could no longer be economically justified. "If drugs are going to be prescribed under generic name, and selected mainly on the basis of price," an advertising expert said, "promoting them—at least in the way we've done it in the past—would be nonsensical."

For many years it had been asserted that the wider use of generics—through repeal of the antisubstitution laws, the encouragement or even requirement of generic prescribing, or other means—would have an enormous effect in reducing the nation's prescription drug bill. The potential savings were often given in terms of at least many hundreds of millions of dollars each year.

In the case of certain products—especially those required for the long-term treatment of certain chronic diseases—it was obvious that the savings to some patients would be very large.[73] The effect on the nation's total drug bill, or on the bill for a particular governmental program, was not so clearly understood. In an attempt to assay such potential savings, the Task Force on Prescription Drugs undertook a special study of the effect of generic prescribing on one proposed program—the provision of out-of-hospital prescription drugs to beneficiaries of the Medicare program. Under hypothetical conditions—which would be virtually impossible to achieve in reality—the potential savings were calculated to be a *maximum* of only about 6 percent at the retail level.[74]

This figure, unbelievably low to some people, reflected the apparently unappreciated fact that, of the most frequently prescribed drugs, about three-fourths were still under patent, with no generic products available. Of the remainder, some were already being prescribed generically, and thus offered no potential savings, while some generic-name products were actually priced as high as the brand-name products or even higher. Savings could be achieved on only about 15 percent of these most widely used drugs. Greater savings could be achieved with the combination of generic prescribing and the use of an effective formulary, which would ban many costly brand-name products of dubious value.

When applied to a nationwide program, savings of even a small percentage could involve tens or hundreds of millions of dollars annually, and obviously cannot be ignored by taxpayers or their governmental representatives. An increase in generic prescribing and a decrease in brand-name prescribing might possibly induce some drug companies to reduce their promotional expenditures. But generic prescribing, however brought about, will not in itself solve all the economic problems associated with prescription drug use.

THE WEINBERGER BOMBSHELL

On December 19, 1973, President Nixon's recently appointed HEW secretary, Caspar Weinberger, appeared before a special senate subcommittee headed by Senator Edward Kennedy and proceeded to drop what one trade publication described the same day as a bombshell. He reviewed the recommendations presented by the HEW Task Force on Prescription Drugs more than four years earlier and described its operations as "landmarks in the consideration of prescription drug issues." He noted that its findings and recommendations had been reviewed and to a large extent supported by a committee of outside experts appointed by the former secretary, Robert Finch, and chaired by Dr. John Dunlop. He described the steps which had already been taken by HEW to implement many of the Task Force recommendations.

Then the bombshell landed. Weinberger agreed that differences in biological equivalency or availability could occur, but he added, "All the evidence to date indicates that clinically significant differences in bioavailability are not frequent." The required use of low-cost generic products in such federally supported programs as Medicare and Medicaid, he said, could yield a saving of 5 to 8 percent in overall reimbursements for prescription drugs—about the same as the percentage the Task Force had estimated. Accordingly, he announced that HEW would soon be announcing proposed regulations to limit drug reimbursement under its programs to "the lowest cost at which the drug is generally available, unless there is a demonstrated difference in the therapeutic effect." [75]

It was clear that the Administration had made its decision. If a brand-name manufacturer were convinced that its product was superior to a generic competitor, it would be up to the brand-name company to prove it.

Weinberger stated emphatically that the proposed new rulings would not interfere with the practice of medicine. "Every physician must be free to prescribe whatever medication he believes is most appropriate for his patient. It is not the business of government to tell doctors what marketed drugs they may or may not prescribe. That is, and must remain, solely a matter of the professional judgment of the prescribing physician." Under the new rulings, if a physician preferred a costly brand-name product rather than a less expensive generic version, he would still be free to prescribe the brand-name drug. The government would simply not pay for it.

The drug industry had known that the bombshell was coming. Copies of the secretary's statement had been circulated in advance to the press and various interested parties. The Pharmaceutical Manufacturers Association and PMA president C. Joseph Stetler were quick to denounce the HEW decision as radical, a gamble, unable to produce the promised savings, and a disservice to the public. Stetler warned that the new proposal would cripple American drug research and relegate Medicare and Medicaid beneficiaries to second-class medical care.

This was not an altogether new warning. It was, as one commentator put it, "old and tired." What remained to be seen was whether the drug industry and its potent lobby, which had effectively blocked such a policy during the first years of the Nixon Administration, could continue to block it.

THE REAL ISSUE

Finally, by 1973 there was growing awareness that such factors as biological availability, prices, and even profits—important as they are—may not be the real issues underlying the generic controversy. Differences in biological equivalency have occurred in the past and will almost certainly occur in the future, although perhaps less frequently. But such differences are not necessarily the only factor of clinical importance. Thus, a variation of 10, 20, or even 50 percent in absorption rates between two brands of penicillin would not be significant if the penicillin were prescribed for the common cold, or if the patient were directed to take a drug before meals but took it after meals, or if he forgot to take it at all, or if the patient were allergic to the product, or if the prescription were based on the wrong diagnosis.

The economic factors obviously cannot be dismissed. Under a national health program, a possible saving in the total prescription bill—now about $10 billion a year—could be sizeable. As we have indicated above, the potential savings might be a maximum of 6 percent. A more reasonable estimate of savings under actual conditions would be 2 or 3 percent, or roughly $250 million a year. Such a sum is certainly large enough to induce brand-name companies to continue, year after year, their campaign to preserve the antisubstitution laws in the various states. Repeal of those laws might cost them not only $250 million in sales but about $23 million in net profits. Yet in a nationwide comprehensive health program, involving as much as $70 billion a year or more, saving or not saving $250 million a year would hardly rank as an earthshaking possibility.

What may be the most important element in the generic controversy, fanned as it has been by industry, consumer groups, medical journals, and others, is the jockeying for prestige, professional pride, and ego-satisfaction between physicians and pharmacists. This basic problem will not be quickly or painlessly solved.

In this broad field of drug quality there is mounting recognition that not even the most careful quality control systems operated by most of the outstanding drug companies in the nation can be expected invariably to protect the public against low-quality products—those that are mislabeled, subpotent, superpotent, adulterated, or contaminated. Although FDA's checks on quality are not necessarily foolproof, the agency has unquestionably performed a valuable service in intercepting those low-quality products that have slipped through a company's screening program. In fulfilling that role alone, FDA has more than justified its existence.

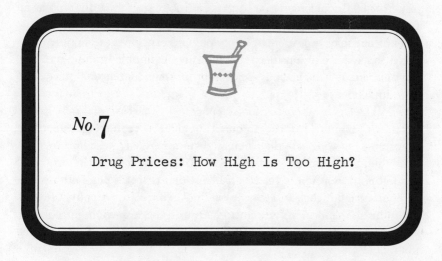

No. 7

Drug Prices: How High Is Too High?

I can't honestly say that drug prices are cheap. I think they're reasonable only for those who can afford to pay the price.

V. D. MATTIA, M.D., *president of Hoffmann-LaRoche,* 1969

THE PRICING structure of prescription drugs in the United States has sometimes been compared to the pricing of rugs in a Turkish bazaar or a Moroccan *souk.* The comparison is unfair. The pricing of drugs is far more complex and confusing and infinitely more irritating. "It is significant to note," George Squibb has testified, "that the industry's pricing policies and practices have not only brought on sharp criticism from those in academic, press, and legislative circles outside the pharmacy and medical professions, but also from those within those professions. . . . Friend and foe alike of the industry point with all sorts of degrees of alarm, shame, disgust, distrust, and perplexity at what is certainly a situation at best hard to justify, and at worst completely unreasonable, chaotic as well as shortsighted and stupid." [1]

Unquestionably, the prices of virtually all aspects of health care have increased at an astounding rate. As is shown in table 8 in the Appendix, the average per capita expenditure for hospital care has soared most dramatically, increasing by roughly six times from 1950 to 1971. Per capita expenditures for physician care have increased about fourfold. This has been accompanied by the rise in median net income of self-employed physicians in private practice: approximately $23,000 a year in 1960, $28,960 in 1965, $32,170 in 1966, $34,730 in 1967, $37,620 in 1968, $40,550 in 1969, and $41,500 in 1970.[2] Although drug expenditures have not increased so rapidly, they have more than tripled. The average price of a prescription has roughly doubled since 1950, and the number of prescriptions per capita dispensed each year has more than doubled.

What has aroused particular concern in the case of drugs is not merely the increased dollar amounts spent each year. First, and most important, is whether the increased numbers of prescriptions are justifiable on clinical grounds. (Some industry representatives have claimed no responsibility for this rise, insisting that it is purely the doing of physicians, but such an attitude overlooks the impact on physicians of the industry's enormous promotion campaign.) A second question is whether the pricing practices of the drug industry are justifiable on any grounds.

The industry, it is often claimed, has set its prices at inordinately high levels so as to reap inordinately high profits. But one authority has suggested that the squandering of resources, illogical pricing, redundancy of products, and other inefficiencies may represent even more money than the manufacturers' profits.[3]

For example, the true economic cost of making and packaging stilbestrol in the form of one thousand 5-mg tablets is about 40 percent more than producing it as one thousand 1-mg tablets. Yet three firms charge at least 160 percent more for the 5-mg tablets, while another charges 600 percent more.

In the case of phenobarbital, the cost of producing one thousand ½-grain tablets is about 15 percent more than for one thousand ¼-grain tablets. Two firms, however, charge 30 percent more for the ½-grain form, four charge 40 percent more, one charges 60 percent more, one charges 70 percent more, and one charges 2,400 percent more. On the other hand, one company charges the same price for both ¼- and ½-grain tablets.

Phenobarbital itself is available in at least nine different colors (one supplier sells the drug in five shades), eighteen different strengths, five dosage forms, seven bottle sizes for standard tablets, and at least six sizes for the drug in solution.

Equally chaotic and confusing is the system of wholesale prices as officially posted, and what happens to those prices in actual practice. In the United States the baseline is generally supposed to be the listing of wholesale prices published annually in the *Drug Topics Red Book* and the *American Druggist Blue Book*. Such listings serve to indicate merely the maximum prices for each product. Otherwise they are meaningless. They represent an umbrella beneath which actual prices to the pharmacist or other outlet are set by quantity discounts, hospital discounts, government discounts, two-for-the-price-of-one deals, annual volume discounts, rebates, and other special arrangements.[4] Often these arrangements are so complicated that the pharmacist is unable to calculate his actual purchase price of a particular drug product—its so-called acquisition cost—without undertaking intolerably expensive and time-consuming accounting procedures.

COMMUNITY PHARMACIES: CONFUSION COMPOUNDED

On top of the acquisition cost, the typical community pharmacist adds a markup to cover his costs of doing business plus a profit. In some instances, notably when governmental programs or private health insurance plans are involved, the markup may be limited or specified by program regulations.[5] In most cases, however, the pharmacist will decide for himself what markup he will use. This has resulted in generally higher retail prices in West Coast communities and in other cities where the cost of living is relatively high, and generally lower prices in the South and in rural areas.[6] The remarkable spread in retail prices was disclosed in a 1972 survey conducted by the Consumer Federation of America, with some pharmacies charging as much as ten times the prices charged by other pharmacies for the same quantity of the same drug (see table 9 in the Appendix).

Even within the same community, surveys have revealed startling differences. For example, a New York City study showed that the average cost for the same prescription in a low-income black area was far higher than that in a low-income white area, and even higher than that in an upper-income "carriage trade" district.[7]

In a large midwestern city, another survey disclosed that the identical prescription—one for fifty tablets of Miltown, 400 mg—cost from $4.25 to $4.50 in five stores owned by one chain, from $3.82 to $4.57 in four stores owned by a second chain, and from $3.95 to $6.50 in fourteen independent pharmacies. In these same stores, when the prescription was written generically, the cost to the patient ranged from $2.38 to $6.35. One pharmacy charged $6.35 for the Miltown prescription and the identical price for the prescription that was filled with a low-cost generic product. Another pharmacy charged $4.50 for the

Miltown prescription and $5.50 for the prescription that ordered a generic but was filled with Miltown.[8]

It is possible, of course, that some of the differences in the prices may justifiably reflect differences in services rendered by the pharmacist —for example, spending additional time to check a patient's drug record or to warn against possible side effects, or making a home delivery—but it is difficult to understand how the same store can charge *more* for dispensing a low-cost generic rather than a brand-name product.

Similarly, it is difficult to explain how the price for the same prescription dispensed by the same pharmacy may vary on different days of the week and even at different times of the same day. Even more distressing was the discovery in a University of Kansas Medical Center survey that the price charged for the identical prescription in low-income black neighborhoods was substantially higher to poorly dressed black patients than to well-dressed whites.[9]

As confused as drug pricing may be at the community pharmacy level, some semblance of order—and, some economists might add, price rigidity and lack of competition among manufacturers—has come from enforcement of the federal Robinson-Patman Act, which prevents manufacturers and wholesalers from discriminating against any individual or class of *retail* vendors. They are required to offer their goods at the same prices and with the same discounts, including quantity discounts. They may not offer a special discount on quantities so huge that only one individual pharmacy or chain can take advantage of it. But the Robinson-Patman law does not generally apply to the prices of drugs sold to nonprofit hospitals, or to federal, state, or local government agencies, or to foreign purchasers, and it is in these areas that price differences become astounding.

THE HOSPITAL PRICE CONTROVERSY

For years the prices set for drugs sold to hospitals have been a thorny problem to hospital officials, community pharmacists, organized pharmacy, and the drug industry. To get his product accepted by a hospital, a manufacturer may cut his price by 30 percent or more below the price offered to a community pharmacy for the same drug in the same quantity. If there is brisk product competition, as among dozens of me-too antihistamines with practically the same clinical value, or if there is price competition between a brand-name product and a generic-name competitor, the price to the hospital may be slashed by more than 50 or 60 percent.

These hospital discounts do not necessarily represent any philanthropic motives. Drug manufacturers are convinced that staff physicians, and especially interns and residents in training, will become accustomed to prescribing a particular product in their hospital practice and then will continue to use it in their private practice.[10] In a way, the hospital-discount system represents a highly valuable form of drug promotion.[11]

Most hospitals have been eager to take advantage of these special discounts, but apparently few have been willing to pass on the savings to their patients. They have set their prices to these patients at roughly the same levels charged by community pharmacies, and sometimes far above, and have thereby added significantly to the hospital income, which in most cases is tax exempt.[12] In our own studies we have found that the pharmacy's profit on hospital-dispensed drugs may be as much as 55 or 60 percent.[13] Sometimes this profit is used to support special activities within the hospital, such as a particular surgery unit or a research project. In other instances it goes into the hospital's general fund.

Such an arrangement, beneficial though it may be to a hospital, means that patients patronizing a community pharmacy are unwittingly subsidizing those inpatients and outpatients who use a hospital pharmacy. This matter has become particularly irritating in the case of hospital outpatient pharmacies, which in a sense compete with community pharmacies. The American Pharmaceutical Association has long argued that this competition is unfair, since the hospital pharmacy can buy at lower costs and pays no taxes, and has urged the application of the Robinson-Patman Act to hospital drug purchases. Similarly, the American Hospital Association has recommended that hospital pharmacies should set their prices to cover their own costs and that they should not be used as a profit-generating activity. In defense, hospital administrators have claimed that this would merely reduce their income and force them to raise their drug prices to patients, stop special programs that are being subsidized by their pharmacy profits, or raise their daily room charges even higher.

In California, legislation was enacted in 1968 requiring drug companies to offer the same prices and discounts to both hospital and community pharmacies. It was hoped that this method of ending discrimination would result in slightly higher prices to hospitals and slightly lower prices to community pharmacies. Apparently its main effect was the raising of drug prices to hospitals.[14] Accordingly, the major beneficiaries have been the manufacturers.

THE NURSING HOME CONTROVERSY: REBATES AND KICKBACKS?

An even more unsavory aspect of drug pricing and the distribution of drug products through institutions concerns the practices of some nursing homes. A Senate inquiry under the direction of Senator Frank Moss of Utah disclosed such devices as these: Some pharmacists have found it necessary to kick back to the nursing home operator as much as 25 percent of their total prescription charges to nursing home patients, or pay a flat $5,000 a year. Others had to rent space in the nursing home, such as a closet, at a cost of $1,000 a month. In some instances pharmacists were pressured into providing drugs, vitamins, and other supplies free to the nursing home, which proceeded to render a full bill to patients. Still others provided personal cosmetics and drugs to nursing home employees and charged the cost to the home, which in turn charged the patients. Several pharmacists, it was revealed, reported outright gifts of large quantities of trading stamps, new cars, color TVs, boats, and prepaid vacations to Hawaii or Europe for nursing home operators, while some were required to advertise in nursing home brochures at ten times the normal rate. The nursing home operators, when faced with such practices, declared that the rebates were all voluntary. On the other hand, Senator Moss told the American Society of Consultant Pharmacists, "If such large discounts are possible, then the product must be overpriced." [15]

THE GOVERNMENT PRICE CONTROVERSY

At least as bizarre has been the pricing system—or nonsystem—for drugs purchased by federal, state, and local governmental agencies. With such institutions, the Robinson-Patman Act does not apply, and the prices bid by manufacturers or wholesalers can vary enormously. For example, one survey disclosed, prices paid by city or county hospitals for sulfadiazine—one thousand 5-mg tablets—ranged from $4.50 in New York to $9.00 in Buffalo, $9.30 in Atlanta, $10.00 in Baltimore, $14.40 in Miami, $15.00 in San Francisco, and $19.20 in Multnomah County, Oregon.[16]

During Senate hearings in 1967, it was reported that CIBA was charging community pharmacies approximately $28 for one thousand 0.25-mg tablets of its Serpasil at the same time it was offering to sell the same product to the Department of Defense for $3.95.[17] Some of these glaring discrepancies were blamed not on the manufacturer but on the wholesaler. Thus, one distributing firm charged $25.50 per unit of chlordiazepoxide to Los Angeles County, but only $18.50 to Philadelphia. In this instance Philadelphia received a greater discount even though it was purchasing smaller quantities.[18]

While some differences could be explained on the basis of high-priced brand-name products versus low-priced generic, most major companies have clearly demonstrated that they will offer even their brand-name products at very low bids to get them accepted by government institutions. "Government agencies purchase pharmaceutical products in large quantities on the basis of competitive bids," it was stated by W. H. Conzen, president of the Schering Corporation. "Such orders may be highly attractive and many companies are convinced that these orders should be sought even at prices which would be unprofitable if normal accounting practices were followed. They do this in the belief that such business should be regarded as incremental business, and that only additional cash out-of-pocket incremental costs directly traceable to the specific order should be considered." [19]

Incremental costs are the specific costs of filling that single order alone, involving primarily raw material and manufacturing expenses. Drugs thus sold to the government are supposedly not required to bear any substantial portion of the research, promotion, and administrative expenses of the company. But occasionally it has been suggested that companies may be so eager to obtain a large hospital or government order that they will put in bids so low that they will lose money. If this ever does happen, industry insiders have commented, it is extremely uncommon. Further, these insiders have suggested that many government orders are filled at a price that covers a fair share of research costs, promotion costs, and administrative costs, and even permits some profit. It is noteworthy that drug companies have practically never been willing to provide government procurement officers with cost information.

Some critics have charged that this whole confused pricing structure at least hints of dishonesty on the part of the industry, or stupidity on the part of governmental purchasing agents, or both. Such critics have insisted that the companies are making at least a small profit on their sales to governments, and accordingly they must be making extortionate profits on their sales to community pharmacies. The prices offered to community pharmacies, they say, should be as low as those offered to government buyers.

It is obvious that the large drug manufacturers have virtually always collected the major portion of their profits from sales to community pharmacies. These sales in most instances are for relatively small quantities, and thus are eligible for relatively small discounts. It seems only logical that sales to hospitals and government agencies, usually involving large quantities, should call for large discounts. What appears totally illogical is that a firm should offer widely different bids on the same product to two different government agencies, or to two different hospitals, even though the quantities involved may be virtually identical.

This situation has been recognized at least in part by one company, Hoffmann-LaRoche, which for several years has had a uniform pricing policy under which government agencies—federal, state, or local—purchasing equal quantities of the same drug product receive the same price.[20] This in effect applies the concept of the Robinson-Patman Act even to government itself. Whether the industry will soon apply the same pricing schedule to all purchasers—community pharmacies, hospitals, and governmental agencies alike—seems doubtful, although one company, Lederle, announced the implementation of such a policy in 1972.

THE INTERNATIONAL PRICE CONTROVERSY

Neither a drug industry leader nor anyone else has yet been able to defend or even satisfactorily explain the disparity in drug prices charged to community pharmacists, hospitals, and government agencies in the United States. Perhaps the most useful defensive maneuver was presented by an industry spokesman who told reporters, "Hell, at least it's legal." Baffling as the domestic situation may be, the differences in prices charged by the same American firm for the same drug product in other countries is even more perplexing.

In 1967, for example, it was reported that while the list price charged to pharmacists for one hundred 0.25-mg tablets of CIBA's Serpasil was $4.50 in the United States, it was $3.00 in Mexico, $1.60 in Brazil, $1.56 in Austria, $1.52 in Italy, $1.24 in Switzerland, $1.19 in England, and $1.05 in West Germany.[21] Schering's Meticorten—one hundred tablets of 5 mg each—was listed at $17.90 in the United States, $22.70 in Canada, $12.26 in Mexico City, $12.20 in Italy, $7.70 in Australia, $5.30 in Brazil, and $4.37 in Switzerland.[22]

These two products, and others with equally inexplicable price differences, were seldom manufactured in the United States and then shipped to foreign countries. In nearly all instances they were produced overseas by a licensee, licensor, subsidiary, or parent company of the American firm. Most frequently, one American drug company official testified, the foreign sales—usually at prices substantially lower than those listed in the United States—were profitable, and often even more profitable than those in this country.[23]

In a more recent and broader survey, conducted on the recommendation of the HEW Task Force on Prescription Drugs, the Social Security Administration undertook a study of the prices to the pharmacist of twenty of the most frequently prescribed brand-name drugs in the United States and eight other nations.

As is shown in table 10 in the Appendix, the American prices for these twenty widely prescribed products were generally far higher than those in any other country studied. For twelve of the twenty drugs the price in this country was the highest, and for three others it was second highest. Canada had the highest prices for three drugs and the second highest for fourteen. Italian prices were also exceptionally high. Lowest prices were found in Ireland for seven drugs, and second lowest for five others.

The great variation from country to country was illustrated by such cases as the following: Lilly's Darvon was priced to druggists in the United States at $7.02 per hundred capsules. The same company's product in Ireland, marketed under the name of Doloxene, was priced at $1.66. Under a license from Hoechst in Germany, Upjohn marketed tolbutamide for the treatment of diabetes in this country under the name of Orinase for $8.23. Hoechst itself marketed the same drug under the name of Rastinon at a price of $2.28 in the United Kingdom and $2.22 in Ireland.

Attempts by drug company officials and others to rationalize these and similar price differences have resulted merely in additional chaos. In some cases it was argued that the lower prices were set in foreign countries because of their poverty, lower standard of living, and lower purchasing power. This hardly explained why Bristol's Polycillin was priced at $41.95 in Brazil and $21.84 in the United States, or why Serpasil was priced at $3.00 in Mexico, and at $1.24 or less in well-to-do Switzerland and West Germany. In their efforts to offer a rational explanation, spokesmen have also mentioned such factors as different wage scales, living costs, taxes, costs of raw materials, size of markets, allocation of research costs, promotional requirements, attempts to forestall inflation, and currency problems.

In the Social Security analysis,[24] it was noted that some of the countries with relatively low prices—Ireland, New Zealand, and the United Kingdom—are able to negotiate with the industry on drug prices.

(These negotiations have not always run smoothly. Thus, a British governmental commission in 1973 attacked Hoffmann-LaRoche for placing exorbitant prices on its Librium and Valium products, ordered the Swiss firm to accept substantial price cuts, and demanded back payments of £1.5 million as "excess profits.")[25] Australia considers the price of a drug before admitting it to the list of products for which the government will provide reimbursement. It also recognizes the fact that some companies undertake significant research programs, thus justifying somewhat higher product costs, while other firms carry on essentially no research operations. Sweden controls the price through established regulatory codes. Both Italy and Brazil actually set prices, but these have been obviously set at relatively high levels.

From the floundering but unsuccessful attempts to find any other convincing explanation, it is conceivable that the widely different international prices are often set on a more elemental basis: they are the highest that the traffic will bear.

Regardless of the reason for these disparities, there is growing interest in what to do about them. During the past few years there has been more and more insistence that the American drug companies should price their products essentially the same in all countries, or offer low prices only in those countries with unquestionably low standards of living. The companies have countered that any attempt to raise their foreign prices would drive them out of foreign markets and add to America's balance-of-trade problems. Similarly, any attempt to reduce their domestic prices to those on foreign markets would be catastrophic to their total financial structure.[26]

An additional facet of the international drug price problem was unearthed in 1970, when Senator Nelson began hearings on the drug purchasing policies of federal agencies. Here it was discovered that American tax dollars were being used in the loan program of the Agency for International Development to purchase bulk drug products at prices far above those listed in Europe.[27]

For example, tetracycline, chlortetracycline, and oxytetracycline had been purchased in bulk from American companies for use in Pakistan and Colombia for $100 to $270 per kilogram, although they could have been bought in Europe for $24 to $30. Ampicillin had been bought at $420 per kilogram when it was available on the European market at $150. Chlordiazepoxide had been bought at $245 per kilogram; its European price was $21.50 to $25.00. Although tetracycline could have been bought for $29 or less per kilogram in Europe, a me-too antibiotic with apparently no great advantages was obtained from an American firm at $2,250 per kilogram.

For such cases a remedy was at hand. On December 31, 1970, AID announced new regulations banning the purchase of any bulk pharmaceuticals at a price more than 10 percent above that at which it is "generally available from any other free world country." At the same time, AID ruled that it would not approve the purchase of a costly me-too drug when a less expensive drug was available to do essentially the same clinical job.[28]

This new policy was viewed dismally by the American industry. Although it involved a potential loss in sales, the loss would probably be relatively small. Total bulk drug transactions financed by AID in 1969 were only about $16 million a year. What hurt was the potential establishment of a precedent. If the government could purchase drugs abroad at a significant saving for use in underdeveloped countries, why couldn't these drugs be purchased in the same way for use in taxpayer-financed health programs in the United States? Any such policy has been denounced on the grounds that it would lead to "reduced research, loss of taxes, elimination of American jobs, and discrimination against American institutions." [29] On the other hand, American taxpayers might view the more economic use of their tax dollars as a reasonably good idea.

PRICE INDICES: UP OR DOWN?

Obviously related to the drug industry's pricing policies and practices—and an aspect at least as controversial as any other—is the matter of actual prices to the consumer. Year after year these prices have changed, and not only the rate of change but even its direction has been hotly disputed.

According to four different indices—those of the *American Druggist*, the *Lilly Digest*, the National Prescription Audit, and *Drug Topics*—the cost of an average prescription has been steadily rising and has increased by about 30 percent since 1958. The rates of increase indicated by these four indices vary somewhat because of differences in the classes of pharmacies surveyed, but they agree that prescription prices have been going up. In striking contrast, according to the Consumer Price Index of the Bureau of Labor Statistics (BLS), drug prices at the retail level increased steadily until 1960, then *decreased* between 1960 and 1968, and only recently began to rise again.

It would seem to be only too apparent that one side or the other must be guilty of gross prevarication, or perhaps computer failure. Actually, both sets of indices are believed to be honest and reasonably accurate. They are measuring different things. Those surveys that demonstrate a substantial rise in average prescription prices have obtained their figures through dividing the total money expended by the total number of prescriptions dispensed. They show generally that the average prescription dispensed in 1960 was priced at about $3.25, and the average in 1970 at nearly $4.00. The drug industry and particularly the Pharmaceutical Manufacturers Association have elected to pay little heed to such figures, but rather have pointed with considerable pride to the price index of BLS.

The BLS indices, highly regarded and frequently used in labor-management wage negotiations, are based mainly on the so-called market-basket technique. With foods, for example, the prices paid by the consumer for given quantities of bread, milk, eggs, potatoes, and the like will be determined and the percentage price changes calculated from one year to the next. For foods and similar commodities this approach has been valid. There have been few differences between the nature of a loaf of bread or a quart of milk in 1960 and the same foodstuffs in 1970.

But, as we have indicated elsewhere,[30] this method does not necessarily apply to drugs. The "market basket" of drugs selected by BLS has, at least until recently, not accurately reflected the drugs actually being prescribed by physicians and purchased by patients. It has given inordinate weight to generic-name products that are no longer under patent and that are therefore subject to more intense price competition. It has given far less weight to drugs still under patent (and relatively immune from price competition) that have maintained their price levels. It was so designed that it did not reflect the impact of new and costly products that may be introduced on the market to replace older and less expensive drugs. It included some products that were introduced under patent and at high prices, and that later lost patent protection, faced more intense competition, and were sold at lower prices. The inclusion of such products would naturally tend to lower the price index. "The Consumer Price Index," we found, "is thus not relevant to the changes which have been occurring in the average price of *all* prescriptions purchased by patients."

It is beyond doubt that the increase in prescription drug prices over the past decades is real and important. More important, of course, is not whether the index has been moving upward or downward, but whether the market price represents a reasonable markup over the actual cost of producing the product. In some cases the newer products not only are more costly per prescription; they may also be better than the products they replaced—safer, more effective, and more rapid in their actions, reducing not only the risk of death from a disease but also the time and severity of pain and disability. Moroever, as economist John Firestone of New York University has reported, the added price may reflect the prescription of larger quantities—more capsules or more tablets—of the same drug.[31] During the past decade, he calculated, the average number of capsules or tablets per prescription ordered by the physician has increased by about 27 percent. If comparative prices are based on identical numbers of units, then the cost of an average prescription on the retail market has actually declined by about 9 percent. (It should be noted that the Consumer Price Index is not involved in such differences as the size of the prescription, since the yearly figures are based on a constant number of capsules or tablets.)

It must also be recognized that a substantial portion of the price increases—from about $2.00 in 1950 and $3.25 in 1960 to $4.00 in 1970—is the result of inflation. Expressed in terms of constant 1950 dollars, the comparable prescription prices would be $2.00 in 1950, $2.50 in 1960, and $2.39 in 1970. These last figures, which cancel out the impact of inflation during the past two decades, demonstrate that—in terms of constant 1950 dollars—the price of an average prescription did increase substantially between 1950 and 1960, and then decreased slightly but unmistakably between 1960 and 1970. In 1970, however, patients were not paying for prescriptions with 1950 currency. They were paying with 1970 dollars, and many of them felt strongly that they were paying with too many 1970 dollars. Drug prices, they insisted, were too high.

TO CUT DRUG COSTS

Whether drug prices are too high, reasonable, or too low is a question on which universal agreement cannot be expected. It is only natural that most drug companies and their stockholders will generally seek higher prices, higher profits, and higher dividends. It is equally natural that patients, and those private or governmental agencies that provide health care for them, will seek lower prices. In this situation, it may be expected that pressure will be placed on the pricing structure of manufacturers, the pricing structure of pharmacists, and the prescribing patterns of physicians, or on all three groups together. And it may be expected that all three, to a greater or lesser degree, will protest.

Insofar as community pharmacies are concerned, there is an often-repeated proposal to reduce pharmacy profits. This route of achieving a saving for the patient may hold some promise. Greater economies, however, might be achieved by increasing the efficiency of pharmacy operations, making use of pharmacy technicians in place of professional pharmacists for routine dispensing chores, and utilizing automatic dispensing equipment, electronic data processing, and related techniques. (These and similar possibilities are discussed in the following chapter.)

Another proposed approach has involved public price-advertising by community pharmacists, a delicate matter that has long been the center of controversy. To some pharmacists such advertising smacks of nonprofessionalism; to others it is merely an accepted method of modern business. On the one hand, we believe the patient has an undeniable right to know *in advance* what prices are being charged by the various pharmacies in his community. Such a policy has long been recommended for doctors' bills; the American Medical Association has urged patients to ask *in advance* what fees their physician intends to charge. For drugs, the method employed—whether it is newspaper advertising, price posting in the pharmacy itself, or circulating price lists to physicians— would appear to be of no great importance, providing it makes comparison shopping possible for those patients who want it.

The value of such shopping may be questioned. It seems unlikely that many patients would be willing to spend fifty cents or more in bus fares in order to save perhaps sixty cents on a four-dollar prescription. The decision on which pharmacy to patronize would probably depend more on convenience and similar factors. In the case of drugs needed for long-term care, the situation might be quite different. With drugs like insulin, thyroid, digitalis, and oral contraceptives, a patient could well decide to shop for low prices in order to save on a three- or six-months supply.

On the other hand, comparison shopping for drugs has its potential drawbacks. It emphasizes only price and ignores the professional services that a pharmacist can render. It weakens the professional status of a pharmacist and makes him seem to be only a pill-counter. "Obtaining health care entirely on the basis of price can be exceedingly dangerous," one pharmacy educator has claimed. "A patient who selects a doctor merely because he charges the lowest price is asking for trouble. A patient who selects a pharmacy in the same way is similarly inviting disaster."

In a drive to reduce drug prices, the drug manufacturer appears to be a far more tempting target. If, for example, the profits of the industry were abolished completely, this in itself would save the nation roughly $800 million a year, an enormous sum by any yardstick. But that amount spread over more than two billion prescriptions dispensed by nongovernmental pharmacies would yield a saving to the patient of about forty cents per prescription. Wiping out drug company profits completely would almost certainly transform the industry into a government-regulated public utility. Reducing drug industry profits to a level more like that of other industries might allow the companies to continue their free enterprise operations; but one of the hazards of moving in this direction is the risk of lowering profits below the level needed to attract investment capital and reward efficiency and creativity.

In our view, an efficient and productive drug industry is deserving of profits—even of relatively high profits—and any efforts to control drug expenditures *solely* by cutting company profits would be damaging to the public. There are, however, other techniques worthy of consideration.

One approach would be to induce or require manufacturers to limit their promotional activities—now estimated to cost about $1 billion a year—and especially those activities which seem to result in irrational prescribing and drug use. A second would be to induce or require manufacturers to limit that portion of their research which is directed primarily toward the development of duplicative or me-too drugs. A third would involve limiting the production, promotion, and marketing of redundant drug products, which are made available in a needless abundance of sizes, strengths, shapes, and colors.

A fourth approach would involve the stimulation of competition—especially price competition—by limiting the period of patent protection, requiring compulsory licensing through an appropriate royalty system, or requiring that all prescription drugs be marketed only under their generic names.

Use of the compulsory licensing approach was urged in 1972 by Senator Nelson in his proposed Public Health Price Protection Act.[32] In the proposed bill, the Federal Trade Commission, upon the certification and advice of the surgeon general of PHS, would be authorized to require that a drug patent become available for reasonable royalty licensing under certain specified conditions. Among the conditions would be the following: (a) The average price to the consumer must be more than five times the cost of manufacture, or higher than the average price in any foreign country; (b) the annual sales of the drug must have been more than $1 million for three or more years; and (c) the existence of a patent must have been found to be a substantial contributing factor to the high price of the product.

Nelson noted that there are already ample precedents for such proposals, especially in the case of atomic energy, the control of air pollution, and the production of fiber, food, and feed. He likewise cited a Department of Justice memorandum that contained this passage: "A patent is not a limitless right; its use is not untrammeled. The patent law does not exist in a vacuum. Its goals must be reconciled and kept in harmony with other goals."

A fifth approach would be the further development of formularies which list approved drug products that meet all necessary quality standards and are available at reasonable prices. Such formularies are already being used in many hospitals and health insurance programs. They might well be used by all prescribing physicians.

A sixth approach, and one that could be explosive in its effects, would call for invocation of a little-known federal law listed as 28 U.S. Code 1498. Enacted during World War I, when it appeared that America's wartime efforts were being crippled by patents on critical military supplies, the law includes the following points:

—The federal government may authorize any company, domestic or foreign, to manufacture a product in violation of an existing patent.
—The product so authorized must be purchased by the federal government itself and must be needed to protect the welfare of the country.
—The patent holder cannot bring suit against the company infringing on his patent, but he can sue the government in the U.S. Court of Claims for his reasonable compensation.

"In this situation," it has been held, "it has been determined that the patentee's monopoly must give way to the public interest where such interest is found to be of paramount importance." [33]

There are two other requirements in the application of 28 USC 1498. First, the price to be paid for the product manufactured under these conditions must be substantially less than the price demanded by the patent holder. And second, when the patent holder appears in court to demand reasonable compensation, he must be prepared to open his books and expose his actual costs and profits to judicial examination.

With drugs, 28 USC 1498 was apparently applied first in the case of tetracycline, at one time available from five American firms—Lederle (a division of American Cyanamid), Pfizer, Bristol, Upjohn, and Squibb (then a division of Olin Mathieson)—under a patent arrangement that would eventually lead to long and bitter civil and criminal suits in the federal courts.[34]

This drug was of particular interest to the Military Medical Supply Agency during the late 1950s. MMSA had the responsibility for the purchase of drugs for all military services. The cost of tetracycline represented the largest expenditure for any single drug. Although the antibiotic was nominally being marketed by five competing firms, vigorous price competition was singularly absent. Whenever MMSA asked for bids, the low bid almost always seemed to be $17.25 per bottle of one hundred 25-mg capsules. Unable to stimulate more competition, and thus get a better break for American taxpayers, Rear Admiral William Knickerbocker, chief of MMSA, investigated and found that an Italian firm was willing to supply tetracycline at a price of $8.50 per bottle.

With the approval of top Department of Defense officials and their attorneys, and over the anguished protests of the American tetracycline producers, MMSA placed an order with the Italian company for about ten thousand pounds of tetracycline powder. With this as a precedent, MMSA later placed purchase orders for other essential drugs with low-cost suppliers. In about a three-year period, MMSA utilized this procedure for approximately fifty drug purchases, saving American taxpayers roughly $21 million. Other federal agencies have also taken advantage of 28 USC 1498 when drugs could be obtained at a fraction of the official American price,[35] but insiders insist that such agencies, at least in recent years, have not taken full advantage of the law. In some cases, the patent holders went to court and received judgments that still allowed very large savings for the federal government.[36] In others, out-of-court settlements were reached.[37] In still others, the patent holders evidently decided not to sue and no claims were filed.

So far, 28 USC 1498 has been utilized mainly for drug purchases by federal agencies. The law, however, could be modified as necessary to apply to governmental payment for drugs prescribed for beneficiaries of such federal health programs as Medicare and Medicaid. Thus, the government could serve as the procurement agent for all drugs needed for Medicare or Medicaid patients, obtaining the lowest bids and the highest discounts available. There appears to be no reasonable excuse for the government to pay $3 for a bottle of twenty capsules of a drug for a patient in a VA hospital, while at the same time it is paying $10 for the same amount of the same drug for a Medicare patient in a community hospital. If a national health insurance or health service program is enacted, the law could be modified to apply to virtually all prescription drugs. (A similar law has long been on the books in England and has actually been put into effect.)[38] "If such events should come to pass," one drug company attorney has commented, "the results could be fantastic. It would open up the damnedest can of worms you've ever seen."

Among the various methods that might be considered for reducing drug expenditures, probably the best can be applied by the physician, either on his own or in cooperation with a pharmacist. He can use more restraint in the size of his prescriptions and refrain from ordering a thirty-day supply of a drug when it seems logical that only a ten-day supply will be needed. For long-term maintenance drugs, he can prescribe enough to last the patient for many months. He can help the patient save money by not prescribing drugs that are listed as only "possibly effective." Utilizing the information that is now available on product quality (and far more will undoubtedly be available in the future), he can select from dozens or scores of comparable products and choose the one available at the most reasonable price. Except in rare instances, such as when a patient's particular idiosyncrasy is involved, he can prescribe generically or authorize the pharmacist to fill the prescription with a low-cost generic product. He can view every promotional claim with skepticism. And, of the greatest importance, he can refrain from prescribing any drug when no drug is really needed. While this in itself would not cut the price of a prescription, it would save the patient from buying a needless prescription.

"Too often," one of our clinical colleagues has admitted, "I've ordered a drug, not because it was clinically indicated, but because the patient wanted it—or I couldn't think of anything else to do—and I wanted to get the patient off my back. This may have been the easy way for me, and satisfying for the patient, but it wasn't good medical practice."

Medicine has faced such situations before. In the case of surgery, for example, we have come to the realization that the most costly operation is not necessarily the one which carries a high fee to the surgeon. Rather, it is the one which is not clinically justifiable, or is not performed competently, and does more harm than good. In the same way, we must recognize that simply cutting the price tag on a prescription—or arranging to have the bill paid by government or an insurance program—will not solve the major problem of high drug expenditures. Physicians, pharmacists, industry, patients, and taxpayers alike must keep in mind that the costly drug is the one that is prescribed for the wrong diagnosis, or in the wrong amounts, or at the wrong time, or with no consideration of cost. And the most costly of all—economically, clinically, and sociologically—is the one that is prescribed when no drug at all is needed. Even though an occasional patient may be able to afford such irrational drug therapy, society cannot.

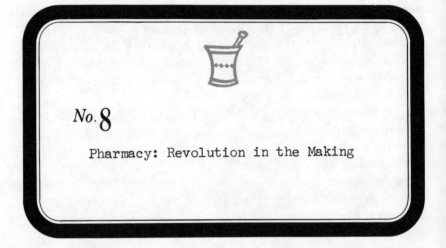

No. 8

Pharmacy: Revolution in the Making

IT IS impossible to suggest when, where, and by whom the practice of medicine was invented. The beginnings of pharmacy, at least as a separate profession, may be indicated with somewhat more precision. In the year 754 A.D. the first public apothecary shop was established by formal orders of the caliph of Baghdad, thus divorcing drug prescribing from drug dispensing. In Western Europe the beginning of pharmacy is generally dated as 1240 A.D., when Frederick II, ruler of the Holy Roman Empire, directed the separation of the two professions. Thereafter, apothecaries rather than physicians took the major role in compounding and dispensing drugs, although some medical men still continue to dispense drug products to their own patients. At the same time, physicians took the major role in diagnosing and treating patients, although pharmacists have often served as "physicians to the poor," and still advise patients on the use of nonprescription remedies.

The cleavage between the two professions has thus never been clear and complete. Further, the resultant ambiguity has frequently been marked by acrimonious dispute, jockeying for positions of prestige and power, and—especially since the middle of the twentieth century—a disruptive failure to agree on what the respective functions of pharmacist and physician should be.

On the one hand, pharmacists have demanded with increasing vigor that physicians should refrain completely from selling drugs or giving free samples to their patients, owning pharmacies or drug-repackaging companies, controlling drug manufacturing companies, or otherwise profiting financially from the prescriptions they write. On the other hand, some physicians have countered that such activities make it possible to provide better health care to their patients. In fact, some medical men have insisted that pharmacists should not diagnose, even when only a nonprescription product is involved, or interfere in any way with their orders.

It would appear that, except in emergencies and in isolated areas without adequate pharmacy services, drug dispensing by physicians may represent a waste of their already limited time in performing work that can be done at least as well by others; and it offers a dangerous potential incentive to overprescribing. Although the American Medical Association has decided it is not unethical for a physician to dispense so long as the patient is not exploited, the AMA is in a position of insisting that the patient must have free choice of physician, but need not have free choice of pharmacist. Similar objections hold for physician-owned pharmacies, again with an obvious potential conflict of interest and an evident risk of excessive prescribing. An even more serious threat is posed by physician-ownership of a so-called repackaging company—one which purchases a drug product from a manufacturer, usually at relatively low prices, and then repackages it under its own label and at its own price. If such a firm is controlled by one or more physicians who set the price at an extraordinarily high level and who then prescribe its products under the repackaging company brand name—thus requiring the pharmacist to dispense them—the profits to the company and its physician-owners can be extraordinarily rewarding. For example, it has been reported that one physician-owned repackaging firm sold dextro-amphetamine for $11.30 a thousand, while a standard wholesaler sold it for 85¢ a thousand. Both companies purchased the identical product from the same supplier.[1]

But these and similar inter- and intraprofessional squabbles, which sometimes pit pharmacists against physicians, sometimes pharmacists against pharmacists, appear to be relatively unimportant. Although these issues may be described in such noble terms as ethics and the optimum care of the patient, too often the fundamental dispute involves who is going to get the patient's dollars.

More crucial is the role of the pharmacist and his relations both with physicians and with patients. It is the pharmacist who can play a vital role in assisting physicians to prescribe rationally, who can help see to it that the right drug is ordered for the right patient, at the right time, in the right amounts, and with due consideration of costs, and that the patient knows how, when, and why to use both prescription and nonprescription products.

It is the pharmacist who has been most highly trained as an expert on drug products, who has the best opportunity to keep up to date on developments in this field, and who can serve both physician and patient as a knowledgeable adviser. It is the pharmacist who can take a key part in preventing drug misuse, drug abuse, and irrational prescribing.

ROLE OF THE PHARMACIST

Within the profession of pharmacy there are serious differences on the appropriate role of the pharmacist. One segment has urged that the pharmacist should restrict his activities largely if not entirely to professional activities, while another group has defended the role of the pharmacist as a combination of health professional and retail merchant. Some pharmacists—especially the more recent graduates—have asserted (and often demonstrated) that they are now more knowledgeable than most physicians in the complex field of drugs and can serve patients best by serving as health educators to the community, especially in matters relating to drugs, and by acting as the drug information experts on the health team. Such a proposal has been warmly supported by some physicians but blasted as clinical heresy by others.

Thus, to some observers, pharmacy is now a profession wracked by the turmoil of trying to find itself. In theory, the problem has been settled once and for all by making the pharmacist an official member of the so-called health team. In reality, this supposedly logical solution has done little but irritate many pharmacists, who feel that they are members of the "team" in name only and have actually been relegated to third-string status.[2]

Many factors have contributed to the creation of this situation. For example, many American pharmacists have found it difficult if not impossible to make a suitable living by devoting themselves exclusively to dispensing prescriptions or even to selling both prescription and nonprescription drugs. Accordingly, they also sell such items as liquor, cigarettes, magazines, handbags, hosiery, cameras, and gardening equipment. For some, such a career as combination professional and merchant has brought adequate compensation. For others, who feel such activities represent a waste of their long professional training, this livelihood has brought mainly frustration.

Another factor has been the change in the nature of drug products themselves. Before World War I, about 90 percent of all prescription orders required the pharmacist to compound the final product himself, combining the active ingredients with the appropriate flavoring material, coloring matter, and other ingredients into the specified powders, solutions, or ointments. By the early 1960s the drug industry had taken over most of these tasks and was able to deliver to the pharmacist the final product in solid or liquid form, ready for consumption. Now specially compounded prescriptions represent only about 1.5 percent of a pharmacist's prescription practice.

As an inevitable consequence, the pharmacist has come to be viewed by the public as one who devotes most of his professional time to counting pills out of a large bottle into a small one, typing the label, and calculating the price—including a presumably extortionate profit—while he is completely protected against any competition by state and federal laws and by professional "ethics." Valid or not, this concept has been so generally accepted that the pharmacist has felt himself rejected by the public, the medical profession, and the drug manufacturers.[3] Perhaps more important, this attitude has also served to blur the important distinctions between the value of the drug product itself and the value of the professional services involved in dispensing it.

Probably as a result of this confusion, some have asserted that the typical community pharmacy is an antiquated institution that has long since outlived its usefulness and must therefore be replaced. Others have defended it as a highly valuable institution, even in its present form, and one that needs to be continued. And still others have predicted that the community pharmacy is destined to continue, but will be gradually modified by economic, clinical, and social factors.

THE NATURE OF RETAIL DISTRIBUTION

Some changes are already apparent. For example, the number of active registered pharmacists in the United States, which remained virtually unchanged at about 100,000 between 1940 and 1950, has now increased to roughly 130,000. The independent community pharmacy—the typical "corner drug store" of past decades—is still dominant, but it is facing increased competition from other vendors. Thus, of the slightly more than two billion prescriptions dispensed in 1970, approximately 46 percent were handled by some fifty thousand independent community pharmacies, 39 percent by hospital pharmacies dispensing to both inpatients and outpatients, and 7 percent by chain pharmacies (generally defined as four or more outlets centrally owned and operated).[4] The remainder were dispensed by a small number of mail order pharmacies, by the physicians who dispense drugs to their own patients, and by approximately fifteen hundred pharmacies operating in department stores, supermarkets, discount houses, and similar establishments. Also included were several hundred prescription pharmacies or pharmaceutical centers handling mainly or exclusively prescription drugs.

Nearly all such retail outlets add a markup averaging roughly 100 percent to the cost of prescription drug products charged by drug manufacturers or wholesalers. A markup of such proportions, along with the high retail price of many drug products, has led some critics to denounce pharmacists in general for making enormous profits. But for the total operations of the average pharmacy, the overhead costs—in-

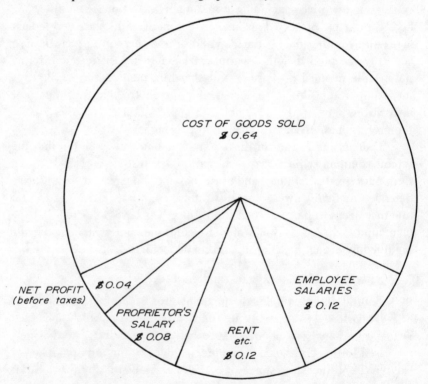

Figure 15. Distribution of Pharmacist's Sales Dollar
Source: *Lilly Digest* (Indianapolis: Eli Lilly and Co., 1972), p. 10.

cluding rent, salaries, and other operating expenses—are so large that net profits before taxes, as based on sales, were about 3.6 percent in 1972 (figure 15), down from the peak figure of about 6 percent in 1965.[5] Net profits *before* taxes, as based on net worth, were approximately 20 percent. The latter figure is somewhat higher than the average of about 15 to 17 percent for grocery stores and other retail outlets. (In contrast, net profits *before* taxes for the drug manufacturing industry were roughly 20 percent as based on sales and 35 percent as based on net worth.)

If, however, attention is directed to the profits made on prescription sales alone, the picture is quite different. On the average, approximately 47 percent of a pharmacist's gross income is derived from the dispensing of prescription drugs, a proportion that has tripled since 1946.[6] One study, conducted in a midwestern state, showed that the average retail price of a prescription was $4.37 in 1970 and $4.47 in 1971. The average net profit on such sales was $0.65, or 14.9 percent, in 1970, and $0.68, or 15.2 percent, in 1971.[7] Thus, although few pharmacists have become affluent as a result of their overall activities—involving not only drugs but also cosmetics, liquor, cigarettes, magazines, and the like—their percentage profit on prescription drugs alone cannot be dismissed as trivial.

The nature of retail drug distribution is now being influenced by other factors which may be far more significant than the type of ownership or the profit structure. For example, there is a growing but probably limited use of automated devices to dispense prescription drugs in precounted, prepackaged, and prelabeled containers.

There is the inevitable development of electronic data processing systems destined to take over a substantial portion of the procedures needed for accounting, invoicing, maintaining patient drug records, and even inventorying. Without the use of such systems, any large-scale drug insurance plan would be overwhelmed in paper work, would involve unacceptable delays in reimbursement, and would raise program costs to an intolerable level. With an appropriate system linking all community and hospital pharmacies into statewide or regional networks, accounting costs and reimbursement delays would be minimized. At the same time, the electronic framework would be available for the rapid detection of possibly irrational prescriptions, and the alerting of physicians and pharmacists to take the necessary corrective steps.

There is a growing willingness to train and employ pharmacy technicians, working under the supervision of licensed pharmacists, to handle many of the routine dispensing tasks.

There is a growing tendency among pharmacists to add to the

wholesale cost of a product a fixed dispensing or professional fee rather than a percentage markup to cover the cost of their services. This has done more than strengthen the pharmacist's professional status. It has helped stimulate the use of low-cost generic-name products where this is possible, since it abolishes the profit incentive for a pharmacist to dispense a high-cost brand-name product.[8] For instance, if he had the choice between either a brand-name product with a wholesale cost of $10 or a generic product costing $5, and used a percentage markup, he might be tempted to dispense the more costly product. But if he would add the same fixed fee—say, $2—he would have no financial reason to select the brand-name drug.

Use of the dispensing fee method may help to alleviate the paradoxical situation in which traditionally a physician is paid when he provides services or advice, while a pharmacist is paid only when he sells a product. Thus, if a pharmacist advises a patient that a certain over-the-counter product is useless for his condition, he receives no compensation. He may spend many minutes discussing a health problem with a patient and then sell him only a twenty-five-cent bottle of aspirin. He may advise a physician over the telephone, only to have the patient take his prescription to a different pharmacy.

This strictly product-oriented approach has done little to enhance the professional status of the pharmacist and has made him less than enthusiastic about offering free advice based on his many years of professional training and experience. Use of a professional fee system for services rendered would make it possible to compensate him for his services, even though these might involve his refusal to dispense an obviously irrational prescription—for example, one calling for a drug to which the patient is known to be allergic. Such a fee-for-service concept has already been implemented in at least one third-party program, partly on the grounds that the pharmacist's fee under such conditions might well save the program many hundreds or thousands of dollars for the treatment of an adverse drug reaction.[9]

These and similar developments could free pharmacists from much of the time-consuming drudgery long associated with filling prescriptions and allow them more hours to apply their professional knowledge and judgment. Such a prospect is challenging and exciting to some pharmacists. To others it is threatening.

In this connection, it has become painfully apparent that many pharmacists now in practice were trained under an antiquated educational system that required them to devote many hours acquiring a detailed knowledge of herbs, crude plant extracts, microscopic root structures, and the like—a knowledge which they practically never applied during their professional careers. In contrast, in many pharmacy schools and in postgraduate courses, students and practicing pharmacists have now been given valuable training in such subjects as drug metabolism, drug interactions, and the detection and prevention of adverse drug reactions, yet—except in rare instances—they have found only limited opportunities to utilize their knowledge.

Some pharmacists, of course, have already demonstrated their ability to do more than read a doctor's prescription, fill it, label it, and charge for it. Some have kept valuable family drug records, indicating all drug products—prescription and over-the-counter—obtained by the family members, and recording all known drug allergies and other idiosyncracies. They have used these patient files to detect prescriptions that might induce an allergic reaction, produce dangerous interactions, or signal drug abuse, a potential suicide attempt, or the acquisition of drugs for eventual sale on the black market. Some have helped patients with advice on how to use a prescription product, warning against overdosages and other irrational use, thus strengthening or even clarifying a physician's instructions. Some have undoubtedly saved lives by intercepting irrational prescriptions—the wrong drug for the patient, or the wrong amount—and immediately alerting the physician.

Many pharmacists have made important or even lifesaving contributions by referring patients to professional medical care. A New Jersey survey disclosed such pharmacy reports as the following:

> Patron requested a first aid cream by name. The pharmacist recommended immediate attention at the hospital as it was apparent there was blood poisoning in the patron's arm. The hospital made the patient aware that he might have lost his arm if proper attention had not been given.
>
> Customer wanted citrate of magnesia and questioned if it was good for gas pains for her son. After questioning . . . found patient had abdominal pains . . . suggested doctor. Patient operated for appendicitis.
>
> Patron requested something for a raspy throat that he had for two months. The pharmacist suggested a physician at once. The advice was taken and the condition was finally diagnosed as a cancer of the larynx. Surgery was performed to remove the growth.[10]

Unfortunately, such laudable actions are not universal. Thus, a survey of thirty-six metropolitan pharmacies showed that thirty were willing to sell a so-called cold remedy, Dristan, to a known diabetic patient, even though the ingredients of Dristan are contraindicated in diabetes. The same survey revealed that eleven out of twelve pharmacists were willing to dispense to the same patient prescriptions for two antidepressive drugs, imipramine and tranylcypromine, although the two products in combination can cause death. The investigators concluded, "It is painfully and deadly obvious that the pharmacists in our sample utterly failed the tasks presented them—failed to the point of exposing their patients to the unnecessary risk of possible death." [11]

In a Los Angeles survey of 133 pharmacies, it was found that when a "patient" said, "I've had some bleeding and pain with my bowel movements for the last few weeks, and I was wondering if you've got something for it"—symptoms that should alert any health professional to the possibility of rectal cancer—21 percent of the pharmacists recommended an over-the-counter antihemorrhoid product without even suggesting the "patient" should seek medical advice.[12]

The Los Angeles study indicated that, by and large, the tendency to sell a product—the urge for the fast drug dollar—appears to be greater among pharmacists who own their pharmacies than among those who work on a salary.

There is, therefore, at least some evidence to indicate that while some pharmacists are eager to get more professional responsibilities and others are unwilling to expand their roles, there are some pharmacists who are professionally competent to participate more actively in health care and others whose competence is at least open to question.

This situation has become particularly important in the 1970s, when there is a critical shortage of physicians, with many overworked doctors unable to keep abreast of the avalanche of new drug products, unable to see patients without long and frustrating delays, unable to find time to become drug experts themselves, and heavily dependent on the possibly prejudiced advice of drug detail men and drug advertising. At this very same period, although there are some pharmacists whose incompetency represents a serious health hazard, there are others by the tens of thousands—most of them recent graduates—who are well trained, highly competent, highly motivated, and looking forward to becoming accepted members of the health team, serving as drug information specialists, and even undertaking the management of patients who do not, in fact, require the direct care of an already overburdened physician.

The executive director of the American Pharmaceutical Association has said, "In our pharmacy manpower pool of some 120,000 actively engaged practitioners, we have some 35,000 pharmacists who graduated in the last decade who . . . could be trained rapidly to take over higher order functions. . . . If we could save only one hour per week for each of

100,000 actively engaged physicians by employing a more efficient model of communicating drug information, we would be adding the equivalent of another 2,000 physicians available 50 hours per week for diagnosis and treatment." [13]

It seems evident that dispensing physicians are dissipating much of their limited time in tasks which, in most cases, can be carried out at least as well—and possibly even better—by a *competent* pharmacist working under the minimal supervision of a *competent* physician. Actual trials in both military and civilian practice, and notably in Public Health Service hospitals,[14] have shown that it scarcely requires five years of medical school, plus a year or two of postgraduate training, to provide routine follow-up care for most patients with diabetes or pernicious anemia, give routine immunizations, or diagnose and treat most cases of poison oak, impetigo, and other simple skin ailments. These and many other procedures are being handled admirably by pharmacists. It is not clear why physicians continue to waste their precious hours on such matters. Perhaps the patient demands it. Perhaps the physician insists, possibly for financial reasons, but more probably to maintain his ego-satisfactions. But this is a luxury which neither physicians nor patients in particular nor society in general can any longer afford.

THE ADVENT OF CLINICAL PHARMACY

A new role must be found for pharmacists, not simply to maintain or enhance *their* ego-satisfactions, but to improve the delivery of high quality health care. In this connection, growing interest has been focused on a challenging but sometimes confusing concept known as clinical or patient-oriented pharmacy. Much of the confusion among both pharmacists and physicians has stemmed from the fact that there is yet no specific definition of this approach. Additional confusion has resulted from the fact that, in one sense, the concept of clinical pharmacy is new, untested, and therefore threatening, whereas many of its aspects go back to the very beginning of pharmacy. Wherever the pharmacist's major objective is not simply the dispensing and sale of a drug product but rather the health of the patient, clinical pharmacy is at work.

During the early 1960s, one observer has noted, mention of "research in the area of clinical pharmacy" appeared with increasing frequency.[15] Primarily, these discussions in technical publications urged the development, training, and effective use of the patient-oriented pharmacist as opposed to the product-oriented pharmacist. From the diversity of the pilot programs which began to appear after 1965, it is apparent that there was no immediate agreement on how such patient orientation could best be achieved without needlessly upsetting patients, physicians, nurses, hospital administrators, and those pharmacists who were disturbed by any attempts to modify classical pharmacy practice.

In most of these early programs, the so-called clinical pharmacists have been trained in university hospitals or other large medical centers, working alongside of medical students, and have been used mainly in such institutions. This training is given best in the hospital, it was emphasized by Dr. Robert Miller of the University of California at San Francisco. There the student learns why a drug is given and what results the physician expects, and then observes the patient's actual response to the drug.[16]

Clinical pharmacists trained at our medical center, and at such other centers as those in Pittsburgh, Detroit, Los Angeles, and Cleveland, have functioned effectively in a variety of ways. They have conducted admission interviews with entering patients to discover which drugs—prescription or nonprescription—each has been taking and any drug allergies of which he is aware. In a study of such interviews at a Minneapolis hospital, it was demonstrated that the pharmacist is often far more successful than the physician in turning up data. Thus a patient will respond to the usual question from a physician, "What drugs have you been taking during the last six months?" by replying, "None." The same patient, however, will offer far different, and often highly valuable, information when a pharmacist asks such questions as "What do you take when you have a cold? What do you do for a headache? Do you ever take any medicine for an upset stomach? Do you take any laxatives, or use any drops or sprays? What do you take when you can't go to sleep?" [17]

Similarly, a patient may deny the existence of any drug allergy. But when one such individual was interviewed by a clinical pharmacist and was asked, "Did you ever feel sick after taking any medicine?" he replied, "Did I? The last time my doctor gave me a shot of penicillin, I swole up and like to die!"

In some institutions, the clinical pharmacist provides information to the physician on the relative efficacy, safety, cost, and quality of a number of products that may be under consideration, so that the patient will get not merely a good drug but the best one for him.[18] Sometimes the pharmacist's suggestions will result in only a financial saving to the patient or the hospital, as when a low-cost product is proposed in place of an expensive brand-name or me-too drug that offers no clinical advantage. Far more significant is advice that clearly influences the patient's health care and may save his life. Thus, pharmacists have often been able to help the patient dramatically by intercepting an order for a drug to which he is allergic, alerting the physician to the potential hazards of combining two drugs that may interact adversely, suggesting laboratory tests needed to monitor the effects of a drug, indicating those drugs that may interfere with routine laboratory tests, and in general serving as the physician's immediately available storehouse of up-to-date and unbiased information on drug safety, efficacy, quality, and costs.

This kind of drug monitoring has been defined as the pharmacist's review and analysis of a patient's drug therapy. The analysis will either indicate that the drug treatment is right for the patient or "result in the pharmacist suggesting alternatives to the physician to improve the patient's drug therapy." [19]

Often the hospital-based clinical pharmacist will pick up an early warning of a potentially hazardous situation merely by routine review of a patient's chart. In other instances the pharmacist will be alerted during routine visits to the patient himself, seeing to it that the latter is actually getting the right drug in the right dosage at the right time, and making sure that the drug is having the desired effects. In still other cases, the pharmacist will be able to help by taking part in regular ward rounds, along with the attending physicians. One experienced clinical pharmacist comments:

> Here everything can depend on your personal relations with the physician. When you find he is prescribing a drug that is useless for a particular patient, or is planning to order an adult-sized dose for a child, or is unaware that another doctor is also prescribing for the patient, you don't point this out to him in the hearing of a nurse, or another doctor, or the patient himself. You take him aside, if you possibly can, and ask him if he's sure he really wants to prescribe that way.

Where excellent physician-pharmacist relations have been established on the basis of experience and mutual trust, it is frequently the physician who will turn to his pharmacist colleague and ask for advice. In one such hospital, which recorded some twelve thousand drug consultations per year, in more than 60 percent of the cases it was the physician who was the one to seek guidance.[20]

Not all physicians in all hospitals have yet demonstrated their willingness to seek advice on drug therapy from even a well-trained clinical pharmacist, and certainly not all physicians have found it comfortable to accept such advice when it is offered. Nevertheless, the concept of the clinical pharmacist is winning more acceptance each year. It has been applied with excellent results in many Public Health Service and other government hospitals.[21] It has been approved for use in some institutions by the influential Joint Commission on Accreditation of Hospitals.[22] Increasingly, it is being used in community and teaching hospitals.

It has been repeatedly emphasized that the hospital-based clinical pharmacist is able to practice his profession with more intensity than his community-based colleagues.[23] One reason is that detailed information on the patient's condition is always available for the pharmacist in the hospital record. Another is the close proximity of patient, physician, and pharmacist. But it has also been emphasized that the clinical pharmacist can likewise play a vital role in nonhospital pharmacies.[24] He can keep patient records of all prescription and nonprescription drugs obtained by the patient, support the physician's instructions, warn against possible drug interactions, and see to it that the patient is taking the drugs as prescribed and obtaining renewals when they are indicated.

The practice of patient-oriented pharmacy outside the hospital is obviously a totally different operation. The patients themselves are different. More often, they are afflicted with chronic illness. Some may be required to take maintenance drugs for many months or years, and perhaps for the rest of their lives. The patient, the physician, and the pharmacist may see each other only infrequently. There is rarely a nurse to see that the patient is taking his medication in the right amounts at the right time. The patient may neglect to report any adverse effect of the drug. Rarely has the pharmacist any access to the patient's record chart. He may not even be aware of the diagnosis—a matter of vital importance.

One community-based clinical pharmacist, Dr. Paul Lofholm of the Ross Valley Medical Clinic near San Francisco, recently stated, "Though the pharmacist does not make the diagnosis, he must understand it so he can continually evaluate the patient and can monitor the use of the drug. . . . He consults with the physician not only when it may be legally necessary, but far more important, when it is therapeutically necessary." [25] A major problem at the outset is establishing pharmacist-physician communications. "But that need not be so difficult," he said.

> If you're working in a hospital, and are always available on the wards, the doctors will ask you questions. The same thing can happen if your pharmacy is located in a community group practice environment. In the community, you start by trying to line up informal sessions with a group of physicians, and bring them up to date on new drug developments. Soon

you find that the physicians are coming to you and asking you to talk to them. As a matter of fact, you can do some of the best jobs of physician-educating—and pharmacist-educating—over a cup of coffee in a nearby restaurant.[26]

Although some physicians have resisted this kind of education, apparently preferring to get their advice and guidance from a drug detail man, most have been delighted to take advantage of it. As one physician in the Ross Valley Clinic commented, "In the complexity of the drug world today, it's awfully handy to pick up the intercom and say, 'Paul, is it OK to give this drug to that patient?' and get a fast and informative answer." [27]

In the same way, the pharmacist is in a particularly strategic position to answer questions that the patient never got around to asking the physician, or was too embarrassed to ask, such as: "How long will I have to take the medicine? It says to take it before meals, but does that mean fifteen minutes before, or an hour, or two hours? Is it going to make me feel nauseated? Will it give me a rash? If it makes me feel sick, should I call you, or stop taking it, or what? What should I do if I forget to take a couple of doses? The doctor said I shouldn't have my usual cocktail before dinner while I'm taking this stuff, but what about beer or wine?" The pharmacist must be prepared not only to answer these and similar queries but also to alert the patient to the signs of serious side effects or adverse reactions that may result from the prescribed drug itself or from interactions with other drugs, foods, soaps, industrial chemicals, and other substances.[28]

The community pharmacist can place additional emphasis on the necessity for taking the drug in the right amounts at the right time. As two Veterans Administration pharmacists have commented, "The patient is not receiving optimum care when the correct diagnosis is followed by selection of the appropriate therapeutic agent but this continuum of therapy is not followed. . . . Several earlier studies have suggested that in general patients are somewhat unreliable when charged with the responsibility for self-administration of their prescribed drugs." [29] In the VA study, a survey was conducted simply to determine whether patients took the prescribed number of doses per day. It was found that there was an average error of 25 percent, with some patients taking the wrong doses on the wrong day. With some patients, errors of more than 50 percent were discovered.

Working in the community, the clinical pharmacist may be in a key position to learn that a patient may be receiving a multiplicity of prescriptions from different doctors. In one such instance, Dr. Joseph McEvilla of the University of Pittsburgh reported the case of a woman who was simultaneously receiving eleven different prescriptions from ten different physicians, not one of whom was aware that other physicians were also treating the patient.[30]

Finally, the clinical pharmacist in the community can serve effectively as health educator, provide advice to forestall the irrational use of nonprescription drugs, keep community physicians informed on the relative quality and the relative costs of competitive drug products, and induce patients to seek professional medical care when this seems indicated. One physician has written:

> In a true team approach of the future, one could visualize the pharmacist's role as encompassing supervision of long-term medication, recognition and reporting of adverse drug effects, and scheduling of routine laboratory work for periodic checks. . . . The pharmacist on the team may be the first to be aware that the patient is not taking the medication as prescribed. He may be the first to sense that a suicidal patient is stockpiling drugs, or to spot a conflict in action of multiple drugs. . . . The question would not be how the pharmacist could help the physician but how he, as part of a comprehensive health team, could best help the patient.[31]

Recently, Dr. Robert Ebert, Dean of the Harvard Medical School said,

> I see no reason why the pharmacist working with the physician might not assume primary responsibility for long-term care of certain patients, particularly those requiring continuous drug therapy. . . . The future of the pharmacist lies in the direction of clinical medicine and the education of the pharmacist must reflect this need. The pharmacist in training needs to have a greater exposure to patients, a better understanding of disease, and a greater opportunity to work with the physician in the direct provision of medical services.[32]

In any consideration of future pharmacist-physician relations, an editorial view published in a leading medical journal is particularly pertinent:

> Physicians are apt to take it for granted that if there are to be health teams, they will always be the captains. In certain situations, as when a life is in the balance on the sickbed or in the operating room, for example, this will be uncontested. . . . But in less critical circumstances this traditional command authority may become more diffuse and other professionals are

found more directly involved in the decision-making processes of patient care. The thought—perhaps specter is a better word—of patient care being directed by committees of health professionals, very possibly with consumers added as voting members, inevitably comes to mind. Yet this in fact already occurs . . . and the experience has been by no means all bad.[33]

If the clinical pharmacist is to achieve acceptance in the community, he must be aware of what the public expects. Public attitudes toward pharmacy and pharmacists have been somewhat illuminated by the results of a survey conducted by the Dichter Institute for Motivational Research. In the survey most consumers demonstrated that they have little understanding of what a pharmacist actually does. The word "pharmacist" carries with it the concept of professional status, while the word "druggist" does not. Many individuals noted that physicians and attorneys have "offices," while pharmacists have "stores"; physicians have "patients," while pharmacists have "customers." The interviews disclosed that most people were reluctant to comparison shop for prescriptions. Most were unimpressed by the need for price advertising, although they approved the idea of price posting in each pharmacy. Most were willing to pay a higher price if they felt they were getting personal attention from the pharmacist. More than two-thirds wanted to receive the pharmacist's assurance that the prescription being dispensed was right for them, with no risk of adverse reactions, interactions with other drugs, or the possibility of allergic reactions.

Two decades ago, in a survey conducted for a California county medical society to examine public attitudes toward medicine, the Dichter group emphatically recommended the concept of a "personal physician" for each individual or each family. In the recent survey they urged pharmacy to stress the role of the "personal pharmacist" to the public.[34]

Many decisions bearing on the role which the pharmacist will fill in the future are yet to be made—and yet to be accepted—but the signposts are becoming more clear. Under the pressure of economic, clinical, and social forces, the pharmacist will be required to participate more actively in the provision of health care. In such circumstances, there will naturally be instances in which the pharmacist should function under the supervision of a physician. There may be others, especially in the selection of the right drug, in which the physician should prescribe under the supervision of a pharmacist. It may well mean a revolution to bring about such changes.

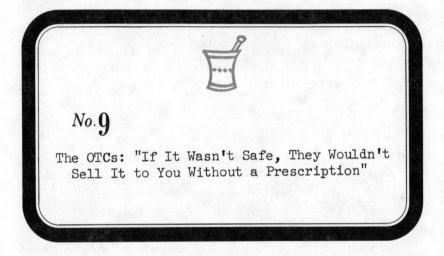

No. 9

The OTCs: "If It Wasn't Safe, They Wouldn't
Sell It to You Without a Prescription"

IN MODERN times relatively little
attention has been devoted by industry critics to over-the-counter drugs,
or OTCs. These are the products which, upon approval of the Food and
Drug Administration, may be dispensed by any pharmacy—or any
grocery, supermarket, liquor store, or other vendor—without a prescription. Their use may be recommended by a physician or a pharmacist, as
in the classical advice, "Go home and take some aspirin," but ordinarily
the patient diagnoses his own problem and selects the supposedly
appropriate remedy, with or without the advice of spouse, grandmother,
distant relatives, next-door neighbors, or television commercials.

Most OTCs are useful, or at least used, mainly for mild and
presumably self-limiting ailments: headache, hangover, hay fever, the
common cold, "nervous tension," indigestion, muscular aches, sunburn,
poison ivy or poison oak dermatitis, hemorrhoids, constipation, and
insomnia—or what the patient judges to be insomnia, such as the
inability to fall asleep within ten or fifteen minutes. Since the numbers
of victims suffering from these and similar complaints remain relatively
constant and cannot be readily augmented by standard promotional
campaigns, some OTC manufacturers have sought to expand their

markets by the ingenious device of inventing new diseases, such as the "blahs," which ostensibly can be alleviated by their intensely advertised products.

But not all OTCs are limited to use in minor conditions. Aspirin for example, remains not only one of the most popular remedies for pain but also the drug most effective and most frequently recommended by physicians for the treatment of rheumatoid arthritis and osteoarthritis.

Since the cost of a typical OTC product is usually small, especially in contrast with that of many prescription drugs, there has not yet been any significant public outcry against OTC prices and profits. Competition has been brisk, and prices are often widely advertised by both manufacturers and retail stores, which serves in some cases to keep prices low. But some OTCs are priced at a relatively high level, considering the prices of competitive products on the market, either under the same or a different name. Further, the expenditures for these products are not insignificant, especially among elderly patients and those with chronic disease or recurrent symptoms. The average per capita expenditure for OTCs is now about $20 a year. For the elderly the average is probably $40 a year or more. Rarely are the costs of out-of-hospital OTCs covered by health insurance or other third-party programs.

By accident or design, an impenetrable barrier has seemingly been erected between the major prescription drug companies and the OTC companies, and the two groups supposedly do not converse. The prescription drug makers refrain from advertising their products directly to the public and accordingly refer to themselves as the ethical drug firms. Most OTC companies do advertise to the public, and might therefore be termed the unethical drug firms, but technically they are often known as proprietary companies. Because of certain characteristics, notably their apparently limited scientific research on new OTC products and their enormous public advertising, the OTC firms seem to be excluded from the upper echelons of the pharmaceutical industry or treated as undesirable distant relations.

The barrier separating OTC companies and prescription drug companies is, in fact, nonexistent. Almost every major prescription drug firm is also a major manufacturer of OTCs, which are produced under its own name or—perhaps for reasons of delicacy—under the name of a subsidiary. For example, Glenbrook Laboratories (Bayer Aspirin, Phillips' Milk of Magnesia, Vanquish for headaches, and Cope for "nervous tension headaches") and Lehn & Fink (Lysol) are subsidiaries of Sterling Drug, as is the Winthrop Laboratories division that specializes in

prescription products. Whitehall Laboratories (Anacin, Dristan, Preparation H for hemorrhoids, and Preparation W for warts) is a subsidiary of
American Home Products, which also owns such prescription drug
makers as Wyeth and Ayerst. Leeming/Pacquin (Ben-Gay, Desitin for
athlete's foot, and Visine eyedrops) is a division of Pfizer. Vick Chemical
(NyQuil, Vick cough drops, Vick Formula 44 for coughs and colds, Sinex
nasal spray, and Lavoris mouthwash) is a division of Richardson-Merrell.
Plough (Di-Gel antacid, Feen-A-Mint laxative gum, St. Joseph Aspirin,
and Solarcaine) is now a member of the Schering-Plough group. Menley
& James (Contac for colds and Sine-Off for sinus headaches) is owned by
Smith Kline & French.

There are, in addition, some companies whose business is largely if
not exclusively devoted to OTCs. Some of these have been in business
for a century or more. There are believed to be more than twelve
thousand firms now marketing OTC drugs. Unfortunately, no one—neither FDA nor spokesmen for the proprietary companies—seems to know
the number of OTC products on the market, and estimates have run
from 100,000 to 200,000 or more. It has been fascinating to some
observers to note that essentially all of these products are formulated
from only about 250 significant active ingredients.[1]

THE ORIGINS OF DO-IT-YOURSELF THERAPY

Since the beginning of written medical history, and undoubtedly
long before, man has demonstrated an irrepressible desire to treat his
own ills.[2] The use of some of these early remedies was based on centuries
of empirical trial-and-error observations. In their early search for food
under primitive conditions, Dr. Chauncey D. Leake has written, people
tried everything in their environment, whether of plant, animal, or
mineral origin.[3] Some of these substances proved to be nutritious. Others
caused vomiting or catharsis and were therefore applied for digestive
complaints; some controlled pain and were used for every discomfort
from headache to battle injuries; some reduced fevers; some could be
applied as poultices to reduce skin irritation; some caused abortion or
induced labor in pregnant women.

Most of these early drugs have long since disappeared from the
pharmacies and apothecary shops of the civilized world, but some of
them—such as opium, cinchona, ergot, the salicylates, mercury salts,
digitalis, belladonna, lime juice, and animal organ extracts—today, in
one form or another, have maintained acceptance in modern medical
practice. There were others whose use was based seemingly only on

superstition. For example, many of these ancient remedies incorporated cow dung, sheep dung, wolf dung, or even human excreta; such an ingredient supposedly made the patient's body so unpalatable that the demon causing the trouble would be induced to leave the premises. Some plant and animal products won at least temporary acceptance—for perhaps a few centuries—because of the shape of the plant's leaves or the reputed strength, bravery, or sex life of the particular animal species.

At some point in the history of medication—especially of self-medication—an additional element was introduced when imaginative merchants clearly recognized that there was much gold to be made in these pills. Accordingly, some individuals took a useful drug and multiplied their profits by diluting the active ingredient with such low-cost adulterants as sugar, flour, clay, or sawdust. Still other entrepreneurs discovered the vast profits that could be garnered by putting together a drug product—the ingredients were inconsequential, providing a catchy name could be attached—and promoting it to the public through testimonials, billboards, and other advertising techniques. These promotional methods have not yet totally vanished. In many societies, at least up to the nineteenth century, these and similar products were commonly taken as folk remedies. Only when they failed was the patient likely to seek the aid of a medicine man, or of a physician or surgeon.

Some of these publicly advertised products represented something new—a truly original invention, with real or imagined values—and their composition was maintained as a trade secret. In England a royal letter of patent could be obtained from the king—at a price—to protect the manufacturer from competition. In other instances there was nothing new about the product, but it was patented—at a price—nonetheless. This procedure represented a valuable source of revenue to the crown, but in 1624 British patents by royal favor were abolished by statute. Thereafter patent medicines need not have been safe or effective, but they must have represented new inventions.[4]

The name "patent medicine" has lingered on in the English language, although it has become almost meaningless. Few drug products of this class are now under patent, although many are marketed under a trademark or brand name. Today, they are variously called proprietary medicines, home remedies, family medicines, nonprescription drugs, or OTCs. In turn, the OTC products are sometimes subdivided into the "ethical" OTCs, which need no prescription but are not advertised at all or are advertised only to physicians and other health professionals, and the ordinary OTCs, which are advertised directly to the public. Among the ordinary OTCs there seems to be a pharmaceutical pecking order depending on whether the product is promoted through huge, costly, nationwide newspaper, magazine, radio, and television advertising, or merely by means of a discreet counter display in the neighborhood pharmacy. Regardless of nomenclature, OTCs have long been widely used in this country. In fact, until the 1930s there were few drugs which could *not* be bought without a physician's prescription.

Federal governmental efforts to influence the sale, quality, promotion, and use of OTC drugs go back at least as far as 1848, when the Congress ruled that all medicines shall be "examined and appraised, as well as any reference to their quality, purity and fitness for medical purposes, as to their value and identity specified in the invoice." [5] This, however, applied only to products imported from foreign countries. In the case of American-made drugs, the customer was on his own. In 1888 the Congress ruled against the manufacture or sale of adulterated foods or drugs in the District of Columbia and prohibited adulterations that were (1) injurious to health; (2) injurious in quality or nature or substance; or (3) intended fraudulently to increase bulk, weight, or measure or to conceal inferior quality. But OTCs were exempted from the act.

During the next decade or so, as the result of the efforts of some physicians, pharmacists, and responsible manufacturers, and the muckraking exposés of the *Ladies' Home Journal, Collier's,* and other publications, federal agencies took increasing interest in adulterated drugs and in those that were falsely or fraudulently labeled or promoted. Those efforts led eventually to enactment of the 1906 Pure Food and Drugs Act, which provided some help in controlling drug adulteration, and the 1912 Sherley Amendment to the act, which marked a further step to stop deceptive labeling. Unfortunately, as government attorneys were quick to learn, it was difficult enough to convince a judge and jury that a promotional claim was false. It was even more difficult—and often impossible—to convince them that the claim was fraudulent, put forth with deliberate intent to deceive.

Somewhat tighter restrictions were incorporated in two pieces of legislation enacted in 1938. One was the Wheeler-Lea Amendment to the Federal Trade Commission Act, which theoretically made it possible to control the advertising of OTCs. The other was the 1938 Food, Drug, and Cosmetic Act, which gave FDA authority to require proof that any new product—prescription or OTC—was at least safe.

Both bills had been opposed at the outset by the drug industry.

OTC manufacturers first declared that the law would put them out of business, although they endorsed the final form of the legislation. The House of Representatives committee report on the legislation gave this reassurance: "The bill is not intended to restrict in any way the availability of drugs for self-medication. On the contrary, it is intended to make self-medication safer and more effective." [6]

It was this 1938 law—along with the Durham-Humphrey Amendment of 1951—that confirmed the authority of FDA to divide all drugs into two classes, those sold only on prescription and those sold over-the-counter. For the prescription products, the instructions for use were to be given to the patient by his physician. For OTCs, the instructions for use were to be printed on the label.

Further controls on drug safety, labeling, and also efficacy—again for both prescription and OTC drugs—were incorporated in the Kefauver-Harris Amendments of 1962. Many elements of the original bill were strongly denounced at the outset by OTC manufacturers, who warned that the legislation would put them out of business.

By 1972 spokesmen for the Proprietary Association—the trade association for the OTC drug industry—admitted that the industry had not been wrecked by any of this federal legislation. A few products had been taken off the market, some had needed to be reformulated with different ingredients, and some had required labeling changes. Few companies had been forced to close their doors, and many were making more profits than ever. "The 1938 law," they said, "did not put the industry out of business. It updated the industry. The 1962 law is not wrecking the industry. It is modernizing it."

Industry leaders could take some comfort in repeated assertions that federal agencies had no intentions of interfering with mankind's apparently God-given right to self-medication, and to dose itself, cure itself, and—if this should happen—kill itself with home remedies. "Self-medication is an essential part of our health care system," FDA commissioner Charles Edwards told a Senate hearing in 1971. "Man has a basic urge to help himself when he is sick or discomforted. If his complaint arises out of temporary, self-limiting conditions that yield to drugs safe enough for non-professional use, it makes good sense in our judgment to encourage self-medication rather than unnecessary visits to an already overworked physician." [7]

Such an expression might well have provided complete reassurance to the OTC drug industry, but even in 1972 not all members of the industry were reassured. Some were fully aware that—unlike the case of prescription drugs—the provisions of the 1962 law had not yet been fully applied to OTC drugs. The supposed efficacy of their products, the nature of their advertising, and the possible relation of OTC advertising to drug abuse were yet to undergo governmental trial by fire.

"Those of our companies that get through relatively unscathed will have it made," one OTC company official told us. "They will practically have the government on their side, and at least be able to suggest that their products and their advertising are government-approved. But until all the decisions are in, some of us may be a little nervous."

THE OTC INDUSTRY: SALES AND PROFITS

One of the more perplexing aspects of the OTC market is that there is little or no agreement on its size. Depending on definition, sales may now be as small as $2.7 billion a year, or as large as $10 billion or more. In some cases there can be no question about classification. By virtually any yardstick, such products as nonprescription antacids, laxatives, and agents for the relief of pain would be accepted as OTC drugs. Presumably most cosmetics would not. But there is less certainty on the proper classification of medicated soaps, baby powders, deodorants, and vaginal jellies, creams, and foams used as contraceptives. Toothpastes and mouthwashes might not be viewed as drugs, but they have been promoted by the use of health claims that have attracted the attention of FDA.

One widely accepted classification is published annually by *Drug Topics*. According to its reports, OTC sales at the consumer level were about $3.1 billion in 1972 (see table 11 in the Appendix). Not included in that total, however, were such items as $13.1 million for hair medicaments; $13.0 million for dandruff rinses; $41.8 million for foot powders, salves, and ointments; $59.2 million for medicated shampoos; $95.6 million for baby powders, oils, lotions, suppositories, and diaper rash preparations; $89.2 million for feminine hygiene medications and nonprescription contraceptives; $245.4 million for mouthwashes and gargles; and $408.2 million for tooth pastes and powders. (Also missing from the list were perhaps the oldest of all over-the-counter remedies, alcoholic beverages, with retail sales of more than $15 billion a year.) These figures cover mainly community pharmacies, supermarkets, department stores, and other retail outlets. They do not include drugs dispensed by hospital or government pharmacies.

It may be assumed, therefore, that—depending on definition—nationwide sales of OTCs in 1972 were at least $4.0 billion, and may have been far higher (see table 12 in the Appendix). For domestic sales in 1970, it had been estimated that twenty-seven companies had 85 percent of the total, and five firms—American Home Products, Bristol-Myers, Miles Laboratories, Sterling Drug, and Warner-Lambert—controlled 45 percent.[8] On 1970 sales at the retail level of about $3.5 billion, about $2 billion represented the gross receipts of manufacturers. Approximately $160 million, or 8 percent, represented net profits after taxes.[9]

Sales of OTC products have been increasing steadily over most of the past quarter-century, but the rise has not matched the meteoric increase in the sale of prescription drugs, especially since the early 1960s. (See figure 16.) While OTCs had about 86 percent of the total drug market in 1921, as measured at the manufacturer's level, they repre-

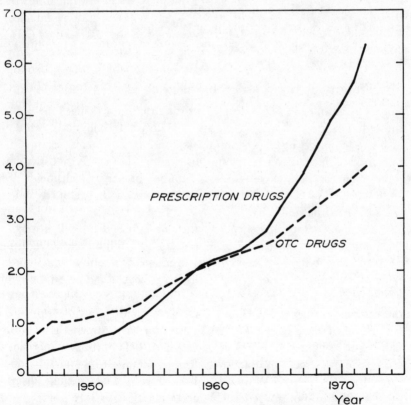

FIGURE 16. Retail Sales of Prescription and Over-the-Counter Drugs, 1945–1972
SOURCE: *Drug Topics*, various issues.

sented about 60 percent in 1937, 38 percent in 1947, 28 percent in 1963,[10] and probably less than 25 percent in 1972.

Research in the field of OTC products is difficult to measure. Large sums may be invested in market research, consumer acceptance surveys, and the development and testing of novel shapes, flavors, and coloring matter, but probably less than $1 million a year is put specifically into the development of new active ingredients for OTC use. It is difficult if not impossible to isolate these expenses from the cost of research of new prescription drugs being undertaken at the same time by the same companies.

As one result of this minimal research effort, few recent discoveries of new medicinal agents for use in self-medication have been reported. Officials of the American Pharmaceutical Association have estimated that less than a dozen significant new active ingredients for OTC products have been permitted by FDA to reach the market during the past fifteen years.[11] Far more significant, at least in its impact on stimulating sales, has been the industry's support of OTC promotion, which has long since reached the point of enormous proportions, dubious accuracy, and questionable taste.

PROMOTION: THE QUESTION OF VOLUME

The amount of OTC drug advertising that now deluges the public through newspapers, magazines, radio, television, billboards, window displays, counter displays, pamphlets, and other media cannot be measured with precision. Some authorities have indicated that it is now more than $1.2 billion a year.[12] A number of surveys, although not complete and not necessarily comparable, offer some detailed indications of the situation.

An *Advertising Age* survey of the one hundred top advertisers in the United States—with sales of more than $280 billion and advertising of nearly $5.3 billion—disclosed that drug and cosmetic manufacturers ranked first among major groups, with 1972 advertising investments of $1.1 billion, representing 10.9 percent of sales.[13] The greater portion of these expenses involved OTC products. (See table 13 in the Appendix.) An official of the Federal Trade Commission has testified that, on the basis of 1969 figures, domestic advertising for OTC products represents more than 37 percent of domestic sales.[14] According to *Advertising Age*, three drug companies—Warner-Lambert, with 1972 advertising expenditures of $134 million; American Home Products, with $116 million; and Bristol-Myers, with $115 million—ranked among the ten leading advertisers in the nation.[15] (See table 14 in the Appendix.)

A *Product Management* study, based on only about five hundred of the many thousands of "drugs and other health aids" available over the counter for human use, and not covering all media, analyzed so-called identifiable advertising expenses totaling $481 million—about one-third of the estimated total of OTC promotion.[16] Approximately 57 percent was used for network TV advertising, 25 percent for TV spot commercials, 13 percent for magazines, and 5 percent for newspapers and radio.

A breakdown by drug class, as shown in table 15 in the Appendix, demonstrates that a large amount—nearly $100 million—was used in efforts to capture shares of the half-a-billion-a-year market for headache remedies and other internal analgesics, $77.4 million was used to tout cough and cold remedies, $45 million was used in the praise of antacids, and $16.8 million for laxatives.

American Home Products spent about $26 million for its Anacin, $17 million for its Dristan products, and $5 million for its antihemorrhoid Preparation H. Bristol-Myers spent $11 million for its Bufferin advertising and $11 million for its Excedrin. Miles Laboratories spent $24 million for its Alka-Seltzer line and $8 million for its One-A-Day vitamin products. Sterling spent $24 million for its Bayer Aspirin products and $6 million for Phillips' Milk of Magnesia. Warner-Lambert spent $10 million to promote its Listerine products and $5 million for Rolaids. J. B. Williams spent $5 million for its Geritol products and $5 million for Sominex.[17]

Any efforts to limit OTC advertising on the grounds that use of the products "may be dangerous to your health," or for any other reason, would probably not receive the warm endorsement of the advertising media and particularly that of television. In 1970, before cigarette commercials were banned from television, all tobacco advertising amounted to $313.6 million. In contrast, advertising for OTC drugs amounted to approximately $1.2 billion, of which roughly $960 million was allocated to television.

PROMOTION: THE QUESTION OF QUALITY

Although the extent of OTC advertising has been vigorously denounced by physicians, pharmacists, consumer groups, educators, and government officials, the most forceful attack has been leveled against the nature and content of that promotion. It is only too clear that much public drug advertising ranks somewhere between odious and *O Deus!*

For decades, enormous sums have been spent to convince the public that failure to have a daily bowel movement is a medical emergency, perspiration odor and bad breath represent offenses as heinous as treason and child-beating, spooning a laxative into a child can be equated with giving mother-love (and *not* giving such a laxative is tantamount to withholding parental affection), sleeplessness for a few minutes needs treatment for insomnia, tension is both bad and quickly curable, mouthwashes and gargles are effective in the treatment and even prevention of the common cold, home cold remedies actually cure or shorten the cold infection, and it is wise to ingest a pain remedy for the relief of "imperceptible pain."

"All too often," FDA commissioner Edwards told the 1971 meeting of the Proprietary Association,

> basically good products with long and useful histories are being altered, added to, reformulated and reshaped with no purpose but promotional advantage. And promotion all too often is being conducted in ways to make a snake oil salesman green with envy.
>
> I can sympathize with the competitive pressures which perpetuate this situation. At the same time, I understand the frustrations of a public besieged with claims and counterclaims, with testimonials and with doubtful assertions of comparability.
>
> When drug promotion reaches that point where antacids are offered like martinis and laxatives are implied as essential to everyday happiness, then the time has come to take a good hard look at the situation.[18]

More than half a billion dollars has been spent by the makers of Anacin, Bufferin, Excedrin, the various brands of aspirin, and other pain remedies to extol their products on the basis of what are mostly trivial formulation differences. For example, Anacin—a combination that now consists of approximately $6\frac{2}{3}$ grains of aspirin and $\frac{1}{3}$ grain of caffeine per tablet—has been held out to be vastly superior to 5-grain tablets of aspirin alone, although the value of caffeine in control of headache pain is reportedly without significant scientific support.

Another headache remedy, Excedrin PM—a combination of three traditional analgesics, aspirin, acetaminophen, and salicylamide, plus caffeine and an antihistamine, methapyrilene fumarate—made its bid in this field with a promotional campaign that will long be remembered. Based on what was reported to be a "major hospital study," the Excedrin PM story was related night after night in a dramatic, moving, and highly effective presentation by TV actor David Janssen. The manner in which

Mr. Janssen spoke his lines cannot be faulted. The campaign itself came to a disastrous climax when the physician who directed the "major hospital study" demanded that his findings be disassociated from the promotion, since he had tested the product only on postchildbirth pain. Soon afterward, the National Broadcasting Company refused to accept the advertising on its network, and eventually the campaign was dropped.[19]

Headache remedies are by no means the only products whose advertising has earned scathing criticism. In some instances the promotion has attracted barbs because of the "phony folksiness" of the presentation, or the intense sincerity expressed by radio or TV spokesmen. Many of these campaigns bring to mind the old adage "At all costs be sincere—whether you mean it or not." Still other campaigns, notably for laxatives and hemorrhoid remedies, have been delivered in a vocal wrapper more customarily associated with sepulchral phrases beginning, "Dearly beloved, we are gathered here to . . ."

Some promotional campaigns have deserved criticism because of the scientific—or unscientific—nature of their content. Thus, antacids have been promoted with visual demonstrations of their ability to coat glass surfaces; but the human stomach is not lined with glass, and there is no evidence to demonstrate that the product acts in this fashion under clinical conditions. Tonics for the elderly have been praised on the basis of their vitamin and mineral content, although it seems probable that their beneficial effects may be more related to the fact that these vitamins and minerals are contained in a solution consisting mainly of 20 percent alcohol.

Such tonics as Geritol and SSS have received particular attention from Senate investigators and representatives of the Federal Trade Commission. For example, an FTC order—later affirmed by a federal court—ordered the SSS Company to "cease and desist from false and misleading advertisements" such as the following radio commercial:

> Do you find yourself missing out on the fun in life? Do you feel dull, draggy . . . just "too tired" to do things? Then maybe you're suffering from iron deficiency anemia—low blood power. If so, what you need is Three-S Tonic! New formula Three-S tonic—now with B vitamins—is rich in iron to help build back your blood power . . . restore your energy . . . help you feel better fast! Three-S tonic goes to work within 24 hours. And if you don't feel better in just six days the Three-S Company will refund your money . . . every cent of it! So don't miss out on the fun in life. Don't let yourself feel "too tired" to enjoy things. Deficiency anemia, take

Three-S Tonic! Yes, yes, yes . . . get SSS! Get started on new-formula, iron-and-vitamin-enriched Three-S Tonic . . . in liquid or tablet form . . . right away.

From the FTC's findings, the court quoted this statement:

As we have noted, the evidence in this case overwhelmingly supports the conclusion that iron deficiency and iron deficiency anemia cannot be self-diagnosed. The evidence also supports the examiner's parallel conclusion that vitamin deficiency is virtually non-existent and cannot properly be diagnosed without a physician. Representations to the contrary are false and deceptive and cannot be condoned on the ground that Congressional policy favors self-medication on a trial-and-error basis.[20]

A 1971 advertisement for Vivarin, promoted as a non-habit-forming stimulant, was based on the following "case history":

One day it dawned on me that I was boring my husband to death. It wasn't that I didn't love Jim, but often by the time he came home at night I was feeling dull, tired and drowsy. [Then Vivarin tablets came upon the scene.] All of a sudden Jim was coming home to a more exciting woman, me. We talk to each other a lot more. . . . And after dinner I was wide-awake enough to do a little more than just look at television. And the other day—it wasn't even my birthday—Jim sent me flowers with a note. The note began: "To my new wife . . ."[21]

According to FDA, a Vivarin tablet contains mainly caffeine and sugar in amounts roughly equivalent to those in a half-cup of sweetened coffee.[22] In 1972 the Federal Trade Commission obtained a consent order that banned the manufacturer of Vivarin from making what were termed false advertising claims.[23] In 1973 the same firm, J. B. Williams Co., was fined $812,000 for violating an earlier FTC cease-and-desist order involving its Geritol and FemIron advertising; spokesmen for Williams declared that the judgment was wrong and the penalty excessive, and announced their intent to appeal.[24]

Common OTC sedatives, such as Sominex, Compoz, and Tranquil, have as their major ingredient an antihistamine that produces drowsiness as a side effect. According to The Medical Letter, these may be useful in some individuals. "On the other hand," it was stated, "the likelihood that they will be ineffective, the great variability of reaction of different persons to the same antihistamine, and the frequency with which antihistamines cause undesirable, and sometimes serious, side effects, hardly make them products to recommend as hypnotics."[25]

In a new series of hearings chaired by Senator Nelson on OTC promotion, Dr. Edwards expressed his particular exasperation with OTC manufacturers who launch huge promotional campaigns designed to convince the public that their latest product is "new-new-new." But, he said, when such companies were charged in court with failure to get FDA approval of their new wonder drug, they contended that the product was nothing new at all—that it consisted of well-known ingredients.[26] Thus the companies sought to have it both ways, telling the public that the products were "new-new-new," while simultaneously telling the judge that they really were "old-old-old."

One of the difficulties has been the reticence of some OTC manufacturers to give quantitative data on the composition of their products, claiming that such information is a trade secret. For example, when the APhA was compiling its authoritative *Handbook of Non-Prescription Drugs* in 1967, the makers of 40 percent of the leading OTCs on the market declined to divulge such secrets. In 1971 the makers of 20 percent of these products were still refusing to provide the information.[27]

Special concern has been expressed over the potential impact of public drug advertising on drug abuse, and particularly its impact on children. "One of the messages children receive from such advertising is that medicines have magical qualities," it has been claimed by Dr. David Lewis, of the Harvard Medical School. "They watch on television as a pill causes the instant transformation of a sufferer's face from glumness to glee. My concern is that such widespread promotion of drugs, their magical qualities, and the immediacy of their effects, may be factors that encourage our children to experiment with their own array of drugs." [28]

To spokesmen for the APhA the matter of excessive drug advertising is already out of hand. "When people are coaxed into taking a pill each time a stressful situation occurs, when Brand X is touted as the solution to all family health problems . . . we do indeed have a public health problem," Dr. Richard Penna told the Nelson subcommittee.[29] James Bicket of the APhA added, "We feel that OTC drug advertising is out of control. . . . It is often erroneous, it exaggerates claims, and it even attempts to convince people that they have non-existent diseases. Most critically, we feel that OTC drug advertising contributes substantially to the 'drug orientation' of our culture, and we believe something should be done about it." [30]

John Ingersoll, head of the former Bureau of Narcotics and Dangerous Drugs, declared that irresponsible drug advertisements have encouraged the American public to develop a "take something syndrome" that invites people to seek relief through drugs for even the least discomfort.[31] The Proprietary Association has denied that there has been any significant evidence to demonstrate the misuse of OTC products, or to link OTC advertising—especially on television—with drug abuse.[32] In fact, PA spokesmen have emphasized, drug abuse existed long before the rise of modern drug advertising, and drug abuse occurs now in countries such as Sweden where drug advertising is banned from TV.[33]

The PA defense may be somewhat persuasive if drug abuse is considered to be the use of only such illegal agents as heroin, LSD, and marijuana. The situation is strikingly different if drug abuse is considered to include also the abuse or misuse of such legal drugs as tranquilizers, sedatives, stimulants, and other products available either with or without a prescription, and the growing tendency of the public to take a pill for every ill, real or imagined.

Without admitting its concern that there may be a very significant association between drug advertising and this broader type of drug abuse, the PA voted in 1971 to tighten its recommended guidelines to give "new assurances of higher standards of advertising." [34] The added recommendations were the following:

(1) Depiction of consumers continually relying on medicines as simplistic solutions to emotional or mood problems should be avoided.

(2) Advertising for proprietary medicines should avoid representations by word or picturization which, in reasonable construction, are commonly associated with the "drug culture" or which imply a casual attitude toward the use of drugs.

(3) Exaggeration or dramatization which misrepresents the product's capabilities should be avoided.

(4) Claims of product effectiveness should be supportable by clinical or other medical evidence *or experience through long use* [italics ours].

(5) Proprietary medicine advertising directed toward young children and encouraging them to use such medicine should be avoided.

(6) Advertising of proprietary medicines on programs or in publications which are specifically directed toward young children should be avoided.

In short, the industry, while denying the existence of a problem, has indicated its desire to help solve it, but only by voluntary self-regulation. Several firms have already taken steps to discontinue drug advertising in TV programs directed to children. Early in 1973 the Proprietary Association joined with the National Association of Broadcasters in establishing voluntary codes that would affect all TV drug advertising. The codes would presumably make it easier for broadcasters to reject unacceptable advertising material—a step that many broadcast-ers felt was essential if they were to avoid a congressional ax on all TV drug advertising.[35] "It happened to us with cigarettes," a TV network official stated. "It could happen to us with drugs."

But the historical record of such voluntary efforts does not provide grounds for much optimism. No major industrial group (such as automobile makers, food manufacturers, the movie industry, and the oil industry) and no major professional group (including physicians, pharma-cists, lawyers, journalists, and even clergymen) have yet been able to keep all of its members in line solely by self-regulation.

In the case of the OTC industry, it may be essential for the government to lay on its heavy hand—or perhaps two or three of its heavy hands. Unlike prescription drugs, which are under FDA control for their composition, safety, efficacy, and advertising, OTC products are now under the theoretical control of three different agencies: FDA, for composition, safety, and efficacy; the Federal Trade Commission, which controls all advertising aimed at the public; and the Federal Communi-cations Commission, which controls radio and TV stations through its power to license or unlicense each broadcasting station.

The record of FCC in cleaning up the drug advertising mess has long been, in the words of one of its own commissioners, less than overwhelming. It has argued that the commission must not act too hastily to remove drug advertising from the airwaves because this produces millions of dollars a year for the broadcasters. To such a view, Commissioner Nicholas Johnson commented, "If these network execu-tives, who are rich beyond their wildest dreams of avarice, would put some of that money back into programming, we might feel differently about their purported plight. But when they demonstrate such brazen indifference to public interest in programming, as well as commercials . . . any coin thrown in their wishing well leaves a hollow echo indeed." [36]

The outspoken commissioner told Senator Nelson, "I do not see how anyone who is seriously concerned with the effect of television on children can ignore the testimony you have heard, or fail to move, now, against the commercial exploitation of children, both in the lifestyle that television purveys to them, and the specific drug and drug-related products—candy aspirin, cough medicines, animal or cartoon vitamins—that are huckstered on programs designed to capture children for advertisers." [37]

Johnson himself recommended that FCC propose rules that would ban much OTC drug advertising, particularly for analgesics and mood-altering drugs, and that in any case all OTC advertising should be cleared in advance by both FDA and FTC, and stripped of emotional and psychological appeals. Drug advertising in programs viewed especially by children should promote the company name rather than a specific product. The commission's Fairness Doctrine should be extended so that deceptive advertising could be attacked by counteradvertising. And the advertising record of each radio and TV station, including its broadcasts of false, misleading, or deceptive claims, should be reviewed by independent experts each time the station applied for license renewal.

Unfortunately, many of these proposed FCC moves would require the Trade Commission to act first—notably to determine precisely which advertising claims were actually false, misleading, or deceptive— and FTC has so far won few plaudits for moving forcefully or quickly against drug companies. For example, it took the commission sixteen years to get the word "liver" out of Carter's Little Liver Pills. It began investigating J. B. Williams' advertising for Geritol in 1959, and yet it was only in 1973 that the courts acted. FTC investigations of analgesic commercials began in 1955, and investigations of cold remedy advertising began in 1962, and by 1972 no case in these fields had yet yielded even an opinion from a hearing commissioner.

"Part of this," said Robert Pitofsky, director of FTC's Bureau of Consumer Protection, "may be due to the agency's shortcomings and part a tribute to the way top-notch lawyers occasionally can run the government ragged. But I do not think either of those factors is the main problem." [38] Mostly responsible is the fact that any litigation in this field is lengthy and can often tie up an agency in snarls of red tape that will take at least a year, and often many years, to unravel. In contrast, an advertising campaign may last only twenty-six weeks. At the end of that time, while government officials may still be struggling to halt one bad campaign, the company may be embarked on a new one.

Nevertheless, in the spring of 1972 FTC embarked on a new campaign to halt some of the blatantly misleading advertising claims for competing OTC products. Among the primary targets of this campaign were such promotional assertions as "Our Brand A product is best for headaches because it contains pure aspirin, and nothing is better than pure aspirin," and "Our Brand B product is best for headaches because its aspirin is combined with gentle buffers." Obviously, FTC held, one of the two claims must be false—an exceedingly strange situation, since the two firms involved were subsidiaries of the same parent company.

A major phase of this new FTC intervention was directed at heavily advertised claims for cough and cold remedies—"sinus relief in seconds," "quiets your cough from cold or flu up to eight hours," "relieves major cold symptoms for hours," "contains a special antihistamine to help control sneezing," "for children and adults, recommended by many doctors," "a cough suppressant as effective as codeine, but not narcotic," "relieves more major cold symptoms than the leading capsule," "more MDs recommend it than any other product," "relieves sore throat pain fast." To the manufacturers who promulgated these and similar statements, the FTC said, "Substantiate them." A leading trade journal forecast that the manufacturers would be facing a rough regulatory future.[39]

The third potential participant in this area, FDA, is virtually powerless under existing law. It may keep an OTC drug off the market if the product is relatively unsafe or ineffective, but it has no direct authority over OTC advertising.

Except for the simple but drastic technique of banning all public advertising of drugs, any solution to this complex problem will be complex and probably less than completely satisfactory. Nonetheless, there are corrective steps which are urgently needed and which, alone or in combination, can alleviate the situation.

(1) The companies can be induced to tone down their promotional efforts, both in volume and in intensity of claims.

(2) They can be induced to refrain from using promotional devices that contribute to public dependence on drug products for every real or fancied ailment, physical or emotional, medical or social.

(3) Under its existing authority, FCC should require stations to provide appropriate time for counterattacks against drug advertising that is false, misleading, deceptive, or otherwise unfair. This antidote is already available for political candidates. It should also be available in matters vitally affecting the public health. Here it should be emphasized that the radio and television channels do not belong to the stations or networks. They are owned by the public.

(4) Of probably most practical importance, the companies can be required to obtain preclearance of their advertising, not by FTC or FCC, but by FDA. This last approach, which would require congressional action, would assign the responsibility for making drug advertising decisions to drug experts. FDA is already charged with rendering such decisions on the advertising of prescription drugs, and has developed apparently tolerable working arrangements with the prescription drug industry. It seems reasonable to expect that it could develop similar

arrangements with the OTC drug industry. Under current financing, FDA does not have the money to pay for such advertising reviews—especially for preclearance—but it can be given the needed additional funds. It does not have the necessary personnel, but—again, with adequate financing—it can train and recruit the needed experts.

Logically, the industry should pay for such operations. It can meet the costs in several ways, such as by reducing its overall investment in promotion, or more probably by passing on the costs to the consumers. If, however, the results would be a reduction in false, misleading, or deceptive advertising, or a reduction in promotion that contributes to drug abuse by both children and adults, the public will be getting a bargain.

OTC SAFETY

It is widely believed by the public, and apparently by some health professionals, that all OTCs are innocuous. ("If it wasn't safe, they wouldn't sell it to you without a prescription.") But no OTC, if it has any biological effect whatsoever, may be considered totally safe. The position of the OTC makers is clear. "Most over-the-counter preparations—both single ingredient and combination—have an impressive history of safety through actual use," the Proprietary Association has stated. "Many of them have been used for upwards of a quarter of a century; others for a much greater length of time. . . . Through use, experience and substantiated general effectiveness, their safety and efficacy have been established." [40]

Industry spokesmen have testified that OTC preparations, designed for use by the general public, and for use as directed in the labeling, must be safe when used as so directed. If they are not, they are in violation of the law, and there is no justification for their sale on an over-the-counter basis. "The margin of safety must be substantial," PA representatives have said, "and it is."

In general, the industry has adopted the posture that its OTC products are relatively harmless "when used according to directions." But many patients do not follow directions, and some products—even when used according to directions—have caused injury or death. Antibacterial agents in soaps and other products have induced serious or incapacitating sensitivity to light.[41] Oxyphenisaten acetate, a chemical contained in such laxatives as Evasof, Hydrolose Fortified, Prulose Complex, Syncelax, Urbalax, and Vio-Lax, has been linked to jaundice and hepatitis.[42] Laxatives containing phenolphthalein may cause itching, burning, and blistering in hypersensitive patients, and even deaths following respiratory depression and collapse have been reported.[43] Continued use of mineral oil laxatives will interfere with the absorption of vitamins A and D. The use of any laxative in the presence of abdominal pain may cause death from a ruptured appendix.

Antacids taken over a prolonged period can cause either constipation or diarrhea, along with nausea. They are contraindicated for patients with high blood pressure, kidney disease, or a history of urinary stones or gastrointestinal bleeding. Magnesium-containing antacids can produce severe reactions, including lethargy, coma, circulatory collapse, and respiratory paralysis.[44]

The AMA's *Drug Evaluations* has described most OTC cold remedies as combination products having "more sales appeal than actual usefulness." In many instances, the AMA said, "they are irrational or even dangerous." [45] At a Senate hearing, Dr. Sol Katz of Georgetown University indicated that OTC cough and cold remedies should be removed from the market. On the other hand, he said in reply to a question, "Hot chicken soup is very good." [46] Vick's "night-time cold remedy" NyQuil came in for special attention when it was described as a "witch's brew" containing an antihistamine known to have "tremendous side effects." This unflattering comment came from Dr. Donald La-Brecque, former director of clinical research for Vick Laboratories. He noted that it served as an effective sedative because it contains 25 percent alcohol, and he suggested that a glass of sherry would be equally effective. In his testimony he said he had left Vick because of a disagreement over general policy, and he observed that medical directors were too often asked to prove claims already made by the sales department.[47] Company officials countered that its NyQuil product "has been used safely and effectively by millions of people in the United States." [48]

Aspirin, the leading cause of poisoning in children under the age of five,[49] has been held responsible for asthma, skin eruptions, anaphylactic shock, and other allergic reactions. "Although the incidence of such reactions to aspirin is quite low," Dr. Richard Penna of the APhA has reported, "the mortality rate of aspirin-sensitive asthmatics is high."

More widespread is the gastroduodenal bleeding and ulceration resulting from use of aspirin, alone or in combination. "This incidence of bleeding is significant," he told a Senate hearing.

Nearly 70 percent of patients taking aspirin show a daily recurrent blood loss of two to six milliliters (half to one teaspoonful), and 10 percent of these patients lose daily as much as ten milliliters (two teaspoonsful). Scientists investigating this effect note that aspirin ingestion may be the precipitating factor in 50 percent of the cases that were hospitalized because of hemorrhage. . . . In addition to being a causative culprit in bleeding, aspirin has been shown to be a contributing agent in peptic ulcer conditions. The amount of blood loss involved in the occasional use of aspirin is probably not clinically significant. However, with geriatric patients, with individuals ingesting large doses of aspirin over prolonged periods of time, and with patients who have ulcers or are ulcer-prone, blood loss and gastric ulceration may be of great significance.[50]

At least as serious are the undesirable or dangerous results caused by the combination of many common OTC preparations with prescription drugs. Among such interactions are the following: [51]

Patients taking salicylate-containing analgesics (aspirin, Alka-Seltzer, Anacin, Bufferin, Cope, Doans Pills, Excedrin, Fizrin, Measurin, Midol, Resolve, Vanquish, and so forth) may risk a drop in blood sugar levels if they are also taking antidiabetic drugs, gastrointestinal bleeding if they are taking alcohol, and aplastic anemia if they are taking methotrexate.

Those taking such antiasthmatic remedies as Asthmanefrin, Breatheasy, Bronkaid Mist, or Primatene Mist may develop high blood pressure if they are also using furazolidone, monamine oxidase (MAO) inhibitors, antihypertension agents, procarbazine, or *l*-Dopa, and a rise in blood sugar levels if they are being treated with antidiabetic agents.

With such antihistamine- or sympathomimetic-containing cough remedies as Cheracol, Coldene, Novahistine DH, Romilar CF, Sudafed, Super Anahist Syrup, Triaminic, Triaminicol, and Trind, they may develop central nervous system depression if they are also taking alcohol, reserpine, or sedative agents, and severe sedation if they are taking doxepin, MAO inhibitors, or barbiturates. In addition, these cough remedies may block the action of anticoagulants used to prevent blood clotting.

With antihistamine- or sympathomimetic-containing cough and cold tablets and capsules (4-Way Cold Tablets, Allerest, Bromo Quinine, Bronkaid, Cheracol Capsules, Contac, Coricidin D, Dristan, Ornex, Sinutabs, and so forth) they may risk central nervous system depression if they are simultaneously using alcohol, procarbazine, reserpine, or sedatives, sedation if they are using doxepin or MAO inhibitors, and a blocking of the effect of anticoagulants or steroid hormones.

Such nose drops and sprays as Alconefrin, Contac Spray, Coricidin

Mist, Neo-Synephrine, Privine, Sinex, Super Anahist, and Vick's Vantro-nol can cause a rise in blood sugar levels if the patients are being treated with any antidiabetic agent, and high blood pressure if they are using furazolidone, MAO inhibitors, antihypertension agents, procarbazine, or *l*-DOPA.

Dormin, Nytol, Sleep-Eze, Sominex, and similar sleeping aids incorporating antihistamines, or an antihistamine plus an alkaloid like belladonna, can induce central nervous system depression in patients also taking alcohol, reserpine, or sedatives, profound sedation if they are under treatment with doxepin, MAO inhibitors, or barbiturates, and an interference with the action of anticoagulants and steroids.

Some—although certainly not all—of these unhappy or even lethal results might be prevented if all patients would follow directions and "use only as directed," if they were more informative in telling their physician which OTC drugs they were customarily using, if physicians were generally aware of the composition of OTC products, and if more physicians were better aware of the potential dangers of drug interaction. Unfortunately, many patients misdiagnose their own ailments. They select remedies, with or without professional or nonprofessional guid-ance, for reasons that may be dubious or totally idiotic. They do not "use only as directed." They overdose themselves in the apparent belief that if the recommended three pills a day don't work, they should take six—or if three pills do work, then nine pills should work three times as well; or if the label warns against use for more than a week, they take the product for four weeks "to give it a little more time to have an effect."

They use OTCs continuously for weeks or months without seeking professional consultation, and thereby may delay the proper diagnosis and early treatment of a serious disease. They ply themselves each day for months with a remedy to ease a constant headache, only to find too late that their problem was not a simple headache but a growing tumor in the brain. They try for months or even years to alleviate their "indigestion" or "constipation" with antacids, digestives, or laxatives, and call for medical consultation only after their intestinal cancer has become inoperable. They have combined antihistamine-containing cold remedies, nose drops, or sleep aids with presumably moderate quantities of alcohol or a barbiturate, and killed not only themselves but other victims in automobile collisions. They have applied an ointment to relieve a minor skin irritation and have developed an allergic reaction to the product or a contact dermatitis; instead of stopping the product, they have continued to apply more and more of it until they have produced a serious, disfiguring, and sometimes life-threatening reaction.

They misuse these products by ingesting enormous quantities, month after month, of cough remedies or liquid preparations consisting largely of alcohol in concentrations as high as 80-proof. In this connection, Dr. Maven J. Myers of the Philadelphia College of Pharmacy and Science has noted, "While most states restrict alcoholic beverage purchases to persons either 21 or 18 years of age, there is generally little restriction on use if the product is called a drug." [52]

Such employment of OTCs usually does not represent "use only as directed," and the manufacturer can thereby be technically absolved from moral blame or legal liability. The manufacturer has lived up to the letter of the law if he includes appropriate warnings, as required by FDA, in the label—although they may be printed in type so small that they appear only as an almost undecipherable blur. There is as yet no law to compel the manufacturer to print the potential hazards in letters large enough to give them equal billing with the recommended uses. Similarly, there is yet no law to require the inclusion of warnings in advertisements to the public.

The inclusion of these warnings in drug advertisements has been stubbornly resisted by OTC manufacturers. The publication of such material, they insist, would needlessly alarm many people who could benefit from proper use of the drug. It would discriminate against drug companies, requiring them to disclose the dangers inherent in their products while not applying a similar burden on makers of such items as alcoholic beverages, foods, home appliances, and automobiles. Further, it has been asserted—and can be proved only too readily—that publicizing a warning is no guarantee that it will be followed or even read. "The possession of correct health information is no assurance that the possessor will use such information to protect his health," one medical expert has said. "Any one of us knows at least one physician who gives sound advice about diet and overweight, yet possession of this knowledge does not keep him even within 20 percent of the desirable weight for his height and age." [53]

A considerable share of the responsibility for misuse of OTC products, and for the drug interactions between OTC and prescription drugs, must clearly be shouldered by physicians and pharmacists. Many of these professionals are apparently unaware of the interactions that can involve OTCs. Many pharmacists appear to be unwilling to recommend that a patient should not purchase an OTC product, although some—especially those who maintain family drug records—have evidently felt that it is their responsibility to offer advice on such matters. In some cases serious drug reactions have occurred when the physician has failed to cover both OTC and prescription drug use when working up his patient's past medical record, or when he has failed to give adequately clear, comprehensive instructions. In such events the failure has sometimes resulted from a disastrous breakdown in physician-patient communications.

Thus, one patient declared that he was taking no drugs or medicines at home, in the belief that products like cold remedies, antacids, laxatives, and headache tablets "didn't really count." Another, advised by her physician to take no drugs or medicines of any kind except the ones he prescribed, was found to be taking large amounts of aspirin every day. "But aspirin isn't a medicine," she explained. "You can buy it at the corner grocery."

OTC EFFICACY

When the drug safety amendments were enacted in 1938 and the drug efficacy amendments in 1962—both providing "grandfather clause" protection to products introduced before 1938—it was fervently hoped in some quarters that these laws would be applied mainly if not entirely to prescription drugs. Most OTC products, since they had obviously passed the so-called test of time and had won widespread consumer acceptance, would presumably receive minimal attention—if any at all.

For some years, FDA indicated that it would go along with this attitude. The safety of OTC products was obviously a matter of some concern, but their effectiveness was far down on the priority scale. Strapped by small budgets and limited manpower, the agency had its hands full with prescription drug problems. Further, it seemed obvious that home remedies were hardly of life-and-death importance; if they were pharmacologically useless, few patients would be seriously harmed. At the worst, they would be paying out their dollars for worthless products. At the best, they might feel better simply for having ingested a pill, even an ineffective pill.

By the mid-1960s FDA recognized that such an easy-going approach did not represent the intent of the Congress. The law said that the safety and efficacy of all drugs, prescription and nonprescription alike (except for the old pre-1938 products), must be documented. In 1966 the effectiveness of OTCs began to be seriously questioned when FDA contracted with the National Academy of Sciences/National Research Council to examine the efficacy of about four thousand products and to classify them into half a dozen different categories of effectiveness. Included in this first batch of products were about four hundred OTCs. Of these, the NAS/NRC panels decided that, on the basis of all available evidence, only about one-fourth could be rated as "effective."

This in itself was a bitter pill for the OTC manufacturers to swallow, but it was only a small pill. The good name of an additional 100,000 or more OTC products remained unsullied. Moreover, it seemed all too clear that a survey of this enormous number of products would require an enormous number of years. Since it had taken the NAS/NRC panels roughly two years to examine 4,000 products, a comparable survey of 100,000 OTCs on a product-by-product basis would take at least a quarter of a century and possibly much longer.

But FDA had learned a few lessons. Early in 1971 Commissioner Edwards presented a preview of the planned OTC study. First, he said, there must be a census of all products available without prescription in the United States. (Legislation calling for a census of all drugs, prescription and OTC, was enacted in 1972.) Second, all the products— whether there might be 100,000 of them, or 200,000, or possibly 500,000—would be divided into a reasonable number of therapeutic classes, such as analgesics, laxatives, and "mood drugs." Third, the industry would be invited to provide all the available data concerning the safety and especially the efficacy of their products. Finally, FDA would assemble the best scientific experts in the country to consider the evidence—not product by product, but class by class. Dr. Edwards said:

> Where there is adequate evidence for experts to agree that the drugs are safe and effective, we would permit continuing marketing. Where such evidence is lacking or inadequate to make such judgment, we would have no choice, under the law, but to require adequate studies to establish the drug's efficacy. Of course, if a drug were found to be effective, before permission for continued marketing could be granted, it would be necessary to establish that the labeling for the product was adequate to permit safe and effective use by the lay person without medical supervision.[54]

Dr. Edwards proposed that the expert panel judging each therapeutic group would recommend certain formulations and labeling that would be acceptable for each category. Manufacturers of products not conforming to these criteria would have two choices: either change their formulations and modify their claims, or be prepared to undertake additional research and submit the requisite scientific data to support their stand. (There was a third possibility, which, although perfectly apparent, was not mentioned by any party: file suit to block the government in the courts.)

"Beyond any question," the FDA commissioner said, "the OTC's differ legally, medically, and in method of use from prescription drugs. They just as clearly require a different approach and a different order of evidence to establish efficacy." He emphasized, however, that FDA had no intention of applying a double standard of effectiveness to OTC and prescription products.

> I have repeatedly tried to emphasize in every way I can that the problem for proving efficacy for OTCs is different than for prescription drugs. But, the point that needs to be stressed is that no matter what the variations in kind and magnitude, the proof of efficacy must be no less valid and no less reliable than for prescription drugs. It must be proof which can be medically documented. It must, in this final analysis, allow the consumer a reasonable expectation that the product he buys will give him the relief he seeks.

In a carefully worded position paper, the Proprietary Association expressed its support of the efficacy review and agreed wholeheartedly with the FDA's plan, with a few intriguing exceptions. The PA recommended that the efficacy of a product could be demonstrated by *any* of the following procedures:

—Scientifically designed objective or subjective clinical studies
—Bioavailability of individual ingredients
—Documented clinical experience and/or uncontrolled clinical studies
—Properly designed consumer and market research studies and surveys
—Pharmacological data obtained from scientifically designed studies in animals
—The general medical and scientific literature as well as published or unpublished laboratory or clinical data
—Experience through long use by the medical profession and/or consumers
—Common medical knowledge.

FDA quickly indicated that it would not go along with measuring drug efficacy on the basis of uncontrolled studies of any kind, or on such popularity polls as consumer acceptance surveys and long use by either physicians or patients. The agency had already fought this battle in the affair of prescription drugs, and was committed to the policy that popularity or large sales could be disastrously misleading as evidence of efficacy.

In January 1972 FDA spelled out the details of the program. It announced that the investigations would take up the products in about two dozen therapeutic classes, beginning with antacids, laxatives, cold remedies, dentifrices, antiperspirants, and sunburn lotions. Pain killers, stimulants, sedatives, and other "mood drugs" were scheduled for later examination. Optimistically, it was suggested that since the 100,000 or more products contained only about 200 or 250 active ingredients, the entire review could be completed within three or four years.[55] The Proprietary Association issued a statement that said it generally supported the plan. "We have no complaint nor suggestion on how better to do it." [56]

Most of the companies were already reconciled to the probability that some of their products would have to be dropped and some would require the omission of needless constituents or other changes in formulation. Some claims for effectiveness would need to be softened or radically changed. As a result, some firms might suffer painful though probably only brief economic trauma. But the products that were cleared, with or without change, would carry a virtual guarantee for both safety and efficacy by both the manufacturer and the federal government.

Learning from past experience, FDA officials planned the OTC hearings so that they would provide full opportunity for all interested drug experts, company representatives, and spokesmen for consumer groups to present whatever factual material they had, together with their views, opinions, and recommendations. Before the final rulings would be handed down, all interested parties would have ample opportunity to comment on the proposed drafts of the regulations, the revisions of those drafts, and even the revisions of the revisions. FDA officials as well as officials of the Proprietary Association strongly and repeatedly urged every interested party—especially representatives of the drug companies —to keep in the closest possible touch with all proceedings.

In this environment, with almost every participant anxious to give everyone his full say and eager to prevent costly, lengthy court battles, the panels began their work in relative peace and quiet. By January 1974, peace on the OTC front had not broken out, and FDA was still caught in a crossfire between consumer groups and industry representatives. This time, however, the FDA officials were not visibly shaken; most had been toughened in the earlier battles over prescription drugs.

To review the OTC products, fifteen panels of experts had already been organized and were in operation. One, concerned mainly with antacids, was nearing the end of its long investigation. This had been essentially a pilot group. It had received all the available scientific evidence, submitted a proposed monograph, published this for comment by all comers, next published a tentative final report, offered this for comment and agreed to hold public hearings if requested, and then would be ready to prepare the final monograph. Once the final version was published, the only recourse for unhappy consumers or drug companies would be the courts.

Of special strategic importance, consumer and industry representatives had been invited to participate fully in the deliberations of the panel experts, although without having any vote on the decisions. As a result, it appeared that a few OTC antacids would be forced off the market, and many or most of the others would be required to change their formulations, their labels, or both. Changes in advertising were already becoming evident. But significantly, there had been few emotional explosions.

"Everybody got gored a little," one observer said. "Nobody came out completely happy. But there wasn't the expected bitterness. I'm keeping my fingers crossed, but I think that the right tone has been set—that the process works."

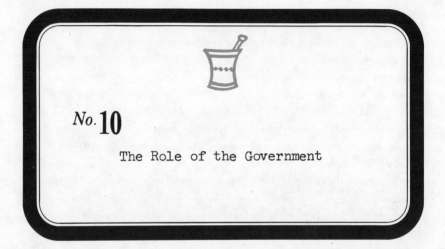

No. 10

The Role of the Government

ACCORDING to its numerous and outspoken critics, the government's record in fostering the discovery and rational use of drugs has been little better than wretched. There is, however, no agreement among these critics on the reason for reaching such a verdict.

The government has been charged, for example, with being stingy in supporting research, and with frittering away tax dollars in providing research support. It has been accused of doing too much basic research, and of not doing enough. It has been attacked for failing to pour tens of millions of dollars into a research program of interest to only a small pressure group, or to only one congressman. It has been denounced for harassing the drug industry, and for being too soft on industry; for letting unsafe drugs reach the market, and for banning useful drugs; for moving too slowly, and for moving too fast; for tampering with the freedom of the press by interfering with drug advertising, and for letting advertisers pollute the environment with misleading drug claims; for allowing drug profits to soar, and for trying to keep drug prices low; for interfering with the seemingly divine right of a physician to prescribe as he alone sees fit, and for failing to control disastrously irrational prescribing; and, in general, for being bureaucratic, vacillating, dictatorial, inconsistent, addicted to nit-picking, and basically incompetent. Because of all these sins, real or imaginary, it is claimed that the health of the public has been grievously harmed.

It is probable that this lack of unanimity among critics stems largely from the fact that there has never been widespread agreement, and perhaps never will be, on what role the government should play in the main areas concerned: drug research, drug regulation, and drug purchasing. In any consideration of this inevitably controversial subject, two points may well be kept in mind. First, since this country was created, blaming any branch of government for doing the wrong thing in the wrong way at the wrong time has remained one of the most cherished pastimes of Americans. And second, while most of the participants in this controversy proclaim their unswerving devotion to the cause of health, there is at least a slim possibility that some of them may be thinking more, although talking less, about money. As a newspaper columnist advised many years ago, "When you see a lot of folks debating with noble arguments over which policy will do most to benefit the public, you'd better look first and see which policy will do most to benefit whose pocketbook."

There is certainly no evidence, however, to indicate that governmental policies and actions in this field have done serious harm to the public. This may be because, as a commentator has noted, "God usually looks after children, drunks, and the United States of America," or because, at least some of the time, the government has done the right thing in the right way at the right time.

GOVERNMENT RESEARCH SUPPORT

By two yardsticks—the amount of money invested and the number of new drugs obtained as dividends—the federal government has apparently failed to take a leading part in supporting drug research. Where the American drug industry is now spending more than $700 million a year in research related directly or indirectly to drugs, including about $100 million for basic research, the government is spending a total of about $100 million a year. Where the industry—American and foreign—has introduced several dozen important new drugs (plus a hundred or more me-too or duplicative products) during the past decade, government-supported scientists have introduced only a dozen or less. But the impact of this tax-supported activity, involving mostly basic or fundamental studies, has been far from negligible. As industry scientists themselves have stated, without the enormous foundation of basic knowledge created with the help of government funds, government-financed screening programs, and government-developed testing techniques, the introduction of new drugs by industry—both in the United States and abroad—would have been difficult if not totally impractical.

Most of the government's drug-related research has been conducted within the National Institutes of Health, or supported by NIH grants or contracts to universities, medical schools, and other research centers.[1] To a considerable degree, such studies have made possible the development and evaluation of drugs for the control of hypertension and other cardiovascular disease, arthritis, asthma, systemic fungal diseases, congenital defects, diseases of the eye, various types of leukemia, Hodgkin's disease, choriocarcinoma, Burkitt's lymphoma, and other forms of cancer.[2] The National Cancer Institute alone has spent more than $250 million to develop a framework for research on anticancer drugs. Much of the development of drugs for the treatment of schizophrenia, depression, and other mental illness has been built on research supported by the National Institute of Mental Health. NIH research, both basic and applied, has contributed significantly to the development and evaluation of new contraceptive drugs. The development of improved drugs for the treatment of malaria and other tropical diseases, and of radiation sickness, has been aided by research supported by both NIH and the Department of Defense. Scientists at the Atomic Energy Commission's Brookhaven National Laboratory were responsible for the development of l-Dopa for the treatment of parkinsonism. Programs financed by the Public Health Service and the Veterans Administration have been vital in the mass-testing of a wide variety of drug products. In addition, primarily through support from the Public Health Service's Communicable Disease Center, the National Institute of Allergy and Infectious Diseases, and the PHS Division of Biologics Standards (transferred in 1972 to FDA and named the FDA Bureau of Biologics), government funds have been utilized to develop and evaluate improved vaccines for the prevention of mumps, measles, German measles, and various respiratory infections.

It also seems reasonable to believe that other aspects of the government's biomedical research program, now totaling about $1.5 billion a year, eventually will also have some bearing on future drug development, even though the biomedical research itself is not specifically related to drug research.

Whether the government's drug-related research is appropriate in direction and size is currently a matter of dispute. It has been proposed, for example, that NIH should restrict itself entirely to high-level, ivory-tower fundamental research, leaving drug development and testing to the drug industry and nongovernmental institutions. In contrast, it has been urged that NIH should devote far more of its activities to practical drug development—not because NIH can do the job better than industry, but presumably because NIH scientists would not waste time and money in turning out me-too products, and because government-discovered drugs could be made available without patent and at a lower price to the patient. It has also been proposed—even demanded—that NIH should embark on huge crash programs, such as $100-million-a-year projects to discover new drugs for cancer, alcoholism, or narcotic addiction. As attractive as such all-out attacks might appear, their prospects generally are dim, since the major need is not merely for money but rather for brilliant investigators with brilliant ideas.

GOVERNMENT DRUG REGULATION

Although the government's activities in the field of drug research have occasionally been the center of dispute, its actions in drug regulation—by the Division of Biologics Standards for vaccines and other biological products, and by FDA for drugs in general—have repeatedly been under far more vigorous attack. In the case of FDA, the hostilities began during the early days of the Kefauver hearings, when for the first time the Congress began to show particular interest in precisely how the agency was operating.

At that time FDA was under the direction of George Larrick, a longtime government employee who had been named commissioner in 1954. Under this leadership FDA had apparently worked with at least modest success and practically no fanfare. Only when the Kefauver investigation began was it seriously charged that, at least under Larrick's administration, FDA had worked without fanfare because it had not been doing much work at all—certainly in the case of drugs—and that the regulators had become entirely too friendly with the industry to be regulated.[3] The industry, it appeared, had been delighted to have Larrick appointed commissioner, and in 1958 the PMA had given him its award for "devoted service to the public welfare" and for "understanding our mutual problems." The Larrick regime was described in a trade journal as "one of sweetness and light, togetherness, of loving one's neighbor."[4]

This era came to an abrupt end in January 1966, when Larrick retired and was replaced by a career PHS officer, Dr. James Goddard. He stayed in office for only two and a half years. To many in the drug industry it must have seemed like two and a half centuries. It took him less than three months to signal his intentions. He appeared before a PMA convention and denounced the drug industry as suffering from a long-standing case of irresponsibility.[5] He called some companies to task for their slovenly research and misleading promotion.

Soon he took the new authority provided by the 1962 Kefauver-Harris Amendments—authority which his predecessor had never implemented in force—and put the law into effect. He and his staff cracked down on false advertising and misleading claims. They intensified the "Dear Doctor letter" approach, which required manufacturers to write every physician in the country to retract their unsubstantiated claims. They demanded that every prescription drug advertisement carry appropriate information on hazards and contraindications. They enacted regulations requiring informed consent from subjects participating in research projects. To put the new drug efficacy rules into effect, they set up the Investigational New Drug and New Drug Application programs. They arranged the contract under which the National Academy of Sciences/National Research Council would review the efficacy of drugs introduced since 1938. Dr. Goddard himself was personally villified for pointing out the dangers of LSD and other potent psychedelic drugs, for declaring that marijuana was far less dangerous to society than alcohol, and for suggesting that the current laws against marijuana use were too harsh and impractical.

Within a few months after he embarked on this multifaceted campaign, there were the first demands that John Gardner, then secretary of Health, Education, and Welfare, should fire the commissioner. Month after month, these demands became more insistent, but the secretary stood behind Dr. Goddard. "I'd rather have a man I have to slow down once in a while," he said, "than a man I have to wake up." In 1968, for reasons which have never been made public, Gardner himself resigned. Soon after, Dr. Goddard submitted his resignation. To many drug company officials, his departure was viewed as a long-awaited victory for the drug industry.

Next to become commissioner was Dr. Herbert Ley, who had been one of Dr. Goddard's right-hand men. His tenure was memorable for at least three reasons. First, it lasted for only a little more than a year. Second, during the first half of his time in office, he gave no speeches and held no press conferences. Third, it was marked by what became known as the Adriani affair.

Dr. John Adriani, professor of surgery and pharmacology at Louisiana State University, professor of surgery at Tulane, and chairman of the AMA's Council on Drugs, had long been considered one of the most eminent authorities on drugs in the United States. In addition, he had expressed his feelings that drugs should be advertised and prescribed by their generic names,[6] a view that was scarcely palatable to the brand-name drug industry. In May 1969, he later told reporters, he had been offered the post of Director of FDA's Bureau of Medicine. Three weeks after he accepted, he was notified that he was no longer being considered.

It was hardly a secret that elements of the drug industry had forcefully opposed the appointment, and one trade paper had predicted that industry opposition was so strong that Commissioner Ley "will have to . . . search for another candidate."[7] But when the offer was retracted, an official of the PMA told the *New York Times* that he was "not aware of any activity by the industry or PMA" concerning the appointment.[8] Following a time-honored tradition, Dr. Roger O. Egeberg, the HEW assistant secretary for health and scientific affairs, was tapped to be the scapegoat, and issued a press statement saying that Dr. Adriani had "exhibited poor judgment in announcing his candidacy." Dr. Egeberg assured the public that "political sensitivity and special interest groups must not and will not become factors in the selection of a Director of the Bureau of Medicine."[9]

Neither the PMA's assurance nor that of Dr. Egeberg won wide credibility. Both statements could be rated only as "possibly effective." According to the *Times*, Dr. Adriani himself had been told by one HEW official that "the pressure against his appointment from the pharmaceutical industry was too great for the Nixon Administration to withstand."

The Adriani affair in itself was probably not responsible for any major shakeup in FDA. But late in 1969, after he had become involved in the controversy over the removal of Panalba from the market and the furore over cyclamates, Dr. Ley was requested to resign. He declined, and he was fired. His successor was Dr. Charles Edwards, a Mayo-trained surgeon, one-time head of the socioeconomic department of the AMA, and later vice-president for health affairs of a Chicago management consultant firm, Booz, Allen, and Hamilton.

What he inherited was described variously as a "disaster area," an agency lurching defensively from crisis to crisis, traumatized by both internal and external attacks, downgraded by the administration, and with few supporters in industry, medicine, the Congress, and the White

House. The morale of the FDA staff dropped to a new low when the draft report of an internal study group was leaked to the press. The report concluded, "The American public's principal consumer protection is provided by the Food and Drug Administration, and we are currently not equipped to cope with the challenge." [10]

When Dr. Edwards took office, some members of his staff were circulating automobile bumper stickers reading, "Pray for FDA." The new commissioner did more than appeal to heaven. He managed to attract top new assistants to replace those who had left the agency. He succeeded in getting his budget nearly doubled, with the sum allocated for drug regulation increased from about $25 million to more than $40 million a year. "Considering that the price of drugs at the retail level is now more than $10 billion a year," he said recently, "that investment—about four hundredths of one percent of sales—must be the cheapest insurance policy around. Perhaps it's too cheap, because good science and good regulation don't always come at bargain prices." [11]

He urged strengthening of the campaign against misleading prescription drug advertising—a campaign that had visibly slowed down under his precedessor. He achieved a victory of sorts against some of his former associates at the AMA when he insisted that every package of oral contraceptive pills must carry a warning directed not to the physician but to the patient. He expressed his belief that both physicians and patients should have ready access to prescription drug prices. He demonstrated his keen interest in the problem of adverse drug reactions and admitted that industry, organized medicine, and his own agency had all failed to do an adequate job in disseminating information to physicians and patients. He tried valiantly to explain to scientists some of the harsh realities of life in a regulatory agency, and the need to make decisions sometimes on the basis of incomplete or inconclusive scientific knowledge. "There are often times," he said, "when regulation cannot wait on science—when an urgent regulatory decision must be made before all the facts are in, or before the facts are agreed upon by scientists." [12]

Dr. Edwards openly and strongly supported the expressed opinions of his staff members who claimed that much present-day prescribing is wasteful, dangerous, or otherwise irrational.[13] But the solution to the problem, he insisted, does not lie in the direction of dictating to physicians how they should prescribe.

> As I see it, our responsibility in FDA is to guarantee that no drug will get on the market—or stay on the market—unless there is adequate

evidence of its safety and efficacy, and its values and hazards are honestly and accurately described to physicians. If the doctor wants to ignore the information available to him—to use an approved drug for an unapproved use, or to use other than the recommended dosages—that's his responsibility, and the responsibility of his brother doctors. We have no thought of dictating the practice of medicine.[14]

We believe, however, that FDA should give careful consideration to proposals for guiding prescribing by creating four classes of drugs: (1) those that can be dispensed over the counter without a prescription by any vendor, (2) those that can be dispensed without a prescription, but only by a pharmacist, (3) those that can be prescribed by any physician, and (4) those that can be prescribed only by physicians who are specially trained, or who are practicing in a hospital or other approved center where they are under the surveillance of their peers.

That fourth class might well be distasteful to some physicians in the United States, although it has been established in several foreign countries, for it recognizes that not all medical men are equally competent in drug prescribing. As one medical leader noted many years ago, "Everyone with a medical degree and a license is legally entitled to do anything in medicine. Some of them are damn fools enough to try it. They harm or kill people by doing surgery for which they're not trained, giving psychiatric treatment without any experience, and prescribing powerful medicines they know little or nothing about." More recently, there has been general recognition that some forms of therapy—brain surgery, for example—should be undertaken only by experts working in a properly equipped center, and that the care of a patient with severe paranoid schizophrenia should usually be directed by a psychiatrist. It seems only logical that the administration of such potentially hazardous agents as some of the powerful new anticancer drugs should likewise be limited to qualified experts.

Early in his regime, Dr. Edwards warned that some generic-name products might be biologically nonequivalent to their brand-name competitors. Later, however, he added that there was no evidence to show that significant lack of biological equivalence among generic products was a frequent phenomenon.[15]

He urged that the details of manufacturing processes—the so-called trade secrets—submitted by a drug firm in a New Drug Application should continue to be kept secret, but that the results of all animal and human trials and similar clinical data should be made public. He expanded the use of outside experts to provide technical advice and guidance to FDA and promptly faced the charge that he was selling out to industry. It was true, of course, that many of the experts utilized by the agency—chemists, pharmacologists, physiologists, and clinicians— were also serving as consultants to drug companies, or had so served in the past. Some had received substantial research support from industry. Some were members of company boards of directors. Use of their services by the government might well be considered a serious conflict of interest.

"But here again, you've got to look at the facts of life," the commissioner said. "There are not many first-class experts in this field—not enough to go around. Naturally, industrial firms have looked to them for advice. If we refused to take advantage of their knowledge, we'd have only one other option—call on those with less experience and less knowledge. But obviously, you use your advisers to give consultation, and not to make your decisions for you." [16] Further, he noted, many of these outside advisers had been even tougher on industry than experts inside the agency.

In mid-1973 Dr. Edwards left his FDA post to become assistant secretary for health. To the amazement of many—and occasionally Dr. Edwards himself—FDA had not disintegrated. Morale had improved markedly, and the agency had rewon considerable respect. "God knows, we've made mistakes," he said, "but we must be doing something right." The agency was still hamstrung by shortages of manpower and money; to do the job it was then required to accomplish would take at least $75 million a year. It finally obtained legislative authority to get an up-to-date census of every drug on the market and its maker. It needed to solve the continuing internal debate over whether FDA should be primarily a regulatory agency—an FBI of foods, drugs, and cosmetics— or primarily a scientific agency, like the National Cancer Institute, or something in between. It needed a reduction in the demands placed on its top officials to report constantly before investigative congressional committees and defend their every day-to-day action. And before any new era of sweetness and light could dawn, a solution reasonably acceptable to all parties needed to be found for the long-playing argument over the approval of new drugs and of drug promotion.

In the matter of drug promotion and advertising, the policy of FDA was clear: the approved label (including the so-called package insert) must stand as the gospel. If a physician wanted to use the drug for an unapproved use, that would be his responsibility, but it would be the responsibility of the manufacturer to tell him in the label which uses were approved. If the manufacturer wanted to advertise or otherwise promote the product for additional applications, let him submit substantial evidence to show that it is sufficiently safe and effective for these other uses.

It is quite possible that the typical package insert is unduly complex, giving page after page of information on approved uses and all known side effects, hazards, and contraindications. Some physicians have claimed that this descriptive matter goes into such exquisite detail that they cannot find time to read it. But few doctors use more than a few score different drugs to treat most or all of their patients. Keeping up with drugs in such relatively limited numbers would not seem to be too much to ask of a physician who may hold in his power the life or death of a patient.

In the matter of approving drug advertisements before they are published, the present policy of FDA is also clear. "As desirable as such preclearance may appear," said FDA's legal counsel Peter Hutt, "it would be too cumbersome and impractical. The cost-to-benefit ratio now wouldn't justify it." [17]

As irritating as the dispute over drug labeling and promotion may be, far more noise has been generated by the controversy over the long delays—sometimes two or three years, or even longer—in getting FDA approval of a new drug. In some instances such delays have meant that a new drug will be introduced in foreign countries before it is cleared for use in the United States. It is evident that this has been irksome to the drug companies, since it has postponed the date at which they could begin recouping in the American market on their research investment, but rarely is this point emphasized. Instead, it has been charged by the drug industry and by many nonindustry scientists (some of whom work closely with industry) that the delay has created a "therapeutic gap," with foreign patients enabled to benefit more promptly from new discoveries, and with foreign companies able to challenge the preeminence of the United States in pharmaceutical developments.[18]

In 1971, for example, PMA president Joseph Stetler cited a report showing that forty-seven out of a total of eighty-four new drugs discovered by American firms since 1962 had been made available to European doctors before they could be prescribed in America. "Altogether," he said, "we find that over half of the drugs discovered in this country are not available for prescription use here until months and sometimes years after their introduction abroad." [19] But the PMA's own analysis indicated that when a product was first introduced elsewhere than in the United States, the culprit was not necessarily FDA. Some companies applied for approval first in foreign countries. Some felt that their proposed products—such as those indicated mainly for the treatment of tropical diseases—did not seem to be suitable for the American market.

More recently, such critics as Dr. Stephen DeFelice—a former medical director of Pfizer—declared that current FDA restrictions on new drug investigations have "cost the public many drugs that could have aided diseases still untreatable." [20] He offered no proof of his allegations. Economist Sam Peltzman of the University of California at Los Angeles attacked FDA for what he described as the agency's overzealous preoccupation with drug safety and asserted that on a cost-benefit basis it would be better for the public if the drug industry were left free to market its new products and take the risk of an occasional thalidomide-like disaster.[21] Another economist, Milton Friedman of the University of Chicago, wrote in a *Newsweek* column that the Kefauver-Harris Amendments must be repealed. "To comply with them," he said, "FDA officials must condemn innocent people to death. . . . Indeed, further studies may well justify the even more shocking conclusion that the FDA itself should be abolished." [22] For support he cited two drugs that were available in England but not in the United States.

A less tempestuous suggestion came from a committee of distinguished physicians and scientists headed by Dr. Robert Dripps of the University of Pennsylvania. "We have concluded that the procedures by which new drugs are evaluated and approved for use in this country [are] causing us to fall behind in this important area of medical science," the committee stated. "We believe a change in the drug regulatory system is badly needed." [23] The Dripps committee statement, which called for a careful, dispassionate review by the Congress, was promptly picked up by a number of throwaway journals, all heavily supported by drug advertising, and interpreted as calling for the demolition of FDA. Dr. Dripps said afterwards that he was appalled by such an interpretation. "We did not begin our efforts to inspire a congressional study of FDA," he said, "in order to destroy, dismember or disrupt an on-going agency." [24]

Particular attention has been focused on such drugs as lithium carbonate for the control of manic depressive psychoses (approved in this country after forty other nations had accepted it), rifampin for the treatment of tuberculosis (discovered in Italy, first sold there in 1968, introduced in England and France in 1969, and in the United States in

1971), carbenoxalone for the treatment of gastric ulcer (voted the drug of choice by British doctors but, at least by late 1973, still not approved in the United States), and fenfluramine as an appetite depressant (developed by an American firm, A. H. Robins, approved for marketing in France in 1963 and the United Kingdom in 1964, and approved in the United States only in mid-1973).

"In our opinion, positive action on the drug has been hung up on the generic question of the role of appetite suppressants in medical practice," said Dr. Frederick Clark of Robins.[25] To these and similar criticisms, Dr. John J. Jennings of FDA replied, "The primary cause of the much touted delays in FDA decision-making is beyond all question the poor quality of the data, particularly of the clinical investigations, submitted to us." [26]

The issue here is not whether there has been a relative lag in getting new drugs approved in the United States. The existence of that delay is obvious. Its painful effect in postponing lucrative American sales campaigns is equally evident. But a more important issue is at stake. Has that lag significantly harmed American patients? Has it actually resulted in needless disability and pain, in delayed recovery, in needless deaths? Is the machinery for drug approval in this country so slow, cumbersome, and inefficient that it calls for radical surgery?

"If there is evidence that American patients have been significantly hurt because they didn't have access to a new drug available first in other countries," Dr. Edwards said in 1972,

> we have not seen it. After the record of Chloromycetin misuse, the early widespread acceptance of combination antibiotics, and the disastrous thalidomide experience, we would hope that most American physicians now realize that a popularity poll—unless it's supported by substantial scientific evidence—can't necessarily be accepted as proof of safety and efficacy. Too often, we've all seen how these popularity votes can be determined and manipulated by intensive promotion campaigns. Too often, we've seen a drug widely or even universally accepted as safe, until somebody decided to study its toxicity. If other countries want to accept a drug without the evidence we demand, that's their business—but God help their patients.[27]

The tough, play-it-safe, and sometimes agonizingly slow drug approval procedures and policies of FDA have often been compared—and usually unfavorably—with the generally simpler, quicker, more relaxed, and supposedly equally safe techniques used in other countries.

To critics of FDA—and of the laws which it is required to implement—
the American system is to blame for stifling creativity, raising research
costs to intolerable levels, slowing the introduction of new drugs,
limiting the array of drugs available to physicians, interfering in the
practice of medicine, and making decisions which are too often based on
political rather than scientific reasons. As a result, it has been charged,
American drug companies are being forced to move their operations
abroad, which will result in lost American jobs; American doctors are
faced with increasing government dictation; American science is losing
out to foreign science; and, of most importance, the greater array of
drugs available to foreign physicians means that foreign medical care
may be better than American medical care. The last is a particularly
fascinating argument, since it has occasionally been voiced by the
identical individuals who declare at the same time that American
medical care is the best in the world.

To some, much of this criticism represents "merely static—the
natural reaction of the regulated to strong regulation." [28] The howls of
outrage at what are termed capricious decisions of FDA are often much
like the agonized protests of a baseball player sliding into third base who,
knowing he was out by five feet, will nonetheless argue with the umpire,
realizing full well that such histrionics are expected of him by his
teammates, his manager, his opponents, the audience, and the umpire,
too—and also realizing that the umpire will not reverse his decision on
that play but may be more charitable on the next one. FDA officials,
serving as umpires themselves, are apparently well aware of the situation,
and do not expect applause when they label some "evidence" as
inadequate.

To other observers it is noteworthy that most—though not
all—scientific journals have rarely bothered to participate in this dispute.
Detailed accounts of the attacks against FDA have been carried mainly
in throwaway publications that exist primarily on drug advertising. To
still others, the constellation of charges leveled against the agency is
reminiscent of programs carefully contrived by experienced political
public relations firms for the candidates they guide in an election, and
based on the principle *Offer something to everybody.* Thus, interference
with research may be viewed as a threat to the scientific community.
Moving drug establishments outside of the United States may be a
threat to labor unions. Raising the cost of drug development may reduce
dividends and therefore be a threat to company stockholders. Government intervention of any kind may be a threat to physicians. A hint that

foreign drug research may possibly be more productive than American research may appear as a threat to the national security of the United States. And even the suggestion that a foreign country has drugs that might possibly be more useful in the treatment of arthritis, atherosclerosis, hypertension, cancer, or old age can be virtually guaranteed to upset the millions of Americans suffering from arthritis, atherosclerosis, hypertension, or cancer, or who are getting old—and all of whom are likely to write to their congressman.

Although much criticism of the American system may be dismissed as static, there are some points that deserve further consideration. It is true, for instance, that the cost of introducing a new drug has escalated in the United States—presumably because of FDA's slowness in approving new drugs—but a British authority, Michael Cooper, has noted, "The fact that this tendency is certainly equally true throughout Europe, casts some doubt on the claim that this is the sole reason." [29]

The productivity of the American drug industry, as measured by the number of new drugs introduced annually, has dropped noticeably over the past decade or two. Yet, with the exception of Italy and Japan, the same situation has occurred in other countries. Physicians in some countries may have more drugs at their disposal than do their American counterparts, but there is no evidence that the number of available drugs—or the date at which they became available—is a yardstick of the quality of health care. For example, the numbers of drugs on the market in France and Germany far exceed those in Sweden and Holland, but there is no evidence that Swedish and Dutch patients receive medical care that is substantially less effective than that which the French and Germans receive. In fact, from our own observations, we would be inclined to rate the quality of medical care in Sweden as probably the highest in Europe.

Another aspect of this they've-got-more-drugs approach has been stressed by Paul de Haen of New York, whose periodic box score of new drugs is internationally recognized. "What is frequently forgotten," he claims, "is the fact that because of the activity of the Food and Drug Administration, the American physician is spared being confronted with the promotion of irrational drug mixtures and drugs of dubious efficacy which are marketed by the hundreds in [many] countries." He also reported that almost half of the new chemical entities that originated in England, France, Germany, and Italy were not marketed outside their "native" countries.[30] Numerous surveys have shown that many drugs introduced in England were not marketed in the United States, but at the same time many drugs introduced in Sweden were not marketed in England, many introduced in France were not marketed in Sweden, many introduced in Germany were not marketed in France, many introduced in Italy were not marketed in Germany, and many introduced in the United States were not marketed in Germany.

In 1973, when Dr. Edwards resigned as FDA commissioner to become assistant secretary for health, he was succeeded by Dr. Alexander McKay Schmidt of the University of Illinois. The latter was not visibly impressed by any "drug gap" between the United States and other countries. He said,

> I am still new in my job, and am still opening closet doors, but the evidence I have discovered to date simply doesn't support the view that Americans are being denied valuable new drugs because of FDA bumbling, procrastination, or for any other reason. I will change my mind as the facts might require, but as of now I believe that this problem—if it exists at all—is secondary to the need for wiser use of the many remarkable drugs that are now available on the American market.[31]

Unquestionably, drug makers have been able to get their products accepted in most foreign countries more easily, more quickly, and at less expense than in the United States, and the governmental requirements they faced were fewer and simpler. It has been frequently suggested, therefore, that this country might well scrap its cumbersome, time-consuming system of drug approval and instead adopt such a simple, streamlined system as that instituted in Great Britain in the early 1960s. The British method was described to American physicians in 1966 in a series of reports commissioned by *Medical Tribune* and written by Dr. Joseph Cooper, professor of government at Howard University. Labeled as a "lean and spare apparatus," the British system was based on the operations of a Committee on Safety of Drugs under the chairmanship of Sir Derrick Dunlop. Working without an elaborate structure of laws, regulations, and similar red tape, the Dunlop Committee had apparently reached an amicable voluntary understanding with the drug industry so that new drugs could be cleared for safety with a minimum of fuss and fanfare and in a fraction of the time required in the United States. In comparison with the British system, Dr. Cooper concluded, "The present FDA may be found to be an anachronism—out of tune with the decision-making needs of modern biological science."[32]

One of the most curious cases in this field—and, at least for a time, one of the most baffling—concerned a sudden and severe rise in deaths attributed to asthma. In England and Wales the asthma mortality rate had remained relatively stable for about a century. Then, beginning about 1960, the rate skyrocketed. At the peak, in 1966, it had more than tripled. Similar increases were quickly noted in other countries—Ireland, Australia, New Zealand, and Norway. In Norway the rate increased almost tenfold.

British investigators suggested that a newly introduced antiasthma product—isoproterenol marketed in an aerosol nebulizer—might be responsible, and accordingly governmental agencies moved to restrict its use. Gratifyingly, the asthma death rate promptly dropped, but still not back to preepidemic levels. "Before that, however," said Dr. Paul Stolley of Johns Hopkins, "at least 3,500 asthmatics—most of them below the age of thirty-five—died suddenly during the 1960s in Britain alone. In children between the ages of ten and fourteen, asthma had become the fourth leading cause of death. It was the worst therapeutic drug disaster on record. There's nothing else—not even thalidomide—that ranks with it." [33]

But the problem was not yet solved. Isoproterenol nebulizers had also been widely used in the United States, Canada, Sweden, West Germany, Japan, and other countries, and yet none of these nations experienced such a disaster. Why had they been spared? Dr. Stolley became involved in this mystery while he was vacationing in a small town in England and was asked to see a twenty-four-year-old asthma patient who had suffered an acute attack in church. When he arrived at the patient's house, the victim was dead—with a nebulizer clutched in his hand. Dr. Stolley decided to launch a small investigation. In 1972 he published his findings.[34]

In the United States, Canada, Sweden, and most of the other countries which had escaped the epidemic of sudden asthma deaths, he found that the products licensed for marketing contained 0.08 mg of isoproterenol per spray. In Britain, Australia, New Zealand, and Norway, a superproduct—containing five times as much, or 0.40 mg per spray—had been approved for use. (In Belgium and Holland, which also had little or no increase in the rate of asthma deaths, the potent product had also been approved but apparently was never widely prescribed.) "The evidence does not suggest that this highly concentrated isoproterenol preparation was the sole cause of the increased mortality," he concluded. "Rather, it might have contributed to the severity of the epidemic of asthma mortality in countries in which the preparation was widely used."

The affair of the isoproterenol nebulizers[35] does not in itself prove the superiority or greater wisdom of FDA. The manufacturer had never requested FDA's approval of the high-potency product. But the event does demonstrate that at least some of the highly praised drug testing systems used in other countries have had tragic defects.

To the discomfiture of those who felt that the United States should dump FDA in favor of something like the relaxed laissez-faire operation in Great Britain, it was the British who dumped their system in favor of one surprisingly like FDA. The Dunlop Committee, said a British official, had "functioned very well with the sole exception that one or two very un-English gentlemen, selling pharmaceuticals from abroad, have taken advantage of its voluntary nature." [36] For that reason, and "to some extent for administrative tidiness," the voluntary scheme was replaced by statutory controls, rules, regulations, and the inevitable red tape under the Medicines Act of 1968. Dr. Dunlop was named chairman of the new Medicines Commission established by the law. To him FDA represented a vital operation. He described it as "the premier drug regulatory organization in the world which has done so much to protect the public—and not only the public of the USA." [37]

To Dr. Mark Novitch of FDA the change in Great Britain is typical of new attitudes becoming apparent in other countries. "In these nations—Sweden, the Netherlands, Norway, Australia, New Zealand, and others—regulations have already become more strict," he says. "Legislators and government officials, backed by the medical profession, have found they cannot place full reliance on any voluntary program that depends essentially on self-regulation by the drug industry." [38]

The contributions of industry to improved methods of drug testing and quality control have been substantial, here and abroad, he told a 1969 conference, but "there remains an evident need to increase the responsibility of government to assure the safety, efficacy, and quality of marketed drugs." [39] Even in countries with less stringent requirements, Dr. Novitch says, officials freely acknowledge that they are often able to operate their streamlined systems because they can adopt as guidelines the findings of FDA on drug safety and efficacy.

The tendency of some countries to model their drug approval programs on the American system does not indicate that FDA is a model of what a governmental agency should be. There is much room for improvement in FDA operations, especially where the handling of New Drug Applications is concerned. The scientific capability of the agency, and especially of its review officers, needs substantial strengthening, and stronger ties should be forged with the National Institutes of Health, universities, research centers, and the scientific and medical communities in general. Decisions could be speeded. FDA-industry relationships could be substantially changed from the it's-them-against-us approach to more effective cooperation, and the customary delaying tactics of FDA examiners could be modified.

To a considerable extent, these delaying maneuvers—often described as nit-picking—represent the regrettable but completely understandable response of any governmental group that is constantly being badgered by industry, consumer groups, the press, and the Congress. In FDA this has led to what is known among staff members as Rule One, or PYOT—Protect Your Own Tail. "Any time you approve a new drug," says a former FDA examiner, "you're wide open for attack. If the drug turns out to be less effective than the original data showed, they can nail you for selling out to a drug company. If it turns out to be less safe than anybody expected, some congressman or a newspaper writer will get you. So, there's only one way to play it safe—turn down the application. Or at least stall for time and demand more research."

One step to correct the situation, already being implemented by the agency, is the scheduling of FDA-drug company conferences before testing begins and midway during the testing program, so that both parties are clearly aware of what the company intends to do and what FDA will demand in the way of essential evidence to demonstrate safety and efficacy. Another is a clearly defined and rigidly enforced FDA policy to give top priority in evaluating applications to those products that are urgently needed in medical practice, second consideration to those that are supported by "elegant" research—research that is well planned and well executed—and lowest priority to applications for new me-too drugs, or to low-quality research.

There is ample proof to show that FDA can move quickly when necessary. For example, although a new drug application usually requires many months or years for processing, the application for an urgently needed new oral contraceptive product—Searle's Demulen—was cleared in about ten days. The application for l-Dopa, urgently needed for the treatment of parkinsonism, went through in a few weeks.

To achieve more efficient operations, the United States should work toward reciprocity with drug-licensing bodies in selected countries, such as Sweden, Denmark, Norway, the Netherlands, and Great Britain. Consideration should be given to the possibility that not every bit of data submitted by a company should be reviewed by FDA. With companies that have established good records for reliability, it may be desirable merely to spot-check the data and call for extensive review only when the check reveals inconsistent or inaccurate statements.

A third step would be more rigorous control of private laboratories and individual investigators whose reports are submitted by drug companies as evidence. The need for such control is obvious. For example, one spot check turned up the case of an assistant professor of medicine who had reputedly tested twenty-four drugs for nine different companies. "Patients who died while on clinical trials were not reported to the sponsor," an audit showed. "Dead people were listed as subjects of testing. People reported as subjects of testing were not in the hospital at the time of the tests. Patient consent forms bore dates indicating they were signed by the subjects after the subjects died." Another audit disclosed the notable case of a commercial drug testing facility that had ostensibly worked on eighty-two drugs for twenty-eight sponsors. "Patients who died, left the hospital or dropped out of the study were replaced by other patients in the tests without notification in the records. Forty-one patients reported as participating in studies were dead or not in the hospital during the studies. . . . Record-keeping, supervision and observation of patients in general were grossly inadequate." [40]

Still another productive step would be the frank admission by FDA—regardless of any congressional or press criticism that might ensue—that the requisite safety levels of a new drug must depend on the uses for which the product is intended. For example, a drug that caused serious or even fatal side effects in one out of a hundred patients might be banned for use in the treatment of acne, athlete's foot, or the common cold, but might well be approved for treatment of bubonic plague, meningitis, or pulmonary carcinoma. There have been instances in which FDA has faced up to such realities. When, for instance, the applications for one new drug were undergoing review, it was clearly demonstrated that this agent was relatively safe for mice, rats, guinea pigs, cats, and monkeys. It would apparently be a boon for tens or hundreds of thousands of victims of a grievously incapacitating disease, no longer able to benefit from other therapy, and fated to undergo miserable months of increasing disability ending in death. Unfortunately, the drug had produced what seemed to be high blood sugar levels in two out of a large series of dogs.

One FDA scientist said, "We can't approve the drug. The company should be required to undertake another survey—at least for six months—to clarify this effect on dogs." The scientist's supervisor was somewhat exasperated. "All right," he said. "Maybe it caused hyperglycemia in those two dogs. But, for heaven's sake, there are thousands and thousands of people who could be helped by this drug. Without it, they're going to die. Whether you like it or not, I'm going to approve the application." But he added, "In deference to you, I'll put in one recommendation on the label. I'll make it read: 'Don't give to dogs.'"

Perhaps the most useful step, worthy of trial on at least a pilot basis, would be the establishment of FDA drug research and evaluation facilities in selected medical schools or other centers. "In such centers," says FDA's Dr. Novitch,

> the investigators would be working in a scientific environment. They would hold academic positions, and be able to teach and carry on their own investigations to improve drug knowledge and regulation. They would be able to consult, day by day, with their scientific colleagues. They would not, however, receive any drug company funds. An application for a major new drug could be assigned by FDA to a drug research and evaluation center for the review of specific aspects and, in some cases, confirmation of the data. We would have an opportunity to bring FDA and the medical community closer together in a way that could really improve the objectivity, the quality, and the credibility of drug reviews.[41]

Under such conditions, with each new drug assigned by FDA to a testing center on the basis of staff competence and available facilities, no investigator would be under any temptation to take questionable shortcuts, tamper with the evidence, or present conclusions that were not supported by adequate evidence. In the long run, this procedure could make testing a lot more efficient, quicker, and less costly for everybody. It might even prevent a few arguments.

GOVERNMENT DRUG PURCHASES: THE BIG STICK

It has become generally obvious that the federal government has influenced the development and use of drugs through its research activities and through the regulatory operations of FDA. What has remained unappreciated is the fact that the government can have a far more substantial impact when it acts as a drug purchaser. "This is where the government has its real muscle," an industry leader has told us. "If ever the government decides to use that power, it can revolutionize the drug business."

For many years the federal government has been the largest single buyer of drug products in the United States, and one of the largest in the world. Through its direct purchase for the military services, the Veterans

Administration, the Public Health Service, and other agencies, and its reimbursement for drugs under existing Medicaid and Medicare programs, it has been buying about 19 percent of the prescription drug industry output.[42] During the three fiscal years of 1967 through 1969, estimated annual federal expenditures for drugs climbed from $514 million to $975 million.[43]

Under Medicare, however, government payments for drugs until now have been restricted essentially to those prescribed for hospitalized patients. If that program should be extended to include all out-of-hospital drugs for the elderly, the government would be paying for an estimated 43 percent of the industry output. And if—or when—a national health insurance or health service program is enacted, and substantial drug coverage is included, the government may well be paying for 80 percent or more. In such a situation, with annual governmental drug expenditures running to $2 billion a year—and perhaps far more—it would be inconceivable for the Congress *not* to set guidelines so that the money will be expended prudently. Those guidelines may well have a massive effect on both drug prices and profits, and even on the practice of medicine and the quality of health care.

The many guideline options available for an expanded Medicare drug program were studied by the Task Force on Prescription Drugs, working under these instructions from HEW secretary Gardner:[44]

> The Task Force has no prior commitment to recommend for or against the inclusion of prescription drugs in the Medicare program. Its directive is first to investigate and then to make whatever recommendations it considers appropriate.
>
> The Task Force will examine a wide range of factors which are involved in the use of prescription drugs and will offer its recommendations within six months. The problems are numerous and complex. Some answers may be found speedily; others may take many months, possibly even years, of work, including laboratory research and clinical trials.
>
> In all of its work, I have asked the Task Force to measure the value of possible solutions not only in terms of dollars to be saved, but in the quality of health care to be delivered.

In our final report, published in 1969, we noted that the secretary had by no means exaggerated the scope and complexity of the assignment. "Inevitably," we stated,

> as formal operations were begun by the Task Force, and as additional information was requested by the Congress, it became essential to broaden

the study to cover a large number of closely interrelated factors—the use of prescription drugs by the elderly, and their ability to meet drug expenses; the health needs of the elderly; the prescribing patterns of physicians, and the sources of drug information available to them; the nature of drug manufacturing, and of drug promotion, drug pricing, and drug profits; the nature of drug distribution; the pharmacological aspects (including the hotly controversial matter of clinical equivalency); the role of formularies; the nature of current drug insurance programs, private and governmental, in this country and abroad; and the various alternatives involved in program financing, administration, reimbursement, classification, coding, and other aspects of drug insurance.[45]

Our major finding was this: *a drug insurance program under Medicare is needed by the elderly, and would be economically and medically feasible.*

The elderly—those aged sixty-five or more—were obviously in a difficult position. Although they represented a relatively small proportion of the total population, their inordinate health needs, their high health care costs in general and high drug costs in particular, and their limited financial resources combined to create a serious and sometimes a devastating medical and economic problem far out of proportion to their numbers.[46] They made up only 10 percent of the population, but they accounted for the use of roughly 25 percent of all out-of-hospital prescription drugs. It was estimated that the elderly were then receiving some 262 million prescriptions a year for out-of-hospital drugs, at a total cost of roughly $1.0 billion.[47] (In 1972 it was estimated that a comprehensive out-of-hospital drug program under Medicare could involve as many as 430 million prescriptions a year, at a total cost for the drugs of about $2 billion plus administrative costs of several hundred million dollars.[48])

In order to find ways to keep such expenditures at acceptable levels, the Task Force and its consultants examined a variety of techniques. Some of these concerned drug prices set by the manufacturer. Others concerned limiting the size and nature of the program.

In the control of drug prices, several options were open. One would be acceptance of the present pricing system, letting each manufacturer establish his own prices to the community pharmacy, hoping the manufacturer would set these prices at the "usual and reasonable" levels, and counting on normal competition to keep prices low. It was not the most attractive possibility, since the drug industry had not been particularly noted for keen price competition. A second option would be the establishment of a federal drug formulary containing only those products for which the government would approve reimbursement and which presumably would be available at relatively low prices. Such a system, involving industry-government negotiating, had already been used in such countries as Australia and New Zealand.[49] A third option would have the government serve as the legal purchaser of the drugs for all Medicare beneficiaries, and possibly for all Medicaid beneficiaries, just as it was serving for the Department of Defense, the Veterans Administration, and the Public Health Service. This would open a number of intriguing possibilities, including government purchase only on competitive bids and even government purchase in violation of patent, with the patent holder able to secure reasonable reimbursement by filing suit in the federal courts.[50] None of these methods would prevent a physician from prescribing any product he desired for a Medicare patient. If an unapproved drug were prescribed, the government would simply decline to pay for it.

In its analysis of these approaches, the Task Force said, "Prices paid for drugs must be fair both to the industry and to the taxpayer by providing for a fair profit to the drug makers without incentives for inflationary price increases to the public." [51] Here it was all too clear that if the company were forced to sell its product for Medicare patients at a minimal profit, or perhaps no profit at all, it might retaliate by skyrocketing the price to non-Medicare patients.

Other techniques were available to hold down costs by limiting the size or nature of the program, or by invoking cost-sharing methods long used by many insurance plans. One option would be the establishment of an annual deductible, with each patient required to pay for the first $50, $75, or $100 of his drug costs each year. Another would require the patient to pay a fixed amount—for example, $1.00, $1.50, or $2.00—or a fixed percentage of the cost of each prescription. Limits could be set on the size of an individual prescription, such as not more than a thirty-day supply, or on the maximum cost for any prescription.[52]

Another method, used in many private and governmental programs, would ban coverage for certain classes of drugs, such as multivitamins, antiobesity products, and antacids. In some of these other programs, tranquilizers were covered only for a patient discharged from a mental hospital and whose diagnosis of mental illness was apparently beyond question. Consideration was given to proposals that coverage be provided only for certain chronic ailments, such as arthritis, hypertension, or coronary disease, or to such specific drugs as insulin, reserpine, or prednisone, but it was suggested that these limitations would serve only as invitations to fraud.[53] It was also noted that some drug insurance programs banned the inclusion of oral contraceptives, but it was felt that this approach would not be of great significance to a Medicare population. In the application of these and similar controls, the Task Force again urged caution: "While drug program expenditures would thus be reduced, the quality of health care would suffer and costs in other parts of the Medicare program could well increase as a result of increased physician and hospital services required." [54]

Finally, there were two approaches which, used alone or together, could have the most significant impact, especially in improving the quality of medical treatment—the use of a program formulary and the implementation of utilization review. (Both of these methods are discussed more fully in chapter 13.) These are aimed not so much at preventing excessive drug costs but rather at stopping bad prescribing. They are urgently needed. If they are adopted as an integral requirement in any federal drug insurance program or health plan, the impact on the quality of health care will justify all the work it will demand.

Many of the program options studied by the Task Force were contained in proposed legislation introduced in the Congress during the past several years. By late 1973 all of these plans were still matters of heated debate. At the center of the controversy were such issues as which drugs for which diseases should be covered, price controls, the portion of each prescription cost that the patient would be required to pay, and the use of a formulary. The eventual fate of any such legislation cannot be predicted with certainty. Nevertheless, we believe that the creation of an out-of-hospital prescription drug program for Medicare patients, either as part of the Medicare program or as part of a more inclusive national health program, is now inevitable.

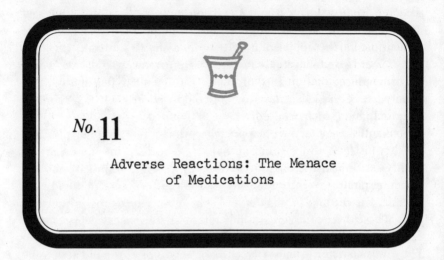

No. 11

Adverse Reactions: The Menace of Medications

I firmly believe that if the whole materia medica, as now used, could be sunk to the bottom of the sea, it would be better for mankind and all the worse for the fishes.

OLIVER WENDELL HOLMES, M.D.,
Address before the Massachusetts Medical Society, 1860

CASE: Patient, aged six, visiting San Francisco with parents. Seen in motel by physician, who diagnosed condition as streptococcal throat infection. Parents either neglected to inform physician that patient highly allergic to penicillin or were unaware of fact. Physician administered penicillin by injection. Child suffered anaphylactic shock, recovered only after intensive treatment with epinephrine and corticosteroids.

CASE: Male, aged fifty-nine, suffering from bladder infection, treated with long-acting sulfonamide. Developed well-defined skin lesions, characterized by concentric circles with hemorrhagic centers, symmetrically located over palms, soles, wrists, and ankles. Soon developed high fever, severe irritation of mucous membranes of mouth, hemorrhagic crusting on lips, irritation of eyes and nose, probably kidney damage (later diagnosed as Stevens-Johnson syndrome, or severe bulbous erythema multiforme, with reported death rate of 5 to 18 percent). Patient recovered after prolonged hospitalization.

CASE: Adult male, treated with phenylbutazone for gout. Developed generalized rash, with large layers of necrotic skin, patient acutely ill (later diagnosed as "scalded skin syndrome," Lyell's disease, or toxic epidermal necrolysis, with estimated mortality rate of about 30 percent). Patient died after prolonged hospitalization.

CASE: Hospitalized patient recovering from heart attack, stabilized on coumarin to prevent further blood clotting. Expected hospital stay, twenty-one days. On fifteenth day, given indomethacin to control arthritic pain. No change ordered in coumarin dosage. Patient suffered serious intestinal hemorrhage. Recovered and discharged from hospital on sixty-first day.

CASE: Female, aged twelve, treated with chloramphenicol for mild upper respiratory infection of undiagnosed origin. Developed aplastic anemia. Patient died.

These five cases illustrate what are now termed adverse drug reactions. Until a decade ago it was known that they could be serious, but it was commonly believed that they were so rare as to be practically insignificant. Today we realize that they occur by the thousands or tens of thousands every day.

They kill more victims than does cancer of the breast. They rank among the top ten causes of hospitalization. In the United States alone, they are held accountable for as many as fifty million hospital patient-days a year. They may interfere with diagnostic tests, causing a missed or erroneous diagnosis.

They may spare a patient's life but leave him blind or deaf, afflicted with kidney, liver, or brain damage, bone necrosis, ulceration of the bowel, intestinal hemorrhage, skin scars, extreme sensitivity to sunlight, or other disabilities that may last for months or years.[1] Only during the past ten years have we begun to recognize the magnitude, seriousness, and complexity of the problem. Today it is only too obvious that adverse drug reactions represent a major public health menace of alarming proportions.

The failure of many physicians in the past—and of some even today—to appreciate the nature of the situation has come in part from a failure to agree on a precise definition of an adverse drug reaction. In some instances, it has been held to be any reaction to a drug that is unpleasant, disabling, or deadly. According to this view, any case of diarrhea resulting from use of a laxative would, in fact, be branded as an adverse reaction. Some writers have felt that adverse drug reactions should include the unhappy results of administering the wrong drug to the wrong patient, ingesting enormous quantities of alcohol, taking huge overdoses of a barbiturate accidentally or for suicidal purposes, the "bad trips" resulting from the use of LSD and other illicit psychedelic drugs, or the addiction caused by morphine, heroin, and other narcotics.

More recently, there appears to be growing acceptance of the concept that an adverse drug reaction might well be considered to be one marked by these characteristics:

—It is adverse—that is, noxious, unfavorable, untoward, pathological.

—It is unintended or unanticipated, and not sought as a goal of therapy.

—It results from the use of a legally available drug in normal dosages, administered for the diagnosis, prevention, or treatment of a disease, or to modify bodily functions.

—It is not mild or trivial in degree, but serious enough to cause obvious disability, call for hospital admission or additional hospitalization, or require significant changes in the planned strategy of treatment.

As will be noted below, such a reaction may stem from the administration of a single drug, or of two or more drugs in combination. It may involve a prescription drug or an over-the-counter product.

The new concern with this age-old problem has stemmed mainly from two factors. First has been the realization that an unpleasant reaction seen in a patient under drug therapy is not necessarily a symptom of the disease, nor an inadvertent administration of the wrong drug or the wrong dosage, nor the underlying uncooperativeness of the patient, but instead may be caused by the drug itself. The second factor has been the rise in drug use, with more people taking more drugs than ever before. Between 1950 and 1972 the average number of prescriptions dispensed by community pharmacies alone to each man, woman, and child in this country has jumped from about 2.4 to 5.5 per year. If all prescriptions are counted, including those dispensed by hospital pharmacies, the total number is more than 2.4 billion and the average number per individual per year is close to ten.

When viewed against some two billion prescriptions a year, the occurrence of even five or ten million adverse reactions may appear to be relatively infrequent. But any event, although it involves a fraction of 1 percent of all prescriptions, that strikes millions of patients is no trivial matter.

There are other aspects which have also delayed understanding of the situation. Thus, it was difficult at first for many clinicians to link a drug applied to the skin with rare damage showing up in the kidney, or to relate a drug taken to control a kidney infection with an uncommon but devastating skin rash. Competent physicians would be alert to a reaction marked by an excessive degree of the expected response—for example, severe diarrhea caused by the customary dose of a laxative, or a profound drop in blood-sugar level caused by insulin—but they were not prepared to accept readily the possibility that a laxative could be the cause of a skin rash, hepatitis, respiratory collapse, or death, or that use of an antidiabetic agent could be associated with a higher rate of deaths from heart disease. They found it hard to understand the long time delays which were sometimes involved, as in the case of blindness that occurred many months after the use of an antimalarial or a phenothiazine tranquilizer had been terminated.[2] They were not prepared to accept the possibility that two drugs long known to work with relative safety when given alone could interact with serious or fatal consequences when given to the same patient. They were unaware that certain patients, genetically lacking a vital enzyme, could not safely take drugs that worked without danger in other individuals.

Still other elements have served to complicate matters. Because of the multitude of different drugs being taken at the same time by the same patient, it often seemed impossible to relate a drug reaction to any one product. A physician could never be certain that the patient, either in the hospital or at home, was actually taking the drug as ordered, and might be tempted to explain any adverse reaction as the result of a failure to follow directions. Adequate laboratory studies to prove or disprove a tie between drug use and reaction were usually not available. In addition, many physicians were not emotionally prepared to believe that a reaction could have been caused by a drug they had prescribed.

"Poor documentation of drug reactions has minimized the apparent frequency of drug toxicity in the United States," it has been claimed by Dr. Kenneth Melmon of the University of California at San Francisco. "Reporting in the past has relied on the volition of the physician or hospital staff; the quality of the data gathered is deplorable." Too many physicians have a low index of suspicion, he said. "A physician is naturally reluctant to think that his treatment contributes to a patient's disability. . . . Too frequently, laboratory data of new symptoms that do not 'fit' into the anticipated course of the disease are ignored." [3]

SCOPE OF THE PROBLEM

Although the magnitude of the problem remains unclear, there is ample evidence to show that it is serious. The 2.4 billion prescriptions dispensed each year to an estimated 150 million people give only one aspect of the situation. There are no reliable figures on how many people take OTC products, but the number may well equal or exceed the number using prescription drugs.

For the thirty million patients hospitalized annually, the risk of adverse drug reactions is especially great. They are relatively older than nonhospitalized patients, they are usually more seriously ill, and they are exposed to more drugs during their hospital stay. It has been estimated that of the patients admitted to the medical services of general hospitals in the United States, each will receive an average of eight or more drugs during their hospitalization. As many as 28 percent of them may suffer an adverse reaction. Perhaps 3 to 5 percent of the patients in those medical services were admitted because of adverse reactions.[4]

If admitted to the hospital for any other reason—a heart attack, a fractured leg, childbirth, or even a diagnostic procedure—a patient runs a substantial risk. In one early epidemiological study conducted in 1960, Dr. Elihu Schimmel of Yale found that of more than a thousand patients admitted during an eight-month period, 13 percent developed adverse drug reactions caused by diagnostic procedures or therapy. At least 1 percent of all admitted patients in this study died of an apparent drug reaction.[5] Complicating the situation for hospitalized patients is the fact that from 2 to 8 percent of all drug doses given in hospitals are in error—wrong drug, wrong dose, wrong route of administration, wrong patient, or failure to give the prescribed drug.[6]

In an important study undertaken by Dr. Leighton Cluff and his colleagues at Johns Hopkins Hospital in 1964, it was disclosed that 13.6 percent of patients developed "documented" or "probable" adverse drug reactions during hospitalization. About 5 percent of their patients had been hospitalized because of such a reaction, and of this group nearly a third developed an additional drug reaction during hospitalization.[7]

Drug reactions, they reported, rated seventh among all causes for hospital admission, outranking diseases of the blood system, the musculoskeletal system, the genitourinary system, and the skin. A reaction caused by an over-the-counter product accounted for about 20 percent of the cases. Among the most frequently observed reactions were nausea, vomiting, diarrhea, mental depression or agitation, low blood sugar, cardiac arrythmia, low blood pressure or shock, rashes, and bleeding disorders.[8]

The research method developed by the Johns Hopkins group, which later served as a pattern for many other studies in this country, Canada, and Europe, did not depend on the retrospective technique of reviewing hundreds or thousands of more or less complete patient records—an approach which obviously depended on the ability of a physician, nurse, or intern to detect a reaction in the first place and then on their willingness to include this possibly embarrassing information on the patient's chart. Instead, a prospective method was used, with selected samples of patients monitored daily for the occurrence of a reaction. With this approach, the odds were high that if a reaction were detected—whether or not it could be linked to a specific drug—at least the event was recorded.

In one Canadian study a survey showed that 30 percent of hospitalized patients either suffered an adverse drug reaction or were victims of an error in drug administration.[9] In another, it was reported that 18 percent of all patients admitted to the public medical wards of Montreal General Hospital developed adverse reactions, most of which either were so serious as to require specific corrective therapy and prolonged hospitalization or resulted in death. Nearly 7 percent of all entering patients had been admitted because of a serious drug reaction.[10]

A detailed five-hospital study in Boston conducted by Dr. Hershel Jick and his associates found about 31 percent of all hospitalized patients on the medical wards suffered adverse effects that were probably or definitely drug-related. In four-fifths of the cases the reaction was rated as moderate or severe.[11]

Using a different approach, Dr. Jan Koch-Weser and his colleagues at Massachusetts General Hospital found that most cases of adverse reactions were of little clinical significance. Only 5.3 percent of the drug-reaction patients showed any residual effect when they left the hospital, and few of them suffered permanent damage. Yet in the case of 20.3 percent of these patients, hospitalization was significantly prolonged.[12]

An apparently contrasting situation was found in a five-hospital study in Philadelphia, with hospital-acquired adverse drug reactions reported to strike less than 1 percent of the patients. All patients—not merely those on the medical services—were studied. In this investigation, however, an adverse drug reaction was defined as "a response to a drug that is unintended and undesired by the physician who prescribed it, and which is severe enough to be commented upon in the progress notes." [13] A later study in one of the cooperating Philadelphia institutions disclosed that most physicians were putting into the patient's record only a small fraction of the adverse reactions they had actually observed.[14] Here, it seems painfully evident that "if you don't look for an adverse drug reaction, you won't see it; if you see it but don't report it, nobody can count it; and if you're apprehensive about a possible malpractice suit, you may be tempted to ignore the whole thing." [15]

One of the major reasons for the high rates reported in most of these surveys is the relatively large number of drugs administered to hospitalized patients, with a clear relation between the numbers of drugs given and the adverse drug reaction rates. Thus, Dr. Cluff noted in his studies[16] that the rate of these reactions was 4.2 percent among patients receiving fewer than five drugs but 45 percent in patients using twenty-one or more drugs. In one drug reaction case fifty-two different drugs were prescribed for the same patient—"which," he said later, "I think is a little hard to justify."

In a recent report covering a six-year study of 11,526 patients in nine hospitals, an adverse reaction either caused or strongly influenced hospital admission in 3.7 percent of the patients. In all patients the adverse drug reaction rate was 28 percent, but only 10 percent of the reactions were classified as of serious proportions. Approximately 1.2 percent of the adverse reactions resulted in death.[17]

A particularly disquieting report from six cooperating hospitals indicated that the rate of fatal hospital-acquired drug reactions in all *medical* patients was 0.44 percent. Patients admitted to the hospital because of an adverse reaction or who suffered such a reaction while being treated in the surgical, pediatric, obstetrical, or other wards were not included. If this figure of 0.44 percent were applied to all patients admitted to all hospitals in the United States—a total of about 32 million admissions per year—it would indicate an annual total of more than 130,000 deaths.[18]

The cost of adverse drug reactions in hospitalized patients is not easy to measure. Thus far, it has proved difficult to place a price tag on the additional physician services that may be required, the additional laboratory services, the additional costs for drugs used to control a drug reaction, the loss of wages by the patients, the pain, the disability, and the temporary or permanent tissue damage. No exact price can be placed on the estimated 130,000 deaths caused annually by adverse drug reactions. In 1970 Dr. Donald Brodie, of the National Center for Health Services Research and Development, stated that the annual costs of these reactions are in excess of $1 billion.[19] More recently, Dr. Melmon noted that a drug-reaction patient would be hospitalized approximately twice as long as a comparable patient with the same disease but without a reaction. "The economic consequences are staggering," he said.

"One-seventh of all hospital days is devoted to the care of drug toxicity." He estimated the extra room-and-board charge for hospital care, using a base of about $60 a day, at $3 billion.[20] If it is assumed that the hospital treatment of drug reactions involves a minimum of fifty million patient-days per year, at an average charge of $90 a day, the cost to patients, third-party agents, or taxpayers merely for hospital room and board would be at least $4.5 billion a year.

Not all of this expenditure is avoidable or preventable. Some adverse drug reactions occur as an inescapable aspect of the last-ditch therapy of cancer and similar diseases. In such instances, the chance of drug-induced disease is one of the risk-to-benefit decisions which a physician must make in planning any therapeutic strategy. "Some adverse reactions to drugs are the price of progress in effective drug therapy," it has been emphasized. "Regrettably, however, today's sum total of drug-induced disease greatly exceeds the irreducible minimum. . . . All of us have seen too much serious illness from drugs for which the patient had no real need." [21]

What transpires outside a hospital is not well known. If a patient suffers a serious drug reaction but does not appear at a hospital or even mention it to his physician, the incident will remain unknown to any researcher collecting data. Even if the patient does describe the event to his physician, but the latter fails to report it, no one else will be aware of the reaction.

Nevertheless, some significant information is available. For instance, in 1953 Dr. Gerald Jampolsky surveyed the use of penicillin among a randomly selected group of outpatients at the Stanford University Hospital, and found that more than 50 percent of the individuals had received penicillin (almost 20 percent for treatment of the common cold) and almost 10 percent had developed a rash following use of the drug.[22]

In a study at the University of Florida Medical Center at Gainesville, Dr. Henry Meleney and Dr. Mary Lynn Fraser reported that 37 percent of five hundred outpatients interviewed had noted a drug reaction some time in the past. Most frequently blamed were penicillin (sixty-two of the patients afflicted), a sulfa-drug (thirty-four patients), codeine (eighteen patients), tetanus antitoxin (thirteen patients), and aspirin or an aspirin-like product (thirteen patients).[23]

The exposure of this group of five hundred patients to drugs was probably not unusual. They took a total of 1,776 drug products—an average of about 3.6 apiece—in the two months before their examination. Of the 497 different drugs taken by the group, only 67 percent had been prescribed by a physician. The largest number taken by any individual was 16. Only 9 percent reported they had taken no drugs during the two-month period under study. The investigators came to this conclusion:

> Although the results of this study, except for the observation of adverse reactions at the time of admission, are dependent solely on information furnished by the patients, it is felt that they present a reasonably accurate picture of drug usage by the clinic population and of the experience of this group with adverse drug reactions. With the rapidly increasing availability of new therapeutic agents, their combination under slightly differing trade names and their promotion by advertising and salesmanship, a bewildering proliferation of chemotherapy is developing. This continuing trend deserves a warning that the benefits to the patient may be more than offset by the danger of adverse reactions as well as by the increasing cost of therapy.

The economic costs of these out-of-hospital reactions are also difficult to assess. Even with a severe reaction, the patient may not seek medical care. He may continue to work. But it seems reasonable to suppose that, if a million or more drug-reaction victims are hospitalized each year, then at least several million others are stricken but stay at home or visit a physician in his office. Many of them undoubtedly lose days or weeks of pay, or function with reduced efficiency. Among dermatologists, for example, there are many who believe that half the patients in their waiting rooms are there because of a drug reaction.

Of the very large number of serious adverse drug reactions, which may be estimated to total more than five million and perhaps as many as ten million a year, about 20 to 30 percent seem to be acts of God. At the present state of knowledge, no one can easily foresee the first time a patient will show an allergic reaction to penicillin (although the second time should be readily predictable). No one can predict that a newly developed drug will cause a reaction that had never before been reported. It is difficult to predict a long-delayed response that will appear only after a drug has been used for many years. It is likewise difficult to predict a drug-induced genetic change that will appear only in the next generation. Nevertheless, even though the state of knowledge in this field is imperfect, one fact seems clear: from 70 to 80 percent of these reactions could have been predicted, and most of these might therefore have been prevented.[24]

THE PATIENTS AT RISK

Although the frequency of adverse drug reactions cannot yet be calculated with any precision for the population as a whole, certain groups seem to run an inordinate risk. To a considerable extent, the explanation seems apparent—the more drugs used, the greater the danger.

The elderly, those aged sixty-five or more, are in a more hazardous state than younger adults, at least in considerable part because their per capita consumption of drugs is more than double that of men and women under the age of sixty-five. Perhaps for the same reason, the rate for women is greater than that for men, and is especially high for older women.[25]

In the presence of certain chronic diseases, drug metabolism may be substantially modified. Thus, as a Temple University study showed, when kidney function is impaired, the rate at which a drug is excreted from the body may be slowed and dangerously high concentrations may be built up in the tissues.[26] The presence of gastrointestinal disease, liver disease, acute or chronic infection, allergies, and a previous history of adverse drug reactions should alert a physician to the possibility that a drug may react in bizarre and unpredictable ways.

Alcoholism, one of the most widespread and serious chronic diseases, poses still another prescribing problem and a special risk to the patient who both drinks and takes medication. When imbibed in large quantities, alcohol inhibits the metabolism of other drugs in the liver, often with dire results. Dr. Emanuel Rubin and Dr. Charles Lieber have stated:

> The high incidence of alcoholism, and the fact that many alcoholics are not recognized as such, magnify the importance of this problem. More than half of the fatal automobile accidents in the United States directly involve intoxicated drivers, many of whom may suffer from a synergism between alcohol and other commonly ingested drugs such as barbiturates and tranquilizers. An interaction between alcohol and other drugs may also contribute to accidental or suicidal deaths in individuals who have consumed barbiturates while they were inebriated. Indeed, more alcoholics die from drug intoxication than from acute alcohol intoxication.[27]

Although children generally use drugs far less often than their elders, they present another set of complex prescribing problems.[28] Some drugs, for example, are far more toxic in newborns than in adults, while others are safer. Drug absorption is usually more rapid in very young children, but drug metabolism and excretion may be slower than in adults. There may be significant differences in the rate at which drugs pass from the blood into the brain. A drug that has no influence on the skeletal and sexual systems of an adult can have a catastrophic effect on the developing skeletal system and sexual organs of a child.

Still other hazards may come from genetic deficiencies. For example, it has been demonstrated that 10 to 15 percent of black males develop hemolytic anemia following the use of primaquine, sulfa-drugs, or phenacetin—the result of a genetic lack of an enzyme, glucose-6-phosphate dehydrogenase. Patients with porphyria, an inborn error of metabolism, may have acute attacks of the disease precipitated by the use of barbiturates.

In recent years, particularly, concern has been expressed over the use of apparently benign drugs in pregnant women. Malformation or death of the unborn child has been associated with the mother's use of such products as barbiturates, opiates, anticoagulants, sulfa-drugs, streptomycin, antithyroid agents, some antihistamines, and excessive quantities of Vitamin C and Vitamin K. "Unless a drug is urgently needed," it was recommended by *The Medical Letter*, "it should not be administered during pregnancy, especially during the first trimester or close to the time of delivery." [29] Dr. Edward Quilligan of the University of Southern California estimated that 90 percent of the drugs now given pregnant women should probably not be used except in cases of extreme urgency.[30]

A list of the tissues, organs, and functions which can be damaged by drug reactions in these high-risk groups would be a catalogue of practically all the parts and functions of the body, from bones to brain and from digestion to sex drives.

In recent years particular attention has been directed toward adverse drug reactions involving the skin, the organ which is often held to be a mirror reflecting changes in other parts of the body. Some of these dermatological reactions involve only the skin, while others are a manifestation of a serious systemic disorder. Certain of these skin reactions may result from irrational prescribing by physicians, or their failure to warn patients to stop treatment and call for immediate help if any reactions occur. But many are the result of irrational self-medication by patients. Dermatologists are well aware of patients who treat a seemingly minor skin ailment—for example, a poison oak or poison ivy irritation, or impetigo—with a "healing" ointment, prescription or nonprescription, only to find that the condition becomes worse, where-upon they daub still more of the preparation on the afflicted area, which apparently results in still more irritation, which they treat with still more medication. Other patients develop a skin reaction after use of a laxative, and for some incredible reason they blame this on constipation and treat it with more doses of the same laxative.

The majority of patients, and apparently many physicians, seem inclined to dismiss adverse drug reactions involving the skin as irritating, uncomfortable, or at the worst temporarily disfiguring. There appears to be little realization that some of these reactions may lead to death. At Stanford, Dr. Eugene Farber and Dr. Fred Rosewater have noted that at least six drug-induced reactions are important to dermatologists.[31] These include allergic urticaria secondary to anaphylaxis, Stevens-Johnson syndrome, Lyell's disease, exfoliative dermatitis, allergic vasculitis, and drug-induced lupus erythematosis. All can cause death.

A list of drugs responsible for disabling or fatal reactions would encompass virtually every drug product legally on the market, and some that are available only illegally. With few if any exceptions, any drug that will influence living tissues can also damage those tissues. Most frequently implicated in adverse reactions resulting in hospitalization are digoxin, aspirin, prednisone, warfarin, and guanethidine, one survey indicated. The drugs most commonly causing adverse reactions in hospitalized patients were headed by heparin, prednisone, spironalac-tone, hydrochlorothiazide, digoxin, and neomycin.[32]

In the past, many a physician prescribed a drug on the comforting basis that "it may not do any good, but it won't hurt you." Some physicians still do. But in this direction lies potential disaster. In this connection, a number of products deserve special consideration: the antibiotics, among the most widely prescribed and probably most widely misprescribed of all drugs; the psychoactive products, both prescription and nonprescription; digitalis; and aspirin.

THE TROUBLE WITH ANTIBIOTICS

Prescribed for 20 to 40 percent (depending on the season) of all hospitalized patients, antibiotics represent one of the most popular of all drug groups. The rationale of this popularity has been seriously questioned, notably the use of these sometimes hazardous agents for treatment of the common cold and similar trivial infections, and their increasing use as a preventive in patients about to undergo simple, uncomplicated surgery. Dr. Leighton Cluff testified:

In the surveillance of the use of antibiotics at the Johns Hopkins Hospital in the months of December and January, it is not at all uncommon for 40 percent of the patients in the hospital to receive at least one antibiotic, and it is inconceivable to me, because one of my major interests is infection, to believe that 40 percent of the patients in the hospital require an antimicrobial drug. . . . I think that there is no question but that these drugs are . . . used excessively.[33]

The massive application of antibiotics has long been a matter of wonder and irritation to experts on infectious disease. In 1971 about 2.4 million kilograms of antibiotics—roughly 26,400 tons—were produced in the United States and certified for distribution by FDA. This is the equivalent of some ten billion doses, or enough to supply fifty doses per year for every American. In that same year, physicians wrote 160 million antibiotic prescriptions, an increase of 35 percent over the preceding four years.[34]

When utilized appropriately, antibiotics have clearly served as some of the most valuable drugs ever discovered. Their record in controlling a wide variety of once disabling or even fatal diseases has been thoroughly documented. Equally well documented but apparently unappreciated by many patients and physicians alike is the fact that no antibiotic—in fact, no antibacterial substance of any kind—can be accepted as completely safe. In his authoritative *Diseases of Medical Progress*, Dr. Robert Moser has discussed the seemingly limitless complications that have followed twenty years of "antibiotic abandon." [35] They have caused illnesses more severe than the diseases they were intended to combat. They have directly led to kidney, gastrointestinal, pulmonary, liver, and nervous system destruction, and to disfiguring, disabling, and sometimes lethal skin reactions. They have injured the bone marrow—here chloramphenicol is the most renowned offender—and have caused aplastic anemia, agranulocytosis, hemolytic anemia, and other blood dyscrasias, which sometimes are fatally irreversible. They have triggered serious anaphylactic or other allergic responses, including asthma, serum sickness, and skin disorders.

In many instances they are administered to manage the common cold, influenza, virus pneumonia, and other virus infections of the upper respiratory tract, in which they are useless. Frequently the justification for their use is said to be preventive, but such prophylaxis may subject the patients to superinfection and other adverse effects, with little prospect of success in averting infection. Often this application wipes out susceptible organisms and leaves the patient unprotected against infections by fungi or previously benign bacteria. Bacterial mutations are encouraged, and the development of antibiotic-resistant strains is fostered. In combination with steroids, antibiotics can cause a proliferation of fungi which may produce a disseminated fatal infection. It has been estimated that from 2 to 7 percent of hospitalized patients receiving antibiotics will develop a serious or even deadly superinfection.[36]

Of special ecological importance, antibiotics can indirectly upset the balance of microorganisms—to most of which we have become resistant over the centuries—not only in an individual but also in a ward, a hospital, or an entire community. Dr. James Philp has accordingly noted that antimicrobial agents are among the most dangerous environmental pollutants. "Unfortunately," he said, "the full impact of this is seldom felt by the prescribing physician, who is not only a prime polluter but also is in a key position to minimize the dangers." [37]

The problem of safe antibiotic therapy and the proper approach to antibiotic prescribing have been well summarized by two eminent pharmacologists, Dr. Louis Goodman and Dr. Alfred Gilman:

> The fact that harmful effects may follow the therapeutic or prophylactic use of antibiotics must never discourage the physician from their administration in any situation in which they are definitely indicated. It should, however, make him very careful in their use when they are required, and very hesitant to employ them in instances in which indications for their application are either entirely lacking or, at most, only suggestive. To do otherwise is to run the risk, at times, of converting a simple, benign, and self-limited disease into one that may be serious or even fatal. It must always be kept in mind that the use of any powerful therapeutic agent is accompanied by a calculated risk. The antibiotics are no different; to be concerned with only their potential dangers is no less unrealistic and unwise than to accept them as universally applicable, completely benign, and entirely harmless.[38]

THE TROUBLE WITH PSYCHOACTIVE DRUGS

Since its inception, the human race has been plagued by emotional or sociological problems that may be divided into four major groups: those that can be solved with reasonable ease, those so incapacitating that they require intensive psychotherapy, those that are insoluble but relatively unimportant, and, of particular interest, those that are insoluble but seriously frustrating. To cope with this last group, man has developed a limited number of procedures. A truly adult individual will recognize that the problem exists, and that it is insoluble; he will probably say, "The hell with it," and go on to something else. Tragically, very few of us can follow such an approach, and most will need to find a suitable crutch of one kind or another.

Over the past several hundreds or thousands of years not many suitable crutches for this purpose have been found. Some cultural groups have turned to the excessive use of alcohol. Some have turned to narcotic drugs. Some have turned to excessive eating, as in the accepted admonition, "You've got troubles? So take a little chicken soup." Some have turned to sexual excesses—"You have a problem? Take a new lover." Some have turned to excessive religious activities. Since the mid-1950s, however, especially in Western Europe and the United States, a new escape route has won popularity—the use of such legally available psychoactive drugs as sedatives, tranquilizers, antidepressants, stimulants, and antitension remedies.

To some clinicians and pharmacologists the utilization of psychoactive agents represents a highly satisfactory if temporary solution. These drugs are not illegal, immoral, or fattening. They enable many patients to live with such problems as an unhappy marriage, a frustrating job, the fear of getting a tooth extracted, a snub at the country club, the generation gap, racism, pollution, and war. They help frantic mothers cope with young children who insist on behaving like children. They let many individuals stay awake all day and sleep all night. They serve as an antidote to emotional tension—as if emotional tension always calls for an antidote. They alleviate depression. In some cultures or subcultures, their use serves as a mark of belonging. They can bring peace and tranquility to a household, a schoolroom, an old people's home, a psychiatric institute, an entire hospital ward. Such a result may be viewed as a blessing by parents, teachers, nurses, hospital attendants, and other caretakers, but the value to the children or patients concerned may be seriously questioned.

To a considerable number of physicians the very act of prescribing one of these mood-altering agents—even though it is not clearly indicated—brings satisfaction. It represents a positive act that supports their image in their patients' eyes—and in their own—as a healer, and may also be justified by the attitude that it may not help but it probably won't hurt.

But the prescribing of psychoactive drugs is not without hazard. It may lead to the dangerous belief that one of these agents not only will alleviate the symptoms for a brief period, but will actually solve the woes, griefs, and problems of everyday living. The attitudes surrounding the prescribing and use of these drugs can easily lead to a way of life based on the conviction that all personal and interpersonal relations can be readily and safely regulated by chemistry. The admittedly dramatic effects of the psychoactive drugs have certainly played a role in their abuse. It is noteworthy that the majority of patients brought to a hospital for detoxification are victims not of such illicit drugs as LSD, heroin, or marijuana, but of amphetamines, barbiturates, and tranquilizers.[39]

These agents have similarly been implicated in still other adverse reactions. One of the first tranquilizers, reserpine, induced a suicidal depression so often that its use in the treatment of emotionally disturbed patients had to be radically curtailed. Amphetamine produces not only dependence or addiction but interference with blood-cell production and mental changes that are clinically indistinguishable from paranoid states.[40] Although the accepted indications for this drug have now been limited to its use mainly in narcolepsy, as a central nervous system stimulant for the treatment of some hyperactive children, and possibly the short-term treatment of obesity, it still is widely used for long periods—partly as the result of pressure from patients—for conditions in which it is irrational and unsafe.[41] No one knows how many of the prescribed doses of amphetamine find their way into illegal channels, but some have estimated that as much as 50 percent reaches the black market.[42]

With such widely used tranquilizers as chlordiazepoxide (Librium) and diazepam (Valium), there may be reactions like jaundice and other signs of liver damage, blood dyscrasias, blurred vision, hallucinations, changes in blood clotting, nausea, constipation, a drop in blood pressure, skin eruptions, excessive stimulation, and acute rage. There may be physical or psychological dependence, and termination of treatment may be marked by convulsions and other withdrawal symptoms. One of the serious consequences of the widespread use of phenothiazine tranquilizers such as chlorpromazine for the long-term treatment of the mentally ill, particularly in mental hospitals, nursing homes, and similar institutions, has been the occurrence of tardive dyskinesia in many patients.[43] Not only does this have devastating physical consequences for the victim—uncontrollable, involuntary movements of tongue, lips, hands, and even the entire body—but it also markedly affects interpersonal relationships.

Barbiturates can induce skin rashes and a variety of other unpleasant adverse reactions. In some patients they can lead to serious or fatal respiratory or circulatory collapse. All of them are believed to be potentially addictive.

The use of such antidepressants as imipramine (Tofranil) has been associated with such effects as dizziness, nausea, vomiting, agitation or manic episodes, hallucinations, tremor, low blood pressure, skin rashes, depression of blood-forming tissues, and epileptic-like seizures. Imipramine was one of the drugs—the others were methylphenidate (Ritalin) and dextroamphetamine (Dexedrine)—that were reportedly administered to roughly 5 to 10 percent of the 62,000 grade school children in Omaha who were identified by their teachers as "hyperactive" and "unmanageable."[44] Imipramine also figured in an advertising campaign directed to physicians which was based on this message:

"Dear Doctor: For parents, inability to communicate with their children is a significant loss. The 'What did I do wrong' lament of the parent may be accompanied by feelings of incapacity, inferiority, guilt, and unworthiness. Many may, in fact, be suffering from symptoms of pathological depression. What can Tofranil, imipramine hydrochloride, do for your depressed patient?"

Currently, about 17 percent of all prescriptions—roughly one in six—calls for a psychoactive drug.[45] Some workers estimate that the ratio is closer to 20 percent or more. Moreover, many of these drug orders call for 800, 1,000, 1,200 or 1,500 capsules or tablets at a time. These are presumably aimed at controlling emotional problems. The disabling nature of many such problems may clearly justify a call for help. But in many cases, they do not seem to call for medical help. A prescription for a mood-altering drug can provide relief for awhile, but at a price that does not seem justifiable. That drug companies have participated in promotional campaigns to encourage the use of their products to solve common emotional problems may be understandable. After all, as one drug promotion expert has indicated, the sale of psychoactive drugs has become very big business indeed. Patients have waged their own campaigns, requesting or even demanding prescriptions for psychoactive drugs, often as a means of legitimizing their complaints. But that physicians have allowed themselves to be swayed by such campaigns is exceedingly difficult to condone. On the other hand, it must be recognized that some psychiatrists and other mental health workers believe that psychoactive drugs are underused rather than overused.[46]

THE TROUBLE WITH DIGITALIS

Among the most valuable of all therapeutic agents, digitalis and such other drugs as digoxin, digitoxin, and their chemical relatives are used daily by several million Americans for the treatment of cardiac failure and abnormal cardiac rhythms. They are also among the most dangerous of all drugs. There is only a narrow margin of safety between the effective dose and the toxic dose. The therapeutic level is 60 percent of the toxic level.[47] The toxic level, moreover, may vary considerably between one patient and another. It may vary in any one individual from time to time. Absorption may be radically changed by a number of different diseases also afflicting the patient.

For these reasons, finding the right dose of digitalis for the right patient—and modifying it correctly and promptly when necessary—represents one of the more difficult of all pharmacological balancing acts. The physician must constantly bear in mind that patients needing digitalis may be seriously and chronically ill. Many cannot function adequately without medication. For some the only alternative to the continued use of digitalis is death.

For these reasons, and others, the number of adverse reactions caused by digitalis products is high. Studies have shown that 21 percent of all in-hospital adverse drug reactions have been caused by these drugs, and in nearly one-third of these the reaction was fatal.[48] Other investigations have revealed that from 20 to 25 percent of all hospital patients taking digitalis show signs of toxicity, and one author has declared that "digitalis toxicity appears to have reached epidemic proportions." [49]

Various factors have contributed to this situation. Some overzealous physicians have exceeded the recommended dosages of digitalis.[50] Some have placed their patients on rigidly predetermined dosage schedules, neglecting to determine through appropriate observation and tests whether such a schedule is actually correct for an individual patient. Many have failed to recognize that more lives are lost from overdosage than from underdosage. There has been, as one authority put it, a lack of prudent and mature judgment of the clinical problem at hand.[51]

The trouble with digitalis is intensified when the cardiac patient is simultaneously treated with mercurial or thiazide diuretics to enhance the excretion of excess salt and water and help combat hypertension. These drugs may also induce the secretion of potassium salts from the body, and lead to low blood-potassium levels. With low blood-potassium levels, the rate of adverse reactions to digitalis becomes even greater. Accordingly, physicians have long been advised to see that their patients who are treated simultaneously with a digitalis-like product and a diuretic are given protection with supplemental potassium salts. For one reason or another, too often the advisory message to prescribers has not gone through. Of patients taking both digitalis and a diuretic, from 17 to 35 percent are stricken by an adverse drug reaction.[52]

One possible explanation was revealed in a 1971 California survey which showed that of sixteen hundred patients treated with both digitalis and a diuretic, slightly more than 72 percent were not given a prescription for the recommended potassium supplement.[53] "Under these circumstances," said Marcel Laventurier, who conducted the survey, "the reported occurrence of an adverse reaction in only 35 percent of such patients must be looked upon as a miracle."

Recognition of the problem by physicians and patients, with meticulous attention to details of management, are the keys to reducing digitalis intoxication to the lowest possible level.

THE TROUBLE WITH OTCs

It has already been noted (see chapter 9) that over-the-counter drugs, or OTCs, are relatively safe—although relative to what has never been completely clarified—but they are not entirely safe. Adverse reactions to these products, obtained without a prescription and most often used without a physician's knowledge, have been held responsible for about one-fifth of all drug-caused hospitalizations.[54] The OTC reactions that are not sufficiently serious to require hospitalization but are severe enough to cause significant tissue damage and disability undoubtedly number in the millions each year. Most frequently incriminated have been headache remedies and other analgesics, laxatives, and antacids, not necessarily because they are peculiarly dangerous but because they are so widely used.

Particularly important is the case of aspirin, which many people seemingly believe can be swallowed frequently and in enormous quantities without any danger. In fact, aspirin is responsible for 5 percent of all fatal poisonings in the United States each year and for 15 percent of all poisoning deaths of children aged five years or less.[55] When taken in nonlethal but nonetheless excessive amounts, this drug can interfere with the body's blood-clotting mechanism, damage hearing, cause cardiac difficulties and have a devastating effect upon the gastrointestinal tract. According to Dr. René Menguy of the University of Chicago, one out of every seven patients brought to hospital emergency rooms with massive stomach bleeding can trace their trouble to indiscriminate use of aspirin. In his opinion, anyone who takes even eight to ten aspirin tablets a week is inviting damage to the lining of his stomach, and accordingly there may be grounds for reclassifying aspirin as a prescription drug.[56]

In the same way, Dr. W. A. Bleyer and Dr. R. T. Breckenridge of the University of Rochester have found that aspirin taken by a woman during the last three weeks of her pregnancy can result in bleeding problems in her newborn child.[57] Research at the Merck Institute for Therapeutic Research and other centers has demonstrated that aspirin can interact dangerously with other drugs, blocking the action of anti-inflammatory agents used in the treatment of arthritis, stepping up the action of anti-blood-clotting drugs, blocking the sedative effect of phenobarbital, interfering in the action of gout remedies, and producing dangerously low blood-sugar levels in patients using oral antidiabetic drugs.[58]

The adverse reactions caused by OTC products are presumably infrequent, but no risk that disables or endangers hundreds of thousands or millions of victims a year can be ignored. In this case, little can be accomplished by educating and alerting physicians, since they are usually unaware of the nonprescription products being ingested by their patients. The companies that manufacture OTCs could place greater stress on these dangers in their labels and advertising, but this approach has not been greeted with any enthusiasm by the drug companies. "Is it reasonable to emphasize such a possible risk when it occurs perhaps five or ten times out of a thousand?" an official of the Proprietary Association has asked. "Probably all you'd do would frighten a lot of people from taking a drug that could be of benefit to them."

Further, is it reasonable to single out drug advertising—along with cigarette advertising—as the only promotional campaigns that must carry appropriate warnings? Should automobile advertisements that describe the power, economy, and sleek lines of a new car be required to mention also the fact that the engine may drop out? Should travel advertisements extolling the beauty and glamor of some tropical paradise be required to note that visitors will be exposed not only to beauty and glamor but also to typhoid fever and amebic dysentery? And should every bottle of liquor be required to carry a label statement indicating that ingestion of the contents may lead to intoxication, liver damage, and alcoholism?

Perhaps the most effective step could be taken by clinically oriented pharmacists, especially if they keep adequate patient records and are willing to devote time to keeping every patient posted on the proper use and potential dangers of any drug, prescription or nonprescription. Or perhaps all people, starting in early childhood, could be educated to treat every drug with the care and caution it deserves.

THE TROUBLE WITH DRUG INTERACTIONS

All medical men are aware, or at least should be, that two or more different drugs administered to the same patient may interact to cause one kind of reaction or another. Sometimes this interaction may be intended and beneficial, producing desired results that no individual drug can yield. Thus, triple-sulfas—sulfadiazine, sulfamerazine, and sulfamethazine—have won an accepted role in treating many infections. Two steroid hormones have been successfully combined to serve as an effective oral contraceptive.

But sometimes the interaction may be unintended and far from beneficial. One drug may react chemically with another. One may have an effect on the rate of absorption, metabolism, or excretion of another—thus giving what may be dangerously high or low blood levels—or it may alter the action of the second drug on the target tissues or organs. In some instances the result may be an additive effect, as when three different physicians prescribe three different tranquilizers—each in the standard dosage—for the same individual, each physician unaware that his colleagues were also treating the patient.

In other cases the result may be an antagonism or blocking of one drug by another. Typical is the instance in which a patient being treated with tetracycline to combat an infection is also given an antacid containing calcium, magnesium, or aluminum for indigestion. These metallic substances block the absorption of tetracycline and render it ineffective. In still other cases there is a potentiating effect. Thus, a patient given a standard dose of an anti-blood-clotting agent together with an antiarthritis remedy may develop a serious or fatal hemorrhage.

Strangely, the seriousness and extent of many of these interactions remained virtually unknown for many years. In the case of the dangerous interactions between the coumarin anticoagulants and phenobarbital, for example, Dr. Jan Koch-Weser of Harvard has pointed out that these unhappy phenomena escaped detection for fifteen years while the two drugs were used together, and another ten years passed before the importance and mechanism of the reaction was understood.[59] The morbidity and mortality due to the interaction during the many years before its clinical recognition, he said, must have been tragically high. Largely because of the reports by Dr. Koch-Weser and such other writers as Dr. Eric Martin[60] and Dr. Michael Crick,[61] the attention of the medical profession has finally been drawn to this long-ignored problem. The American Medical Association, in its recently established *AMA Drug Evaluations*,[62] has given it special attention, and physicians are now being alerted to the hazards involved.

Although any drug may conceivably interact with any other, the most frequently involved products seem to include barbiturates, sulfa-drugs, oral antidiabetics, digitalis and related cardiac drugs, monoamine-oxidase (MAO) inhibitors used in the treatment of mental depression, and especially the coumarins administered orally to prevent blood coagulation and the occurrence of blood clots.

The coumarins lose much of their effect when they are given to a patient who is also taking such drugs as phenobarbital, butabarbital, some antihistamines, glutethimide, chloral hydrate, griseofulvin, and oral contraceptives. The result may be clot formation in the legs, lungs, brain, or heart. In contrast, the effect of the coumarins is enhanced—with the risk of hemorrhage—by interactions with oral antibiotics, indomethacin, phenylbutazone, quinidine, quinine, salicylates, and sulfa-drugs. A physician wanting his patient to take two potentially interacting drugs—for example, coumarin and phenobarbital—can sometimes take appropriate precautions. Knowing that the phenobarbital limits the action of coumarin, he can step up the coumarin dose. But if the patient forgets to take his phenobarbital for a few nights, the results may be catastrophic.

Not only prescription drugs are involved in these interactions. MAO inhibitors used in the treatment of depression can result in a dangerous high blood pressure crisis if the patient is also taking amines contained in many over-the-counter cold, cough, and sinus remedies. The same hypertensive effect can result from the combination of MAO inhibitors with the tyramine contained in aged cheeses, Chianti wines, beer, sherry, pickled herring, yeast extract, chicken liver, and chocolate.[63]

All during the 1960s, while growing emphasis was being placed on the potential dangers of drug interactions, there remained great doubt that any appreciable number of physicians were actually prescribing interacting drugs. This comforting idea was abruptly ruptured by two reports from California. In 1971 Dr. Robert Maronde and his colleagues published an analysis of 52,733 prescriptions dispensed to outpatients by the Los Angeles County–University of Southern California Medical Center. Included in their findings were these:[64]

—Of 283 patients given an oral anticoagulant, 22 (about 8 percent) also received phenobarbital.

—Of 64 patients given guanethidine for hypertension, 6 (9 percent) also received ephedrine, pseudo-ephedrine, or amitryptiline, which act to raise blood pressure.

—Of 640 patients given meprobamate, 78 (12 percent) simultaneously received another tranquilizer.

—Of 430 patients given chlorpromazine to control severe emotional tension, 206 (48 percent) also received trifluoperazine or thioridazine, which are designed to have the same effect.

How many of the patients given these injudicious and potentially dangerous combinations actually took the drugs, and how many suffered serious reactions, was not known. Nevertheless, the findings were upsetting to those who had postulated that physicians, once they had been warned, would act appropriately. "Presumably," one of the Los Angeles investigators said later, "you'd figure that one doctor would look at the patient's chart and check on what else had been prescribed for him before writing a new prescription. But, as the data show only too clearly, you can't count on it."

An even more disconcerting report was presented early in 1972 before the American College of Physicians by Dr. Robert Talley, of the San Joaquin Foundation for Medical Care, and Marcel Laventurier, of Paid Prescriptions, Inc. The San Joaquin Foundation had contracted with the State of California to provide medical care to nearly 42,000 patients under the Medicaid program. Paid Prescriptions had been retained under a subcontract to handle compensation for prescription drugs dispensed under the program. Over a twelve-month period, the patients had received about 420,000 prescriptions. Some of the results of the analysis were the following:[65]

—Of 10,818 patients given tetracycline, 572 (about 5 percent) also received tetracycline-blocking antacids. (The number of those patients who obtained such an antacid product on their own without a prescription was not known.)

—Of 183 patients given guanethidine, 14 (8 percent) also received potentially interacting antidepressants.

—Of 342 patients given probenecid or a similar drug for the relief of gout, 98 (29 percent) also obtained prescriptions for products containing salicylates. (The number of patients obtaining salicylates in the form of aspirin and other nonprescription drugs was unknown.)

—Of 2,667 patients given oral antidiabetic drugs, 815 (31 percent) also received sulfa-drugs, salicylates, chloramphenicol, phenylbutazone, and other interacting drugs.

—Of 148 patients on oral anticoagulants, 79 (53 percent) were given barbiturates and other sedatives, salicylates and similar analgesics, quinine, quinidine, and other interacting products.

—Of 1,601 patients on combined treatment with digitalis and a potassium-depleting diuretic, 1,158 (72 percent) did not get a prescription for supplementary potassium.

Of the 42,000 patients, potentially interacting prescriptions had been dispensed to nearly 8 percent. "What is most surprising and most alarming," a trade journal commented, "is the fact that the more serious the interaction, the more likely seemed its chances of occurring. . . . If nothing else, these figures indicate a threshold of risk that would seem to be clearly unacceptable. More important, they suggest that the interaction problem is at least as severe as some people have been warning." [66]

From even this brief review it already seems evident that the cost of adverse drug reactions—most of them predictable and preventable—represent clinically and economically a fringe detriment to our total drug bill that society can no longer tolerate. They also represent a challenge to the medical and pharmacy professions as well as the public to find practical methods that will minimize adverse drug reactions without interfering with the rational use of drugs. To reach this objective a number of far-reaching and perhaps painful decisions may be required. Physicians may find it helpful to take advantage of the knowledge of new and highly skilled technical experts, such as clinical pharmacologists and clinical pharmacists. They may even call on a computer to corroborate a therapeutic decision.

On occasion, physicians, pharmacists, and patients alike may be forced to adopt new and apparently heretical viewpoints. For a beginning, they might accept the fact that the most dangerous as well as the most costly drug—like the most dangerous and costly surgical operation—may well be the one the patient didn't need in the first place.

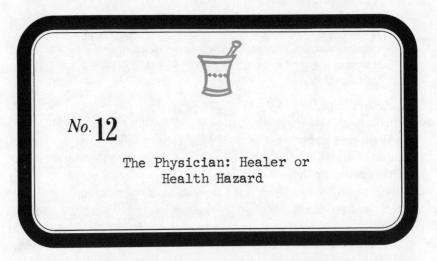

No. 12

The Physician: Healer or
Health Hazard

Rational prescribing—the right drug for the right patient, at the right
time, in the right amounts, and with due consideration of relative costs.

IN 1968 the HEW Task Force on
Prescription Drugs devised this definition, and expressed the conclusion
that rational prescribing as so defined was far from universal in medical
practice.[1] This was possibly something of an understatement. There was
already some evidence to support that view, and leading clinicians and
medical educators were expressing their grave concern. "It is my belief,"
said Dr. Jan Koch-Weser of Harvard, "that lack of knowledge in the
proper therapeutic use of drugs is perhaps the greatest deficiency of the
average American physician today." [2]

These and similar comments were not welcomed by organized
medicine, and some AMA spokesmen lashed out in attacks against
"arrogant pharmacologists" who criticized their clinical brethren. In the
ensuing years, however, the evidence of dangerously widespread irrational prescribing has steadily mounted.

—Highly dangerous drugs have been prescribed when equally effective but
safer products were available.

—Drugs effective in the treatment of one disease have been prescribed for
conditions in which they are worthless.

—An estimated 25 percent of the nation's drug expenditure has gone for
drugs whose efficacy has never been substantially proved.[3]

—Drugs have been prescribed with inadequate precautions against adverse reactions or addiction.

—Costly products have been prescribed when equally safe and effective products were available at lower cost.

—In some instances, patients have been undermedicated—that is, effective treatment was available but not prescribed, or the treatment was for too brief a period.

By and large, in most countries, the problem has been viewed as overmedication. Dr. Mark Novitch of FDA has stated it in these words: "We shall have to realize that overmedication is not simply overconsumption of drugs. When the more toxic of two equally effective drugs is used, that is overmedication. When a fixed combination drug is used and only one of the components is indicated, that is overmedication. And when a costly drug is prescribed where a less costly one of equal effectiveness is available, that, too, in a sense, is overmedication." [4]

It might be presumed that modern physicians have available or could easily get the essential unbiased facts on the value and hazards of any drug, and would make their prescribing judgments accordingly. The record does not justify such a comforting attitude. The physician is, in fact, besieged with information. He may obtain it from detail men, drug advertisements, medical journal articles, books, consultation with colleagues, government reports, and attendance at scientific meetings. Some of this information may be excellent; some may be adequate; some may be inaccurate, biased, or blatantly misleading. This torrent of information is at least in part a reflection of the explosion in scientific knowledge that has occurred during the past forty years and particularly of the pharmacological revolution that has provided an unprecedented number and variety of drug products.

Such a situation has posed inescapable problems to the physician. He must attempt to keep abreast of these developments at the same time that he must deal with increasing numbers of patients who are more and more aware of new drug discoveries. But these problems cannot justify the failure of individual physicians or the medical profession itself to anticipate and deal with the irrational prescribing and use of potent drugs.

THE EVIDENCE: CHLORAMPHENICOL

The medical profession has long cherished and defended its independence and autonomy, and especially the privilege of an individual physician to prescribe drugs as he alone sees fit. It is difficult to defend such a privilege if the profession is unable or unwilling to provide the public with greater protection than it did in the case of chloramphenicol, marketed originally by Parke-Davis under the name of Chloromycetin. The company's activities in promoting this drug, praising its real or proposed applications and minimizing its hazards, have been discussed in previous chapters. But in addition, the Food and Drug Administration and the physicians who prescribed chloramphenicol to millions of patients must bear their share of the blame.

Chloramphenicol was discovered in 1947, and in the following year became the first antibiotic to be prepared synthetically. In 1949 it was approved for marketing by FDA. Almost from the start, it won enthusiastic recognition for use against typhoid, typhus and other rickettsial infections, brucellosis, and urinary tract infections caused by those gram-negative organisms sensitive to the drug. Most of these were serious and occasionally fatal diseases. In the United States, however, most of them were exceedingly uncommon. Yet, to the delight of Parke-Davis and its promotion experts and detail men, sales soared from $9 million in the first year of marketing to $52 million in 1952.

Even in 1949 the first warning was sounded, with a report that blood damage had been detected after chloramphenicol administration.[5] Other reports of adverse effects were published both in medical journals and the lay press in 1950 and 1951. In June 1952 an editorial in the *Journal of the American Medical Association* transmitted the warning to all physicians:

> A second and more serious type of reaction that has been encountered is production of a true aplastic anemia. In the experience of one group, this anemia has occurred in patients who have previously received one or more courses of chloramphenicol without untoward effect. When the drug was subsequently administered, even in small doses, a severe blood abnormality has appeared. Even deaths have been reported. Whether chloramphenicol continues to remain as one of the more useful antibiotics or whether it will be relegated to a place where its use will be confined to the treatment of patients with typhoid or serious infections for which no other therapy is available, remains to be seen. Further observations are in order. In the meantime, physicians should be on the alert.[6]

A strong warning of possible blood damage was carried in the 1953 edition of *New and Non-Official Remedies*.[7] Promptly FDA, in cooperation with the National Research Council, investigated the situation, documented the relation between chloramphenicol and blood damage, and ordered tightened label warnings. As a result of these warnings, and FDA's strong recommendation that it should not be used indiscriminately or for trivial infections, sales of the drug plummeted—for a brief period. Then Parke-Davis intensified its promotion, physicians were apparently convinced, and sales soared again.

In 1954 FDA undertook a second survey. Its report contained these memorable statements:

> From the information we have gathered, there is every reason to believe that the medical profession has been alerted to the possible hazards involved when this drug is employed so that the decision to use it in a given situation rests with the physician where it properly belongs. . . . Misuse of the drug, so noticeable in the first study, appears to have been practically eliminated as judged by the second more extensive survey.[8]

This reassuring appraisal scarcely fitted with production figures. FDA approval of chloramphenicol batches rose dramatically from about 6 million grams—enough for twelve million doses—in 1953 to 19 million grams in 1955, 41 million in 1958, 50 million in 1959, and 55 million in 1960. By 1960 it appeared that the drug had been administered to forty million patients in a little more than ten years.

The production record was a brilliant testimonial to the skill of Parke-Davis promotion. It could also be read as a scathing indictment of the prescribing judgment of physicians. Some of their attitudes may be understandable. Physicians were in most instances too ready to look at only the beneficial effects of chloramphenicol, and it was abundantly clear that the drug was often highly effective. But they rarely considered the irrationality of prescribing a drug that was unnecessary or inappropriate, and in most instances they placed minimal importance on its potential hazards. It was only rare that an individual physician even saw a patient suffering from chloramphenicol-induced aplastic anemia. Accordingly, it seems, his own limited experience and that of a few colleagues had more influence on his prescribing judgment than did the data analyzed and publicized by the AMA, FDA, and the National Research Council.

The AMA's Council on Drugs published its second chloramphenicol report in *JAMA* in 1960:

> Although the warning statement specifically cautions against the indiscriminate use of the drug or against its use for minor infections, an examination of the reports received by the registry reveals that the drug has been used in such conditions as upper respiratory infections, including the common

cold, bronchial infections, asthma, sore throat, and tonsilitis, miscellane-
ous urinary tract and ear infections, undiagnosed low-grade fever, and even
disseminated lupus erythematosis, gout, eczema, malaise, and iron deficiency anemia.[9]

The National Research Council and FDA once again stressed the
need for more caution and for better physician education. A flurry of
damage suits filed against Parke-Davis and some of the chloramphenicol-
prescribing physicians slightly cooled the company's ardor. Perhaps more
important were the disclosures of chloramphenicol-induced blood damage during the Kefauver hearings on the drug industry. According to the
president of Parke-Davis, those hearings "caused some very unfavorable
publicity, I may say unjustified and ridiculous, which cost us a volume
loss on Chloromycetin of about fifteen million dollars." [10]

The prescribing of chloramphenicol declined and sales were
obviously off in 1961, but the drop was short-lived, and by 1962
prescriptions and production were rising once again. It was only too clear
that the efforts of AMA, FDA, and the National Research Council had
little sustained impact against Parke-Davis promotion. In 1967, with
chloramphenicol production reaching near-record levels, the AMA's
Council on Drugs published an analysis showing that among chloram-
phenicol-treated patients suffering blood damage, the drug had been
prescribed properly in only 6 or 7 percent.[11] (Even with this record, the
JAMA continued to carry chloramphenicol advertisements.)

Then, in November 1967 the Nelson hearings took up the matter
of antibiotics in general and chloramphenicol in particular. Those
hearings—and the newspaper accounts they evoked—apparently had a
greater restrictive effect on the production, promotion, and prescription
of chloramphenicol than did any other factor in the previous eighteen
years. The public as well as the medical profession had finally appreci-
ated the hazards of chloramphenicol. Nelson did not challenge the
usefulness of chloramphenicol. He freely admitted, on the basis of much
scientific evidence, that it was of very great value, but only for certain
infections. His targets were the manner in which Parke-Davis had
promoted it, and the manner in which physicians had prescribed it.

One spokesman for the AMA—although not for its Council on
Drugs—took the senator to task for his attacks. Said Dr. Clinton McGill,
an AMA trustee:

Now, when the first reports of aplastic anemia and blood dyscrasias came
out and were reported in 1951 to the medical profession, the use of

Chloromycetin dropped almost to zero. It dropped very sharply because of this potential danger, once the facts were known. My point is this information is not wasted. This does reach the medical profession, and any doctor that has practiced in the last fifteen years and does not know that Chloromycetin can produce serious blood dyscrasias must be blind, dumb, and deaf because there have been all these warnings.

Nelson replied, "That is exactly what the experts' testimony has been—that many doctors have been blind, dumb, and deaf. It has been a horrible tragedy in this country and it is an indictment of the medical profession." Dr. McGill indicated he was not impressed by some of those experts. "This committee," he said, "has given a public forum to certain arrogant professors of pharmacology who have openly discredited the drug-prescribing abilities of the American physician. I deeply resent this insult to our clinical integrity." [12]

By mid-1968 it was evident that production of chloramphenicol—a reflection of chloramphenicol prescribing—was dropping precipitously. That drop has continued more or less steadily at least to 1973. Most of the chloramphenicol still being used was prescribed by a very few physicians—usually general practitioners working in isolated settings—who considered it their favorite antibiotic.[13] Recently, Dr. Harry Dowling—long a leading member of the AMA Council on Drugs—summed up the affair by saying: "Perhaps the most flagrant example of bad therapeutic judgment has been the failure of some doctors to desist from the unnecessary use of chloramphenicol." [14]

The record of chloramphenicol production from 1950 to 1972 is shown in figure 17. It is a record compounded in part from complacency, laziness, stupidity, carelessness, deceit, and greed. It likewise poses questions that must be answered by physicians. Why did all the efforts of the AMA, the National Research Council, FDA, and even the courts fail for almost two decades, and why did the promotional strategy of a drug company succeed? Why did the hearings of the Nelson committee have such a dramatic impact on physicians' prescribing of chloramphenicol? Is it possible that informed consumers, rather than organized medicine or government, are best able to determine when and where to set the limits?

The chloramphenicol affair poses still additional questions. Should FDA limit the use of this and similar hazardous drugs to hospitalized patients or to patients who are undergoing continuing treatment after hospital discharge? Do patients have a right to know both the values and hazards of any drug prescribed for them? And what impact would the

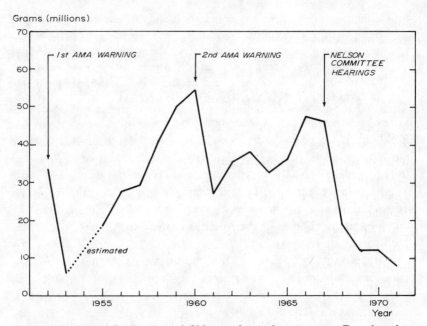

Grams (millions)

FIGURE 17. Annual Production of Chloramphenicol, 1952–1971. Data based on quantities certified annually by Food and Drug Administration.
SOURCE: James L. Goddard, statement in U.S. Senate, Select Committee on Small Business, Subcommittee on Monopoly, *Present Status of Competition in the Pharmaceutical Industry* (Washington, D.C.: U.S. Government Printing Office) 6:2630 (1968); Mark Novitch (Food and Drug Administration), personal communication, 1972.

implementation of such a right have on patient-physician relations? It has long been traditional for hospitals to require the informed consent of a patient before any elective surgery may be performed. A recent California Supreme Court decision would hold that similar informed consent should be required when any potentially dangerous drug is prescribed.[15] Should a similar requirement be established throughout the nation?

THE EVIDENCE: ANTIBACTERIAL THERAPY

By no means is chloramphenicol the only antibacterial agent whose irrational use has been clearly demonstrated. For many years, experts in infectious disease have been decrying the overprescribing of nearly all antibiotics, sulfa-drugs, and similar agents, alone or in combination. "The concept that if one antimicrobial is good, two should be better and three will virtually cure anybody of anything has long been refuted," two modern workers have noted, "although it is still being employed." [16] Approximately one-third of all hospitalized patients on any given day receive some type of systemic antimicrobial by injection or oral administration, they said.

Similar findings have been reported by other investigators.[17] Most indicate that in the overwhelming proportion of treated patients, the antibacterial drugs were prescribed without any reported evidence of bacterial infection. These potentially dangerous drugs were therefore given not to treat an infection—for which their use is usually rational— but to prevent an infection, which might not occur in any case. Accordingly, it seems, they were used as a pharmaceutical version of propitiating the gods.

The growing use of antibiotics to prevent infection has apparently been the principal reason for the rapid and indeed alarming increase in the prescribing of these drugs during the last few years. Some physicians justify this use on the basis that the risk is slight, the cost to the patient is usually not great, and the patient is pleased to see that his physician is doing something for him—and thus is not likely to turn to another physician. Evidence does not support such a belief. The best thing that might be said about the prophylactic use of antibiotics is that in most instances it is not clinically justifiable. It presents needless risks and causes unnecessary expense. At the worst, it may be fatal for the patient. The added risk clearly outweighs any hypothetical benefits.

Examples of apparently irrational administration of antibiotics for prevention are now appearing frequently in medical journals. Thus, in one study of twenty-four hospitals conducted on patients undergoing surgery for uncomplicated inguinal hernia, it was reported that 38 percent received one or more antibiotics. In a third of these patients, the drug was used to prevent infection. The range of antibiotic use in these patients was remarkable, with 3 percent of the patients being treated with antibiotics in one hospital as compared with 82 percent of the patients in another.[18] It was not possible to justify these differences on the basis of any rational standards of medical care.

The irrational use of antibiotics and other antibacterial agents has recently been documented in another hospital study conducted by Andrew Roberts and Dr. James Visconti of Ohio State University. In an analysis of 1,035 patient records it was found that 340 had been given antibacterial treatment. A team of experts reviewing the records judged that the prescription had been rational in only 12.9 percent of the cases, questionable in 21.5 percent, and irrational—wrong drug, wrong dosage, wrong route of administration, or no indication for a drug in the first place—in an astonishing 65.6 percent. Of the 340 patients, 48 developed an adverse drug reaction. In 44, or 92 percent of these, the prescribed treatment was rated as questionable or clearly irrational. The Ohio investigators said:

> If the antibacterials were completely innocuous drugs with a potential only for doing good, the sole objection to their irrational use shown in the study would be cost—admittedly an important consideration in some instances. . . . Unfortunately, cost is not the sole objection or in fact the most significant objection to the irrational use of antimicrobials. . . . Antimicrobials may harm the patient by giving rise to undesirable side effects, they may harm the patient by interfering with the development of antibodies, and they may harm by sensitizing the patient to the antibiotic so that, at some time in the future when he really does need it, he experiences an unpleasant reaction. From the point of view of the population as a whole, the widespread and unnecessary use of antimicrobials is most undesirable because it encourages the emergence of resistant strains.[19]

Such resistant varieties, presumably arising from the excessive use of antibiotics and other antibacterial drugs, are responsible for devastating infections that may sweep through some hospitals like epidemics. They are charged with roughly 100,000 deaths each year.[20]

When the Ohio study was reported, it was denounced for exaggerating the situation. On the other hand, there is evidence that the problem may be even more serious. For example, at the Los Angeles County–University of Southern California Medical Center, a study of fifty-four patients treated with cephalexin—one of the newer and more expensive antibiotics, costing the hospital an average of about $12 per prescription—showed that the treatment was irrational in fifty, or nearly 93 percent. In these fifty inappropriately treated cases, either a safer or more effective drug should have been chosen, or there was no need for an antibacterial drug of any kind.[21]

The irrational prescription of antibacterial drugs for the common cold is an all too common practice. In a 1969 report, for example, Dr. Paul Stolley and Dr. Louis Lasagna of Johns Hopkins presented data indicating that "most physicians (about 95 percent) will issue one or more prescriptions to a patient whom they diagnose as having the 'common cold.' Almost 60 percent of these prescriptions are for antibiotics, with the tetracyclines and penicillin the most popular choices. Sulfa drugs are also prescribed in significant numbers.[22]

The irrational prescription of combination antibacterial products —two or more antibiotics, or an antibiotic plus a sulfa-drug, in a ratio fixed by the manufacturer—has been discussed in an earlier chapter. Use of these products has long been branded as unacceptable medical practice by the AMA's Council on Drugs. This stand was further supported by the National Academy of Sciences/National Research Council in its 1969 report to FDA:

> It is the principle of medical practice that more than one drug should be administered for the treatment of a given condition only if the physician is persuaded that there is substantial reason to believe that each drug will make a positive contribution to the effect he seeks. Risks of adverse drug reactions should not be multiplied unless there be overriding benefit. . . . Multiple therapy using fixed ratios determined by the manufacturer and not by the physician is, in general, poor practice.[23]

As the record has shown, the medical profession has been split on this issue. Many practicing physicians have ignored the attitude of the AMA Council on Drugs and the views of the NAS/NRC and have continued to prescribe fixed-ratio antimicrobial products as long as they were available on the market. Official spokesmen for the AMA have maintained a position defending the drug industry that produced and promoted these products. Yet, in stunning contrast, virtually every specialist on drug therapy and infectious disease has opposed their general use.

The position of the top level of organized medicine—the Board of Trustees of the AMA—in apparently defending the widespread use of antibiotics and other antibacterials can scarcely be taken as evidence that the AMA has come out in favor of irrational prescribing. The problems faced by the individual physician, and his attitudes and beliefs, were also considered. The physician must satisfy his patients. He has been led to believe that the typical patient would prefer to get almost any prescription rather than no prescription at all. He must diagnose and then lay out a strategy of treatment in a relatively few minutes. Only infrequently does he have access to adequate laboratory facilities for the prompt diagnosis of infectious disease, and he may be convinced that the cost of a laboratory test to diagnose or detect the infection may exceed the cost of the antibiotic used to treat it. He may have been convinced that the risks to the patient of antibiotic therapy were slight. In situations of uncertainty such as this, he often decides to treat rather than to wait. The physician is more likely to be criticized by patients and colleagues alike for failure to treat than for overtreatment or unnecessary treatment. Some physicians may prescribe antibiotics as "defensive medicine"; for example, a surgeon may prescribe an antibiotic in the hope of preventing not only a postoperative infection but also the possibility of a malpractice suit. These factors, together with the fact that some physicians practice in virtual isolation from their professional colleagues, and yet are fully exposed to detail men and other means of drug promotion, may well explain much of the unjustified use of antimicrobial products.

As was noted above, many of the overriding policies of the AMA have long been vigorously opposed by the AMA's own Council on Drugs. This divergence in views was settled late in 1972 when the AMA simply disbanded the drug council. The move was officially explained as an economy measure, but one critic put it this way: "The AMA could no longer keep both an effective Council on Drugs and the support of drug advertisers. One of them had to go."

THE EVIDENCE: PSYCHOACTIVE DRUGS AND OTHERS

There are still other examples of irrational prescribing which bring little credit to physicians. One concerns Vitamin B_{12}, which is effective for only one condition—pernicious anemia. Each year it is prescribed in quantities at least a thousand times the estimated amount needed for all pernicious anemia patients in the country. Millions of injections of Vitamin B_{12} are given for a remarkably wide spectrum of diagnostic conditions, it has been reported by Dr. Stolley and Dr. Lasagna, with the drug ordered as a "stimulant," a "sedative," or a placebo.

Another involves the widespread use of meperidine (Demerol) rather than morphine for the control of severe pain in the treatment of terminal cancer, biliary or urinary colic, heart disease, or postsurgical distress. There is no evidence that meperidine is less addicting than morphine. There is no evidence that meperidine causes less respiratory depression than morphine, or that it is more effective in reducing pain. "The heavy promotion of a drug such as meperidine in medical journals and by detail men," it was emphasized by *The Medical Letter*, "has a marked and apparently lasting effect on the prescribing habits of physicians." [24] Such promotion has similarly had an impact on the pocketbook of the patients; for example, the retail price for clinically equivalent prescriptions is approximately $3.45 for morphine and $7.40 for meperidine.

It is difficult to explain the undermedication of patients with high blood pressure. Most physicians are aware of the value of drugs in the control of severe hypertension, with diastolic pressures of 130 mm or more. They seem less aware that antihypertensive drugs can also be valuable in moderate cases, with pressures between 100 and 130, reducing the incidence of complications and prolonging the life of the patient. A recent study by the Veterans Administration has clearly established their value in patients with pressures between 90 and 115.[25] It is in this last group that treatment is often inadequate or not even attempted.

One of the most confusing and difficult areas of therapeutics has been the prescribing of psychoactive drugs—major tranquilizers, minor tranquilizers, sedatives, stimulants, and antidepressants. At community pharmacies in the United States, they account for more than 200 million prescriptions per year at a retail cost of nearly one billion dollars. For this whole group of drugs, use increased by 44 percent from 1964 to 1970. For the minor tranquilizers alone, use increased during that period by nearly 78 percent.[26]

A similar pattern has been observed in Canada, Sweden, and other countries. In Great Britain psychoactive drugs account for about 20 percent of all prescriptions dispensed under the National Health Service. In terms of both numbers and cost, they make up the largest single class of drugs prescribed. From 1961 to 1971 there was a 78.8 percent increase in prescriptions for these agents in Great Britain. Although there was a 32 percent decrease in the use of barbiturates and a 43 percent decrease in that of stimulants and appetite suppressants between 1965 and 1971, the prescribing of nonbarbiturate hypnotics increased by 166 percent, that of antidepressants by 103 percent, and that of tranquilizers by 70 percent.[27]

Relatively little criticism has been directed at the use of major tranquilizers, such as the phenothiazines, for the treatment of patients with severe schizophrenia or other serious psychotic disorder. What has been attacked is the prescription of the minor tranquilizers, or antianxiety drugs, such as meprobamate, chlordiazepoxide, and diazepam, especially for such conditions as "environmental depression," "not fitting in," "a child's fear of the dentist," or the "tired mother syndrome." Most of these minor tranquilizers are prescribed not by psychiatrists but by general practitioners, many of them overworked and under constant pressure to "do something" for their patients. Dr. Henry Lennard of the University of California, San Francisco, and Dr. Mitchell Rosenthal of New York's Phoenix Houses described the situation in these terms:

> It has been estimated that 60 percent of the patients who appear in a general practitioner's office or clinic do so for largely nonmedical reasons.

They come because they are lonely, depressed, anxious, dissatisfied, or unhappy. They are troubled because they are finding it difficult or impossible to measure up to prevailing social prescriptions as to what one ought to get out of life. They are not as popular, successful, sweet-smelling, thin, vigorous, or beautiful as they have been led to believe (by the advertising arms of industry and the media) they ought and deserve to be.[28]

It is clear that such individuals need help. It is not so clear that all of them need chemotherapy.

There are at least some signs that anxiety-ridden patients can receive significant nonchemical aid when a family has access to a competent doctor who is available twenty-four hours a day. This method has been tested at Harvard's family health care program, where a student physician serves as such a family physician. "He assumes responsibility for total care and comes to know the family intimately. In this setting where emotional disorders are common, prescribing of tranquilizers is so unusual, it is a cause for comment. When psychotropics are used, they are one part of total management, not the sole treatment." [29]

On the other hand, Dr. Mitchell Balter and Dr. Jerome Levine of the National Institute of Mental Health have claimed that these psychoactive agents are being underprescribed. Basing their conclusions on a study of 2,552 patients, they reported that 22 percent—29 percent of the women and 13 percent of the men—had used a psychotherapeutic prescription drug during a one-year period. They said:

> If the question is whether physicians are contributing to drug abuse by creating physical dependence among their patients, we see little to be alarmed about. Our data indicate that most private practitioners, if anything, err in the conservative direction. . . . Only 4 percent of the males and 6 percent of the females had ever used drugs of these classes on a regular daily basis for two months or more. . . . In terms of the incidence of high levels of psychic distress, one could make a good case for the point that population needs for drug treatment are not being met.[30]

The report by the NIMH workers, and similar views expressed by others,[31] were welcomed by the drug industry and widely publicized by various medical publications. They were less warmly received by Dr. Lennard and his colleagues. It is possible that the percentage figures reported—4 percent of the men and 6 percent of the women—may be too low. But even if they are accepted, the admitted daily use of psychoactive drugs for prolonged periods by what would be many millions of individuals cannot easily be accepted as rational.

A similar controversy exists in England, where some physicians have expressed their dismay at the widespread use of psychoactive drugs to enable patients to cope with the tensions of modern life, while other medical men claim that they have no responsibilities for those tensions but only the obligation to help their patients deal with them.[32]

A particularly thorny problem has centered on the use of amphetamines and other stimulant drugs. Dr. Balter and Dr. Levine reported that the number of prescriptions filled for such products has remained relatively constant over the past eight to ten years.[33] Considering the increase in population, they said, this indicates a decline in usage. In striking contrast, however, Dr. Lester Grinspoon and Peter Hedblom declared that the reported legal production of amphetamines had risen from 3.5 billion tablets in 1958 to more than 10 billion in 1970 and more than 12 billion in 1971. "Indeed," they said, "many published studies continue to report amphetamine use rates that are gross underestimates because they ignore the incredibly widespread black-market distribution system that continues to thrive despite federal efforts to seal up the massive leakage from pharmaceutical companies, wholesalers, druggists, and even physicians' offices." [34]

The amphetamine controversy has likewise been intensified by a long-standing debate over whether these drugs are technically addictive. Regardless of this dispute, they are clearly dangerous. A similar debate has raged over the rationality of permitting the promotion and prescription of the amphetamines for the general treatment of obesity. Here again, the medical profession is split. Although many physicians seem to approve restrictions in the production and use of amphetamines, others have denounced these restrictions as a dictatorial effort by both government and some medical groups to control the practice of medicine and to interfere with a physician's traditional right to prescribe as only he decides. Whether such prescribing is tolerated by other physicians is one matter. Another is whether, under government-financed programs, the taxpayers should be forced to pay for it.

THE EVIDENCE:
THE HOSPITAL-BASED SUPER-PRESCRIBERS

Another aspect of irrational prescribing has been illuminated by a special series of studies at the Los Angeles County–University of Southern California Medical Center. One of the largest hospitals in the world, it serves a patient population of approximately one million. In the outpatient clinics alone, about 600,000 prescriptions are written annually by about nine hundred physicians. Most of the patients receive their drugs without cost. Most of them are indigent and have no need for large supplies of medication to take on extended travel. Since late in 1967 outpatient prescriptions have been processed by computer techniques, thus making possible one of the first major investigations on precisely how hospital-based physicians actually prescribe.

In one study,[35] directed by Dr. Robert Maronde, attention was focused on the seventy-eight most frequently prescribed drugs, which together accounted for more than 80 percent of all outpatient prescriptions. A total of 52,733 consecutive prescriptions for these drugs was dispensed during the research period. In each case the quantity of the drug prescribed was compared with a level arbitrarily set to represent the maximum for rational therapy. (The limits were established by a group of five physicians and two pharmacists, who worked for a year and a half in frequent consultation with representatives of all the medical specialties and subspecialties in the hospital.) Of the 52,733 prescriptions, it was reported that 13 percent called for drug amounts in what were defined as excessive quantities.

"It is noteworthy," the Los Angeles researchers said, "that the percentage of excessive-quantity prescriptions was especially high in the case of frequently prescribed sedatives and tranquilizers." Nearly 40 percent of the prescriptions for meprobamate-400 mg were listed as calling for excessive quantities. The same was true for 33 percent of those for chlordiazepoxide-10 mg, 33 percent of those for diazepam-5 mg, and 30 percent of those for phenobarbital-30 mg.

"It likewise seems noteworthy," they said, "that these sedative or tranquilizing agents were involved in prescriptions written for what would seem to be exceedingly large quantities. Thus, prescriptions for meprobamate-400 mg and chlordiazepoxide-10 mg, each with a defined limit of 100, were prescribed in quantities as high as 800. For phenobarbital-30 mg, with a limit of 200, prescriptions for as many as 1,300 were found."

Some of the case records turned up in the study were remarkable:

Over a 112-day period, one patient received fifty-four prescriptions, including twelve individual prescriptions dispensed on one day and eleven on another. He received during this time 1,130 capsules of propoxyphene, 870 capsules of chlordiazepoxide, 700 capsules of diphenylhydantoin, 620 capsules of griseofulvin, 520 tablets of sodium salicylate, 500 tablets of phenobarbital, 500 tablets of nitroglycerine, 300 tablets of thyroid, 300 tablets of multiple vitamins, 300 tablets of furosemide, 300 tablets of acetaminophen, 240 tablets of triamcinolone, 230 tablets of hydrochlorothiazide, 200 tablets of phenobarbital-ephedrine-theophylline, 200 tablets of acetylsalicylic acid, 40 tablets of sulfamethoxazole, 40 tablets of chlorpromazine, and 26 tablets of aluminum hydroxide-magnesium hydroxide gel, for a total of 7,416 units. In addition, he was given 6,800 ml of potassium chloride 10 percent syrup, 480 ml of elixir terpin hydrate, 240 ml of hand lotion, and 600 ml of thymol 4 percent chloroform. "This individual," it was reported, "received nine separate prescriptions for propoxyphene. None of these exceeded the approved limit of 300 capsules—one was for 30, five were for 100 each, and three were for 200 each—but the total of 1,130 capsules would appear to be substantial."

Over a 105-day period, another patient was given six prescriptions for meprobamate, totaling 720 tablets, and six for propoxyphene, totaling 760 capsules. On one day, he received one prescription for 100 tablets of meprobamate and another for 100 capsules of propoxyphene, both written by the same physician. On the following day, he received from a second physician a prescription for 200 meprobamate tablets and another for 300 propoxyphene tablets.

Over a 100-day period, a diabetic patient received five prescriptions for tolbutamide, totaling 1,320 tablets. Included were three prescriptions dispensed over a 23-day period for 200, 120, and 300 tablets, respectively, written by three different physicians.

Significantly, approximately 50 percent of the excessive-quantity prescriptions were written by only thirty, or 3.4 percent, of the prescribing physicians. Most of these "super-prescribers" were physicians hired solely for the purpose of caring for outpatients. Beyond that, they seemed to have few characteristics in common. Some had been trained at the most highly regarded medical schools in the country, while others had gone to less esteemed institutions. Seven of the thirty had been in practice for one year or less, but four had been practicing for twenty years or more. One was a specialist in internal medicine, serving on the medical school faculty.

Generally, it was found, when a super-prescriber wrote excessive-quantity prescriptions for one drug, he followed the same pattern with other drugs. For example, slightly more than 51 percent of all prescriptions written by one physician were judged to call for excessive quantities. The Los Angeles workers concluded:

> It is suggested that these types of irrational prescribing may be controlled in a medical center or hospital environment. This would require

(1) agreement among the clinical staff that such an approach is both clinically and economically necessary; (2) agreement through peer judgment on the limits of each major drug that may be rationally prescribed (with provisions to permit the prescription of apparently excessive quantities under exceptional circumstances); and (3) the availability of an adequate computer system or other method of data processing.

With their computer the Los Angeles group was able to detect an apparently excessive-quantity prescription within seconds after it reached the pharmacy. The pharmacist could then alert the physician and discuss the matter with him. "In most such cases," Dr. Maronde said later, "the physician would explain the exceptional circumstances which made the prescription appropriate, or he would order a reduction in the quantity, or he would cancel the prescription completely." [36] When they were so notified, most physicians cooperated immediately. Many made such a comment as, "Good Lord, I didn't realize!" or "I didn't have the patient's chart. I didn't know he was getting prescriptions from another doctor." But there was a small core of super-prescribers who were less cooperative. "Don't tell me how to prescribe," one of them told a pharmacist. "I write the prescriptions. You fill 'em."

In a later study,[37] Dr. Maronde and his colleagues used the computer-based system to analyze prescriptions for those drugs considered most likely to be abused. Most frequently involved, they found, were diazepam, chlordiazepoxide, phenobarbital, and propoxyphene. In some cases, they were dispensed in a single excessive-quantity prescription. In others, they concerned multiple prescriptions for the same drug, each calling for a reasonable quantity but dispensed at remarkably frequent intervals. Many of the patients could be classified as prescription-shoppers.

One patient obtained two prescriptions for diazepam, each for a 150-day supply, from two physicians in different clinics on the same day. Another obtained one prescription for a 66-day supply of chlordiazepoxide and a second, four days later, for a 50-day supply. Both were written by the same physician.

Still another received two prescriptions for phenobarbital, one for a 150-day supply and the other for a 167-day supply, ordered by two different physicians in the same clinic on the same day. One woman received a 25-day supply of diazepam, a 33-day supply of phenobarbital, and a 16-day supply of propoxyphene, all on the same day. Two days later, she received a 15-day supply of diazepam, a 50-day supply of phenobarbital, and a 16-day supply of propoxyphene. All six prescriptions were written by the same physician.

"The ultimate fate of the drugs involved in these excessive-quantity prescriptions is not known," the Los Angeles group said.

> In some cases, the prescribed quantities may actually be ingested by the patients for whom the prescriptions were written. In others, they may be discarded. In some instances, they may be kept in the family bathroom cabinet, providing a lethal invitation to potential suicides and inquisitive children. Some of these excessive quantities may be shared with other members of the family or with neighbors. Some may be sold.

Whether any effective means to control drug abuse by minimizing this variety of irrational prescribing—involving what may be the right drug but certainly the wrong amounts—is yet to be determined. They said:

> There is no reason to expect that minimizing the number of excessive-quantity prescriptions by means of a complex computer system can be justified simply on the basis of direct financial savings on the cost of drugs. The major influence of any control method will probably be in the direction of identifying and correcting grossly irrational prescribing, preventing legally prescribed drugs from reaching the black market, and identifying and eventually treating prescription-shoppers and other drug abusers.

THE EVIDENCE:

PHYSICIANS IN PRIVATE PRACTICE

The problem of irrational prescribing has been further highlighted by studies of private physicians as they actually practice. In one pioneering study, for instance, Dr. O. L. Peterson and his co-workers found that 43 percent of physicians prescribed rationally for the treatment of hypertension, 33 percent for infections and for obesity, 25 percent for congestive heart failure, 17 percent for emotional problems, and only 15 percent for anemias.[38]

The errors disclosed in this investigation could scarcely be dismissed as nit-picking. They included the administration of digitalis in dangerously slovenly fashion, the use of borderline or totally ineffective shotgun preparations for anemia patients, the administration of a variety of drugs for nonexistent organic disease to patients suffering from emotional illness, the use of the wrong dosage or the wrong treatment schedule of drugs for high blood pressure, and the prescription of penicillin for the common cold.

The doctors who prescribed rationally also did a superior job in diagnosis, prenatal and child care, surgery, and obstetrics. "There was a remarkable consistency in the performance of the individual physician. That is to say, if he scored high on history-taking, his performance in the other categories tended to be of the same order. If he did not perform a careful examination, it was unlikely that he would obtain a good history or prescribe rational treatment." A somewhat similar study on Canadian general practitioners by Dr. K. F. Clute indicated that 85 percent prescribed rationally for cardiac failure, 45 percent for infections, and 25 percent for hypertension.[39] It is apparent that the reported percentages of irrational prescribers in the two groups were far from the same. It is also apparent, however, that the prescribing patterns of the two groups left much to be desired.

Numerous investigations in both this country and abroad have demonstrated wide variations among the prescribing patterns in various hospitals. In some institutions, for example, antibiotics and tranquilizers are infrequently used, whereas in other hospitals they are administered to the overwhelming majority of patients. In some communities the number of prescriptions written per patient is nearly twice the number ordered in other areas.[40] The fact that these differences occur does not necessarily prove that one method is irrational and the other rational. Neither or both may be appropriate. The differences, however, are an invitation for objective study.

A particularly significant survey was conducted by Dr. Stolley and his associates on the characteristics of physicians whose prescribing patterns were judged to be the most rational. In general, these rational prescribers were younger and busier than their colleagues. They had been in practice a shorter period of time, tended to refer more patients for consultation, attended more postgraduate courses, and were inclined to rely more on articles in medical journals than on drug advertising or drug detail men for their information on prescribing. "The better prescriber," it was said, "is more cosmopolitan and modern in his approach to medical care, oriented to a concern with quality, and with the psychosocial dimensions of treatment." [41]

In our view, and in that of many of our colleagues, the problem of irrational prescribing can no longer be ignored, covered up, or dismissed as trivial, for it represents not merely an unwise expenditure of funds but a serious hazard to health and even life.

Thoughtful observers have pointed to the wide discrepancy in the prescribing habits of the average physician as compared with those recommended by panels of medical experts.[42] They have pointed to the continued use by the average physician of products found unnecessary or unacceptable by specially qualified therapeutics committees selected by their peers and serving in hospitals and clinics.[43] They have pointed with considerable concern to the fact that the most widely used sources of prescribing information are drug detail men and a book that is essentially a compilation of advertising for the most heavily promoted drugs.[44]

In 1968 the HEW Task Force on Prescription Drugs published the results of a nationwide survey to indicate the relative frequency with which drugs were dispensed to elderly patients. It was the first time such information had been assembled. Before publication, we submitted advance copies of the findings to expert clinical pharmacologists and requested their comments. Generally, they first expressed their disbelief —until they had an opportunity to review the data—and then their dismay. One of them told us, "I suppose we have to believe you," and then added, "If that's the way American physicians really prescribe, then God help American patients." [45]

WHO IS RESPONSIBLE?

The responsibility for this situation has been placed on many factors. For example, as Dr. Koch-Weser and others have claimed, many if not most medical students are inadequately trained in the clinical application of drug knowledge. When the typical physician enters private practice, knowingly or unknowingly he becomes the key figure in drug market strategy. "He must choose from a very large number of competitive and often duplicative products," the HEW Task Force stated. "He must deal with a very large amount of advice, biased or unbiased, from detail men, advertisements, and other forms of promotion. Substantial efforts are made on his behalf by the drug industry and others to prevent any interference with his right to prescribe as he sees fit." [46]

At the same time, the average physician has had inadequate sources of objective, up-to-date information in useful form on both drug properties and drug costs. The drugs he was taught to prescribe early in his career may soon become obsolete and be replaced by newly introduced products. He has only limited time to examine, evaluate, and keep up-to-date on the claims for old and new drugs. He comes to place increasing reliance for his continuing postgraduate education on the promotional materials distributed by drug manufacturers.

And also, at the same time, there is constant insistence—emphasized by both the drug industry and organized medicine—that the average physician, without guidance from expert colleagues, does in fact possess the necessary ability to make scientifically sound judgments in this complicated field. "It is assumed," the Task Force said, "that he has the training, experience, and time to weigh the claims and available evidence, and thus to make the proper selection. Everything, of course, hinges on the validity of this final assumption."

The assumption could not go unchallenged. "We find that few practicing physicians seem inclined to voice any question of their competency in this field of therapeutic judgments. We also find, however, that the ability of an individual physician to make sound judgments under quite confusing conditions is now a matter of serious concern to leading clinicians, scientists, and medical educators." [47]

In general, these findings were disputed by industry leaders and ignored by spokesmen for the American Medical Association. Nevertheless, one AMA president, Dr. Dwight L. Wilbur, did break with tradition when he told a small scientific meeting that medical students "should be educated so that during the years of practice they will be oriented to the continuing education of pharmacologic experts in medical schools and not to the advertising of pharmaceutical manufacturers." [48]

In the mounting concern over irrational prescribing by physicians, much criticism has been heaped on the drug industry. This is not a new development. In 1887 a German pharmacology professor complained that "a great number of physicians, without rhyme or reason, go after every new remedy that is recommended to them. If an industrialist is but shrewd enough to advertise sufficiently, he usually succeeds in increasing the sale of his product—for some time at least—and thus enriching himself." [49]

But drug company promotion, as overwhelming as it has been, is not the only influence that induces—or allows—a physician to prescribe irrationally. The mass media have whetted the public appetite for the latest wonder drug and have tended to strengthen the belief of many physicians in their own infallibility. Drug advertising, especially on radio and television, must accept at least a considerable amount of blame for the irrational self-drugging of patients with over-the-counter remedies. The government has not exerted its full powers quickly and forcefully enough to get unduly dangerous or ineffective products off the market, control irrational promotional claims, and block false and deceptive advertising. Too often, pharmacists have refused to accept their professional responsibilities and have acted as if their major concern was not helping a patient but selling a product.

Unfortunately, in this complex, confusing, and difficult situation, studies of medical innovation—particularly the introduction of new drugs—tell us relatively little that can lead to an effective strategy to reduce to a minimum irrational prescribing by physicians.[50] Too often the consequences of introducing a new drug are not adequately considered by those responsible for its introduction or diffusion into clinical practice. Two perceptive authorities have described the problem accurately: "Almost no innovation comes without any strings attached. The more important, the more advanced, the more 'modern' the innovation (and therefore the more desire by the change agent for its rapid adoption), the more likely its introduction is to produce many consequences—some of them intended and manifest, others unintended or latent. A system is like a bowl of marbles; move any one of its elements and the position of all the others is changed." [51]

In addition, much of the responsibility rests on the patient, especially the one who expects too much of his physician. The problem has been well summarized in a recent report to the Director General of the World Health Organization:

> The insistent demand of the public to take medicines for every ailment undoubtedly contributes to drug misuse and abuse. Expectations of miracle drugs and magical cures have been partly responsible for the defensive attitude of some physicians, who, instead of concentrating only on the well being of the patient and on minimal therapy, especially in trivial conditions, prescribe unnecessarily active drugs. Furthermore, the indiscriminate use of new drugs which provide symptomatic relief for the patient, without devoting the necessary time and attention to the diagnosis of the underlying disease, has sometimes impaired medical care because such symptomatic therapy can make the diagnosis and render the subsequent outcome more hazardous. Drug misuse—or sometimes drug abuse—is also due to the tendency among some patients to expect too much from modern drugs, which have been regarded not only as a means of treatment of disease but also a way of changing moods and improving life, and a substitute for self-control. Better education and information on the use of modern drugs would certainly contribute to the solution of these problems. In order to delineate the misuse of modern drugs, there is need for a thorough investigation of drug consumption and its relationship to health services in some selected areas, based on uniform methodology.[52]

The very act of writing a prescription, rational or not, may serve a role in a tacit conspiracy between physician and patient. The typical physician, Dr. Charlotte Muller has noted, can spend an average of only seventeen minutes with each patient. At the end of that time, even though a patient's problem may not be completely discussed, understood, or solved, it is necessary for the physician to turn his attention to the problems of the next patient who is sitting in the waiting room. But the physician must first get rid of the patient then in his office, and in a manner which will make all parties comfortable.

"Prescribing is, theoretically at least, a means of terminating the interview in a fashion that satisfies both doctor and patient," Dr. Muller said. "The prescription is a signal for the approaching end to the encounter, it both summarizes and carries forward the relationship, it is an expression of concern, and it deals with interests of both parties in a manner perceived as equitable." [53] This, she noted, would appear to be excellent psychological strategy. It may or may not be good medical practice.

Another aspect of the fundamental but generally unmentioned role of the prescription has been analyzed by Dr. Michael Balint and his associates at University College Hospital, London, in a study of patients who obtain repeat prescriptions of drugs—especially of psychoactive drugs—and a parallel study of their doctors.[54] "On the basis of our results," Dr. Balint said,

> we think that in reality repeat prescription is a diagnosis, not of the patient, nor of his doctor, but of the doctor-patient relationship. This is the reason why doctors in general find this condition so difficult to treat; treatment in the traditional sense means that there is something "wrong" in the patient, an illness, which either must be put right or its consequences counteracted. Since the cause of the trouble is only partly in the patient, all attempts at the traditional form of therapy are likely to fail. If, however, it is realized that repeat prescription is a diagnosis that something has gone wrong with the patient-doctor relationship, new possibilities open up for a new kind of therapy. When devising this new therapy, two important factors must never be lost from sight. One is that in a repeat-prescription regime, the drug has become a representative of the "something" that the patient so badly needs. It must, therefore, be respected, and the repeat prescription cannot be simply taken away without replacing it by something equally valuable. The second factor is the collusion between patient and doctor, which means that it is never the patient alone who must be helped to change but also his physician.

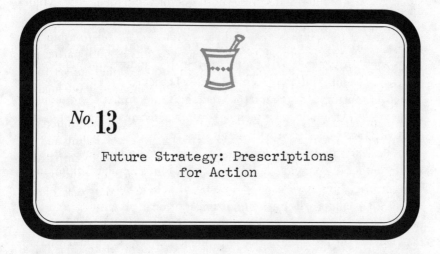

Future Strategy: Prescriptions
for Action

MUCH of the use of pharmaceutical
agents in this country has been rational and brilliantly successful. Lives
have been saved, pain has been alleviated, the anguish of severe mental
illness has been tempered, crippling has been prevented, recovery has
been made quicker, and some age-old plagues have been essentially
obliterated.

But it is only too evident that a significant portion of drug use,
both prescription and over-the-counter, is unnecessary and irrational.
This misuse is largely the result of (1) the lack of skepticism or the
outright naiveté of both physicians and patients; (2) the flood of
advertising and other drug promotion that has too often been unobjec-
tive, incomplete, or misleading; (3) the lack of readily available drug
information that is objective; (4) the widespread use of a drug on the
usually false premise that "it may not help but it won't hurt"; and (5) the
equally widespread belief among the public that there is or must be a pill
for every ill.

Unfortunately, irrational drug use has often been condemned
principally on economic grounds. To those who focus their attention
solely on the financial aspects of the problem, the solutions are

self-evident: cut the price of drugs, slash the profits of the drug industry, revolutionize the drug patent system, or turn the pharmaceutical industry into a national public utility. The high prices of some drug products and the incredible inconsistencies of drug pricing in general cannot be readily justified by ordinary economic arguments, and not even by the industry's constant emphasis on the riskiness of its operations. The present drug patent system is not perfect, and the advantages and disadvantages of changing it should be carefully weighed by the health professions, economists, the drug industry, the Congress, and society in general. The profits of the drug industry are large, but there is no substantial agreement on whether they are too large. Moreover, putting a discriminatory ceiling on the profits of an industry might well place a similar ceiling on inventiveness, ingenuity, and creativity that would eventually harm society.

To our minds, any attempt to solve the problem just to save money, either the patient's or the taxpayer's, is of secondary importance. The primary objective is not lower costs but better health. The significant challenge lies in minimizing irrational prescribing and irrational self-medication in order to improve the quality of health care and the patients' health, limit drug dependence of any kind, and prevent needless drug-induced illness and drug-induced death.

In any consideration of the steps that might be taken, it must be emphasized at the outset that the drugs now available, when used appropriately, can be a boon to mankind. Society must see to it that every patient needing drugs for the prevention, control, or treatment of disease can obtain them. Access to these vital products should be assured by insurance programs, government subsidy, or whatever other technique may be practical.

Society urgently needs new drugs that are better than the ones we have today—more effective, safer, less costly, able to prevent or alleviate diseases that are now uncontrollable. But there is no great need for drugs that are only new. Such me-too drugs, offering no substantial clinical or economic benefits, merely litter the pharmaceutical landscape.

The achievement of these primary goals will require action by physicians, pharmacists, industry, and government, and especially by the public—as patients, as purchasers of drugs, as taxpayers, and as voters. The public must take far more vigorous action and accept far more responsibility than it has ever taken or accepted in the past.

THE PHYSICIAN

Medicine is too important to leave exclusively to the doctors, but medical problems both on a day-to-day basis and in terms of long-term policy can scarcely be solved without them. The record has shown that the prescribing attitudes and practices of many physicians are marked by serious deficiencies. The factors that contribute to such deficiencies have been analyzed by the HEW Task Force on Prescription Drugs,[1] and by many writers in and out of medicine, and were discussed in earlier chapters of this book.

As a vital step in controlling irrational prescribing, the need to improve the teaching of pharmacology and especially clinical pharmacology for medical students and medical residents in training has been stressed repeatedly.[2] Equally important are programs of continuing education for physicians already in practice, especially where these can be conducted in community hospitals, teaching hospitals, and university medical centers.

To improve the accessibility of objective, accurate drug information, a number of options are open. The package insert, which is now financed by the industry, should be replaced by an industry-financed, medically edited, and government-approved compendium listing and describing every prescription drug product legally on the market. It should be updated periodically and be supplemented with price information. Special journals dealing specifically with prescribing (*The Medical Letter* is an outstanding example) should be published by private groups of experts, should not be dependent on any drug advertising, and should be distributed at the expense of the government to all physicians in practice.

A major step would be achieved by enabling major medical journals to publish without the support of advertising. Some editors have welcomed this proposal in theory, for it would leave them free to comment as they saw fit on irrational prescribing and misleading drug promotion; but they sadly admitted that they could not give up their advertising revenues without facing bankruptcy. At least two solutions are possible. On the one hand, the journals that eliminated drug advertising could simply raise their subscription prices to physicians, who would probably pass on the additional cost to their patients. On the other, a few major foundations might well decide to subsidize at least some advertising-free journals on the grounds that this could minimize the cost of irrational prescribing.

Since 1966, when FDA commissioner James Goddard began his crackdown on drug promotion, there has been a visible decrease in the total volume of prescription drug advertising and a substantial improvement in its quality. There are, nevertheless, many loopholes yet to be closed. In the case of OTC advertising to the public, forceful action should be considered by the Congress. Control of all OTC advertising might well be transferred from the Federal Trade Commission to FDA, and preclearance by FDA be required by law. Any company violating the rules should be obliged to make an open retraction in the form of a "Dear Public" letter, prominently published or broadcast. The medical profession should take the lead in examining the consequences for patients of the indiscriminate use of OTC drugs and the relationship of these problems to OTC advertising, and it should then suggest appropriate solutions.

Physicians face another problem—the detail man. This industry representative, or salesman, is the source of much excellent information for physicians on brand-name drug products. But biased, inaccurate, or overzealous detail men pose problems for which practical solutions remain to be found. To improve the situation, it has been proposed that all detail men be trained and recruited from the ranks of pharmacy graduates, that they be required to undergo continuing education, that they be licensed by a government agency, that they be required to provide each physician with an FDA-approved statement summarizing those claims that are based on fact, and even that local medical societies establish "truth squads" that will follow up a detail man's presentation with whatever corrective material may be necessary.

The most effective control, however, will rest on the ability of the individual physician to view all claims with a high degree of skepticism and sophistication. One drug industry spokesman has described the situation in these words: "Effective promotion, heavy promotion, sustained promotion has carried the day. The physicians have been sold. So has the country. . . . The best defense the physician can muster against this kind of advertising is a healthy skepticism and a willingness, not always apparent in the past, to do his homework." [3]

As an expedient, the physician can make more use of the homework already being done by his colleagues. In many hospitals, there is now a Pharmacy and Therapeutics Committee—which usually includes both pharmacists and physicians—that seeks to guide the prescribing patterns of all physicians on the staff. In some instances, they may offer only informal suggestions, which any physician is free to accept or reject. In others, the hospital committee has clear authority to permit or ban the use of any product.

In many hospitals, the committee decisions are reflected in a formulary, or list of the approved drugs that may be prescribed and that will be stocked in the hospital pharmacy. Often, they ban costly brand-name or me-too products which, in the committee's view, are not clinically needed. Similar formularies have been adopted by some voluntary health insurance systems and by various state and federal health programs. Any substantial extension of the formulary system, especially in Medicare and other federal programs, has been vigorously opposed, however, by the drug industry. Industry spokesmen have charged that a formulary may dangerously interfere with the practice of medicine, result in second-class medical care, and do great injury to patients.

In its *Final Report*, the Task Force on Prescription Drugs reached these conclusions:

> In general, the Task Force finds, American physicians have found a formulary acceptable and practical, especially when it is designed by their clinical and scientific colleagues serving on expert committees, when quality is considered at least as important as price, when the formulary can be revised at appropriate intervals, and when there are provisions for prescribing unlisted drug products where special clinical conditions so demand.
>
> We find that the use of a formulary is not a mark of second-class medicine, but is, in fact, associated with the provision of the highest quality of medicine in the outstanding hospitals in the Nation.
>
> Although use of a formulary is not a guarantee of high-quality medical care, rational prescribing, effective utilization review, and control of costs, we find that the achievement of these objectives in a drug program is difficult if not impossible without it.[4]

We continue to believe that this conclusion was a sound one and that drug formularies can have an important place in improving the quality of medical care.

The next obvious step must be the extension of the formulary system and the involvement of the clinical pharmacist outside of the hospital. These community programs could best be undertaken by group practice clinics and by county medical societies. Such a step, involving reasonable guidelines established by the physicians themselves with the advice of pharmacists and other experts, should be begun on a voluntary basis. But if the guidelines are not set up by health professionals in the community, under growing federal health programs they will almost certainly be set up by government. Indeed, the Professional Standards Review Organization section of the Social Security Amendments of 1972 (Public Law 92-603) allows just three years for guidelines to be implemented. Although organized medicine was officially opposed to these amendments, physicians in local and state medical societies and medical-society-sponsored medical care foundations are now actively involved in developing the guidelines and the procedures to make them work.

Medicine and its allied professions must take a more careful look at the prescribing competence of particular individuals or groups of prescribers. Just as medicine has reached the painful but inevitable conclusions that not all physicians are competent to perform surgery, that not all surgeons are competent to perform open-heart surgery, and that some physicians should be allowed to operate only when a skilled expert stands alongside, the welfare of patients may demand similar decisions in the use of drugs. For instance, there are some drugs that are valuable under certain conditions but so hazardous that their use—except in cases of emergency—might well be limited to specially trained physicians practicing in approved medical centers. There are some physicians whose records of constantly irrational prescribing are so deplorable that a hospital or a local medical society might require that each of their prescriptions be reviewed and countersigned by a drug expert. In the past there have been physicians whose prescribing of narcotics has been so atrocious that they have been prohibited from prescribing such drugs for many years or even for life. It is conceivable that the prescribing patterns of certain physicians have been so irrational, and have resulted in so much injury to their patients, that all their prescribing rights must be banned. And these are responsibilities which must be accepted by the medical profession itself.

Finally, physicians must make a searching examination of the role largely forced upon them by society—a role in which they feel obliged to function as universal healers. They should seek nonchemical methods to assist patients suffering from the social and emotional stresses of life.

THE PHARMACIST

In the hospital, the pharmacist can function most effectively in the control of irrational drug use by serving as consultant and adviser to nurses, to patients, and most significantly, to physicians. Out of the hospital, in community pharmacies, the pharmacist must also play a more responsible role. Here his advice can also be helpful to prescribing physicians in the community, but often it will be he alone who can serve as consultant to the patient, particularly where OTCs are concerned.

He can function as perhaps the most readily available source of information on OTCs in the community. He can refuse to stock and sell remedies he considers ineffective or inappropriate. He can advise all potential purchasers that such products as OTC headache remedies, available at a wide range of prices, have essentially no difference in clinical value. He can also alert the patient to the problems he may encounter because of drug interactions, particularly if he keeps adequate drug records on the patients who consult him.

Many pharmacists—particularly recent graduates—have been trained to serve as clinically oriented professionals and are eager to do so. Under a system that rewards them only by success in merchandizing— the more sales, the higher their income—they face economic penalties that make clinical pharmacy a career that may be emotionally satisfying but financially disastrous. There would appear to be one clear-cut solution. The system must be so changed that the professional pharmacist, like his colleagues in other health professions, will receive compensation based on the value of his knowledge, his skill, and his time.[5] For the community-based pharmacist, this calls for a fee-for-service approach, under which the pharmacist would receive the identical professional fee regardless of the price of the product he dispenses. It would be appropriate—but more difficult to achieve—if the pharmacist were to receive compensation whether the patient elects to buy a drug or not to buy. (For the pharmacist associated with a prepaid group practice, of course, the professional compensation is a simple matter and can be readily determined within the organization.)

Since pharmacists are already involved in filling prescriptions under federally financed programs, and since the likelihood is great that this involvement will increase over the coming years, consideration should be given to legislation and regulations that could enable pharmacists to contribute even more effectively to the quality of health care. Thus, as a requirement for participation in federal programs, it might well be made mandatory for pharmacists to maintain drug records on all out-of-hospital patients and to consult these records before dispensing any prescription. They should similarly be required to counsel these ambulatory patients on the nature of each prescription, the reason why it was ordered, the results that are expected, the adverse reactions that might occur, and any special precautions needed for proper use and storage of the drug. In order for the pharmacist to offer the most helpful guidance, it should be required that all prescriptions carry the physician's diagnosis, either spelled out or given in code symbols, if the prescription is to be accepted for reimbursement under any federal program. Under such programs, no prescription should be approved for reimbursement if it carries such vague instructions as "take as directed."

Pharmacy schools should be urged or required to give their students sufficient training in measuring blood pressure, pulse rate, and similar physical signs, so that, with the approval of the physician, the pharmacist can carry on effective surveillance of patients undergoing long-term drug treatment for such chronic diseases as pernicious anemia, diabetes, and hypertension—permitting refills as indicated, calling for laboratory tests, and urging the patient to seek a physician visit when this is indicated. Consideration should be given to the proposal that practicing pharmacists be required to take periodic postgraduate courses as a prerequisite for license renewal—a suggestion that has already been made for physicians and other health professionals—or that pharmacists voluntarily taking postgraduate refresher courses should qualify for higher professional fees. Some states are already implementing requirements for continuing education in pharmacy.

INDUSTRY

A responsible drug industry should undertake on its own the following steps:

—Reexamine its research directions, company by company, to determine if they are in the best interests of both the company and the public
—Minimize efforts to develop and market me-too products
—Improve the quality of evidence submitted to obtain FDA approval of a new drug
—Relinquish its position as chief educator of the medical profession on drug use, and return this role to the health professions, providing no-strings-attached grants for the development of programs in clinical pharmacology and clinical pharmacy, as well as in continuing education
—Eliminate the practice of distributing free drug samples unless these are requested by prescribers (Some companies have already abolished this practice on their own. California has banned it by state law.)
—Reduce the quantity and improve the quality of drug promotion, facing up to the fact that at least some detail men have been far overstepping the boundaries of objectivity
—Moderate the quantity of OTC promotion directed at the public, and

be prepared to face the possibility that the public may demand that drug advertising be shown to be as safe and effective as the drug itself
—Consider the evidence that the industry has perhaps unwittingly taken a leading role in inducing physicians to overprescribe antibiotics, psychoactive drugs, and other products, and the charges that it is involved in a campaign of "mystification" aimed at dreaming up new diseases to be controlled by old drugs and to use medical treatment for nonmedical ailments
—Phase out the use of brand names and instead, if the companies have the pride in their own firms which they so fervently claim, let them market drugs labeled only by generic name plus company name.

It seems likely, however, that the industry will make what we believe to be essential changes only when these are required by law, or when the industry discovers that a continuation of some of its practices has become unprofitable. We may now be on the verge of witnessing the application of such an economic lever through the further expansion of government-financed health programs.

THE FEDERAL GOVERNMENT

In each of the three broad categories in which the federal government plays a role—research, regulation, and purchase or reimbursement—existing programs can be strengthened and policy alternatives should be considered. In research and research training, it has been difficult to generate the kind of public and congressional support for pharmacology, pharmaceutical chemistry, and related fields that has long been available for more glamorous assaults on cancer, heart ailments, and such crippling diseases as poliomyelitis and arthritis. There is now a need to strengthen university and independent, nonprofit research institute programs in such areas as pharmacology and toxicology. Here such a group as the Institute of Medicine/National Academy of Sciences might well review present federal, industry, and university policies and programs involving drug research, and then make recommendations for appropriate action.

Within FDA itself, research and regulation sometimes seem to be in conflict, yet they should both serve the same broad national goals. The criticism of FDA by such a distinguished pharmacologist as Dr. Walter Modell of Cornell cannot be dismissed lightly. In 1970 he expressed a view widely shared then and now by many of his colleagues. He wrote:

The FDA should have been the protector of the public, adviser to the medical profession, collaborator of the clinical investigator, and guide and consultant to the pharmaceutical industry. Now, sixty years after its inception, the public still needs better protection against the hazards of new drugs, the medical profession still needs expert advice on drugs, clinical investigators still need assistance in pursuing research on drugs for man, and the pharmaceutical industry would welcome an efficient guide to the manufacture of new drugs.[6]

What steps might be taken to enable FDA to reach such desirable goals? Certainly nothing can be accomplished by a continuation of the intense political pressures placed on the agency or by the highly publicized efforts to make FDA the whipping boy in the constant disputes among the drug industry, organized medicine, and consumer groups. The FDA leadership must rightfully be held to account for its deeds and misdeeds, but not every week on the week.

More efforts must be made to strengthen the scientific capability of FDA, improve its decision-making processes, and move it into the mainstream of biomedical research and training. Within FDA there must be a broader research base linked to clinical pharmacological units in medical schools. Intramural and intermural educational programs must be expanded. There should be greater use of independent nongovernmental consultants. Internal managerial changes are needed to streamline review processes and remove the current incentives for procrastination and buck-passing.

Many of the current federal activities concerning drugs could be dramatically modified by a series of proposals introduced by Senator Gaylord Nelson in what has become known as his omnibus drug bill.[7] His proposal calls for the establishment of a national drug testing and evaluation center, where tests of new drug products for safety, efficacy, and biological availability would be conducted by investigators supported by government rather than industry funds. No new drug would be accepted unless it were demonstrably safer, more effective, or less costly than any similar product on the market. A national drug compendium would describe all drugs legally on the market, with the products listed by their generic names. A "Formulary of the U.S." would list only those products which could be purchased by federal agencies or whose cost would be reimbursed in Medicare, Medicaid, or any other tax-supported program. A new drug plant must pass inspection *before* it goes into production. The secretary of HEW would be authorized to call for batch-by-batch certification—now required mainly for antibiotics and insulin—for any product when this seems necessary.

Whether any or all of Senator Nelson's proposals, and similar recommendations made by others, will be adopted into law remains to be determined. In any case, neither apathy nor the opposition of any self-interested group should be allowed to prevail and to prevent careful congressional examination.

DRUG INSURANCE

In the opinion of many longtime observers of the political scene, it is only a matter of time before some version of national health insurance or national health service will be enacted. It is not yet clear whether such a program will involve an insurance approach, with reimbursement provided by the government for most or all health expenditures; a national health service approach, with physicians and other health workers directly employed by the government; or the compulsory payment of premiums to private companies by employer and employee, with government subsidy provided where needed.

Under any of these methods, it seems almost certain that the coverage will include prescription drugs. Depending on how the ground rules are written, such drug insurance will have a major impact—possibly a revolutionary influence—on the prescribing and dispensing of drugs and on the drug industry itself.

It seems essential that any government insurance program involving drug coverage must be based on the use of a formulary listing those products that the program will cover. The formulary might be wide open, including all drugs legally on the market, but such an all-inclusive approach could be economically disastrous. As a more probable alternative, the formulary would include only those drugs which are demonstrated to be not only necessary, safe, and effective but available at a reasonable price. The government—the representative of the people paying the bill—would ultimately have to determine what prices are reasonable.

Herein lies one mechanism for controlling the unjustified use of needless, costly, me-too drugs. Presumably, the physician might ignore the formulary and continue to prescribe me-too drugs, and the pharmacist would continue to dispense them, but unless valid clinical evidence were presented to justify their use on an individual patient, the program would simply not pay for them. Under such conditions, it seems reasonable to assume that a company would quickly find that developing these duplicative products and marketing them with costly promotion campaigns would be economically unsound.

A second vitally important technique would call for what has become known as drug utilization review. This has been described as a dynamic, constantly modified process aimed first at rational prescribing and the consequent improvement of the quality of health care, and second at the minimizing of needless drug expenditures.[8] Since the Task Force on Prescription Drugs strongly recommended its use in any drug insurance program, utilization review has evoked growing interest.[9] A number of physicians and pharmacists, mainly in hospitals and similar centers, have been maintaining surveillance on how physicians actually prescribe, which drugs they order for which diagnosis, the drug quantities they order, the frequency of refills permitted, and the relative costs involved. The information obtained is then reviewed by a group of the physician's peers. Was the prescribed drug actually the one preferred for the patient's condition? Was it prescribed in adequate, inadequate, or grossly excessive amounts? Was the drug prescribed even though an equally safe and effective but less costly product was available? Could the prescribed drug result in an unnecessary interaction with other medications being taken by the patient? Was the prescribing physician aware that the patient was simultaneously taking drugs ordered by other physicians? Did the patient suffer an adverse reaction for which the prescribed drug or drugs might be guilty?

On the basis of this kind of review, physicians found to be writing seemingly irrational prescriptions can be invited to justify their practices; recommendations or regulations can be established to improve prescribing patterns throughout the hospital; errant physicians can be urged to mend their ways; the hospital pharmacist may be instructed not to fill any prescription that a committee of experts considers to be needless or dangerous; and appropriate changes may be made in the hospital's drug purchasing policies. The Task Force on Prescription Drugs stated:

> Although the use of formularies or utilization review may be construed in some quarters as interference with medical practice, such steps would be neither unprecedented nor necessarily disadvantageous. . . . Formularies have been widely and effectively used in many hospitals and in nongovernmental and governmental drug programs, both to improve care and reduce costs. Precedents for utilization review may be found in many hospitals in this country and abroad, in the efforts by numerous hospital pharmacy and therapeutics committees, in the reviews of medical services initiated by some local medical societies, and in the drug review procedures used in Great Britain and other countries.[10]

Effective utilization review usually requires electronic data processing and the computerization of drug prescribing and dispensing. This step is not inexpensive, and may not be justified merely by savings in drug expenditures[11] or by detecting fraud or program abuse. On the other hand, it seems evident that virtually any kind of national drug insurance program in the United States will require the use of source data automation and computers if only to process the tens or hundreds of millions of claims that will have to be handled each year. Using the same computer system for maintaining surveillance on drug utilization, with all its potential benefits for improving the quality of health care, would represent a dividend of incalculable value.

Critics of such drug utilization review (with some governmental Big Brother keeping his eye on the prescription pad of every physician) have proposed that if there must be drug insurance, let it be written by such nongovernmental institutions as Blue Shield, Blue Cross, and the private insurance companies. This view is apparently based on the premise that these nongovernmental institutions would exert no control over a physician's prescribing preferences. But insurance companies have long since learned that they can no more allow a physician to prescribe any quantity of any drug at any cost than they can allow him to charge any fee for any operation he decides a patient may need. To permit such practices could drive a company into bankruptcy or force it to raise its premiums to intolerable levels.

PROFESSIONAL STANDARDS REVIEW ORGANIZATIONS

Utilization and medical care quality review was accorded new status by the Social Security Amendments of 1972. The law provides for the establishment of Professional Standards Review Organizations (PSROs), each reviewing a substantial number of physicians (probably three hundred or more) and assuming responsibility for a comprehensive, ongoing study of services covered under the Medicare and Medicaid programs. Each PSRO will be responsible for assuring that hospital care and other institutional services were both medically necessary and provided in accordance with professional standards. At its option, and with approval of the Secretary of Health, Education, and Welfare, a PSRO may assume responsibility for noninstitutional services.

The development of hospital medical information systems, including drug information systems, will facilitate the work of both hospital review committees and the PSROs. These systems, combined with appropriate utilization review, should eventually become a requirement for hospital accreditation. They might also be the basis for the development of a nationwide medical or drug information system.

A significant aspect of the new PSRO law is that it would presumably allow a local group of physicians to spell out in more or less detail a description of what is acceptable drug therapy in its community. These guidelines would not only serve as an informative aid to prescribing physicians. They would also offer some guarantee to the doctor that, if he follows these locally accepted rules, he cannot be justifiably charged with malpractice.

AND LAST BUT NOT LEAST

Patients themselves cannot escape the charge that they, by their own attitudes and actions, have contributed in a devastating fashion to the incidence of needless drug use, adverse drug reactions, drug-induced injury, and drug-induced death. They have pressured a physician to prescribe, even against his better judgment. They have insisted on getting a prescription mainly on the grounds that their insurance will cover it. They have become prescription shoppers, going from one physician to the next to obtain a multiplicity of medications, and frequently have neglected to mention their use of multiple drugs when giving their medical histories. They have taken a drug prescribed for another member of their family and used it themselves, presumably in the belief that two diseases marked by similar symptoms must call for the identical therapy.

When they have been given a prescription drug with specific directions, the odds have been alarmingly high that they would take far too little or far too much. According to one review, "The percentage of patients making errors in the self-administration of prescribed medications, with few exceptions, has ranged between 25 and 59 percent. . . . In addition, 4 to 35 percent of the patients were misusing their medications in such a manner as to pose serious threats to health." [12]

In the study it was found that more than one-fifth of diabetic patients were taking either one-half or double the prescribed dose of insulin. In one survey, covering only "reliable" patients, 31 percent were taking less than 70 percent of their prescribed medications. In a group of tuberculosis patients, 48 percent admitted they were taking their medications irregularly or not at all. In a group told to take antibiotics regularly for ten days to control streptococcus infections, 56 percent decided on their own to stop therapy by the third day, 71 percent by the sixth, and 82 percent by the ninth. Part of these failures to comply with directions may be the result of inadequate instructions. "In our society," it was stated, "better instructions are provided when purchasing a new camera or automobile than when the patient receives a life-saving antibiotic or cardiac drug." But certainly part may be blamed on the patients themselves.

Patients have contributed to the general confusion in this area by demanding that every drug must be not relatively safe but 100 percent safe. They have pilloried FDA for refusing to allow a drug on the market even though the agency found there was no substantial evidence to show that it was effective. They have demanded an equal voice with scientists in debating such technical matters as the clinical value of Vitamin E, the bioflavonoids, and a variety of what experts have branded as useless "cancer cures." A survey[13] conducted for FDA disclosed such findings as these:

—An estimated fifty million adults would not be convinced by almost unanimous expert opinion that a hypothetical "cancer cure" was worthless.

—Millions of Americans make decisions on their personal health problems on the basis that "anything is worth a try."

—Three-fourths of the public were convinced that supplemental vitamins provide more pep and energy.

—An estimated sixteen million adults reported they had arthritis, rheumatism, asthma, allergies, heart disease, high blood pressure, or diabetes, although they had not been diagnosed by a physician. About the same number indicated that they would medicate themselves for such ailments as sore throat, cough, sleeplessness, or upset stomach for more than two weeks without consulting a physician.

—Two-thirds of all adults believe a bowel movement every day is essential to health.

—Millions of Americans are convinced that drug advertising is so closely regulated that serious distortions are unlikely, and outright fabrications are nearly impossible. "There is a feeling that 'they wouldn't dare' make up 'evidence' to support a claim, or falsify testimonials because 'they would be caught.'"

—In enormous numbers, they decide their own therapy on the basis of self-diagnosis that may or may not be accurate, advertising claims that may or may not be deceitful (or advertising that may, in fact, be honest but misinterpreted by the reader), and the well-intentioned advice of friends, relatives, and neighbors, all in what was described as an epidemic of rampant empiricism.

Some of these attitudes and actions may be attributable to a growing credibility gap in the once close doctor-patient relationship, and an increasing belief that the doctor doesn't always know best. Some may represent a credibility gap between the public and organized medicine, and mounting suspicion that the dependence of organized medicine on the drug industry may be too close for comfort—or too close for safety. Some may be the unhappy results of the town-versus-gown disputes, with some practicing physicians, basing their views on "clinical judgments" and on their implicit confidence in the absolute integrity of all drug companies, pitted against ivory-tower colleagues who base their views on scientific evidence—disputes that weaken the public's confidence in both physicians and scientists. And some are certainly related to the ingrained belief that the average American—regardless of his education or training—possesses a built-in core of common sense that enables him to brush aside all manner of intellectual camouflage and arrive at simple, commonsense answers to what are (or should be) such basically simple problems as the diagnosis of diabetes, the detection of cardiovascular disease, the value of an arthritis "cure," the treatment of cancer, and the spotting of dishonest claims in a drug advertisement.

It is our belief that the government, acting on the best scientific evidence it can accumulate (and not on testimonials, unsupported "clinical judgments," and the views of consumer groups, industry groups, or other special interests), has the authority and inescapable responsibility to determine which drugs may be legally permitted on the market. In addition, the government, through FDA or whatever consumer protection agency may eventually be involved, should have the responsibility for transmitting drug information to the public, and for taking a leading role in this vital field of consumer education.

Patients as well as physicians have the right to know the scientific basis supporting all claims of drug safety, efficacy, quality, and costs. Unless patients have this right, and the wit to act on the knowledge available to them, all the other steps proposed to achieve the goal of rational drug use—improving the education of physicians, modifying the system of pharmacist compensation, controlling drug detail men, and all the rest—will have only limited impact.

Certainly each patient should be able to ask both his physician and his pharmacist about the known values and hazards of any drug he is supposed to take. Each container of an OTC product should be labeled to indicate not only the approved uses of the drug but also its major hazards, and all this information should be presented in simple terms and in suitably large type. Similar information should be included in every advertisement recommending use of the product. Furthermore, the caution should be presented not in such general terms as "The Surgeon General has determined that cigarette smoking is dangerous to your health," or "Any drug you are about to swallow may work against you," but "This drug may cause gastric hemorrhage," "This drug may cause you to fall asleep when you are driving," or "If you are pregnant, this drug may cause you to produce a defective child."

Advertisements for OTC products should state clearly the identity of the active ingredient rather than mask it under some such phrase as "the pain reliever most frequently prescribed by doctors." If the pain reliever is actually aspirin, the public should be so informed. Each individual can then decide for himself whether to buy one hundred tablets of aspirin labeled as aspirin for 69¢, or labeled as something else for $2.50. Advertisements touting a product with such a claim as "approved by four out of five doctors" should be required to disclose whether this ratio involved a survey of five thousand or five hundred or fifty physicians, or whether, in fact, only five physicians were queried.

Some prescription drugs—antibiotics, steroid hormones, sedatives, tranquilizers, digitalis, and the more potent analgesics—should be dispensed only when a brief, simple statement is attached to point out the probable effects, the possible side effects, and the hazards of not taking as directed. The inclusion of such a warning statement with each container of prescribed oral contraceptives has now been required by FDA, and could profitably be applied to other drug classes. No prescription should be dispensed with such easy-to-misunderstand directions as "take as needed" or "take as directed." A patient is entitled to be reminded of precisely why, how, and when a drug is to be used, and when it is likely to deteriorate after storage and should therefore be discarded.

The influence of public disclosure should not be underestimated, as was indicated by the drastic decrease in the prescription of chloramphenicol after the accounts of its dangers were reported by the press. This must be attributable principally to the action of consumers, since physicians had long been informed about the problem but generally failed to halt their irrational use of the drug.

In any nationwide effort to provide long-needed drug information to the public, a vital part must be taken by the public media. Some magazines and newspapers have already become involved, publishing objective accounts of both the good and the bad about drugs. Other publications evidently selected a more discreet policy and maintained tactful silence on the subject. Yet many newspapers and magazines, and certainly most radio and television stations, continued to accept advertising that contained misleading claims. The customary defense of such policies—"We don't censor advertising claims, that's up to the Federal Trade Commission"—may be legally valid, but it scarcely represents a service to the public. We would hope that, on their own, the media will develop and implement practical methods of controlling misleading drug advertising before the public demands that all public drug advertising be terminated.

Prescriptions for action, such as those we have considered, require analysis by a variety of individuals, groups, and institutions. As we have noted, the problems will not disappear if the alternatives we have proposed fall on deaf ears, or are blocked by apathy or the opposition of special interests. There is no single focal point for responsibility, but it is clear that six are central: physicians, pharmacists, the drug industry, government, the mass media, and organized groups of consumers. After studying and living with these problems for the past seven years, we believe that the next round will belong to the consumer.

Generic Name	Brand Name	Drug Class or Major Therapeutic Use
acetaminophen + aspirin + caffeine + methapyrilene fumarate + salicylamide	Excedrin-PM	Analgesic
acetazolamide	Diamox	Diuretic
aminophylline	Aminodrox	Bronchial dilator
amitriptyline	Elavil	Antidepressant
amphotericin + tetracycline	Mysteclin-F	Antibiotic
ampicillin	Polycillin, Principen	Antibiotic
aspirin + caffeine + codeine + phenacetin	Empirin Compound with Codeine	Analgesic
aspirin + caffeine + phenacetin + propoxyphene	Darvon Compound	Analgesic
benactyzine + meprobamate	Deprol	Antidepressant, antianxiety
bishydroxycoumarin	Dicumarol	Anticoagulant
caffeine + sugar	Vivarin	Stimulant
carbenoxalone	Biogastrone	Ulcer therapy
cephalexin	Keflex	Antibiotic
chloral hydrate	Noctec	Sedative
chloramphenicol	Chloromycetin	Antibiotic
chlordiazepoxide	Librium	Antianxiety
chlorothiazide	Diuril	Diuretic
chlorothiazide + reserpine	Diupres	Antihypertensive
chlorpheniramine + isopropamide + phenylpropanolamine	Ornade	Antihistamine, decongestant
chlorpromazine	Thorazine	Antipsychotic
chlorpropamide	Diabinese	Diabetes therapy
chlortetracycline	Aureomycin	Antibiotic
cloxacillin	Tegopen	Antibiotic
cytosine arabinoside	Cytosar	Anticancer-therapy

Generic Name	Brand Name	Drug Class or Major Therapeutic Use
demethylchlortetra-cycline	Declomycin	Antibiotic
dextro-amphetamine	Dexedrine	Stimulant, appetite depressant
diazepam	Valium	Antianxiety
diethylstilbesterol	Stilbetin	Estrogen
digoxin	Lanoxin	Cardiotonic
diphenhydramine	Benadryl	Antihistamine
diphenylhydantoin	Dilantin	Anticonvulsant, epilepsy therapy
doxepin	Sinequan	Antianxiety
epinephrine	Adrenalin	Asthma and allergy therapy, local anes-thetic aid
erythromycin	Erythrocin, E-Mycin	Antibiotic
erythromycin ethyl-succinate	Pediamycin	Antibiotic
estradiol	Progynon	Sex hormone, anti-cancer therapy
ethynodiol diacetate + ethinyl estradiol	Demulen	Contraceptive
ethynodiol diacetate + mestranol	Ovulen	Contraceptive
fenfluramine	Pondimin	Appetite depressant
ferrous gluconate	Fergon	Anemia therapy
ferrous sulfate	Feosol	Anemia therapy
furazolidone	Furoxone	Antibacterial
furosemide	Lasix	Diuretic
glutethimide	Doriden	Sedative
griseofulvin	Fulvicin-U/F, Grifulvin V, Grisactin	Antifungal
guanethidine	Ismelin	Antihypertensive
hydralazine	Apresoline	Antihypertensive
hydralazine + hydro-chlorothiazide + reserpine	Ser-Ap-Es	Antihypertensive
hydrochlorothiazide	Esidrix, Hydrodiuril	Diuretic
hydrochlorothiazide + protoveratrine + reserpine	Salutensin	Antihypertensive
hydrochlorothiazide + reserpine	Hydropres	Antihypertensive
hydrocortisone	Cort-Dome, Cortef	Anti-inflammatory
hydroxyzine hydro-chloride	Atarax	Antianxiety

Generic Name	Brand Name	Drug Class or Major Therapeutic Use
hydroxyzine pamoate	Vistaril	Antianxiety
imipramine	Tofranil	Antidepressant
indomethacin	Indocin	Antiarthritic
isocarboxazid	Marplan	Antidepressant (monoamine oxidase inhibitor)
isoniazid	INH	Tuberculosis therapy
isoproterenol	Isuprel, Proternol	Bronchial dilator
ketamine	Ketalar, Ketaject	General anesthetic
levodopa, *l*-Dopa	Dopar, Larodopa	Antiparkinsonism
lithium carbonate	Eskalith, Lithane	Antipsychotic
MAO inhibitors	(see isocarboxazid, nialamide)	
meclizine	Bonine, Bonamine	Antinauseant
mefenamic acid	Ponstel	Analgesic
meperidine	Demerol	Analgesic
meprobamate	Equanil, Miltown	Antianxiety
mesoridazine	Serentil	Antipsychotic
methadone	Dolophine	Analgesic
methotrexate	Methotrexate	Anticancer, psoriasis therapy
methyclothiazide	Enduron	Diuretic
methyldopa	Aldomet	Antihypertensive
methylphenidate	Ritalin	Stimulant
mithramycin	Mithracin	Anticancer therapy
neomycin	Neobiotic, Mycifradin	Antibiotic
nialamide	Niamid	Antidepressant (monoamine oxidase inhibitor)
nitrofurantoin	Furadantin	Antibacterial
nitroglycerin	Nitro-Bid, Nitroglyn, Nitrostat	Angina pectoris therapy
norethindrone	Norlutin	Abortion preventive
norethindrone acetate + ethinyl estradiol	Norlestrin	Contraceptive
norethynodrel + mestranol	Enovid	Contraceptive
nortriptyline	Aventyl	Antidepressant
novobiocin + tetracycline	Panalba	Antibiotic
oxyphencyclimine	Daricon	Antispasmodic
oxytetracycline	Terramycin	Antibiotic
para-aminosalicylic acid (PAS)	Rezipas, Pamisyl	Tuberculosis therapy
penicillin G	Pentids, Pfizerpen	Antibiotic

Generic Name	Brand Name	Drug Class or Major Therapeutic Use
pentobarbital	Nembutal	Sedative
phenformin hydro-chloride	DBI	Diabetes therapy
phenobarbital	Luminal	Sedative
phenylbutazone	Butazolidin	Antiarthritic
potassium-phenoxy-methyl-penicillin	V-Cillin-K	Antibiotic
prednisolone	Delta-Cortef, Meticortelone Acetate	Anti-inflammatory
prednisone	Deltasone, Meticorten	Anti-inflammatory
probenecid	Benamid	Gout therapy
procarbazine	Matulane	Anticancer therapy
prochlorperazine	Compazine	Antinauseant, antipsychotic
propoxyphene	Darvon	Analgesic
pseudo-ephedrine	Sudafed	Bronchial dilator
reserpine	Serpasil	Antihypertensive
rifampin	Rifadin, Rimactane	Tuberculosis therapy
secobarbital	Seconal	Sedative
spironolactone	Aldactone	Diuretic
sulfamethoxazole	Gantanol	Antibacterial
sulfamethoxypyridazine	Kynex	Antibacterial
sulfisoxazole	Gantrisin	Antibacterial
tetracycline	Achromycin, Sumycin	Antibiotic
tetracycline + phenacetin + caffeine + salicylamide + chlorothen citrate	Achrocidin	Antibiotic, analgesic
tetracycline + nystatin	Tetrex-F	Antibiotic, antifungal
tetracycline + triacetyl-oleandomycin + glucosamine HCl	Signemycin	Antibiotic
thalidomide	Kevadon	Sedative
thioridazine	Mellaril	Antipsychotic
tolbutamide	Orinase	Diabetes therapy
tranylcypromine	Parnate Sulfate	Antidepressant
triacetyl-oleandomycin	TAO	Antibiotic
triamcinolone	Aristocort, Kenacort	Anti-inflammatory
trifluoperazine	Stelazine	Antipsychotic
triparanol	MER/29	Hypocholesterolemic
tripelennamine	Pyribenzamine	Antihistamine
warfarin	Panwarfin	Anticoagulant

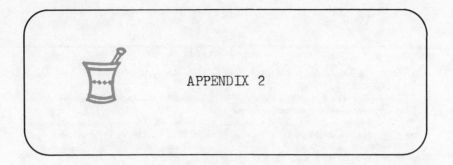

APPENDIX 2

Table 1

THE AMERICAN DRUG INDUSTRY: SALES, RESEARCH, PROMOTION, AND PROFITS, 1950–1972

| Year | Sales | | Worldwide Research and Development | | Promotion | Net Profits | |
	Worldwide (millions)	U.S. (millions)	(millions)	% of Sales	(U.S. only) (millions)	(millions)	% of Sales
1950	$1,430	$1,013	$ 39	2.7	$203	$...	...
1951	1,485	1,148	50	3.4	230	...	...
1952	1,540	1,175	63	4.1	235	129	8.4
1953	1,595	1,213	67	4.2	243	129	8.1
1954	1,650	1,252	78	4.7	250	152	9.2
1955	1,815	1,457	91	5.0	291	191	10.5
1956	2,090	1,676	105	5.0	335	250	11.9
1957	2,420	1,742	127	5.2	348	283	11.7
1958	2,640	1,802	170	6.4	360	301	11.4
1959	2,750	1,805	197	7.2	361	319	11.6
1960	2,860	1,905	212	7.4	381	306	10.7
1961	2,992	1,954	238	7.8	391	314	10.5
1962	3,236	2,199	251	7.8	440	317	9.8
1963	3,469	2,317	282	8.1	464	354	10.2
1964	3,717	2,479	298	8.0	496	401	10.8
1965	4,219	2,779	351	8.3	556	464	11.0
1966	4,660	3,011	402	8.6	602	503	10.8
1967	5,102	3,226	448	8.8	645	515	10.1
1968	5,665	3,655	485	8.6	731	545	9.6
1969	6,208	4,008	549	8.8	811	596	9.6
1970	6,853	4,322	619	8.8	864	664	9.4
1971	7,383	4,667	684	9.0	933	721	9.5
1972 (est.)	8,070	5,031	728	9.0	1,006	734	9.1

Worldwide Sales: Data shown for human and veterinary products, dosage and bulk forms. (SOURCE: Figures for years 1961–1972 taken from Pharmaceutical Manufacturers Association, *Annual Survey Reports,* Washington, D.C. Figures for years 1950–1960 derived from PMA data on dosage forms only plus 10 percent to represent estimated bulk forms.)

(Continued on next page)

Table 1 (Contd.)

U.S. Sales: Data shown for human dosage forms only. (SOURCE: Pharmaceutical Manufacturers Association.)

Worldwide Research and Development: Data shown for human and veterinary studies. (SOURCE: Pharmaceutical Manufacturers Association.)

U.S. Promotion: Based on estimate that 20 percent of U.S. sales represents minimum expenditures for U.S. promotion. (U.S. Department of Health, Education, and Welfare, Task Force on Prescription Drugs, *The Drug Makers and the Drug Distributors,* Washington, D.C., U.S. Government Printing Office, 1968, pp. 27, 28.)

Net Profits: Data indicate net profits after taxes, as based on percentages reported by Federal Trade Commission, Security and Exchange Commission, First National City Bank of New York, and other sources.

Table 2

COMPARATIVE DRUG PROFITS, 1960–1972

Year	Drug Manufacturers (in %)	All U.S. Manufacturers (in %)
1960	17.0	9.3
1961	16.7	8.9
1962	16.7	9.9
1963	17.0	10.3
1964	18.4	11.7
1965	20.5	13.1
1966	20.8	13.6
1967	18.7	11.8
1968	18.4	12.2
1969	18.7	11.7
1970	18.2	9.4
1971	19.3	9.7
1972	18.3	10.6

SOURCE: Calculated from information available in *Quarterly Financial Report for Manufacturing Corporations,* Federal Trade Commission, Securities and Exchange Commission.

NOTE: Average net profits after taxes as a percentage of net stockholders' equity, U.S. drug manufacturers and all U.S. manufacturing corporations, 1960–72. Net stockholders' equity defined as average of beginning and end-of-year stockholders' equity.

Table 3

NET WORTH, SALES, AND NET PROFITS
OF MAJOR DRUG COMPANIES, 1972

Company	Net Worth (millions)	Sales (millions)	Profits After Taxes		
			Net Profits (millions)	% of Net Worth	% of Sales
Abbott Laboratories	$ 293.4	$ 521.8	$ 39.4	13.4	7.6
American Home Products[a]	583.6	1,587.0	172.7	29.6	10.9
Baxter Laboratories	193.4	278.8	22.2	11.5	8.0
Bristol-Myers[b]	420.4	1,201.2	83.9	20.0	7.0
Carter-Wallace	107.0	165.0	10.6	10.0	6.4
Cutter Laboratories	47.5	89.2	2.1	4.4	2.3
International Chemical and Nuclear	38.2	161.4	3.3	8.8	2.1
Johnson & Johnson	732.9	1,317.7	120.7	16.5	9.2
Eli Lilly & Co.	603.6	819.7	126.3	20.9	15.4
Marion Laboratories	21.9	51.0	8.2	37.4	16.1
Merck & Co.[c]	608.2	958.3	147.6	24.3	15.4
Miles Laboratories	60.9	319.0	15.2	25.0	4.8
Morton-Norwich[d]	163.5	367.8	24.4	14.9	6.6
PEPI, Inc.[e]	92.5	203.7	5.2	5.6	2.5
Pfizer, Inc.[f]	635.4	1,093.4	103.2	16.2	9.4
Richardson-Merrell[g]	176.9	446.5	36.5	20.8	8.2
A. H. Robins Co.	73.7	166.7	22.8	30.9	13.7
Rorer-Amchem, Inc.	90.5	166.1	21.0	23.3	12.7
Schering-Plough	323.0	504.2	77.4	24.0	15.3
G. D. Searle & Co.	164.8	271.9	41.9	25.4	15.4
Smith Kline & French[h]	204.0	402.3	48.9	24.0	12.2
Squibb Corp.[i]	416.3	925.9	71.7	17.2	7.7
Sterling Drug[j]	353.9	720.8	69.0	19.5	9.6
Syntex Corp.	165.0	140.3	30.7	18.6	21.9
Upjohn Co.	311.1	511.3	46.5	15.0	9.1
Warner-Lambert[k]	792.7	1,487.5	122.7	15.5	8.3
26-company Totals	$7,674.3	$14,878.5	$1,474.1	19.2	9.9

SOURCE: Derived from data reported by Federal Trade Commission, Security and Exchange Commission, First National City Bank of New York, Value Line Investment Survey, and other sources.

NOTE: The data are reported by leading pharmaceutical manufacturers listed on major United States stock exchanges. They cover the calendar year 1972, or the nearest comparable fiscal year, and reflect company-wide operations, which in many instances include not only prescription drugs but also nonprescription drugs, cosmetics, and so forth.

[a] Includes Wyeth, Ayerst, Ives, Whitehall, Fort Dodge.

[b] Includes Mead Johnson, Clairol.

(Continued on next page)

Table 3 (Contd.)

c Includes Calgon, Baltimore Airfoil.

d Formed by merger of Morton International and Norwich Pharmacal in 1969.

e Formerly Phillips Electronics and Pharmaceutical Industries.

f Includes Coty.

g Includes William S. Merrell, Vick Chemical, National Drug, Hess & Clark, Jensen-Salsbery.

h Includes Love Cosmetics.

i Formed by merger of Beech-Nut and E. R. Squibb & Sons in 1968.

j Includes Lehn & Fink, Winthrop.

k Includes American Optical; merged with Parke-Davis in 1970, but in early 1974 the merger was still being opposed by the Federal Trade Commission.

Table 4

NET PROFITS OF MAJOR DRUG COMPANIES, SHOWN AS A PERCENTAGE OF NET WORTH, 1956–1971

Company	1956	1957	1958	1959	1960	1961	1962	1963	1964	1965	1966	1967	1968	1969	1970	1971
Abbott Laboratories	14	16	15	14	12	12	13	14	15	15	15	14	15	15	16	9
American Home Products	34	36	35	34	32	31	31	31	32	31	30	29	30	31	31	29
Baxter Laboratories	10	14	15	17	14	15	15	14	14	16	16	18	17	12	12	11
Bristol-Myers	14	15	15	18	20	22	25	26	27	28	30	23	24	25	24	21
Carter-Wallace	47	42	38	36	25	27	21	24	23	19	16	13	15	12	12	14
Cutter Laboratories	4	10	10	9	5	7	10	11	13	12	16	15	10	10	10	9
International Chemical and Nuclear	...	...	...	...	...	...	...	...	...	...	...	6	6	13	22	22
Johnson & Johnson	11	11	9	10	10	10	10	10	12	13	14	14	15	15	16	16
Eli Lilly & Co.	20	19	13	13	10	12	14	13	16	19	20	19	21	21	21	19
Marion Laboratories	...	...	...	...	...	...	...	...	...	54	50	44	55	45	38	34
Merck & Co.	15	16	17	17	15	14	14	17	20	24	27	25	24	24	24	24
Miles Laboratories	18	22	22	28	18	20	17	20	20	20	18	17	31	33	22	24
Morton-Norwich	24	24	24	25	25	23	22	26	26	27	28	25	37	16	16	15
PEPI, Inc.	15	...	...	7	4	4	5	4	4	6	8	9	8	6	7	5
Pfizer, Inc.	15	18	18	16	16	16	16	16	17	18	19	16	16	16	17	16
Richardson-Merrell	15	15	18	18	22	22	20	19	20	20	22	21	20	20	21	22
A. H. Robins Co.	...	...	...	...	...	...	22	23	26	28	27	55	43	36	30	33
Rorer-Amchem, Inc.	34	38	40	45	43	39	41	39	42	40	35	33	28	23	23	23
Schering-Plough	37	31	22	18	14	14	14	14	17	19	22	21	24	24	22	22
G. D. Searle & Co.	27	26	23	23	22	26	31	35	38	33	27	30	29	29	28	26
Smith Kline & French	40	38	33	36	31	32	32	32	32	36	32	30	27	26	26	25
Squibb Corp.	15	15	13	13	13	14	15	16	17	18	18	15	14	16	17	17
Sterling Drug	26	26	29	29	28	26	24	23	23	24	24	23	22	22	21	20
Syntex Corp.	...	...	1	...	5	5	9	27	37	36	52	36	29	25	21	17
Upjohn Co.	17	17	18	18	16	15	15	15	16	19	17	14	14	14	12	14
Warner-Lambert	20	23	20	21	20	19	18	19	21	22	22	18	19	20	15	15

SOURCE: Derived from data reported by Federal Trade Commission, Security and Exchange Commission, First National City Bank of New York, Value Line Investment Survey, and other sources.

Table 5

NET PROFITS OF MAJOR DRUG COMPANIES, SHOWN AS A PERCENTAGE OF SALES, 1956–1971

Company	1956	1957	1958	1959	1960	1961	1962	1963	1964	1965	1966	1967	1968	1969	1970	1971
Abbott Laboratories	11	11	11	11	10	9	10	11	11	10	10	9	9	9	9	5
American Home Products	11	11	11	11	6	11	11	11	11	10	10	10	10	10	10	11
Baxter Laboratories	5	4	6	6	6	7	7	6	6	6	8	8	9	8	8	8
Bristol-Myers	6	6	6	7	6	8	7	8	9	8	8	7	7	7	8	7
Carter-Wallace	11	13	14	15	13	14	13	14	14	13	12	10	9	9	8	9
Cutter Laboratories	1	3	4	5	2	3	4	4	5	5	6	6	4	4	4	5
International Chemical and Nuclear	...	...	...	...	...	...	...	...	...	...	...	4	2	3	5	6
Johnson & Johnson	5	5	5	5	5	5	5	6	6	7	7	7	7	8	8	9
Eli Lilly & Co.	17	16	13	12	10	12	12	11	12	13	14	13	15	16	16	13
Marion Laboratories	...	...	...	...	...	2	3	3	5	15	18	19	18	16	16	17
Merck & Co.	12	12	14	14	13	12	12	14	16	18	18	17	16	16	15	15
Miles Laboratories	6	7	6	6	5	6	5	6	6	6	5	5	5	5	4	4
Morton-Norwich	11	12	12	13	13	13	13	13	13	14	15	12	10	7	7	6
PEPI, Inc.	...	...	...	7	3	3	2	2	3	3	3	4	4	3	3	2
Pfizer, Inc.	10	11	11	10	10	10	10	10	10	10	10	9	9	9	9	10
Richardson-Merrell	8	8	9	11	11	11	11	10	9	10	10	9	8	8	8	8
A. H. Robins Co.	...	...	9	10	9	9	12	11	13	14	14	12	12	12	13	13
Rorer-Amchem, Inc.	9	11	12	15	16	16	18	18	20	20	20	20	14	13	13	14
Schering-Plough	20	19	17	15	12	12	12	11	12	12	13	13	13	13	13	16
G. D. Searle & Co.	23	23	21	21	20	22	24	26	28	26	20	20	18	17	16	16
Smith Kline & French	17	18	17	18	17	17	17	17	18	17	16	16	15	13	13	13
Squibb Corp.	6	8	7	7	8	8	7	8	8	8	7	7	6	7	7	8
Sterling Drug	10	10	10	10	10	10	10	10	11	11	10	10	10	10	10	10
Syntex Corp.	21	9	1	...	5	5	7	23	32	29	34	29	27	27	14	21
Upjohn Co.	13	14	14	15	14	14	13	13	14	15	14	11	10	10	10	9
Warner-Lambert	8	10	9	9	9	8	9	10	10	10	10	8	8	8	8	8

SOURCE: Derived from data reported by Federal Trade Commission, Security and Exchange Commission, First National City Bank of New York, Value Line Investment Survey, and other sources.

Table 6

NUMBER OF RECALLS FOR LOW-QUALITY DRUG PRODUCTS, 1966–1971

Year	Label Mix-up	Contaminated or Adulterated	Subpotent or Superpotent	Total
1966	27	92	59	178
1967	18	74	70	162
1968	66	40	104	210
1969	30	116	160	306
1970	82	78	217	377
1971	154	406	142	702
Totals	377	806	752	1,935

SOURCE: Food and Drug Administration, *FDA Weekly Recall Reports.*
NOTE: Prescription and nonprescription products are included.

Table 7

COMPARATIVE WHOLESALE PRICES OF SELECTED BRAND-NAME AND GENERIC-NAME DRUG PRODUCTS, 1972

Product	Price	Price Ratio
Reserpine: 1,000 0.25-mg		
Serpasil (CIBA)	$39.50	
Reserpine (Vita-Fore)	1.10	35.9:1
Chlorpheniramine: 1,000 4-mg		
Chlortrimeton (Schering)	21.66	
Chlorpheniramine (American Quinine)	1.20	18.0:1
Pentaerythrotetranitrate: 1,000 10-mg		
Peritrate (Warner-Chilcott)	27.00	
Pentaerythrotetranitrate (Vita-Fore)	1.50	18.0:1
Meprobamate: 1,000 400-mg		
Equanil (Wyeth)	68.21	
Meprobamate (Interstate)	4.90	13.9:1
Chlorpheniramine, timed disintegration: 500 12-mg		
Teldrin (Smith Kline & French)	32.50	
Chlorpheniramine (American Quinine)	2.50[a]	13.0:1
Oxytetracycline: 100 250-mg		
Terramycin (Pfizer)	20.48	
Oxytetracycline (H. L. Moore)	1.95	10.4:1
Theophylline, ephedrine, and phenobarbital: 1,000		
Tedral (Warner-Chilcott)	32.85	
Theophylline, ephedrine, and phenobarbital (Kasar)	3.90	8.4:1
Tetracycline: 1,000 250-mg		
Achromycin (Lederle)	52.02	
Tetracycline (Interstate)	8.75	5.9:1
Tripelennamine: 1,000 50-mg		
Pyribenzamine (CIBA)	27.16	
Tripelennamine (Columbia)	4.70	5.8:1
Penicillin G: 100 400,000-units		
Pentids (Squibb)	10.04	
Penicillin G (Midway)	1.75	5.7:1

SOURCE: *Drug Topics Red Book 1973*, Oradell, N.J., 1972.
[a] Price for 500 units based on $5.00 per 1,000.

Table 8

PER CAPITA HEALTH EXPENDITURES, 1950–1972

Year	Total	Hospitals	Physicians	Drugs[a] Total	Prescription	Other[b]	All Others[c]
1950	$ 75.66	$ 24.90	$17.76	$11.16	$ 6.74	$ 4.42	$21.84
1955	100.27	35.04	21.91	14.16	8.55	5.61	29.16
1960	137.00	49.46	30.92	19.89	12.00	7.89	36.73
1965	187.58	68.81	44.23	24.53	14.80	9.73	50.01
1966	207.22	77.92	45.78	26.55	16.02	10.53	56.97
1967	232.42	89.76	50.89	27.96	16.87	11.09	63.81
1968	257.28	102.49	54.36	30.19	18.22	11.97	70.24
1969	287.83	117.47	61.37	33.04	19.82	13.22	75.95
1970	318.45	134.22	68.59	35.01	21.00	14.01	80.63
1971	351.50	147.78	74.68	36.62	21.97	14.65	92.49
1972	391.70	161.13	81.59	39.91	23.95	15.96	109.07

SOURCE: Barbara S. Cooper and Nancy L. Worthington, "National Health Expenditures, Calendar Years 1929–1971," *Social Security Administration, Research and Statistics Note*, DHEW Pub. No. (SSA) 73-11701, March 6, 1973, p. 13; 1972 estimated data, Social Security Administration, 1974.

[a] Dispensed by community pharmacies only, not including those dispensed by hospital pharmacies, dispensing physicians, governmental institutions, and so forth. Amounts for prescription drugs represent an estimated 60 percent of total drug expenditures.

[b] Primarily over-the-counter products.

[c] Including expenditures for dental care, eyeglasses, and so forth.

Table 9

COMPARATIVE RETAIL PRICES OF SELECTED PRESCRIPTION DRUGS

Product	High	Low	Median	Ratio of High to Low Price
Penicillin G: 100 400,000-U	$15.00	$1.50	$ 4.75	10.0
Tetracycline: 100 250-mg	20.00	2.50	4.75	8.0
Thyroid: 100 1-gr	3.90	0.63	1.25	6.2
Achromycin V: 100 250-mg	17.94	3.47	6.50	5.2
Tuss-Ornade Spansules: 100	20.00	5.00	12.85	4.0
Insulin Squibb U-80 10-cc—all types	2.98	0.88	1.89	3.4
Actifed: 100	10.00	2.99	5.95	3.3
Equanil: 100 400-mg	13.15	4.60	7.90	2.8
Flagyl: 100 250-mg	25.00	9.20	17.00	2.7
Premarin: 100 1.25-mg	15.89	6.09	7.75	2.6
Sumycin: 100 250-mg	10.00	4.05	6.00	2.5
Pentids: 100 400,000-U	15.95	6.50	11.59	2.4
Benadryl Kapseals: 100 50-mg	6.35	2.77	4.00	2.3
Valium: 100 5-mg	15.00	6.75	9.38	2.2
Diuril: 100 500-mg	11.25	5.09	6.95	2.2

SOURCE: Derived from *Prescription Drug Pricing: An Almost Total Absence of Competition* (Washington, D.C.: Consumers Federation of America), September, 1972.

NOTE: Based on a survey of 147 pharmacies in 81 communities in 17 states and the District of Columbia, July–August 1972.

Table 10

COMPARATIVE INTERNATIONAL PRICES OF SELECTED BRAND-NAME DRUGS

(Prices to Pharmacists[a])

Drug	Country								
	United States	Australia	Brazil	Canada	Ireland	Italy	New Zealand	Sweden	United Kingdom
Achromycin	$ 5.34	$ 9.79	$ 4.22	$12.64	$3.42	$10.84	$13.78	$13.89	$ 5.04
Benadryl	2.22	1.60	0.81	2.77	1.37	2.60	1.29	2.33	1.20
Compazine	7.86	4.44	2.45	6.05	2.87	3.04	2.93	2.28	3.04
Darvon	7.02	2.73	3.72	5.29	1.66	7.86	2.08	3.33	1.92
Declomycin	19.79	11.17	4.93	16.09	8.97	17.88	3.87	19.43	8.20
Doriden	3.00	2.11	1.97	2.67	0.92	1.80	1.23	2.06	1.00
Elavil	8.55	3.33	2.26	6.30	2.26	4.22	4.20	3.09	2.28
Equanil	7.06	4.17	1.91	5.13	1.79	3.65	2.06	1.67	1.74
Erythrocin	26.12	14.51	11.92	25.04	8.56	24.57	10.88	19.21	10.02
Gantrisin	2.94	3.00	1.51	3.06	1.64	2.47	1.11	2.83	1.92
Lanoxin	1.03	0.69	1.31	1.51	0.53	1.73	0.52	0.98	0.38
Librium	6.40	3.74	2.40	5.45	2.05	3.55	1.83	3.11	2.40
Orinase	8.23	2.83	2.77	6.34	2.22	2.86	(b)	4.86	2.28
Ovulen[c]	7.38	4.11	4.82	5.95	3.59	8.20	3.56	4.51	4.10
Polycillin	21.84	20.48	41.95	22.18	9.31	19.15	11.30	16.58	8.23
Stelazine	9.75	4.70	2.42	8.38	2.78	3.82	3.71	4.41	2.59
Terramycin	20.48	9.79	4.63	16.92	7.74	13.27	3.68	13.04	9.06
Thorazine	6.60	2.22	2.47	5.82	1.71	3.47	1.82	2.88	1.68
Valium	8.03	3.74	3.62	6.01	2.46	3.42	2.72	3.71	2.88
V-Cillin-K	8.95	6.11	8.66	10.69	2.77	(d)	2.99	(d)	2.40

Products (U.S. brand name, generic name, U.S. manufacturer, and strength).

Achromycin (tetracycline Lederle) 250 mg
Benadryl (diphenhydramine Parke-Davis) 50 mg
Compazine (prochlorperazine Smith Kline & French) 10 mg
Darvon (propoxyphene Lilly) 65 mg
Declomycin (demethylchlortetracycline Lederle) 150 mg
Doriden (glutethimide CIBA) 250 mg
Elavil (amitryptiline Merck) 25 mg
Equanil (meprobamate Wyeth) 400 mg
Erythrocin (erythromycin Abbott) 250 mg
Gantrisin (sulfisoxazole Roche) 500 mg

Lanoxin (digoxin Burroughs-Wellcome) 0.25 mg
Librium (chlordiazepoxide Roche) 10 mg
Orinase (tolbutamide Upjohn) 500 mg
Ovulen (ethynodiol diacetate with mestranol Searle) 1 mg
Polycillin (ampicillin Bristol) 250 mg
Stelazine (trifluoperazine Smith Kline & French) 5 mg
Terramycin (oxytetracycline Pfizer) 250 mg
Thorazine (chlorpromazine Smith Kline & French) 50 mg
Valium (diazepam Roche) 5 mg
V-Cillin-K (potassium phenoxymethylpenicillin Lilly) 250 mg

SOURCE: Edmond M. Jacoby, Jr., and Dennis L. Hefner, "Domestic and Foreign Prescription Drug Prices," Social Security Bulletin 34:15 (May 1971).
[a] Price to druggists for 100 capsules or tablets, except for Ovulen.
[b] Orinase available in New Zealand, but no price listed in official schedule.
[c] Ovulen price for 6 x 21 tablets.
[d] Data not available.

Table 11

RETAIL SALES OF OVER-THE-COUNTER DRUGS, 1972

		(millions)
Vitamin Concentrates		$ 413.0
Cough and Cold Remedies		660.9
Laxatives		212.7
Internal Analgesics		
Aspirin	$106.1	
Others	525.8	631.9
External Analgesics		136.0
Tonics and Alteratives		126.1
External Antiseptics		72.3
Antacids		116.7
Miscellaneous		
Diarrhea Remedies	75.6	
Suntan Lotions and Oils	64.9	
Acne Remedies	58.7	
Sleeping Aids (Nonprescription)	29.8	
Burn Remedies	27.7	
Hemorrhoid Remedies	26.9	
Motion Sickness Preparations	21.7	
Eye Lotions and Washes	25.4	
Poison Ivy Remedies	21.3	
Athlete's Foot Medication	9.6	
Others	346.0	707.6
		$3,077.2

SOURCE: Drug Topics, 1973 Marketing Guide (Oradell, N.J.: Medical Economics, 1973), pp. 13–15.

Table 12

ANNUAL RETAIL SALES OF OVER-THE-COUNTER DRUG PRODUCTS, 1945–1972

(in millions)

	1945	1950	1955	1960	1965	1966	1967	1968	1969	1970	1971	1972
Packaged Medications	$521.4	$921.0	$1,257.8	$1,703.0	$2,045.2	$2,170.0	$2,268.8	$2,438.2	$2,592.0	$2,688.5	$2,874.1	$3,077.2
Foot Medications	...	...	15.2	21.6	29.3	31.7	33.9	35.0	37.0	38.2	40.2	41.8
Baby Medications	14.9	20.9	33.4	40.8	62.1	66.2	70.5	76.5	80.1	84.8	88.2	95.6
Feminine Hygiene	47.6	47.2	38.8	52.5	62.5	70.9	76.0	86.9	88.8	87.0	89.8	89.2
Dentrifices	75.6	111.4	153.0	242.0	275.6	299.8	316.1	327.4	344.4	360.6	390.9	408.2
Mouthwashes	22.9	25.8	34.5	75.8	128.7	158.4	200.5	212.1	229.3	230.9	240.6	245.4
Medicated Shampoos	...	...	...	20.8	30.2	33.6	36.4	39.4	40.8	45.4	48.1	59.2[a]
Dandruff Rinses	...	...	...	...	12.3	12.7	13.3	13.8	13.5	13.7	13.9	13.0
Hair Medications	4.9	6.0	7.2	8.4	10.5	11.0	11.3	11.4	12.1	12.7	13.0	13.1
Totals	$687.3	$1,132.3	$1,539.9	$2,164.9	$2,656.4	$2,854.3	$3,026.8	$3,240.7	$3,438.0	$3,561.8	$3,798.8	$4,042.7

SOURCE: 1945–1971 data, derived from *Drug Topics*, various issues; 1972 data, derived from *Drug Topics, 1973 Marketing Guide* (Oradell, N.J.: Medical Economics, 1973).

[a] Figure extrapolated from 1971 data.

Table 13

ADVERTISING VOLUME AND SALES OF TOP 100 ADVERTISERS, BY PRODUCT CATEGORY, 1972

Category	Advertising Volume (millions)	Mfgr's Sales (billions)	Advertising as % of Sales
Drugs and cosmetics	$1,130.8	$ 10.4	10.9
Food	862.2	21.3	4.0
Soaps, cleaners, etc.	509.0	5.7	8.9
Cars	460.5	69.1	0.7
Retail chains	311.4	24.8	1.3
Tobacco	285.5	9.7	2.9
appliances, TV, radio	215.2	16.3	1.3
Telephone service, equip't	171.8	25.5	0.6
Oil	165.3	59.3	0.3
Liquor	160.5	4.0	4.0
Soft drinks	147.8	2.3	6.4
Chemicals	131.4	8.6	1.5
Tires	121.0	6.8	1.8
Beer	77.8	2.1	3.7
Photographic equip't	76.6	2.6	2.9
Paper products	51.0	1.8	2.8
Gum and candy	42.8	0.4	10.7
Miscellaneous	353.1	11.3	3.1
Total	$5,273.7	$282.0	1.9

SOURCE: Derived from data in *Advertsing Age* 44:28 (August 27, 1973).

Table 14

ADVERTISING VOLUME AND SALES OF TOP TEN ADVERTISERS, BY COMPANY, 1972

Company	Advertising Volume (millions)	Mfgr's Sales (billions)	Advertising as % of Sales
Procter & Gamble	$275	$ 3.9	7.0
Sears, Roebuck	215	9.8	2.2
General Foods	170	2.0	8.6
General Motors	146	30.4	0.5
Warner-Lambert	134	0.9	14.6
Ford Motors	132	20.2	0.7
American Home Products	116	1.2	9.4
Bristol-Myers	115	1.0	12.0
Colgate-Palmolive	105	0.9	12.1
Chrysler	95	7.3	1.3

SOURCE: *Advertising Age* 44:28 (August 27, 1973).

Table 15

ADVERTISING VOLUME OF SELECTED OTC DRUG PRODUCTS, BY CLASS, 1972

Class	Advertising Volume (millions)
Dental supplies and mouthwashes	$112.0
Headache remedies, sedatives, and sleeping preparations	99.5
Cold, cough, and sinus remedies	77.4
Digestive aids and antacids	45.0
Medicated skin products and liniments	39.1
Vitamin preparations and tonics	29.9
Feminine hygiene	26.8
Laxatives	16.8
Reducing aids	4.0
Other packaged medications	30.5
Total	$481.0

SOURCE: Derived from *Product Management* 2:45 (August 1973).

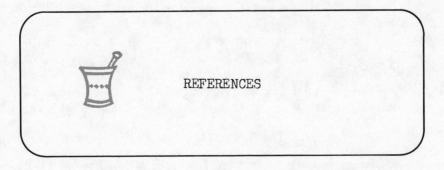

REFERENCES

IN OUR research, much valuable material was obtained from the background papers and reports of the HEW Task Force on Prescription Drugs and the hearings conducted by Senators Estes Kefauver and Gaylord Nelson. In the following pages, these sources are identified and abbreviated as follows:

RxTF, *Drug Users*
U.S. Department of Health, Education, and Welfare, Office of the Secretary, Task Force on Prescription Drugs, *The Drug Users* (Washington, D.C.: U.S. Government Printing Office, 1968).

RxTF, *Drug Makers and Distributors*
Ibid., *The Drug Makers and the Drug Distributors* (Washington, D.C., 1968).

RxTF, *Drug Prescribers*
Ibid., *The Drug Prescribers* (Washington, D.C., 1968).

RxTF, *Current Programs*
Ibid., *Current American and Foreign Programs* (Washington, D.C., 1968).

RxTF, *Insurance Design*
   Ibid., *Approaches to Drug Insurance Design* (Washington, D.C., 1969).
RxTF, *Final Report*
   Ibid., *Final Report* (Washington, D.C., 1969).
U.S. Senate, *Administered Prices*
   U.S. Senate, Committee on the Judiciary, Subcommittee on Antitrust and Monopoly, *Administered Prices in the Drug Industry* (Washington, D.C.: U.S. Government Printing Office).
U.S. Senate, *Competitive Problems*
   U.S. Senate, Select Committee on Small Business, Subcommittee on Monopoly, *Present Status of Competition in the Pharmaceutical Industry* (Washington, D.C.: U.S. Government Printing Office).
U.S. Senate, *Advertising of Proprietary Medicines*
   U.S. Senate, Select Committee on Small Business, Subcommittee on Monopoly, *Effect of Promotion and Advertising of Over-the- · Counter Drugs on Competition, Small Business, and the Health and Welfare of the Public* (Washington, D.C.: U.S. Government Printing Office).

1. The Revolution in Drugs

1. Raoul Jagnaux, *Histoire de la chémie* (Paris: Baudry, 1891); Hermann Schelenz, *Geschichte der Pharmazie* (Berlin: Springer, 1904); A. C. Wootton, *Chronicles of Pharmacy* (London: Macmillan, 1910); Charles H. LaWall, *4000 Years of Pharmacy* (Philadelphia: Lippincott, 1927); Milton Silverman, *Magic in a Bottle* (New York: Macmillan, 2nd ed., 1948); Harry F. Dowling, *Medicines for Man* (New York: Knopf, 1970).

2. Chauncey D. Leake and Milton Silverman, *Alcoholic Beverages in Clinical Medicine* (Chicago: Year Book Medical Publishers, 1966), pp. 9, 10.

3. Silverman, *Magic in a Bottle*, pp. 244–259.

4. RxTF, *Drug Makers and Distributors*, pp. 20–22.

5. New York Academy of Medicine, Committee on Public Health, "The Importance of Clinical Testing in Determining the Safety and Efficacy of Drugs," *Bulletin of the New York Academy of Medicine* 38:417 (1962); Louis Goodman, "The Problem of Drug Efficacy: An Exercise in Dissection," in Paul Talalay (ed.), *Drugs in Our Society* (Baltimore, Md.: Johns Hopkins Press, 1964), p. 63; Jesse W. Markham, "Economic Incentives and Progress in the Drug Industry," in Talalay p.

176; Max Tishler, *Molecular Modification in Drug Design*, Advances in Chemistry, Series 45 (Washington, D.C.: American Chemical Society, 1964), pp. 11, 12; Leonard Schifrin, "The Ethical Drug Industry: The Case for Compulsory Patent Licensing," *Antitrust Bulletin* 12:905 (1967); Calvin M. Kunin, statement in U.S. Senate, *Competitive Problems* 2:710 (1967).

6. Claude E. Forkner, "Medical Intelligence: Drug Mixtures," *New England Journal of Medicine* 259:438 (1958).

7. RxTF, *Drug Makers and Distributors*, p. 18.

8. Walter Modell, statement in U.S. Senate, Committee on the Judiciary, Subcommittee on Antitrust and Monopoly, *Drug Industry Antitrust Act* (Washington, D.C.: U.S. Government Printing Office, 1961), pp. 305–322; Harry L. Williams, statement in U.S. Senate, *Competitive Problems* 2:460, 461 (1967).

9. *Annual Survey Report 1971–1972* (Washington, D.C.: Pharmaceutical Manufacturers Association, 1973).

10. Charles C. Edwards (Food and Drug Administration), personal communication, 1972.

11. U.S. Department of Health, Education, and Welfare, Public Health Service, *Diabetes Source Book* (Washington, D.C.: U.S. Government Printing Office, 1969), p. 57.

12. Leon J. Epstein, Richard D. Morgan, and Lynn Reynolds, "An Approach to the Effect of Ataraxic Drugs on Hospital Release Rates," *American Journal of Psychiatry* 119:36 (July 1962).

13. Henry L. Lennard, Leon J. Epstein, Arnold Bernstein, and Donald C. Ransom, "Hazards Implicit in Prescribing Psychoactive Drugs," *Science* 169:438 (1970); Henry L. Lennard, Leon J. Epstein, Arnold Bernstein, and Donald C. Ransom, *Mystification and Drug Misuse* (San Francisco: Jossey-Bass, Inc., 1971).

14. H. H. Fudenberg, "The Dollar Benefit of Biomedical Research: A Cost Analysis," *Journal of Laboratory and Clinical Medicine* 79:353 (1972).

15. U.S. Department of Health, Education, and Welfare, National Center for Health Statistics, "Births, Deaths, Marriages, and Divorces: Annual Summary for the United States, 1972," *Monthly Vital Statistics Report* 21:8 (June 27, 1973).

16. Ibid., p. 4.

17. Walsh McDermott, statement in U.S. Senate, Committee on Government Operations, Subcommittee on Foreign Aid Expenditures, *Population Crisis*, p. 276 (1968).

18. Barbara S. Cooper and Nancy L. Worthington, "National Health Expenditures, Calendar Years 1929–71," *Social Security Administration, Research and Statistics Note*, March 6, 1973, p. 11.

19. U.S. Department of Health, Education, and Welfare, Social Security Administration, Office of Research and Statistics, *Prescription Drug Data Summary 1972*, DHEW Publication No. (SSA) 73–11900, tables II-2 and IV-2; Vincent Gardner (Social Security Administration), personal communication, 1973.

20. *American Druggist*, various issues.

21. National Prescription Audit, National Hospital Audit, *General Information Report* (Ambler, Pa.: Lea, Inc., 11th edit., 1972).

22. *American Druggist*, various issues.

23. American Hospital Association, Bureau of Research Services, personal communication, 1971.

24. Milton Silverman, unpublished data.

25. T. Donald Rucker (Social Security Administration), personal communication, 1972.

26. RxTF, *Drug Users*, p. 20.

27. World Health Organization, "Drug Consumption in Europe," *WHO Chronicle* 25:458 (1971).

28. U.S. Department of Health, Education, and Welfare, Public Health Service, *Cost and Acquisition of Prescribed and Nonprescribed Medicines—United States—July 1964–June 1965*, National Center for Health Statistics, Series 10, No. 33, 1966.

29. C. Witten, cited in Henry L. Lennard et al., *Mystification and Drug Misuse*, p. 9.

30. Henry L. Lennard et al., *Mystification and Drug Misuse*, p. 13.

31. Editorial, "Treatment by the Whole Individual," *New England Journal of Medicine* 280:271 (January 30, 1969).

2. The Revolution in Drug Making.

1. George S. Squibb, statement in U.S. Senate, *Competitive Problems* 5:1555 (1968); Jonathan Spivak, "Images of the Drug Industry: The Public View," in Joseph D. Cooper (ed.), *The Economics of Drug Innovation* (Washington, D.C.: American University, Center for the Study of Private Enterprise, 1970), p. 10; Henry B. Steele, comment in Cooper p. 145.

2. United States v. Richardson-Merrell, Inc., Crim. No. 1211–63 (D.D.C., June 4, 1964); Thomas M. Rice, statement in U.S. Senate, *Competitive Problems* 10:4202 (1969).

3. Harry F. Dowling, *Medicines for Man* (New York: Knopf, 1970), p. 105.

4. RxTF, *Drug Makers and Distributors*, p. 9.

5. Tom Mahoney, *The Merchants of Life* (New York: Harper, 1959).

6. Donald D. Vogt and Norman F. Billups, "The Merger Movement in the American Pharmaceutical Complex," *Journal of the American Pharmaceutical Association* NS11:588 (November 1971).

7. Dowling, *Medicines for Man*, p. 86.

8. *Annual Survey Report 1970–1971* (Washington, D.C.: Pharmaceutical Manufacturers Association, 1972).

9. RxTF, *Current Programs*, p. 172.

10. RxTF, *Drug Makers and Distributors*, pp. 45–47.

11. Ibid., p. 45.

12. U.S. Senate, Committee on the Judiciary, Subcommittee on Antitrust and Monopoly, *Physician Ownership in Pharmacies and Drug Companies*, 1965, p. 279; Henry B. Steele, statement in U.S. Senate, *Competitive Problems* 5:1909 (1968).

13. Robert Ball, "The Secret Life of Hoffmann-LaRoche," *Fortune* 84:130 (August 1971).

14. *The Value Line Investment Survey* (New York: Arnold Bernhard and Co., August 6, 1971).

15. G. Joseph Norwood and Mickey C. Smith, "Market Mortality of New Products in the Pharmaceutical Industry," *Journal of the American Pharmaceutical Industry* NS11:592 (1971).

16. RxTF, *Drug Makers and Distributors*, p. 48.

17. Simon N. Whitney, comment in Joseph D. Cooper (ed.), *The Economics of Drug Innovation* (Washington, D.C., 1970), p. 156.

18. Ibid., p. 108.

19. William S. Comanor (Harvard University), personal communication, 1967.

20. Willard F. Mueller, statement in U.S. Senate, *Competitive Problems* 5:1816 (1968).

21. A. Dale Console, statement in U.S. Senate, *Competitive Problems* 11:4504 (1969).

22. David M. Kiefer, "Risk and Reward in Ethical Drugs," *Chemical and Engineering News* 46:22 (January 29, 1968).

23. Hubert H. Humphrey, cited in "Fifteen Firms Hide Drug-Testing Fees Paid Doctors," *Washington Post*, March 30, 1964; A. Dale

Console, statement in U.S. Senate, *Competitive Problems* 11:4481 (1969).

24. Leonard A. Scheele, statement in U.S. Senate, *Competitive Problems* 6:2289 (1968); Harold A. Clymer, "The Changing Costs and Risks of Pharmaceutical Innovation," in Cooper, *Economics of Drug Innovation*, p. 123; Vernon A. Mund, "The Return on Investment of the Innovative Pharmaceutical Firm," in Cooper p. 125.

25. Henry B. Steele, statement in U.S. Senate, *Competitive Problems* 5:1928 (1968).

26. Leonard G. Schifrin, comment in Cooper, *Economics of Drug Innovation*, p. 212.

27. Helen B. Taussig, "The Evils of Camouflage as Illustrated by Thalidomide," *New England Journal of Medicine* 269:92 (July 11, 1963).

28. Henry E. Simmons, statement in U.S. Scnatc, *Competitive Problems* 23:9557 (1973).

29. Harry F. Dowling, *Medicines for Man* (New York, 1970), pp. 97–99; Louis Lasagna, comment in Cooper, *Economics of Drug Innovation*, p. 163; Paul de Haen, *New Products Parade 1971. Annual Review of New Drugs* (New York: Paul de Haen, 1972).

30. Henry E. Simmons, statement in U.S. Senate, *Competitive Problems* 23:9559 (1973).

31. Haskell J. Weinstein, statement in U.S. Senate, *Administered Prices* 18:10,254 (1960).

32. A. Dale Console, statement in U.S. Senate, *Administered Prices* 18:10,380 (1960).

33. Ibid., p. 10,373.

34. Henry E. Simmons, statement in U.S. Senate, *Competitive Problems* 23:9407 (1973).

35. Max Tishler, *Molecular Modification in Drug Design*, Advances in Chemistry, Series 45 (Washington, D.C.: American Chemical Society, 1964), pp. 11, 12.

36. Pierre R. Garai, "Advertising and Promotion of Drugs," in Paul Talalay (ed.), *Drugs in Our Society* (Baltimore, Md.: Johns Hopkins Press, 1964), p. 189.

37. RxTF, *Final Report*, pp. 8, 9.

38. Dowling, *Medicines for Man*, p. 114.

39. Michael H. Cooper, comment in Joseph D. Cooper (ed.), *Economics of Drug Innovation*, p. 223.

40. Howard I. Forman, "Drug Patents, Compulsory Licenses,

Prices, and Innovation," in Cooper, *Economics of Drug Innovation*, p. 180.

41. Frederick M. Scherer, comment in Cooper, *Economics of Drug Innovation*, p. 199.

42. Statements in U.S. Senate, *Competitive Problems* 5 (1968): Paul H. Cootner, p. 1618; Gordon R. Conrad and Irving H. Plotkin, p. 1638; Jesse W. Markham, p. 1667; Simon N. Whitney, p. 1725; Leonard G. Schifrin, p. 1863; Henry B. Steele, p. 1901; William S. Comanor, p. 2041; I. N. Fisher and G. R. Hall, "Risk and Corporate Rates of Return," p. 2120.

3. Drug Promotion: "The Truth, The Whole Truth, and Nothing But The Truth."

1. Philip R. Lee, "Prescription Drugs, Public Policy, and the Medical Profession," Aagaard Lecture, presented at the University of Washington, Seattle, February 12, 1968.

2. William Osler, cited in Michael H. Cooper, *Prices and Profits in the Pharmaceutical Industry* (Oxford: Pergamon Press, 1966), p. 212.

3. F. H. Happold, *Medicine at Risk* (London: Queen Anne Press, 1967), p. 134.

4. Calvin M. Kunin, statement in U.S. Senate, *Competitive Problems* 2:714 (1967).

5. Pierre R. Garai, "Advertising and Promotion of Drugs," in Paul Talalay (ed.), *Drugs in Our Society* (Baltimore: Johns Hopkins Press, 1964), p. 195.

6. John G. Searle et al., "The Pharmaceutical Industry," *Journal of Medical Education* 36:26 (January 1961).

7. William J. Hagood and John A. Owen, "The Image of the Drug Industry, as Seen by Town and Gown," *Virginia Medical Monthly* 94:110 (February 1967); Leighton E. Cluff, statement in U.S. Senate, *Competitive Problems* 2:571 (1967); R. W. Fassold and C. W. Gowdey, "A Survey of Physicians' Reactions to Drug Promotion," *Canadian Medical Association Journal* 98:701 (April 6, 1968); Edward R. Pinckney, statement in U.S. Senate, *Competitive Problems* 14:5723 (1969).

8. Harry L. Williams, statement in U.S. Senate, *Competitive Problems* 2:460 (1967).

9. *Drug Topics Red Book* (Oradell, N.J.: Topics Publishing Co., various years).

10. Charles D. May, "Selling Drugs by 'Educating' Physicians,"

Journal of Medical Education 36:15 (January 1961); Harry F. Dowling, *Medicines for Man* (New York: Knopf, 1970), p. 129.

11. May, "Selling Drugs," p. 18.

12. May, p. 2; Martin Cherkasky, statement in U.S. Senate, *Competitive Problems* 2:675 (1967); William B. Bean, statement in U.S. Senate, *Competitive Problems* 10:3917 (1969).

13. F. Roberts, cited in Richard M. Titmuss, "Sociological and Ethnic Aspects of Therapeutics," in Paul Talalay, *Drugs in our Society*, p. 245.

14. James L. Goddard, statement in U.S. Senate, *Competitive Problems* 4:1223 (1967); Robert Oppenheimer, "Ethics is Alive and Well in Medical Ad-Land," *Pharmaceutical Marketing and Media* 3:9 (April 1968).

15. Edwin Funk, "Yesterday, Today and Tomorrow in Drug Advertising," *Pharmaceutical Marketing and Media* 2:13 (March 1967).

16. Bernard Hirsh, statement before U.S. Senate, Committee on Ways and Means, February 26, 1969.

17. Louis Lasagna, "Constraints on Innovation in Drug Development and Use," in Joseph D. Cooper (ed.), *The Economics of Drug Innovation* (Washington, D.C.: American University, Center for the Study of Private Enterprise, 1970), p. 232.

18. Arthur S. Waite, "The Future of Pharmaceutical Drug Promotion," *Medical Marketing and Media* 6:9 (June 1971).

19. James L. Goddard, cited in RxTF, *Drug Makers and Distributors*, p. 28.

20. Pierre Garai, "Advertising and Promotion of Drugs," in Talalay, *Drugs in Our Society*, p. 191.

21. T. Donald Rucker, "Economic Problems in Drug Distribution," *Inquiry* 9:43 (September 1972).

22. C. Joseph Stetler, *Patterns of Prescription Drug Use: The Role of Promotion* (Washington, D.C.: Pharmaceutical Manufacturers Association, 1973).

23. "Medical Education in the United States," *Journal of the American Medical Association* 222:961 (November 20, 1972).

24. RxTF, *Drug Makers and Distributors*, p. 27.

25. Pharmaceutical Manufacturers Association, cited in RxTF, *Drug Makers and Distributors*, p. 29.

26. Sheldon Zalaznick, "Bitter Pills for the Drugmakers," *Fortune* 77:82 (July 1968).

27. A. Dale Console, statement in U.S. Senate, *Administered Prices* 19:10,368 (1960).

28. Fred Danzig (*Advertising Age*), personal communication, 1971.

29. Bernard P. Gallagher, *The Gallagher Report* (New York: The Gallagher Report, Inc.) Vol. 9, No. 6, 2nd Section, 1971.

30. Edward R. Annis, statement in U.S. Senate, *Competitive Problems* 11:4696 (1969).

31. Ernest Howard, cited in U.S. Senate, *Competitive Problems* 12:5021 (1969).

32. Solomon Garb, "Teaching Medical Students to Evaluate Drug Advertising," *Journal of Medical Education* 35:729 (1960).

33. Solomon Garb, cited in RxTF, *Drug Prescribers*, p. 7.

34. D. R. H. Gourley, "Teaching the Evaluation of Drug Advertising to Medical Students," *Virginia Medical Monthly* 93:459 (August 1966).

35. John M. Davis, "Efficacy of Tranquilizing and Antidepressant Drugs," *Archives of General Psychiatry* 13:552 (December 1965); Charles R. Galbrecht and C. James Klett, "Predicting Response to Phenothiazines: The Right Drug for the Right Patient," *Journal of Nervous and Mental Disease* 147:173 (August 1968); Leo E. Hollister, "Clinical Use of Psychotherapeutic Drugs: Current Status," *Clinical Pharmacology and Therapeutics* 10:170 (1969); Richard C. Pillard, statement in U.S. Senate, *Competitive Problems* 13:5414 (1969); Daniel X. Freedman, statement in U.S. Senate, *Competitive Problems* 13:5439 (1969); Henry L. Lennard, Leon J. Epstein, Arnold Bernstein, and Donald C. Ransom, *Mystification and Drug Misuse* (San Francisco: Jossey-Bass, 1971).

36. Cited by Gaylord Nelson in U.S. Senate, *Advertising of Proprietary Medicines* 2:430 (1971).

37. Charles C. Edwards, statement in U.S. Senate, *Advertising of Proprietary Medicines* 2:427 (1971).

38. Robert Seidenberg, statement in U.S. Senate, *Advertising of Proprietary Medicines* 2:539 (1971).

39. Donal F. Magee, statement in U.S. Senate, *Competitive Problems* 2:488 (1967).

40. Ralph O. Wallerstein, Philip K. Condit, Carol K. Kasper, John W. Brown, and Florence R. Morrison, "Statewide Study of Chloramphenicol Therapy and Fatal Aplastic Anemia," *Journal of the American Medical Association* 208:2045 (June 16, 1969).

41. Statements in U.S. Senate, *Competitive Problems* 6 (1968):

William Dameshek, p. 2390; William R. Best, p. 2427; James T. Weston, p. 2474; Paul D. Hoeprich, p. 2516.

42. H. J. Loynd, communication dated March 12, 1952, cited by William C. Hewson in U.S. Senate, *Competitive Problems* 6:2549 (1968).

43. Parke, Davis & Co., "Suggested Details," cited by William C. Hewson in U.S. Senate, *Competitive Problems* 6:2551 (1968).

44. Parke, Davis & Co., memorandum to detail men, cited in Richard Harris, *The Real Voice* (New York: Macmillan, 1964), p. 104.

45. Parke, Davis & Co., "Ideas and Suggestions," cited by William C. Hewson in U.S. Senate, *Competitive Problems* 6:2553 (1968).

46. James L. Goddard, statement in U.S. Senate, *Competitive Problems* 6:2625 (1968).

47. William R. Best, "Chloramphenicol-Associated Blood Dyscrasias. A Review of Cases Submitted to the American Medical Association Registry," *Journal of the American Medical Association* 201:181 (July 17, 1967).

48. Stanford Sesser, "Peddling Dangerous Drugs Abroad: Special Dispensation," *New Republic* 164:17 (March 6, 1971).

49. Gaylord Nelson, statement in U.S. Senate, *Competitive Problems* 6:2223 (1968).

50. Leslie M. Lueck, statement in U.S. Senate, *Competitive Problems* 6:2222 (1968).

51. A. Dale Console, statement in U.S. Senate, *Administered Prices* 18:10,373 (1960).

52. William M. O'Brien, "Drug Testing: Is Time Running Out?" *Bulletin of the Atomic Scientists* 25:8 (January 1969).

53. H. Glassner, "Sales Bulletins, 1965–67," cited by Robert S. McCleery in U.S. Senate, *Competitive Problems* 8:3491–3508 (1968).

54. Henry W. Gadsden, statement in U.S. Senate, *Competitive Problems* 8:3435 (1968).

55. Louis C. Lasagna, cited in *Medical Tribune*, March 29, 1967.

56. *Planning Your Family* (Chicago: G. D. Searle & Co., 1966).

57. William D. Kessenich, cited in Morton Mintz, "The Pill: Press and Public at the Experts' Mercy," *Columbia Journalism Review* 7:4 (Winter, 1968–69).

58. James L. Goddard, "Shared Responsibilities," paper presented at a meeting of the Pharmaceutical Manufacturers Association, Boca Raton, Fla., April 4–6, 1966.

59. Clinton S. McGill, statement in U.S. Senate, *Competitive Problems* 10:4114 (1969).

60. Wallace Laboratories, "Dear Doctor Letter," cited in U.S. Senate, *Competitive Problems* 2:816 (1967).

61. Chas. Pfizer & Co., Inc., "Dear Doctor Letter," dated May 18, 1966, cited in the U.S. Senate, *Competitive Problems* 4:1463 (1967).

62. William W. Goodrich, "The State of the Law and Compliance," paper presented before the Pharmaceutical Advertising Club, New York, October 20, 1966.

63. CIBA Pharmaceutical Co., "Dear Doctor Letter" dated January 20, 1969, cited in U.S. Senate, *Competitive Problems* 10:4128 (1968).

64. Goodrich, "The Law and Compliance."

65. Parke, Davis & Co., "Dear Doctor Letter" dated January 15, 1968, cited in U.S. Senate, *Competitive Problems* 8:3174 (1968).

66. Goodrich, "The Law and Compliance."

67. Morton Mintz, "Drug Ad Exports Pose a Problem," *Washington Post*, May 21, 1968.

68. Charles D. May, "Selling Drugs by 'Educating' Physicians," *Journal of Medical Education* 36:14 (January 1961).

69. Herbert L. Ley, Jr., letter to Gaylord Nelson, cited in U.S. Senate, *Competitive Problems* 4:1321 (1967).

70. Morton Mintz, "Source of Wounds in the Drug Battle," *Washington Post*, December 14, 1967.

71. Arnold K. Carter, "Substitution for Brand-Named Drugs," *Canadian Medical Association Journal* 88:98 (January 12, 1963).

72. James L. Goddard, statement in U.S. Senate, *Competitive Problems* 6:2633 (1968).

73. V. D. Mattia, cited in "A Pill-Giving Maverick," *Life* 66:39 (March 7, 1969).

74. Fred Bartenstein, Jr., "Images of the Drug Industry: The Industry View," in Joseph D. Cooper (ed.), *The Economics of Drug Innovation* (Washington, D.C., 1970), p. 232.

75. Henry B. Steele, cited in U.S. Senate, *Competitive Problems* 5:2002 (1968).

76. James M. Faulkner, statement in U.S. Senate, *Competitive Problems* 10:4056 (1969).

77. Robert Seidenberg, statement in U.S. Senate, *Advertising of Proprietary Medicines* 2:541 (1971).

78. William M. O'Brien, statement in U.S. Senate, *Competitive*

Problems 7:2818 (1968); Morton Mintz, "The Stuff Doctors Read," *Progressive* 33:28 (April 1969).

79. Mintz, "The Stuff Doctors Read."

80. Gaylord Nelson, statement in U.S. Senate, *Competitive Problems* 11:4766 (1969).

81. Mintz, "The Stuff Doctors Read."

82. Morris Fishbein, "Are the New Drug Rules an 'Apotheosis of Absurdity'?" *Medical World News* 8:66 (August 25, 1967).

83. DeForest Ely, cited in Morton Mintz, "The Stuff Doctors Read," *Progressive* 33:31 (April 1969).

84. Jeffrey Bishop, "Drug Evaluation Programs of the AMA: 1905–1966," *Journal of the American Medical Association* 196:496 (1966).

85. Ben Gaffin & Associates, "Report on a Study of Advertising and the American Physician," cited in U.S. Senate, *Competitive Problems* 14:5771 (1969).

86. Julius Richmond, cited in U.S. Senate, *Competitive Problems* 5:2006 (1967–68).

87. Edward R. Pinckney, statement in U.S. Senate, *Competitive Problems* 14:5727 (1969).

88. Dale G. Friend, "Generic Drugs and Therapeutic Equivalence," *Journal of the American Medical Association* 206:1785 (November 18, 1968).

89. Alan B. Varley, "The Generic Inequivalence of Drugs," *Journal of the American Medical Association* 206:1745 (November 18, 1968).

90. Editorial, "Editorials—Editorial Responsibilities—Editorial Procedures," *Journal of the American Medical Association* 209:552 (July 28, 1969).

91. National Academy of Sciences/National Research Council, Division of Medical Sciences Drug Efficacy Study: "Fixed Combinations of Antimicrobial Agents," *New England Journal of Medicine* 280:1149 (May 22, 1969).

92. Edward R. Annis, cited in *AMA News*, March 24, 1969.

93. Franz J. Ingelfinger, statement in U.S. Senate, *Competitive Problems* 10:4027 (1968).

94. George Flesh, "Pharmaceutical Advertising," *New Physician* 20:137 (March 1971).

95. William B. Bean, statement in U.S. Senate, *Administered Prices* 18:10,338 (1960).

96. William W. Goodrich, "The State of the Law and Compli-

ance," paper presented before the Pharmaceutical Advertising Club, New York, October 20, 1966.

97. James L. Goddard, statement in U.S. Senate, *Competitive Problems* 2:750 (1967).

98. RxTF, *Drug Prescribers*, p. 12.

99. *Physicians' Attitudes Toward Drug Compendia. A National Survey Sponsored by Pharmaceutical Manufacturers Association* (Princeton, N.J.: Opinion Research Corporation, 1968).

100. *American Medical News*, June 25, 1973, p. 12.

101. *Medical Tribune*, January 26, 1972.

102. Carl Nathan, statement in U.S. Senate, *Competitive Problems* 14:5557 (1969).

103. Harry F. Dowling, *Medicines for Man* (New York: Knopf, 1970), p. 125.

104. Natalie Shainess, statement in U.S. Senate, *Advertising of Proprietary Medicines* 2:546 (1971).

105. Richard Harris, *The Real Voice* (New York: Macmillan, 1964), p. 111.

106. A. Dale Console, statement in U.S. Senate, *Competitive Problems* 11:4479 (1969).

4. The Impossible Dream:
Search for the Absolutely Safe Drug.

1. Milton Silverman, *Magic in a Bottle* (New York: Macmillan, 2nd ed., 1948), p. 1.

2. Ibid., p. 89.

3. John B. Blake (ed.), *Safeguarding the Public* (Baltimore: Johns Hopkins Press, 1970).

4. James Harvey Young, *The Toadstool Millionaires* (Princeton, N.J.: Princeton University Press, 1961); James Harvey Young, *The Medical Messiahs* (Princeton, N.J.: Princeton University Press, 1967).

5. Young, *Medical Messiahs*, p. 11.

6. William W. Goodrich (Food and Drug Administration), personal communication, 1971.

7. Silverman, *Magic in a Bottle*, p. 242.

8. Young, *Medical Messiahs*, p. 188.

9. Chauncey D. Leake, statement in U.S. Senate, *Administered Prices* 18:10,418 (1960).

10. William Dameshek, "Chloramphenicol: A New Warning,"

Journal of the American Medical Association 174:1853 (December 3, 1960).

11. William R. Best, "Chloramphenicol-Associated Blood Dyscrasias. A Review of Cases Submitted to the American Medical Association Registry," *Journal of the American Medical Association* 201:181 (July 17, 1967).

12. Thomas M. Rice, statement in U.S. Senate, *Competitive Problems* 10:4202 (1969).

13. Beulah L. Jordan, cited in U.S. Senate, *Competitive Problems* 10:4143 (1969).

14. Thomas M. Rice, statement in U.S. Senate, *Competitive Problems* 10:4233 (1969).

15. Edwin I. Goldenthal, statement in U.S. Senate, *Competitive Problems* 10:4206 (1969).

16. Ibid., p. 4207.

17. Ibid., p. 4205.

18. Ibid., p. 4208.

19. Robert C. Brandenburg, statement in U.S. Senate, *Competive Problems* 10:4210 (1969).

20. R. H. McMaster, company memorandum to R. L. Stormont dated April 19, 1960, cited in U.S. Senate, *Competitive Problems* 10:3970 (1969).

21. Robert H. Woodward, company memorandum to F. H. Gelman dated May 20, 1959, cited in U.S. Senate, *Competitive Problems* 10:3971 (1969).

22. R. H. McMaster, company memorandum to [C. A.] Bunde dated June 21, 1961, cited in U.S. Senate, *Competitive Problems* 10:3972 (1969).

23. R. H. McMaster, company memorandum to H. W. Werner dated July 5, 1961, cited in U.S. Senate, *Competitive Problems* 10:3971 (1969).

24. Robert C. Brandenburg, statement in U.S. Senate, 1969.

25. R. H. Woodward, company memorandum to R. H. McMaster dated October 5, 1960, cited in U.S. Senate, *Competitive Problems* 10:4273 (1969).

26. United States v. Richardson-Merrell, Inc., Crim. No. 1211–63 (D.D.C., June 4, 1964).

27. Paul D. Rheingold, "The MER/29 Story: An Instance of Successful Mass Disaster Litigation," *California Law Review* 56:116 (1968).

28. John Wynne Herron, "MER/29—1968—The Goose Is Dead," paper presented at a meeting of the American Bar Association, Philadelphia, 1968; Ralph Adam Fine, *The Great Drug Deception* (New York: Stein and Day, 1972).

29. Ostopowitz v. Wm. S. Merrell Co., No. 5879–1963, N.Y.L.J., January 11, 1967.

30. Toole v. Richardson-Merrell, Inc., 251 A.C.A. 785, 60 Cal. Rptr., 1967.

31. Paul D. Rheingold, personal communication, 1971; Fine, *The Great Drug Deception.*

32. Paul D. Rheingold, "The MER/29 Story—An Instance of Successful Mass Disaster Litigation," p. 146.

33. Fine, *The Great Drug Deception.*

34. Morton Mintz, " 'Heroine' of FDA Keeps Bad Drug Off Market," *Washington Post,* July 15, 1962.

35. Helen B. Taussig, "A Study of the German Outbreak of Phocomelia. The Thalidomide Syndrome," *Journal of the American Medical Association* 180:1106 (June 30, 1962).

36. W. Lenz, "Kindliche Missbildungen nach Medikament-Einnahme während die Gravitat?" *Deutsche medizinische Wochenschrift* 86:2555 (December 29, 1961).

37. W. G. McBride, "Thalidomide and Congenital Abnormalities," *Lancet* 2:1358 (December 16, 1961).

38. Richard Harris, *The Real Voice* (New York: Macmillan, 1964), p. 187.

39. Charles C. Edwards (Food and Drug Administration), personal communication, 1972.

40. Mintz, " 'Heroine' of FDA Keeps Bad Drug Off Market."

41. Harris, *The Real Voice,* p. 98.

42. William W. Goodrich, letter to U.S. Attorney General, dated June 5, 1961.

43. Paul Lowinger, statement in U.S. Senate, *Competitive Problems* 10:3998 (1969).

44. William W. Goodrich, letter to U.S. Attorney General, dated April 20, 1964.

45. Herbert J. Miller, Jr., letter to William W. Goodrich, dated September 28, 1964.

46. U.S. Department of Health, Education, and Welfare, Food and Drug Administration, Advisory Committee on Obstetrics and Gynecology, *Report on the Oral Contraceptives,* August 1, 1966.

47. W. M. Jordan, "Pulmonary Embolism," *Lancet* 2:1146 (November 18, 1961).

48. Edward T. Tyler, "Oral Contraception and Venous Thrombosis," *Journal of the American Medical Association* 185:131 (July 13, 1963).

49. Edmond Kassouf, statement in U.S. Senate, *Competitive Problems* 15:6108 (1970).

50. Herbert Ratner, statement in U.S. Senate, *Competitive Problems* 16:6725 (1970).

51. U.S. Department of Health, Education, and Welfare, Food and Drug Administration, Ad Hoc Committee for the Evaluation of a Possible Etiologic Relation with Thromboembolic Conditions: *Report on Enovid*, August 4, 1963.

52. Morton Mintz, "The Pill: Press and Public at the Experts' Mercy," *Columbia Journalism Review* 7:4 (Winter 1968–69).

53. Edmond Kassouf, statement in U.S. Senate, *Competitive Problems* 15:6110 (1970).

54. Irwin Winter, cited in U.S. Senate, *Competitive Problems* 15:6108 (1970).

55. John Rock, cited in Mintz, "The Pill," *Columbia Journalism Review* (Winter 1968–69).

56. John Rock, cited in Louis Lasagna, "Caution on the Pill," *Saturday Review* 51:64 (November 2, 1968).

57. Gregory Pincus, "Tell Me Doctor," *Ladies' Home Journal* 80:50 (June 1963).

58. *Planning Your Family* (Chicago: G. D. Searle & Co., 1966).

59. G. D. Searle & Co., cited in Mintz, "The Pill," *Columbia Journalism Review* (Winter 1968–69).

60. Alan F. Guttmacher, cited in Morton Mintz, "The Pill: Press and Public at the Experts' Mercy (Part 2)," *Columbia Journalism Review* 8:28 (Spring 1969).

61. Lois Chevalier and Leonard Cohen, "Terrible Trouble with the Birth Control Pills," *Ladies' Home Journal* 84:43 (July 1967).

62. James A. Shannon, cited in Morton Mintz, "Are Birth Control Pills Safe?" *Washington Post*, December 19, 1965.

63. Louis C. Lasagna, cited in Mintz, "Are Birth Control Pills Safe?"

64. Bill Surface, "Controversy Over the Pill," *Good Housekeeping* 170:64 (January 1970).

65. Lord Platt et al., "Risk of Thromboembolic Disease in Women

Taking Oral Contraceptives. Preliminary Report to the Medical Research Council by a Subcommittee," *British Medical Journal* 2:355 (May 6, 1967).

66. M. P. Vessey and W. R. S. Doll, "Investigation of Relation Between Use of Oral Contraceptives and Thromboembolic Disease," *British Medical Journal* 2:199 (April 27, 1968).

67. Celso Ramon Garcia, cited in Bill Surface, "Controversy Over the Pill."

68. Victor A. Drill and David W. Calhoun, "Oral Contraceptives and Thromboembolic Disease," *Journal of the American Medical Association* 206:77 (September 30, 1968).

69. U.S. Department of Health, Education, and Welfare, Food and Drug Administration, Advisory Committee on Obstetrics and Gynecology, *Second Report on the Oral Contraceptives* (Washington, D.C.: U.S. Government Printing Office, 1969).

70. Charles C. Edwards, statement in U.S. Senate, *Competitive Problems* 16:6800 (1970).

71. U.S. Department of Health, Education, and Welfare, Food and Drug Administration, Advisory Committee on Obstetrics and Gynecology, "Chairman's Summary," *Second Report on the Oral Contraceptives* (Washington, D.C.: U.S. Government Printing Office, 1969).

72. Alan F. Guttmacher, statement in U.S. Senate, *Competitive Problems* 16:6619 (1970).

73. Morton Mintz, "The Pill and the Public's Right to Know," *Progressive* 34:25 (May 1970).

74. "Poll on the Pill," *Newsweek* 75:52 (February 9, 1970).

75. U.S. Department of Health, Education, and Welfare, *HEW News*, June 9, 1970.

76. Victor Cohn, "AMA Pledges All-Out Fight Against Birth-Pill Warning," *Washington Post*, June 24, 1970.

77. Collaborative Group for the Study of Stroke in Young Women, "Oral Contraception and Increased Risk of Cerebral Ischemia or Thrombosis," *New England Journal of Medicine* 288:871 (April 26, 1973).

78. "Oral Contraceptives and Venous Thromboembolic Disease, Surgically Confirmed Gall Bladder Disease, and Breast Tumors," *Lancet* 1:1399 (June 23, 1973).

79. University Group Diabetes Program, "A Study of the Effects of Hypoglycemic Agents on Vascular Complications in Patients with

Adult-Onset Diabetes. I. Design, Methods and Baseline Results," *Diabetes* 19 (suppl. 2):747 (1970); "II. Mortality Results," p. 789; "IV. A Preliminary Report on Phenformin Results," *Journal of the American Medical Association* 217:777 (August 9, 1971).

80. John J. Jennings (Food and Drug Administration), personal communication, 1972.

81. Irving Graef, cited in *F-D-C Reports*, October 2, 1972, p. 14.

82. Max Miller, statement in U.S. Senate, *Competitive Problems* 23:9750 (1973).

83. Gerhard Zbinden, "Drug Safety: Experimental Programs," *Science* 164:643 (May 9, 1969).

84. James L. Goddard, "Shared Responsibilities," paper presented at a meeting of the Pharmaceutical Manufacturers Association, Boca Raton, Fla., April 4–6, 1966.

85. Peter Beaconsfield, Rebecca Rainsburg, Julian Huxley, Rudolph Peters, Jacques Tréfouel, Jacques Monod, Raymond Paul, and Hugo Theorell, "Suggestion for a Study on the Implications of Various Chemicals and Non-Disease Specific Drugs," *Experientia* 27:715 (June 15, 1971).

5. Drug Efficacy: The Case
of the Emperor's Old Drugs.

1. Melvin D. Small, statement in U.S. Senate, *Competitive Problems* 1:356 (1967).

2. Ibid., p. 374.

3. Frederick Wolff, statement in U.S. Senate, *Competitive Problems* 3:836 (1967).

4. Thomas Chalmers, statement in U.S. Senate, *Competitive Problems* 23:9756 (1973).

5. Harry L. Williams, statement in U.S. Senate, *Competitive Problems* 2:460 (1967).

6. Henry E. Simmons, "The Drug Efficacy Study: Its Effects on Therapeutics in America," paper presented at a meeting of the American College of Physicians, Denver, March 31, 1971.

7. Herbert L. Ley, Jr., statement in U.S. Senate, *Competitive Problems* 12:5141 (1969).

8. RxTF, *Drug Users*, p. 38.

9. Gifford E. Hampshire, "The NAS/NRC Drug Efficacy Study: A Peer Review," *FDA Papers* 3:4 (November 1969).

10. John Lear, "Taking the Miracle Out of the Miracle Drugs," *Saturday Review* 42:35 (January 3, 1959).

11. Richard Harris, *The Real Voice* (New York: Macmillan, 1964), p. 36.

12. Ibid., p. 55.

13. Ibid., p. 62.

14. John Lear, "The Certification of Antibiotics," *Saturday Review* 42:43 (February 7, 1959).

15. Harris, p. 112.

16. Ibid.

17. Harris, pp. 123, 143.

18. Harris, p. 124.

19. Harry C. Shirkey, statement in U.S. Senate, *Competitive Problems* 23:9616 (1973).

20. Harris, p. 143.

21. Paul Douglas, cited in Harris, *The Real Voice*, p. 215.

22. James Harvey Young, *The Medical Messiahs* (Princeton, N.J.: Princeton University Press, 1967), p. 360.

23. *Unproven Methods of Cancer Treatment* (New York: American Cancer Society, 1966).

24. California Medical Association, Cancer Commission, "The Treatment of Cancer with 'Laetriles,'" *California Medicine* 78:320 (April 1953).

25. Milton Silverman, "Krebiozen: A Serum or a Fake?" *San Francisco Chronicle*, April 1, 1951.

26. Milton Silverman: "History of a 'Hope': The Facts Show Arginase Drug Won't Help Cancer," *San Francisco Chronicle*, April 25, 1952; "Bay Area Cancer Tests Discount Arginase," *San Francisco Chronicle*, April 26, 1952; "L.A. Hospital Halts Cancer Experiment," *San Francisco Chronicle*, April 27, 1952.

27. RxTF, *Drug Prescribers*, p. 35.

28. Joseph F. Sadusk, Jr., "The Impact of Drug Legislation on Clinical Evaluation of Drugs," paper presented at a symposium at the Gottlieb Duttweiler Institute, Ruschlikon-Zurich, August 28–29, 1969.

29. James L. Goddard, "Shared Responsibilities," paper presented at a meeting of the Pharmaceutical Manufacturers Association, Boca Raton, Fla., April 6, 1966.

30. James L. Goddard, "Shared Responsibilities."

31. Richard Harris, *The Real Voice*, p. 219.

32. William W. Goodrich (Food and Drug Administration), personal communication, 1970.

33. National Research Council, Division of Medical Sciences, *Drug Efficacy Study. Final Report to the Commissioner of Food and Drugs, Food and Drug Administration* (Washington, D.C.: National Academy of Sciences, 1969).

34. C. Joseph Stetler, letter dated January 21, 1971, to Gaylord Nelson.

35. R. Keith Cannan, statement in Joseph D. Cooper (ed.), *The Economics of Drug Innovation* (Washington, D.C.: American University, Center for the Study of Private Enterprise, 1970), p. 87.

36. National Research Council, Division of Medical Sciences, *Drug Efficacy Study.*

37. Russell R. Miller, Alfred Feingold, and James Paxinos, "Propoxyphene Hydrochloride. A Critical Review," *Journal of the American Medical Association* 213:996 (August 10, 1970).

38. C. G. Moertel, M. D. Ahmann, W. F. Taylor, and Neal Schwartau, "A Comparative Evaluation of Marketed Analgesic Drugs," *New England Journal of Medicine* 286:813 (April 13, 1972).

39. Charles C. Edwards, "Progress Toward Rational Drug Therapeutics," paper presented at a meeting of the Medical Society of the County of Queens, Queens, N.Y., November 24, 1970.

40. Henry E. Simmons, statement in U.S. Senate, *Advertising of Proprietary Medicines* 3:1052 (1972).

41. Herbert L. Ley, Jr., statement in U.S. Senate, *Competitive Problems* 12:5176, 5230 (1969).

42. J. C. Gauntlett, letter dated January 28, 1969, cited by William L. Hewitt in U.S. Senate, *Competitive Problems* 12:5057, 5067 (1969).

43. Max B. McQueen, FDA memorandum dated April 29, 1969, cited by Herbert L. Ley, Jr., in U.S. Senate, *Competitive Problems* 12:5150 (1969).

44. William W. Goodrich, statement in U.S. Senate, *Competitive Problems* 12:5154 (1969).

45. Charles C. Edwards, paper presented at a meeting of the U.S. Public Health Service Clinical Society and Commissioned Officers Association, Washington, D.C., April 1, 1970.

46. John Adriani, "Ready-Made Fixed-Ratio Drug Mixtures," *Medical Tribune*, November 16, 1970.

47. Louis Lasagna, "The FDA's 'Efficacy' Rule: Does it Work?" *American Medical News*, May 3, 1971.

48. National Academy of Sciences/National Research Council, "Fixed Combinations of Antimicrobial Agents," *New England Journal of Medicine* 280:1149 (May 22, 1969).

49. Lea-Mendota Research Group, *Physicians' Attitudes Towards Combinations. A Research Project for the Pharmaceutical Manufacturers Association* (Ambler, Pa.: Lea-Mendota, April 1971).

50. Heinz F. Eichenwald, statement in U.S. Senate, *Competitive Problems* 12:5017 (1969).

51. C. Joseph Stetler, letter to Jesse L. Steinfeld dated January 21, 1971, cited in U.S. Senate, *Competitive Problems* 20:8083 (1971).

52. Jesse L. Steinfeld, letter to C. Joseph Stetler dated January 28, 1971, cited in U.S. Senate, *Competitive Problems* 20:8082 (1971).

53. Thomas H. Crouch, U.S. Air Force memorandum dated November 27, 1970, cited in U.S. Senate, *Competitive Problems* 20:8230 (1971).

54. Louis Lasagna, "The FDA's 'Efficacy' Rule: Does it Work?"

55. Mark Novitch (Food and Drug Administration), personal communication, 1973.

56. R. Keith Cannan, statement in Joseph D. Cooper (ed.), *Economics of Drug Innovation* (Washington, D.C., 1970), p. 88.

57. Weinberger v. Hynson, Westcott and Dunning, Inc., 412 U.S. 609 (1973); Weinberger v. Bentex Pharmaceuticals, Inc., 412 U.S. 645 (1973); Ciba Corp. v. Weinberger, 412 U.S. 640 (1973); USV Pharm. Corp. v. Weinberger, 412 U.S. 655 (1973).

58. Harry C. Shirkey, statement in U.S. Senate, *Competitive Problems* 23:9582 (1973).

59. "UC Sued: Children Used in Experiments," *San Francisco Chronicle*, September 12, 1973.

60. Shirkey, statement in U.S. Senate, *Competitive Problems* 3:9580 (1973).

61. Karl Evang, *Health Service, Society, and Medicine* (London: Oxford University Press, 1960), p. 127; RxTF, *Current Programs*, p. 187.

6. Drug Quality and the Great Generic Controversy.

1. Glenn Allen Sonnedecker, *Kremer and Urdang's History of Pharmacy* (Philadelphia: Lippincott, 3rd ed., 1963), p. 227.

2. Edward G. Feldmann, statement in U.S. Senate, *Competitive Problems* 1:421 (1967); Lloyd C. Miller, statement in U.S. Senate, *Competitive Problems* 2:499 (1967).

3. Neal Nathanson and Alexander D. Langmuir, "The Cutter Incident: Poliomyelitis Following Formaldehyde-Inactivated Poliovirus Vaccination in the United States During the Spring of 1955," *American Journal of Hygiene* 78:16 (July 1963).

4. U.S. Department of Health, Education, and Welfare, Food and Drug Administration, *Weekly Recall Reports*, 1966–71.

5. Richard M. Furlaud, statement in U.S. Senate, *Competitive Problems* 3:1065 (1967).

6. U.S. Department of Health, Education, and Welfare, Food and Drug Administration, *Abbott IV Solutions*, Washington, D.C., April 2, 1971.

7. U.S. Department of Health, Education, and Welfare, Food and Drug Administration, *"Regulatory History" on Abbott Parenterals*. Washington, D.C., 1971.

8. Margaret Kreig, *Black Market Medicine* (Englewood Cliffs, N.J.: Prentice-Hall, 1967), p. 207.

9. Richard Harris, *The Real Voice* (New York: Macmillan, 1964), p. 31.

10. Austin Smith, cited in Harris, p. 115.

11. Louis Lasagna, "Problems of Drug Development," *Science* 145:362 (July 24, 1964).

12. RxTF, *Final Report*, p. 25.

13. Russell B. Long, cited in Spencer Rich, "Generic Drug Drive Far From Dead," *Washington Post*, December 23, 1967.

14. George S. Squibb, cited in U.S. Senate, *Competitive Problems* 3:947 (1967).

15. Harry L. Williams, statement in U.S. Senate, *Competitive Problems* 2:450 (1967).

16. American Medical Association, "Generic Prescribing Doesn't Guarantee Lower Drug Costs, Chicago Survey Shows," news release, May 26, 1967.

17. Durward G. Hall, statement in U.S. Senate, *Competitive Problems* 1:259 (1967).

18. Martin Cherkasky, statement in U.S. Senate, *Competitive Problems* 2:668 (1967).

19. George S. Squibb, statement in U.S. Senate, *Competitive Problems* 5:1580 (1967).

20. "Tests of Prednisone Tablets," *Medical Letter* 9:41 (June 2, 1967).

21. Sidney Riegelman, "Drug Substitution: Standards and Quality

Control," paper presented at a symposium at the University of California, San Francisco, January 29, 1971.

22. Winton B. Rankin, paper presented at a meeting of the American College of Apothecaries, Boston, October 15, 1966.

23. Edward G. Feldmann, "The Brand Name System: An Intrusion Upon the Profession," *Journal of the American Pharmaceutical Association* NS11:376 (July 1971).

24. Edward G. Feldmann, statement in U.S. Senate, *Competitive Problems* 1:410 (1967).

25. Lloyd C. Miller, statement in U.S. Senate, *Competitive Problems* 2:508 (1967).

26. Henry F. DeBoest, statement in U.S. Senate, *Competitive Problems* 3:971 (1967).

27. Joseph F. Sadusk, Jr. (Parke, Davis & Co.), personal communication, 1967.

28. Edward G. Feldmann, "The Pharmacist's Role in Drug Product Selection," paper presented at a meeting of the Ohio Society of Hospital Pharmacists, Heuston Woods Resort, Ohio, October 1, 1971.

29. John Adriani, statement in U.S. Senate, *Competitive Problems* 12:5128 (1969).

30. C. Joseph Stetler, statement in U.S. Senate, *Competitive Problems* 4:1368 (1967).

31. RxTF, *Drug Users*, p. ix.

32. RxTF, *Drug Prescribers*, p. 21.

33. RxTF, *Final Report*, p. 32.

34. Ibid., p. 31.

35. RxTF, *Drug Prescribers*, p. 48.

36. RxTF, *Current Programs*, p. 19.

37. Ibid., p. 18.

38. Ibid., p. 4.

39. RxTF, *Drug Prescribers*, p. 47.

40. RxTF, *Current Programs*, p. 140.

41. *Bibliography on Biopharmaceutics* (Washington, D.C.: Pharmaceutical Manufacturers Association, 1968).

42. Milton Silverman, letter to Philip R. Lee dated September 13, 1968, cited in U.S. Senate, *Competitive Problems* 9:3729 (1968).

43. RxTF, *Final Report*, p. 32.

44. RxTF, *Drug Prescribers*, p. 23.

45. RxTF, *Final Report*, p. 33.

46. John G. Wagner, "Generic Equivalence and Inequivalence of

Oral Products," *Drug Intelligence and Clinical Pharmacy* 5:115 (April 1971).

47. Edward G. Feldmann, "The Pharmacist's Role in Drug Product Selection."

48. Eldon M. Boyd, "The Equivalence of Drug Brands," *Rx Bulletin* 2:101 (July-August 1971).

49. John Lindenbaum, Mark H. Mellow, Michael O. Blackstone, and Vincent P. Butler, Jr., "Variation in Biologic Availability of Digoxin from Four Preparations," *New England Journal of Medicine* 285:1344 (December 9, 1971).

50. Theodore E. Byers, cited in *Medical Tribune*, March 16, 1972.

51. Jesse L. Steinfeld, statement in U.S. Senate, *Competitive Problems* 20:8107 (1971).

52. S. 2812, U.S. Senate, 92nd Congress, 1st Session, November 4, 1971.

53. Charles C. Edwards, statement in U.S. Senate, *Competitive Problems* 20:7979 (1971).

54. Charles C. Edwards, "The Need for a New Paradigm," paper presented at a meeting of the Academy of Pharmaceutical Sciences, Washington, D.C., April 15, 1970.

55. Charles C. Edwards, letter to C. Joseph Stetler dated March 18, 1971, cited in U.S. Senate, *Competitive Problems* 20:8117 (1971).

56. Charles C. Edwards, paper presented at a meeting of the National Association of Pharmaceutical Manufacturers, Washington, D.C., February 3, 1971.

57. American Pharmaceutical Association, Academy of Pharmaceutical Sciences, "Drug Product Quality," resolution approved by American Pharmaceutical Association House of Delegates, Chicago, November 24, 1969.

58. W. B. Castle, E. B. Astwood, Maxwell Finland, and Chester Keefer, "White Paper on the Therapeutic Equivalence of Chemically Equivalent Drugs," *Journal of the American Medical Association* 208:1171 (May 19, 1969).

59. Henry E. Simmons, directive to staff, Bureau of Drugs, Food and Drug Administration, October 1970.

60. *Federal Register*, January 15, 1971.

61. Henry E. Simmons, "Brands vs. Generic Drugs: It's Only a Matter of Time," *FDA Consumer*, March 1973, p. 4.

62. *A White Paper on the Pharmacist's Role in Product Selection* (Washington, D.C.: American Pharmaceutical Association, 1971).

63. Editorial, "Drug Substitution: How to Turn Order into

Chaos," *Journal of the American Medical Association* 217:817 (August 9, 1971).

64. *The Medications Physicians Prescribe: Who Shall Determine the Source?* (Washington, D.C.: Pharmaceutical Manufacturers Association, 1972).

65. Carl Roberts, paper presented at a symposium at the University of California, San Francisco, January 29, 1971.

66. Editorial, "A Voluntary Delaware Formulary," *Delaware Medical Journal* 42:48 (February 1970).

67. William S. Apple, paper presented at a meeting of Kappa Epsilon Fraternity, University of Minnesota, Minneapolis, August 30, 1971.

68. Edward G. Feldmann, "The Pharmacist's Role in Drug Product Selection."

69. William S. Apple, paper presented at meeting, Minneapolis, 1971.

70. *Weekly Pharmacy Reports* ("The Green Sheet"), January 1, 1973.

71. Russell Roth, cited in Norman Melnick, "AMA Chief Defends His Drug Stocks," *San Francisco Examiner*, August 26, 1973.

72. Mary Lou Andersen (Maryland Pharmaceutical Association), personal communication, 1972.

73. RxTF, *Drug Users*, p. 140.

74. RxTF, *Final Report*, p. 36.

75. *F-D-C Reports*, December 19, 1973.

7. Drug Prices: How High Is Too High?

1. George S. Squibb, statement in U.S. Senate, *Competitive Problems* 5:1572 (1967).

2. U.S. Department of Health, Education, and Welfare, Social Security Administration, Office of Research and Statistics, *Medical Care Costs and Prices: Background Book*. DHEW (SSA) 72-11908, January 1972, p. 43.

3. T. Donald Rucker, "Economic Problems in Drug Distribution," *Inquiry* 9:43 (September 1972).

4. RxTF, *Drug Makers and Distributors*, p. 31; RxTF, *Final Report*, p. 11.

5. RxTF, *Current Programs*.

6. RxTF, *Drug Users*, p. 22.

7. John L. S. Holloman, statement in U.S. Senate, *Competitive Problems* 1:24 (1967).

8. Daniel L. Azarnoff, Donald B. Hunninghake, and Jack Wortman, "Prescription Writing by Generic Name and Drug Cost," *Journal of Chronic Diseases* 19:1253 (1966).

9. Glen E. Hastings and Richard Kunnes, "Predicting Prescription Prices," *New England Journal of Medicine,* 277:625 (September 21, 1967).

10. George S. Squibb, statement in U.S. Senate, *Competitive Problems* 5:1567 (1967).

11. Mark O. Hatfield, statement in U.S. Senate, *Competitive Problems* 5:1566 (1967).

12. RxTF, *Drug Makers and Distributors,* p. 72.

13. Milton Silverman and Mia Lydecker, unpublished data.

14. Robert Johnson (California Pharmaceutical Association), personal communication, 1973.

15. *F-D-C Reports,* October 16, 1972, p. 8.

16. William F. Haddad, statement in U.S. Senate, *Competitive Problems* 1:5 (1967).

17. Gaylord Nelson, statement in U.S. Senate, *Competitive Problems* 5:1611 (1967).

18. Ibid.

19. W. H. Conzen, statement in U.S. Senate, *Competitive Problems* 2:642 (1967).

20. E. B. Anderson, letter to Gaylord Nelson dated January 2, 1968, cited in U.S. Senate, *Competitive Problems* 5:2037 (1968).

21. Gaylord Nelson, statement in U.S. Senate, *Competitive Problems* 3:917 (1967).

22. Ibid., p. 657.

23. Richard M. Furlaud, statement in U.S. Senate, *Competitive Problems* 3:1087 (1967).

24. Edmond M. Jacoby, Jr., and Dennis L. Hefner, "Domestic and Foreign Prescription Drug Prices," *Social Security Bulletin* 34:15 (May 1971).

25. James Poole, "Drug Price Cuts: The Angry Backwash," *Sunday Times* (London), April 15, 1973.

26. RxTF, *Final Report,* p. 12.

27. Gaylord Nelson, statement in U.S. Senate, *Competitive Problems* 18:7330 (1970).

28. U.S. Department of State, Agency for International Develop-

ment, "Determination of Commodity Eligibility for Bulk Pharmaceutical Products," *Federal Register*, December 31, 1970.

29. Editorial, "Right Hand and Left Hand," *Medical Tribune*, October 6, 1971.

30. RxTF, *Drug Users*, p. 15.

31. John M. Firestone, *Trends in Prescription Drug Prices* (Washington, D.C.: American Enterprise Institute for Public Policy Research, 1970).

32. Gaylord Nelson, "Public Health Price Protection Act," *Congressional Record—Senate*, S 16336, September 29, 1972.

33. RxTF, *Drug Makers and Distributors*, p. 41.

34. Michael Pearson, *The Million-Dollar Bugs* (New York: Putnam, 1969).

35. RxTF, *Drug Makers and Distributors*, p. 41.

36. Elmer B. Staats, statement in U.S. Senate, *Competitive Problems* 20:8015 (1971).

37. RxTF, *Drug Makers and Distributors*, p. 42.

38. George Teeling-Smith, "The British Drug Scene," in Joseph D. Cooper (ed.), *The Economics of Drug Innovation* (Washington, D.C.: American University, Center for the Study of Private Enterprise, 1970), p. 5.

8. *Pharmacy: Revolution in the Making.*

1. Philip A. Hart, *Congressional Record* 111:25,238, 89th Congress, 1st Session, September 28, 1965.

2. Jere E. Goyan, "Professional Practice in Transition," paper presented at Wayne State University College of Pharmacy, Detroit, February 16, 1971.

3. Ibid.

4. U.S. Department of Health, Education, and Welfare, Social Security Administration, Office of Research and Statistics, *Prescription Drug Data Summary 1972*. DHEW Publication No. (SSA) 73-11900, 1973, p. 27.

5. *The Lilly Digest* (Indianapolis: Eli Lilly and Co., 1973), p. 16.

6. Ibid., p. 7.

7. T. Donald Rucker (Social Security Administration), personal communication, 1972.

8. RxTF, *Final Report*, p. 16.

9. Marcel Laventurier (Paid Prescriptions, Inc.), personal communication, 1973.

10. Essex County (N.J.) Pharmaceutical Society, "D-Day Pharmacy Diary Digest," Report to Commissioner, Food and Drug Administration, May 18, 1967.

11. D. A. Knapp, H. H. Wolk, D. E. Knapp, and T. A. Rudy, "The Pharmacist as a Drug Advisor," *Journal of the American Pharmaceutical Association* NS9:502 (October 1969).

12. Milton S. Davis and Lawrence S. Linn, "Patterns of Influence Among Pharmacists, Physicians, and Patients," Report to Social Security Administration, March 31, 1971.

13. William S. Apple, "The Changing Role of the Pharmacist," paper presented at a symposium at the University of California, San Francisco, September 10, 1970.

14. Allen J. Brands (Public Health Service), personal communication, 1973.

15. George B. Griffenhagen, "Clinical Pharmacy = Patient Involvement," *Journal of the American Pharmaceutical Association* NS11:45 (February 1971).

16. Robert A. Miller, "Application of Clinical Pharmacy," *Journal of the American Pharmaceutical Association* NS11:46 (February 1971).

17. Mary K. McHale and Andrew T. Canada, Jr., "The Use of a Pharmacist in Obtaining Medication Histories," *Drug Intelligence* 3:115 (April 1969); Vincent E. Bouchard, "Toward a Clinical Practice of Pharmacy," *Drug Intelligence & Clinical Pharmacy* 3:342 (December 1969); Roger S. Wilson and Hugh F. Kabat, "Pharmacist Initiated Patient Drug Histories," *American Journal of Hospital Pharmacy* 28:49 (January 1971).

18. U.S. Department of Health, Education, and Welfare, National Center for Health Services Research and Development, "Report of Task Force on the Pharmacist's Clinical Role," *HSRD Briefs*, No. 4, Spring 1971.

19. William E. Smith, *Clinical Pharmacy Services in a Community Hospital.* U.S. Department of Health, Education, and Welfare, National Center for Health Services Research and Development, DHEW Pub. No. HSM 72-3019, 1972, p. 27.

20. Ibid., p. 31.

21. Allen J. Brands, personal communication, 1973.

22. *Standards for Residential Facilities for the Mentally Retarded* (Chicago: Joint Commission on Accreditation of Hospitals, 1971), p. 73.

23. Richard F. de Leon, "Clinical Pharmacy at the University of

California," *Journal of the American Pharmaceutical Association* NS11:54 (February 1971).

24. Sister Emmanuel, "Community Pharmacy Practice—Its Role in the Education of Clinically Oriented Pharmacists," *Journal of the American Pharmaceutical Association* NS11:48 (February 1971).

25. Paul W. Lofholm, "The Clinical Pharmacist in an Interprofessional Group Practice," in Don E. Francke (ed.), *Perspectives in Clinical Pharmacy* (Hamilton, Ill.: Drug Intelligence Publications, 1972), p. 272.

26. Paul W. Lofholm (Ross Valley Medical Clinic), personal communication, 1972.

27. Lyman Hurlbut, cited in "Pharmacist at the Bedside, MD in the Pharmacy," *Medical World News*, September 26, 1969.

28. Paul W. Lofholm, *Pharmacy Services in a Medical Group Practice*. Rockville, Md., U.S. Department of Health, Education, and Welfare, National Center for Health Services Research and Development, DHEW Pub. No. (HSM) 73-3006, 1973.

29. James C. Clinite and Hugh F. Kabat, "Prescribed Drugs—Errors During Self-Administration," *Journal of the American Pharmaceutical Association* NS9:450 (September 1969).

30. Joseph D. McEvilla (University of Pittsburgh), personal communication, 1971.

31. Dorothy Sved, cited in *American Druggist*, January 12, 1970.

32. Robert H. Ebert, "Changes in the Health System," *Journal of the American Pharmaceutical Association* NS9:402 (August 1969).

33. Editorial, "Of Pharmacists, Physicians and Health Care," *California Medicine* 114:83 (May 1971).

34. *F-D-C Reports*, November 13, 1972, p. 11.

9. *The OTCs: "If It Wasn't Safe,*
They Wouldn't Sell It to You Without a Prescription."

1. Charles C. Edwards, statement in U.S. Senate, *Advertising of Proprietary Medicines* 1:2 (1971).

2. M. N. G. Dukes, *Patent Medicines and Autotherapy in Society* (The Hague: Drukkerij Pasmans, 1963).

3. Chauncey D. Leake, "The History of Self-Medication," *Annals of the New York Academy of Sciences* 120:815 (1965).

4. James F. Hoge, "Legislative History of Home Remedies," *Annals of the New York Academy of Sciences* 120:833 (1965).

5. Ibid., p. 838.

6. H.R. No. 2139, U.S. House of Representatives, 75th Congress, 3rd Session, 1938, p. 8.

7. Charles C. Edwards, statement in U.S. Senate, *Advertising of Proprietary Medicines* 1:2 (1971).

8. C. H. Kline & Co., cited in "American Drug Statistics," *Manufacturing Chemist & Aerosol News* 41:57 (October 1970).

9. Donald J. O'Shea, "Rx Drug Makers' Profits up 12%; Sales Rise 12.5%," *Drug Trade News* 46:1 (September 20, 1971).

10. Jules Backman, "Economics of Proprietary Drugs," *Annals of the New York Academy of Sciences* 120:878 (1965).

11. William S. Apple (American Pharmaceutical Association), personal communication, 1972.

12. C. H. Kline & Co.

13. "Top 100 National Advertisers' Ad Total Reaches $5.27 Billion," *Advertising Age* 44:1 (August 27, 1973).

14. H. Michael Mann, statement in U.S. Senate, *Advertising of Proprietary Medicines* 1:50 (1971).

15. "100 Leaders' Media Expenditures Compared in 1972," *Advertising Age* 44:28 (August 27, 1973).

16. "1972 Ad Expenditures for Health and Beauty Aids," *Product Management* 2:44 (August 1973).

17. "Advertising Marketing Reports on the 100 Top National Advertisers," *Advertising Age* 44:27 (August 27, 1973).

18. Charles C. Edwards, "A Positive Approach to Self-Medication," *Proceedings, Proprietary Association, 90th Annual Meeting* (Washington, D.C.: Proprietary Association, 1971), p. 36.

19. "Up-to-the-Minute Marketing Report on the 100 Largest National Advertisers," *Advertising Age* 42:70 (August 30, 1971).

20. Leslie V. Dix, "Relationship of Research and Development to Regulatory Agency: From the Federal Trade Commission Viewpoint," paper presented before a meeting of the Proprietary Association, New York, December 4, 1969.

21. Vivarin advertisement, cited in U.S. Senate, *Advertising of Proprietary Medicines* 1:229 (1971).

22. Daniel Banes (Food and Drug Administration), personal communication, 1972.

23. *Consumer Reports*, September 1972, p. 589.

24. *F-D-C Reports*, January 29, 1973, p. 6.

25. "Non-Prescription Sleep Aids," *Medical Letter* 1:48 (June 26, 1959).

26. Charles C. Edwards, statement in U.S. Senate, *Advertising of Proprietary Medicines* 1:16 (1971).

27. George B. Griffenhagen and Linda L. Hawkins (eds.), *Handbook of Non-Prescription Drugs* (Washington, D.C.: American Pharmaceutical Association, 1971).

28. David C. Lewis, statement in U.S. Senate, *Advertising of Proprietary Medicines* 2:478 (1971).

29. Richard P. Penna, statement in U.S. Senate, *Advertising of Proprietary Medicines* 1:110 (1971).

30. W. James Bicket, statement in U.S. Senate, *Advertising of Proprietary Medicines* 1:57 (1971).

31. John E. Ingersoll, cited in *F-D-C Reports*, October 9, 1972, p. 15.

32. J. N. Cooke, "President's Report—PA's Positive Approach," *Proceedings, Proprietary Association, 90th Annual Meeting* (Washington, D.C.: Proprietary Association, 1971), p. 26.

33. James D. Cope, "Executive Vice President's Report: PA's Positive Approach," *Proceedings, Proprietary Association, 90th Annual Meeting* (Washington, D.C.: Proprietary Association, 1971), p. 58.

34. J. N. Cooke, "President's Report: PA's Positive Approach," p. 28.

35. *F-D-C Reports*, February 26, 1973, p. 10.

36. Nicholas Johnson, statement in U.S. Senate, *Advertising of Proprietary Medicines* 2:598 (1971).

37. Ibid., p. 617.

38. Robert Pitofsky, statement in U.S. Senate, *Advertising of Proprietary Medicines* 1:45 (1971).

39. *F-D-C Reports*, January 22, 1973, p. 3.

40. *A Position Paper* (Washington, D.C.: Proprietary Association, October 1, 1971).

41. *AMA Drug Evaluations* (Chicago: American Medical Association, 1971), p. 496.

42. Ibid., p. 599.

43. Ibid., p. 600.

44. Ibid., p. 574.

45. Ibid., p. 377.

46. Sol Katz, statement in U.S. Senate, *Advertising of Proprietary Medicines* 3:941 (1972).

47. Donald C. LaBrecque, statement in U.S. Senate, *Advertising of Proprietary Medicines* 3:1029 (1972).

48. *San Francisco Chronicle*, December 7, 1972.

49. U.S. Department of Health, Education, and Welfare, Food and Drug Administration, news release, February 15, 1972.

50. Richard P. Penna, statement in U.S. Senate, *Advertising of Proprietary Medicines* 1:104 (1971).

51. Jack N. Turner, "Some Potential Interactions Between Prescribed Drugs and Over-the-Counter Drug Products," *California Medicine* 117:13 (September 1972).

52. Maven J. Myers, "Distribution Aspects in the Potential Misuse of O-T-C Preparations," *American Journal of Pharmacy* 142:29 (January-February 1970).

53. Herman E. Hilleboe, "Industry's Role in Health Education," *Annals of the New York Academy of Sciences* 120:952 (1965).

54. Charles C. Edwards, statement in U.S. Senate, *Advertising of Proprietary Medicines* 1:12 (1971).

55. Charles C. Edwards (Food and Drug Administration), personal communication, 1972.

56. Proprietary Association, news release, January 4, 1972.

10. The Role of the Government.

1. RxTF, *Drug Makers and Distributors*, p. 15.

2. Robert Q. Marston (National Institutes of Health), personal communication, 1972; Leon Jacobs (National Institutes of Health), personal communication, 1972.

3. Richard Harris, *The Real Voice* (New York: Macmillan, 1964).

4. Morton Mintz, "A Guy in a White Hat," *Washington Post*, January 21, 1968.

5. James L. Goddard, "Shared Responsibilities," paper presented at a meeting of the Pharmaceutical Manufacturers Association, Boca Raton, Fla., April 6, 1966.

6. John Adriani, statement in U.S. Senate, *Competitive Problems* 12:5118 (1969).

7. Washington Drug Letter, cited in William Chapman, "Critic of Industry Rejected for FDA," *Washington Post*, August 26, 1969.

8. William Cray, cited in E. W. Kenworthy, "Doctor Suggests Drug Men Denied Him Post in FDA," *New York Times*, August 26, 1969.

9. Roger O. Egeberg, news release, U.S. Department of Health, Education, and Welfare, August 29, 1969.

10. U.S. Department of Health, Education, and Welfare, Food and Drug Administration, Study Group on FDA Consumer Protection Objectives and Programs, "Draft Report," July 1969.

11. Charles C. Edwards (Food and Drug Administration), personal communication, 1972.

12. Charles C. Edwards, "Federal Health Regulatory Agencies: The Role of the Scientific Community," paper presented at a symposium on National Policy and the Life Sciences, Woods Hole, Mass., August 7, 1971.

13. Charles C. Edwards, "Rational Drug Therapeutics," *FDA Papers* 5:4 (February 1971).

14. Charles C. Edwards, personal communication, 1972.

15. Charles C. Edwards, letter to C. Joseph Stetler dated March 18, 1971, cited in U.S. Senate, *Competitive Problems* 20:8117 (1971).

16. Charles C. Edwards, personal communication, 1972.

17. Peter Hutt (Food and Drug Administration), personal communication, 1972.

18. "American Scientists Charge U.S. Medicine Lags, Urge Major Change in Regulatory Policies," *Medical Tribune*, April 5, 1972; "Growing Therapeutic Gap Worries American Scientists," *Medical Tribune*, April 12, 1972; "Experts Blame FDA for New Drug 'Standstill,'" *Medical Tribune*, April 19, 1972.

19. C. Joseph Stetler, cited in "From Drug House to Doctor via Europe: Why?" *Medical World News* 13:18 (January 28, 1972).

20. Stephen L. DeFelice, *Drug Discovery: The Pending Crisis* (New York: Medcom Press, 1972).

21. Sam Peltzman, statement in U.S. Senate, *Competitive Problems* 23:9814 (1973).

22. Milton Friedman, "Frustrating Drug Advancement," *Newsweek*, January 8, 1973, p. 49.

23. Robert D. Dripps et al., letter to Paul G. Rogers dated February 29, 1972.

24. Robert D. Dripps, cited in *F-D-C Reports*, May 1, 1972, p. 8.

25. Frederick Clark, cited in "From Drug House to Doctor via Europe: Why?" *Medical World News* 13:18 (January 28, 1972).

26. John Jennings, "Government Regulations and Drug Development—FDA," paper presented at a meeting of the American Chemical Society, Chicago, September 16, 1970.

27. Charles C. Edwards, personal communication, 1972.

28. Harry F. Dowling, *Medicines for Man* (New York: Knopf, 1970), p. 224.

29. Michael H. Cooper, *Prices and Profits in the Pharmaceutical Industry* (Oxford: Pergamon Press, 1966), p. 178.

30. Paul de Haen, letter to editor, *Medical Tribune*, December 15, 1971; Paul de Haen, cited in *F-D-C Reports*, January 22, 1973, p. 5.

31. Alexander M. Schmidt, paper presented at a meeting of the Pharmaceutical Advertising Seminar, Chicago, September 13, 1973.

32. Joseph D. Cooper, " 'Lean, Spare' Apparatus Controls Safety in U.K.," *Medical Tribune*, August 22, 1966.

33. Paul D. Stolley (Johns Hopkins University), personal communication, 1972.

34. Paul D. Stolley, "Asthma Mortality: Why the United States was Spared an Epidemic of Deaths Due to Asthma," *American Review of Respiratory Disease* 105:883 (1972).

35. Editorial, "Asthma Deaths: A Question Answered," *British Medical Journal* 2:443 (November 25, 1972).

36. George Teeling-Smith, "The British Drug Scene," in Joseph D. Cooper (ed.), *The Economics of Drug Innovation* (Washington, D.C.: American University, Center for the Study of Private Enterprise, 1970), p. 1.

37. Derrick Dunlop, "Medicines, Governments and Doctors," *Drugs* 3:305 (1972).

38. Mark Novitch (Food and Drug Administration), personal communication, 1973.

39. Mark Novitch, "The Executive Branch View," in Cooper, *Economics of Drug Innovation*, p. 25.

40. Herbert L. Ley, Jr., statement in U.S. Senate, *Competitive Problems* 14:5647 (1969).

41. Mark Novitch, personal communication, 1972.

42. RxTF, *Insurance Design*, p. 20.

43. Elmer B. Staats, statement in U.S. Senate, *Competitive Problems* 20:7996 (1971).

44. RxTF, *Final Report*, p. xxi.

45. Ibid.

46. RxTF, *Final Report*, p. 1.

47. RxTF, *Drug Users*, p. 21.

48. T. Donald Rucker (Social Security Administration), personal communication, 1972.

49. RxTF, *Insurance Design*, p. 19.

50. Ibid., pp. 21, 23.

51. Ibid., p. 21.

52. Ibid., p. 6.

53. Ibid.

54. RxTF, *Insurance Design*, p. 13.

11. Adverse Reactions: The Menace of Medications

1. Dale G. Friend, "Adverse Reactions to Drugs," *Clinical Pharmacology and Therapeutics* 5:257 (1964); R. H. Moser, *Diseases of Medical Progress* (Springfield, Ill.: Charles C Thomas, 1964); Michael F. C. Crick, *Adverse Drug Reactions* (Cambridge, Mass.: Bolt, Beranek & Newman, 1968); Eric W. Martin, *Hazards of Medication* (Philadelphia: Lippincott, 1971); *AMA Drug Evaluations* (Chicago: American Medical Association, 1971).

2. Irving H. Leopold, "Ocular Complications of Drugs: Visual Changes," *Journal of the American Medical Association* 205:631 (August 26, 1968).

3. Kenneth L. Melmon, "Preventable Drug Reactions—Causes and Cures," *New England Journal of Medicine* 284:1361 (June 17, 1971).

4. David P. Barr, "Hazards of Modern Diagnosis and Therapy: The Price We Pay," *Journal of the American Medical Association* 159:1452 (December 10, 1955); Larry G. Seidl, George F. Thornton, Jay W. Smith, and Leighton E. Cluff, "Studies on the Epidemiology of Adverse Drug Reactions. III. Reactions in Patients on a General Medical Service," *Bulletin of the Johns Hopkins Hospital* 119:299 (November 1966); James A. Visconti and Mickey C. Smith, "The Role of Hospital Personnel in Reporting Adverse Drug Reactions," *American Journal of Hospital Pharmacy* 24:273 (May 1967); Leighton E. Cluff, statement in U.S. Senate, *Competitive Problems* 2:560,566 (1967); Natalie Hurwitz and O. L. Wade, "Intensive Hospital Monitoring of Adverse Reactions to Drugs," *British Medical Journal* 1:531 (March 1, 1969); Charles C. Edwards, "Professional Integrity and Health Care for the Future," paper presented at a meeting of the National Association of Retail Druggists, Atlantic City, N.J., October 21, 1970; Russell R. Miller, "Drug Surveillance Utilizing Epidemiologic Methods: A Report from the Boston Collaborative Drug Surveillance Program," *American Journal of Hospital Pharmacy* 30:584 (July 1973).

5. Elihu M. Schimmel, "The Hazards of Hospitalization," *Annals of Internal Medicine* 60:100 (January 1964).

6. K. N. Barker, W. W. Kimbrough, and W. M. Heller, *A Study of Medication Errors in a Hospital* (Fayetteville, Ark.: University of Arkansas, 1966); B. C. Hoddinott, C. W. Gowdey, W. K. Coulter, and J. M. Parker, "Drug Reactions and Errors in Administration on a Medical Ward," *Canadian Medical Association Journal* 97:1001 (October 21, 1967); Clifford E. Hynniman, Wayne F. Conrad, William A. Urch, Betty R. Rudnick, and Paul F. Parker, "A Comparison of Medication Errors under the University of Kentucky Unit Dose System and Traditional Drug Distribution Systems in Four Hospitals," *American Journal of Hospital Pharmacy* 27:803 (October 1970); R. David Anderson, "The Physician's Contribution to Hospital Medication Errors," *American Journal of Hospital Pharmacy* 28:18 (January 1971).

7. Leighton E. Cluff, George F. Thornton, and Larry G. Seidl, "Studies on the Epidemiology of Adverse Drug Reactions. I. Methods of Surveillance," *Journal of the American Medical Association* 188:976 (June 15, 1964).

8. Leighton E. Cluff, statement in U.S. Senate, *Competitive Problems* 2:565 (1967).

9. B. C. Hoddinott et al., "Drug Reactions and Errors."

10. Richard Ian Ogilvie and John Ruedy, "Adverse Drug Reactions During Hospitalization," *Canadian Medical Association Journal* 97:1450 (December 9, 1967).

11. Hershel Jick, Olli S. Miettenin, Samuel Shapiro, George P. Lewis, Victor Siskind, and Dennis Slone, "Comprehensive Drug Surveillance," *Journal of the American Medical Association* 213:1455 (August 31, 1970).

12. Jan Koch-Weser, "Definition and Classification of Adverse Drug Reactions," *Drug Information Bulletin* 2:77 (July–September 1968).

13. Marcus M. Reidenberg, "Adverse Drug Reaction Program of the Greater Philadelphia Committee for Medical-Pharmaceutical Sciences," *Drug Information Bulletin* 2:117 (July–September 1968).

14. Andrew T. Canada, Jr., "Unstructured Retrospective Drug Experience Reports," *Drug Information Bulletin* 2:114 (July-September 1968).

15. Daniel Banes (Food and Drug Administration), personal communication, 1972.

16. Jay W. Smith, Larry G. Seidl, and Leighton E. Cluff, "Studies on the Epidemiology of Adverse Drug Reactions. V. Clinical Factors

Influencing Susceptibility," *Annals of Internal Medicine* 65:629 (October 1966).

17. Russell R. Miller.

18. Samuel Shapiro, Dennis Slone, George P. Lewis, and Hershel Jick, "Fatal Drug Reactions Among Medical Inpatients," *Journal of the American Medical Association* 216:467 (April 19, 1971).

19. Donald C. Brodie, *Drug Utilization and Drug Utilization Review and Control.* U.S. Department of Health, Education, and Welfare, National Center for Health Services Research and Development, 1970, p. 2.

20. Kenneth L. Melmon, "Preventable Drug Reactions."

21. Editorial, "Disease Drugs Cause," *New England Journal of Medicine* 279:1286 (December 5, 1968).

22. Gerald G. Jampolsky, "Attitudes Toward Specific Therapies," *California Medicine* 79:29 (July 1953).

23. Henry E. Meleney and Mary Lynn Fraser, "A Retrospective Study of Drug Usage and Adverse Drug Reactions in Hospital Outpatients," *Drug Information Bulletin* 2:96 (July–September 1968).

24. Melmon, "Preventable Drug Reactions."

25. Miller, "Drug Surveillance."

26. William M. Bennett, Irwin Singer, and Cecil H. Coggins, "A Practical Guide to Drug Usage in Adult Patients with Impaired Renal Function," *Journal of the American Medical Association* 214:1468 (November 23, 1970); Marcus M. Reidenberg, Ingegerd Odar-Cederlöf, Christer von Bahr, Olof Borgå, and Folke Sjöqvist, "Protein Binding of Diphenylhydantoin and Desmethylimipramine in Plasma from Patients with Poor Renal Function," *New England Journal of Medicine* 285:264 (July 29, 1971).

27. Emanuel Rubin and Charles S. Lieber, "Alcoholism, Alcohol, and Drugs," *Science* 172:1097 (June 11, 1971).

28. Jean D. Lockhart, "The Information Gap in Pediatric Drug Therapy," *Modern Medicine* 38:56 (November 16, 1970).

29. "Drugs in Pregnancy," *Medical Letter* 14:94 (December 8, 1972).

30. Edward J. Quilligan, paper presented before a meeting of the California Medical Association, Anaheim, Calif., March 13, 1973.

31. Eugene Farber and Fred Rosewater (Stanford University), personal communication, 1972.

32. Miller, "Drug Surveillance."

33. Leighton E. Cluff, statement in U.S. Senate, *Competitive Problems* 2:569 (1967).

34. Charles C. Edwards, letter to Leighton E. Cluff dated December 5, 1972, cited in U.S. Senate, *Advertising of Proprietary Medicines* 3:1084 (1972).

35. R. H. Moser, *Diseases of Medical Progress* (Springfield, Ill., 1964).

36. F. Robert Fekety, Jr., "Nosocomial Infections," *Postgraduate Medicine* 50:115 (November 1971); James R. Philp, "Untoward Effects of Antimicrobial Drugs," *Postgraduate Medicine* 50:193 (November 1971); Henry E. Simmons, statement in U.S. Senate, *Advertising of Proprietary Medicines* 3:1042 (1972).

37. Philp, "Untoward Effects."

38. Louis S. Goodman and Alfred Gilman, *The Pharmacologic Basis of Therapeutics* (New York: Macmillan, 4th ed., 1970), p. 1169.

39. Robert F. Maronde (University of Southern California), personal communication, 1973.

40. Everett H. Ellinwood and Sidney Cohen, "Amphetamine Abuse," *Science* 171:420 (January 29, 1971); Eric W. Martin, *Hazards of Medication* (Philadelphia, 1971).

41. Editorial, "And Pep in America," *New England Journal of Medicine* 283:761 (October 1, 1970).

42. George V. Mann, "Obesity, the Nutritional Spook," *American Journal of Public Health* 61:1491 (August 1971).

43. George E. Crane, "Clinical Psychopharmacology in Its 20th Year," *Science* 181:124 (July 13, 1973).

44. Alexander R. Lucas and Morris Weiss, "Methylphenidate Hallucinosis," *Journal of the American Medical Association* 217:1079 (August 23, 1971).

45. Henry L. Lennard, Leon J. Epstein, Arnold Bernstein, and Donald C. Ransom, *Mystification and Drug Misuse* (San Francisco: Jossey-Bass, 1971); Mitchell Balter and Jerome Levine, "Character and Extent of Psychotherapeutic Drug Usage in the United States," paper presented before Fifth World Congress on Psychiatry, Mexico City, November 30, 1971.

46. Balter and Levine.

47. Editorial, "Digitalis—Uses and Abuses," *Medical Journal of Australia* 1:723 (April 3, 1971).

48. Larry G. Seidl et al., "Studies on the Epidemiology of Adverse Drug Reactions."

49. James E. Doherty, "Digitalis Serum Levels: Clinical Use," *Annals of Internal Medicine* 74:787 (May 1971).

50. *AMA Drug Evaluations*, p. 2.

51. Doherty, "Digitalis Serum Levels."

52. Kenneth L. Melmon, "Preventable Drug Reactions."

53. Robert B. Talley and Marc F. Laventurier, "The Incidence of Drug-Drug Interactions in a Medi-Cal Population," paper presented before a meeting of the American College of Physicians, Atlantic City, N.J., April 20, 1972.

54. Leighton E. Cluff, statement in U.S. Senate, *Competitive Problems* 2:562 (1967).

55. Joel B. Mann, "Treating Salicylate Intoxication," *California Medicine* 113:16 (December 1970).

56. René Menguy, paper presented before a meeting of the American College of Surgeons, Chicago, October 13, 1970.

57. Werner A. Bleyer and Robert T. Breckenridge, "Studies on the Detection of Adverse Drug Reactions in the Newborn. II. The Effects of Prenatal Aspirin on Newborn Hemostasis," *Journal of the American Medical Association* 213:2049 (September 21, 1970).

58. C. G. Van Arman, cited in "Possible Interaction Occurs with Aspirin and Two Drugs," *Journal of the American Medical Association* 214:39 (October 5, 1970).

59. Jan Koch-Weser and Edward M. Sellers, "Drug Interactions with Coumarin Anticoagulants," *New England Journal of Medicine* 285:487 (August 26, 1971); Jan Koch-Weser and Edward M. Sellers, "Drug Interactions with Coumarin Anticoagulants (Second of Two Parts)," *New England Journal of Medicine* 285:547 (September 2, 1971); Jan Koch-Weser, cited in "Better Detection of Drug Interactions Asked," *Medical Tribune*, April 26, 1972.

60. Eric W. Martin, *Hazards of Medication* (Philadelphia, 1971).

61. Michael F. C. Crick, *Adverse Drug Reactions* (Cambridge, Mass., 1968).

62. *AMA Drug Evaluations* (Chicago, 1971).

63. *AMA Drug Evaluations*, p. 258.

64. Robert F. Maronde, Peter V. Lee, Margaret M. McCarron, and Stanley Seibert, "A Study of Prescribing Patterns," *Medical Care* 9:383 (September–October 1971).

65. Talley and Laventurier, "Incidence of Drug-Drug Interactions."

66. "The Worst Interactions May Happen Most Often," *Drug Topics*, May 8, 1972.

12. *The Physician: Healer or Health Hazard.*

1. RxTF, *Drug Prescribers*, p. 3.

2. Jan Koch-Weser, cited in RxTF, *Drug Prescribers*, p. 3.

3. Henry E. Simmons, paper presented before a symposium at the School of Pharmacy, University of California, San Francisco, September 10, 1970.

4. Mark Novitch, "Overmedication: International Perspectives," paper presented before a symposium on The Overmedicated Society, American Association for the Advancement of Science, Philadelphia, December 28, 1971.

5. Adrian Recinos, Jr., Sidney Ross, Bennett Olshaker, and Ellsworth Twible, "Chloromycetin in the Treatment of Pneumonia in Infants and Children: A Preliminary Report on Thirty-Three Cases," *New England Journal of Medicine* 241:733 (November 10, 1949).

6. Editorial, "Blood Dyscrasia Following the Use of Chloramphenicol," *Journal of the American Medical Association* 149:840 (June 28, 1952).

7. American Medical Association, Council on Pharmacy and Chemistry, *New and Nonofficial Remedies* (Philadelphia: Lippincott, 1953), p. 123.

8. Henry Welch, C. N. Lewis, and I. Kerlan, "Blood Dyscrasias: A Nationwide Survey," *Antibiotics and Chemotherapy* 4:607 (June 1954).

9. American Medical Association, Council on Drugs, "Blood Dyscrasias Associated with Chloramphenicol (Chloromycetin) Therapy," *Journal of the American Medical Association* 172:2044 (April 30, 1960).

10. Harry J. Loynd, cited in Richard Harris, *The Real Voice* (New York: Macmillan, 1964), p. 105.

11. William R. Best, "Chloramphenicol-Associated Blood Dyscrasias. A Review of Cases Admitted to the American Medical Association Registry," *Journal of the American Medical Association* 201:181 (July 17, 1967).

12. Clinton S. McGill, statement in U.S. Senate, *Competitive Problems* 10:4092 (1969).

13. Marshall H. Becker, Paul D. Stolley, Louis Lasagna, Joseph D. McEvilla, and Lois M. Sloane, "Characteristics and Attitudes of Physicians Associated with the Prescribing of Chloramphenicol," *HSMHA Health Reports* 86:993 (November 1971); P. D. Stolley, M. H. Becker, Louis Lasagna, and J. D. McEvilla, "The Relationship Between Physician Characteristics and Prescribing Appropriateness," *Medical Care* 10:17 (January-February 1972).

14. Harry F. Dowling, *Medicines for Man* (New York: Knopf, 1970), p. 279.

15. Cobbs v. Grant, San Francisco 2288, Calif. Supreme Court, No. 352,940, October 27, 1972.

16. Andrew W. Roberts and James A. Visconti, "The Rational and Irrational Use of Systemic Antimicrobial Drugs," *American Journal of Hospital Pharmacy* 29:1054 (October 1972).

17. William E. Scheckler and John V. Bennett, "Antibiotic Usage in Seven Community Hospitals," *Journal of the American Medical Association* 213:264 (July 13, 1970); Calvin M. Kunin, Thelma Tupasi, and William A. Craig, "Use of Antibiotics—A Brief Exposition of the Problem and Some Tentative Solutions," *Annals of Internal Medicine* 79:555 (October 1973).

18. Robert S. Myers, "The Misuse of Antibacterials in Inguinal Herniorrhaphy," *Surgery, Gynecology and Obstetrics* 108:721 (June 1959).

19. Roberts and Visconti, "Rational and Irrational Use."

20. William R. McCabe, Bernard E. Kreger, and Margaret Johns, "Type-Specific and Cross-Reactive Antibodies in Gram-Negative Bacteremia," *New England Journal of Medicine* 287:261 (August 10, 1972).

21. Robert F. Maronde (University of Southern California), personal communication, 1973.

22. Paul D. Stolley and Louis Lasagna, "Prescribing Patterns of Physicians," *Journal of Chronic Diseases* 22:395 (December 1969).

23. National Research Council, Division of Medical Sciences, *Drug Efficacy Study. Final Report to the Commissioner of Food and Drugs, Food and Drug Administration* (Washington, D.C.: National Academy of Sciences, 1969).

24. "The Choice and Dosage of Narcotic Analgesics," *Medical Letter* 15:32 (March 30, 1973).

25. Veterans Administration Cooperative Study Group on Antihypertensive Agents, "Effects of Treatment on Morbidity in Hypertension. II. Results in Patients with Diastolic Blood Pressure Averaging 90 Through 114 mm Hg," *Journal of the American Medical Association* 213:1143 (August 17, 1970).

26. Mitchell Balter and Jerome Levine, "Character and Extent of Psychotherapeutic Drug Usage in the United States," paper presented before the Fifth World Congress on Psychiatry, Mexico City, November 30, 1971.

27. Peter A. Parish, "What Influences Have Led to Increased

Prescribing of Psychotropic Drugs?" in "The Medical Use of Psychotropic Drugs," *Journal of the Royal College of General Practitioners* 23 (Suppl. 2):49 (June 1973).

28. Henry L. Lennard and Mitchell Rosenthal, statement in U.S. Senate, *Advertising of Proprietary Medicines* 2:801 (1971).

29. Richard I. Feinbloom, statement in U.S. Senate, *Advertising of Proprietary Medicines* 2:523 (1971).

30. Balter and Levine, "Character and Extent of Psychotherapeutic Drug Usage."

31. "Dr. Nathan S. Kline Finds Patients in the U.S. Are 'Dangerously Unmedicated or Undermedicated,' " *Medical Tribune*, January 19, 1972.

32. "The Medical Use of Psychotropic Drugs," *Journal of the Royal College of General Practitioners* 23 (Suppl. 2):1 (June 1973).

33. Balter and Levine, "Character and Extent of Psychotherapeutic Drug Usage."

34. Lester Grinspoon and Peter Hedblom, "Amphetamines Reconsidered," *Saturday Review* 55:33 (July 8, 1972).

35. Robert F. Maronde, Peter V. Lee, Margaret M. McCarron, and Stanley Seibert, "A Study of Prescribing Patterns," *Medical Care* 9:383 (September-October 1971).

36. Robert F. Maronde, personal communication, 1972.

37. Robert F. Maronde, Stanley Seibert, Jack Katzoff, and Milton Silverman, "Prescription Data Processing: Its Role in the Control of Drug Abuse," *California Medicine* 117:22 (September 1972).

38. O. L. Peterson, L. P. Andrews, R. S. Spain, and B. G. Greenberg, "An Analytical Study of North Carolina General Practice, 1953–1954," *Journal of Medical Education* 31(Part II):1 (1956).

39. K. F. Clute, *The General Practitioner: A Study of Medical Education and Practice in Ontario and Nova Scotia* (Toronto: University of Toronto Press, 1963).

40. J. P. Martin, *Social Aspects of Prescribing* (London: William Heinemann, 1957).

41. P. D. Stolley, M. H. Becker, Louis Lasagna, and J. D. McEvilla, "The Relationship Between Physician Characteristics and Prescribing Appropriateness."

42. RxTF, *Final Report*, p. 23.

43. Statements in U.S. Senate, *Competitive Problems* 1 (1967): Walter Modell, p. 294; Harry L. Williams, p. 467; Margaret M. McCarron, p. 581; Martin Cherkasky, p. 673.

44. Opinion Research Corporation, *Physicians' Attitudes Toward Drug Compendia. A National Survey Sponsored by Pharmaceutical Manufacturers Association* (Princeton, N.J.: Opinion Research Corporation, 1968).

45. Margaret M. McCarron (University of Southern California), personal communication, 1967.

46. RxTF, *Final Report*, p. 22.

47. Ibid.

48. Dwight L. Wilbur, "Pharmacology and the Practicing Physician," *Proceedings of the Western Pharmacology Society* 11:5 (1968).

49. R. Buchheim, "Ueber die Aufgaben und die Stellung der Pharmakologie an den deutschen Hochschulen," *Archiv für experimentelle Pathologie und Pharmakologie* 5:261 (1876).

50. James Samuel Coleman, Elihu Katz, and Herbert Menzel, *Medical Innovation: A Diffusion Study* (Indianapolis: Bobbs-Merrill, 1966), p. 246; F. Floyd Shoemaker and Everett M. Rogers, *Communication of Innovations: A Cross-Cultural Approach* (New York: Free Press, 2nd ed., 1971), p. 476.

51. Shoemaker and Rogers, p. 333.

52. World Health Organization, *Quality, Safety, and Efficacy of Drugs* (Geneva: World Health Organization, Document EB49/5, November 26, 1971).

53. Charlotte Muller, "The Overmedicated Society: Forces in the Marketplace for Medical Care," *Science* 176:488 (May 5, 1972); S. Albert, cited in Muller, "The Overmedicated Society."

54. Michael Balint, "Conclusions: What Can be Done?" in Michael Balint, John Hunt, Dick Joyce, Marshall Marinker, and Jasper Woodcock, *Treatment or Diagnosis: A Study of Repeat Prescriptions in General Practice* (London: Tavistock, 1970), p. 145.

13. Future Strategy: Prescriptions for Action.

1. RxTF, *Drug Prescribers*, p. 3.

2. Ibid., p. 6.

3. Pierre R. Garai, "Advertising and Promotion of Drugs," in Paul Talalay (ed.), *Drugs in our Society* (Baltimore: Johns Hopkins Press, 1964), p. 199.

4. RxTF, *Final Report*, p. 40.

5. RxTF: *Drug Makers and Distributors*, p. 83.

6. Walter Modell, "Editorial: Requiem for the FDA," *Clinical Pharmacology and Therapeutics* 11:1 (January–February, 1970).

7. S. 2812, U.S. Senate, 92nd Congress, 1st Session, November 4, 1971.

8. RxTF, *Insurance Design*, p. 64; RxTF, *Final Report*, p. 48.

9. Donald C. Brodie, *Drug Utilization and Drug Utilization Review and Control*. U.S. Department of Health, Education, and Welfare, National Center for Health Services Research and Development, 1970; T. Donald Rucker, "The Need for Drug Utilization Review," *American Journal of Hospital Pharmacy* 27:654 (August 1970); Hershel Jick, Olli S. Miettenin, Samuel Shapiro, George P. Lewis, Victor Siskind, and Dennis Slone, "Comprehensive Drug Surveillance," *Journal of the American Medical Association* 213:1455 (August 31, 1970); Paul D. Stolley and James L. Goddard, "Prescription Drug Insurance for the Elderly Under Medicare," *American Journal of Public Health* 61:574 (March 1971); Robert F. Maronde, Peter V. Lee, Margaret M. McCarron, and Stanley Seibert, "A Study of Prescribing Patterns," *Medical Care* 9:383 (September-October 1971); T. Donald Rucker, "The Role of Computers in Drug Utilization," *American Journal of Hospital Pharmacy* 29:128 (February 1972); Robert F. Maronde, Stanley Seibert, Jack Katzoff, and Milton Silverman, "Prescription Data Processing: Its Role in the Control of Drug Abuse," *California Medicine* 117:22 (September 1972); Robert F. Maronde, *Drug Utilization Review with On-Line Computer Capability*, U.S. Department of Health, Education, and Welfare, Social Security Administration, Office of Research and Statistics, DHEW Publication No. (SSA) 73-11853, 1973.

10. RxTF, *Insurance Design*, p. 69.

11. Marcel Laventurier (Paid Prescriptions, Inc.), personal communication, 1973.

12. Ronald B. Stewart and Leighton E. Cluff, "A Review of Medication Errors and Compliance in Ambulant Patients," *Clinical Pharmacology and Therapeutics* 13:463 (July–August 1972).

13. J. W. Buchan, "America's Health: Fallacies, Beliefs, Practices," *FDA Consumer* 6:4 (October 1972).

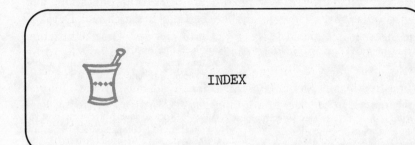

INDEX